American Visions ■ Reading

MW01008088

Consulting Editors

Michael Barton
Associate Professor of American Studies and History
Pennsylvania State University at Harrisburg, Capital College

Nancy A. Walker
Professor of English
Vanderbilt University

This unique series consists of carefully assembled volumes of seminal writings on topics central to the study of American culture. Each anthology begins with a comprehensive overview of the subject at hand, written by a noted scholar in the field, followed by a combination of selected articles, original essays, and case studies.

By bringing together in each collection many important commentaries on such themes as humor, material culture, architecture, the environment, literature, politics, theater, film, and spirituality, American Visions provides a varied and rich library of resources for the scholar, student, and general reader. Annotated bibliographies facilitate further study and research.

Volumes Published

Nancy A. Walker, editor
What's So Funny? Humor in American Culture (1998).
Cloth ISBN 0-8420-2687-8   Paper ISBN 0-8420-2688-6

Robert J. Bresler
Us vs. Them: American Political and Cultural Conflict from WW II to Watergate (2000).
Cloth ISBN 0-8420-2689-4   Paper ISBN 0-8420-2690-8

Jessica R. Johnston, editor
The American Body in Context: An Anthology (2001).
Cloth ISBN 0-8420-2858-7   Paper ISBN 0-8420-2859-5

Richard P. Horwitz, editor
The American Studies Anthology (2001).
Cloth ISBN 0-8420-2828-5   Paper ISBN 0-8420-2829-3

Chris J. Magoc
So Glorious a Landscape: Nature and the Environment in American History and Culture (2002).
Cloth ISBN 0-8420-2695-9   Paper ISBN 0-8420-2696-7

THE AMERICAN STUDIES ANTHOLOGY

THE
AMERICAN STUDIES
ANTHOLOGY

Edited by

RICHARD P. HORWITZ

American Visions ▪ Readings in American Culture

▪

Number 4

▪

A Scholarly Resources Inc. Imprint ▪ Wilmington, Delaware

SR
BOOKS

© 2001 by Scholarly Resources Inc.
All rights reserved
First published 2001
Printed and bound in the United States of America

Scholarly Resources Inc.
104 Greenhill Avenue
Wilmington, DE 19805-1897
www.scholarly.com

Library of Congress Cataloging-in-Publication Data

The American studies anthology / edited by Richard P. Horwitz
    p. cm. — (American visions ; no. 4)
    Includes bibliographical references (p.).
    ISBN 0-8420-2828-5 (alk. paper) — ISBN 0-8420-2829-3 (pbk. : alk. paper)
    1. United States—Civilization—Sources. 2. United States—Literary
collections. 3. United States—Study and teaching. 4. National
characteristics, American—History—Sources. I. Horwitz, Richard P., 1949–
II. American visions (Wilmington, Del.) ; no. 4

E169.1 .A449 2001
973—dc21   2001031069

ABOUT THE EDITOR

RICHARD P. HORWITZ is professor, graduate director, and director of public outreach for the American Studies Department at the University of Iowa. He holds a Ph.D. (1975) in American Civilization from the University of Pennsylvania. For the past twenty-five years his teaching and research have centered on the interpretation of everyday life in the United States now and over the course of the past couple of centuries. He has worked extensively in about a dozen Asian and European nations to contribute to the development of his field and intercultural understanding more generally. Major publications include another anthology, *Exporting America* (1993) (about American Studies around the world, with contributions from eleven countries), and three original volumes: *Anthropology Toward History* (1978) (about interdisciplinarity, applied toward understanding workaday life in a nineteenth-century New England town), *The Strip* (1985) (about highway-oriented commerce, making beds, burgers, cash, and community along a modern Midwestern roadside), and *Hog Ties* (1998) (about the implications of modern agriculture and medical science for the quality of life in America). In the past decade, he has also served as a researcher, writer, photographer, consultant, and public presenter for the Smithsonian Institution (for example, for the Festival of American Folklife) and for several state arts, education, science, and humanities agencies.

Curiously combined with that argumentative national self-consciousness . . . is a profound, imperturbable, unsuspectingness on the part of many Americans of the impression they produce in foreign lands.
—Henry James, "Americans Abroad" (1878)

America has been fully transformed from a country into a trope or a fiction. America is a vast literary playground where sophisticated thinkers exercise their wit and practice their ironic aerobics.
—James Ceaser, *Reconstructing America* (1997)

Because something is happening here
But you don't know what it is,
Do you, Mr. Jones?
—Bob Dylan, "Ballad of a Thin Man" (1965)

I hope to glimpse my own history in relation to the movements of others in a regional contact zone. . . . I want to ask some large and ultimately unanswerable questions in a personal way. To think historically, I need to be both globally aware and locally situated. For the forces—economic, political, environmental—that have brought us all together here are materialized as historical reality only through particular local projects and stories. These are neither uniform nor finally determined. Historical reality, what happens in nonrepeating time, is a changing set of determinations, not a cumulative process or a teleology. This, at least, is my assumption—and hope.
—James Clifford, *Routes* (1997)

CONTENTS

RICHARD P. HORWITZ

Introduction

American Studies
Its Roots
American Studies is a branch of learning. Since
the 1930s people have been gathering in its name
to study and create courses, readings, films, and exhibits. On more than
four hundred college or university campuses in the United States and
many more elsewhere, you can earn a diploma with the words "American Studies" on it. The aim of all of these activities, in one fashion or
another, is understanding America. That is basically all there is to it.

Talking about such a thing as if it had "roots" risks creating some
confusion. Since the mid-1970s, when Alex Haley's book *Roots* and
then a made-for-television translation went blockbuster, the word has
become a cliché. People started using it to mean just about anything
vaguely genealogical or traditional (as in "roots-rock" music). Once
you look for roots in this way, they are too easy to find to be worth
very much. Everything is likely to seem connected to ("rooted in")
just about everything else.

But people often speak as if their roots were a unique, spiritual
home—not just any home, but the one where "our people" (and only
they) were raised. From this perspective, "finding their roots" is
supposed to help folks (for example, initiates to an ethnicity or a
course in American Studies) feel better about who they are. But the

perspective soothes only if they also feel not so much a part of history as a product of it. They treat their origins as if they were their destiny, as if a distant force determined who they would be. Such a pedigree can be revealing, reassuring, or even necessary for self-defense, but it can also conceal the *act* of remembering. In effect, despite Haley's reminders, people forget that *Roots* had to be both researched and made up, both found and invented.

On the other hand, there are lots of people who do not know or much care about their roots. It is, for example, U.S. "minority groups" who embrace (or get stuck with) the roots that put a hyphen in their name: Italian-American, Korean-American, etc. People who pass for white, native-born, and English mother-tongued can easily think that they are just "regular" or "one-hundred percent" American. They do not need "roots" to feel at home. History in effect began when their citizenship was secure. For people who are so comfortable, roots seem merely optional, like fashion accessories. Civility requires only that they endure the pride that less fortunate folks take in such trinkets.

In this respect, the cliché leaves people feeling free to opt out of history altogether. But why should anyone consider ancestors from Brooklyn, Britain, or Germany any more or less rooted than those from Laos or Ethiopia? Why should "regular disciplines" such as philosophy, literature, history, or political science seem any more or less rooted than American Studies? Whatever the therapeutic value of these relations to "roots," they tend to render history a pastime for spectators only.

This book is designed around a more restricted—more literal but still metaphorical—use of the word "roots."

For an actual tree, of course, the roots are the oldest part, buried below ground. Granted, a lot of the action in a plant's life happens above ground, where you can see it, maybe climb its branches, admire new leaves, or taste its fruit. But a lot has happened and continues to happen underground. A hefty taproot digs deep where growth first began. Its grasp allows the trunk to stand tall, even as limbs reach toward the light. With age, the tips of radiating roots stretch for nutrients to touch. Their shape, then, is a record of their route through the soil.

Under decent conditions, they explode out into loam, squeeze between boulders, and fan out over bedrock. They are durable but also degradable. If a major root encounters disease or trauma, it rots and reverts to the soil. Minor roots extend and swell to pick up the slack.

None of them exactly determines the way a tree grows, but every bud is reared below.

In this way, roots are both a fixed record of the past and a dynamic resource for the future. Although normally out of sight, they are among the things most worth envisioning before you prune, graft, climb, or hang a swing. Part of what draws me to this way of introducing American Studies—through a roots analogy—is the lively sense of history that it evokes.

Of course, as a branch of learning, American Studies does not really have roots (at least no more than learning has "branches"). With a little elaboration, the analogy begins to collapse. The field might make more sense if you think of it as a piece of machinery rather than as a plant. Colleges, libraries, and museums are fueled by cash and driven by professionals who are licensed operators. And in some ways every piece of curriculum resembles theater. Regents build the stage, deans do the casting, teachers write the scripts, and students more or less successfully "perform." The history of American Studies might well be introduced as if it were an industry, a city, a game, or for that matter (mindful of the jargon) a foreign language.

But among the distinct benefits of thinking of the field as if it had roots is the insinuation of connections across space and time. The past is at once out of sight and powerfully ever present, both sturdy and pliant.

It is a pretty safe bet, for example, that in times of international conflict, views of America will become politicized and polarized. Every event that might have foreshadowed the conflict, even if only distantly related and vaguely remembered, will be dusted off and stitched into regimental banners. Public officials and their intellectual defenders will review the past and find a legacy that puts God on their side. Foes and their defenders will find the same record satanic. As passions heat up, the latest entry in the "American" record—the goings-on that made it seem so holy or demonic in the first place—will be considered more surely the culmination of a "larger trend." As passions cool, though, these interpretations will likely seem just another in a series of variations on familiar themes. As a simplification of experience—partly researched and partly made up—they may seem regrettable, even forgettable. But they will likely remain ready for recall and refiguring as future events unfold.

To cite just one example, students and intellectuals in urban China in the late 1980s tended to idealize the United States or at least to believe that Chinese officialdom paled by comparison. During the 1989 demonstrations in Beijing's Tiananmen Square, they adapted American symbols to express (to CNN, among others) their hopes for domestic reform. Their "goddess of democracy" was a strikingly pure-white rendering of the Statue of Liberty with her torch held high. (It is worth remembering that the original in New York is a copper-blue figure of nineteenth-century French design.) But barely ten years later, in response to the U.S.-NATO bombing of the Chinese embassy in Belgrade, the same symbols lent themselves to monstrosity. In 1999 students again adapted Lady Liberty for demonstration placards (and CNN). But this time she scowled and wore a swastika while waving a clutch of missiles. U.S. versions of its relations to China for the most part swung on the same gate.

Clearly, these understandings—these nascent American Studies—uniquely befit the two moments. They have their own "historical integrity." But they just as clearly relate to each other and remain available for future reference. We might (just might) expect a variant of one or the other to emerge at other times under comparable conditions. If in engaging in American Studies we find ourselves drawn to kindred impressions, it is worth considering the ways that current circumstances resemble those past conditions. Are we, in effect, drawing on "the same roots"? Should we? Or would other roots be better? What might those be? The main purpose of this anthology is to provide a serviceable sampler.

America

Within modern memory people all over the planet have become remarkably conscious of America. The U.S. dollar is probably the single most convertible currency. Remote villagers have impressions of California and Muhammad Ali. "When America sneezes, the world gets a cold," they say. How that happened, at least over the short run, is fairly easy to explain.

During World War II (1939–1945), Africa, Asia, Europe, and the Pacific were sites of brutal combat. Saturation bombings, fire storms, death camps, disease, nuclear explosions, and radiation destroyed whole cities, paralyzed industry, transportation systems, and agriculture, and left millions of people in mourning, hungry, and homeless. The resource-rich Americas, however, were relatively untouched. Oceans separated them from both the eastern and western fronts. By delaying its declaration of war so long (until December 1941), by methodically gearing up for the fight, and by helping others (especially Europeans) to arm and then recover, the United States experienced the war primarily as a trauma but also as an economic godsend. It helped end one of the worst depressions in history. It left the United States, previously a second- or third-rate power, the dominant force on the planet.

That first taste of preeminence did not last long. As the Soviet Union quickly rebuilt and tightened control over its "satellite" states (1949–1953), the world was soon gripped by another conflict, a "Cold War" that often in fact turned hot. Any anticolonial agitation, boundary dispute, a shift of allegiance or even the hint of one, no matter where it was, could be swept up in the rivalry between the United States and the USSR. From the late 1940s through the 1980s, they were the world's two superpowers, and global, nuclear conflagration was an ever-ominous prospect in their relations.

During the 1980s, however, the greater economic might and symbolic allure of the United States became obvious. As World War II ended, GIs whetted foreign appetites for stateside novelties—chocolate bars, chewing gum, and nylons—tossed from liberating tanks. The U.S. government vigorously promoted its exports in postwar trade policies and the Marshall Plan (1947–1951). But by century's end, trade in Americana had become a multinational enterprise. It became hard to find anyplace on the planet too isolated for distributors of Coke, Marlboros, fast food, Hollywood movies, television series, weaponry, athletic gear, seeds, software, tractors, aircraft, jazz, blues, and rock and roll. Around the world "international youth" donned Levis and Gap T-shirts. Even when designed in Korea, stitched in Honduras, and marketed out of Germany, American style became a global fashion. Whatever their mother tongue, people learned to greet each other with "Hi," "Okay?" "No problem." Quite likely, too, no matter where they were, the U.S. military could rapidly deploy overhead, and the U.S. Federal Reserve in effect set their nation's prime interest rate, too. With the breakup of the Soviet Union at the end of 1991, there was only one superpower left: the United States of America.

You might well think that by now there should be no confusion about where America is or what it represents. Since, now and then, U.S. flag wavers hype "Americanism" and wavers of other flags bemoan "Americanization," you would think these people were talking about the same place.

Not necessarily so.

The problem is not just a matter of perspective, nationality, patriotism, or the issues of the day. The problem is also an ambiguity in the whole notion of place and the name "America" in particular.

In common usage there are at least three distinct senses of the word: geographic, political, and symbolic. Each has somewhat different implications for how anyone could find the place, much less how you should study it. How can you know whether something does or does not belong in a generalization about America? How can you define the place precisely enough to check?

One way to settle this would be to agree on a map. Let the Earth's fixed contours set the boundaries. Draw a line along the waterfronts of the Western Hemisphere, tracing where the earth meets the sea. That gets "America" located, fixed at least at mean tide. Then take account of everything that falls inside the lines. That takes care of what can count as "American." This is a straightforward solution that is also more or less the one used in other fields with "studies" in their names (for example, Cold War-vintage "area studies" such as Asian or African Studies). But for the sorts of issues that have piqued curiosity about America, the no-nonsense solution may be short of satisfying.

The first problem is that the land mass "from sea to shining sea" includes two obvious parts, North and South America. And, beyond the noun in their English names, there is nothing very cohesive about them. Even the seasonal migration of birds tends to separate at the Gulf of Mexico. No colonial power and none of the hundreds of native peoples who have inhabited the two continents for thousands of years has ever claimed the whole of it for a home. Insofar as they have tried —as the Spanish and Portuguese did prior to the fifteenth-century edicts of Pope Alexander VI or in more recent movements for free-trade zones or First Nations rights—the terrain has never been contiguous. For example, the alliances that occasionally bind Inuit, Guaraní, and Cheyenne include Aborigines on the other side of the globe. Hence, the Mexican writer, diplomat, and activist Octavio Paz concludes that "America" exists in the singular only through "an abuse of language."

If we had to choose just one of the Americas to be "America," judging from geography and pedigree alone, it ought to be the one in the south. The word "America" comes to us from the German cartographer Martin Waldseemüller. He coined the name (he literally put it on the map) in 1507 to honor the Florence-born explorer Amerigo (in

Latin, "Americus") Vespucci. In what now appears to be one of the world's greatest examples of false advertising, Vespucci and his imposters claimed to have beaten Columbus in the European race to North America. Waldseemüller was probably among those who believed him, but it is now quite certain that Vespucci lied—that is, if we correct Columbus by tethering his 1492 landfall (Guanahaní/San Salvador in the Bahamas) to North America rather than Asia. Vespucci's first transatlantic ventures (1499–1500) were limited to what is now Brazil, and Waldseemüller's map indicates very little to the north of it. Nevertheless, the name caught on in the south and spread slowly with the European invasion to cover the rest of the hemisphere as well. Scholars at least since Ralph Waldo Emerson have found it amusing that the name for half the world immortalizes a scam.

Ordinary curiosities, though, are usually unproblematically aimed to the north. When people in Pakistan or Peru as well as Peoria talk about "America," they are much more likely to have Chicago or the Rockies in mind than Asunción or the Andes. Obviously, the academic definition of the place should keep such curiosities engaged. But if in response we disregard the crackpot pedigree and restrict "America" to North America, should Mexico, the United States, and Canada share equal billing? And what about the Caribbean? Or U.S. territories such as Puerto Rico and Guam? Or the "American" state of Hawaii? The simple, map-it solution seems to fly in the face of political reality and common sense.

A second option, then, is to credit a political (or geopolitical) rather than strictly topographical definition. We can use "America" as shorthand for the jurisdiction of the United States of America. After all, it is the only nation in the Western Hemisphere with the word "America" in its name. Its contents, we might say, are simply whatever the U.S. Bureau of the Census counts and the Coast Guard or the Immigration and Naturalization Service (INS) let in. The abbreviation is, no doubt, chauvinistic (like calling all gelatin "Jello"), but it is familiar to most people and no more irrational than the average place name.

No doubt, too, the place then becomes a bit more of a moving target. Knowing what belongs in or out of "America" in this sense requires the interpretation of complex legal, military, and diplomatic affairs. At any given moment, reasonable people disagree about where U.S. jurisdiction begins and ends. Currently, for example, Hopi, Mesquakie/Fox, Amish, Puerto Rican, and Nuyorican peoples tend to claim quite different relations to that jurisdiction, all of them with historical justification. Most of Africa's descendants who fell under America's jurisdiction got there by way of kidnapping.

America probably cannot be said to exist as a sovereign entity before the Articles of Confederation or the Constitution was in force (1781 or 1789). The range as well as the substance of its dominion has been contested and changing ever since.

The 49th Parallel became a national northern boundary only through a half-century of warfare and multiple rounds of negotiations with Great Britain (1792–1846). While that boundary remained a blur, "the American West" kept leaping westward—first state by state (for example, Ohio, Tennessee, and Kentucky), then wholesale. Under the terms of the Louisiana Purchase (1803), for a few million dollars, France "sold" to the United States everything between the Mississippi River and the Rocky Mountains, including possessions that were not remotely French. Among the human occupants were Native Americans who had been sovereign for millennia. The expansion of U.S. borders at the expense of native peoples has been a subject of litigation as well as bloodshed from first contact to the present day.

Probably the largest outright land grab was by way of the Mexican War (1846–1848). Again for a paltry sum, with guns drawn and in defiance of competing claims of sovereignty, the United States expanded its boundaries to include everything north of the Rio Grande/ Río Bravo, from the Continental Divide to the Pacific. When forced to sign the Treaty of Guadalupe Hidalgo, Mexico (counting its contestable claims) shrank by about one-third. Other territories in which U.S. jurisdiction has been ambiguous or in dispute include Puerto Rico, the southern Virgin Islands, Hawaii, Guam, more than two thousand islands in the Pacific ("Trust Territory," 1947–1978) as well as Panama and the Philippines for more than a century. When you add to this list the other nations (chiefly in Latin America and the Caribbean) that the U.S. military has occupied for years at a time now and again, the definition of "America" as one polity, the United States, still leaves a great deal unclear. It is certainly hard to think of it as ever neatly corralled on the mainland.

Mindful of this history, it is also hard to come up with a reasonably precise count of how many "Americans" there are, much less where they live or what they are like at any point in time. Every day, thousands of people and a veritable army of attorneys struggle mightily to settle their relationship to the U.S. government. Granted, a lot of prior scholarship on the United States has provided reliable generalizations while dodging such details. But even if the level of uncertainty is restricted to the most obvious cases—Native Americans and citizens of territories other than the mainland states—the number of people affected is large (certainly more than 30 million) and growing fast. When you add the number of illegal aliens or refugees whose citizenship status is pending, the level seems morally as well as numerically far greater than a quibble.

It is worth remembering, too, that even when jurisdiction has been clear, its meaning—the legal significance of citizenship—has been less so. Although the rights of U.S. citizens have been the envy of much of the world, at least since the adoption of the Bill of Rights (1791), domestic access to them has always been uneven. The freedom to move, assemble, worship, or speak at will and the rights to vote, to hold public office, to own property, or to expect equal protection under the law have been doled out in discriminating portions and subject to recall (consider felons or Japanese Americans during their internment, 1942–1945).

For most of U.S. history, certainly all of its first half, full citizenship rights were the preserve of a minority. In the early republic, only free, adult, white male property holders could vote or hold office. Women's civil rights, limited as they were at the end of the eighteenth century, either remained limited or were yet further constricted during the first decades of American jurisprudence. Slaves, of course, had no legally protected property rights; they *were* property. The Constitution mandated apportioning the House of Representatives (where federal revenue bills originate) by counting each slave as only three-fifths of a white person. This "Great Compromise" (1787) was a victory for representatives of slave-holding southern states. According to those from the more populous northern states, slaves did not warrant representation at all.

After the Civil War, government policies haltingly, but in total, immensely expanded legal access to first-class citizenship. The Thirteenth (1865), Fourteenth (1868), Fifteenth (1870), Nineteenth (1920), Twenty-fourth (1964), and Twenty-sixth (1971) Amendments to the Constitution as well as a much larger number of state and local laws, administrative reforms, and judgments greatly reduced legal discrimination based on race, gender, wealth, and age. Of course, the actual experience of citizenship or the way other nations compare is another matter. The point is merely that a definition of "America" as a single nation—a region of clearly marked and consistent jurisdiction—leaves a lot to be desired. Where is the stable subject for American Studies attention? Our sense of place and the bounds of political reality seem ever out of synch.

This muddle about the range and meaning of nationality is not necessarily debilitating for the field. The hunt for practical parameters can itself be enlightening. Many scholars have successfully framed their studies with a serviceable map and some basic political data. The land and the government are important, demanding subjects in themselves. Much of what interests people in studying America is, in fact, on the ground and in its political institutions. It is hard to see how any generalization about the place could make much sense without attention to these realities, complex and volatile as they may be. Hence, history, politics, economics, anthropology, law, geography, technology, sociology, and environmental studies are among the main roots of American Studies.

Often, however, people's curiosity about America, even the way they define it, is not quite (or at least not entirely) a matter of its setting and institutions, its land and legalities. People can, for instance, recognize certain ways of having fun or facing problems, dressing, working, writing, or talking as "typically American." The nationality of your passport, the port of origin of your clothing, or the ground where you stand may not be at issue. "America" can be more abstractly connected to all of these things. This qualitative sense of the place can be detected in fine increments. Details in the way folks set a table, pronounce the letter "A," pose for photographs, or indulge their children can be calibrated as more or less "American."

For centuries, visitors have come to the United States not only to see the land and assess its institutions but also to get a feel for the people. Bold impressions can be gained even at sites far from the United States, say, in an Asian Planet Hollywood or one of those stores built for Yankee executives and GIs on Third World assignment. Such places can be "more American" than any place actually in the United States.

Of course, part of what is going on here is stereotyping. People might cling to these impressions not because they fit reality but because they do not know any better. Demagogues of nearly every persuasion have inflated their agendas or deflated their foes' by associating them with the flimsiest of relations to the United States. Domestic political activists, Freemasons, Mormons, Catholics, Muslims, and immigrants could be more easily persecuted once rendered "un-American." Outside the United States, pious missionaries and patriotic reformers could be silenced as subversive agents of phantom "American" conspiracies.

Flimsy as such connections might be, these, too, are among the roots of American Studies. They are the ones that scholars would prefer to prune. Rather than fostering an understanding of America, they can become a substitute or an obstacle. One of the major challenges of American Studies as an academic field has been to help people appreciate the difference between the sorts of symbols and generalizations that nurture understanding and the stereotypes that do not.

Yet another way to define "America," then, is as a symbolic, heuristic device. It is not quite the place itself but a sense of it, a figuration. It is useful precisely to the degree that it remains a little suspect—simple and true enough to be recognized but also colored or incomplete enough to afford perspective. Less a tangible, whole thing than its attributes, the meaning of "America" is necessarily properly contestable. It is a name for the qualities that, we might well say, "belong" to an elusive, geographic, and political terrain.

Before America can be comprehended in this way, it must (like Haley's autobiography) be both researched and made up or at least molded to sensible shape. The bounds of "America" might be no more (or less) substantial than sentiment, with familiarity on one side and estrangement on the other. Like Alexis de Tocqueville in the 1830s or Robert Bellah in the 1990s, we can wonder if it is fair to say Americans have their "habits of the heart." They might be shaped not only by topography, law, and national power but also by word of mouth, ritual, the circulation of goods, arts, and amusements, flights of fancy, and acts of will. This is the sense of the word "America" to which expressions such as "typically American," "un-American," "Americanism," and "Americanization" appeal. You certainly do not have to "be" American or have any particular feelings about it to understand the place in this symbolic way.

Of the three senses of the word this one is certainly, for better or worse, the most intractable. As fuzzy as it may be, it is the one that has drawn the most widespread, sustained, and passionate curiosity. What does "America" mean? How should it be understood? What has the place—not just its institutions but also the land, its various peoples, and their creations—come to represent? Is that really how it should be understood? To what extent is it wise or stupid to think so?

These are critical and interpretive as well as analytical questions. Help rightly comes from the arts and humanities—literature, philosophy, architecture, dance, painting, sculpture, religion, film, music—as well as history and the social sciences. This symbolic definition of America is the root from which this volume most heavily draws. It is also the root that connects American Studies to culture.

Culture

Insofar as these disciplines of the liberal arts and concepts of place, nation, stereotype, and symbol are the roots of American Studies, culture is their soil. It is what the field's participants feed on and the closest thing to a common ground. Their curiosities are rooted in the culture of America.

In the case of the word "culture," though, such reasoning by analogy is not only awkward but also tough to control. There is no handful of options for defining "culture"; there are hundreds of them.

Nearly every one of the liberal arts has at least a few elaborate theories of the subject. They aim to answer questions in the abstract for once and for all. In what sense can culture be said to exist? Where does it come from? How is it best described? How can competing descriptions be adjudicated? How does culture (or the representation of it) affect people? What makes it persist or change?

Neither simple nor majestic answers remain persuasive for long. Anyone who has taken a course or two in the humanities or social sciences has probably been exposed to a half-dozen definitions, each of them with something to recommend and none of them quite alike.

Amid this variety, though, are some common ideas. By nearly all accounts, culture is a pattern—a regularity of sorts—in the lives of a group of people. It is far from uniform. Individuals, factions, and environments can be related to it in different ways. (The various theories of culture most clearly part company in anticipating the nature of those relationships.) But the pattern is, in one way or another, characteristic of the group as a whole, something they can be expected to know or at least act as if they did. They conform to it or fight it, flee from it or improvise on it every day. They expect their associates—at least if they are "competent" and "one of us"—to do the same. Their fortunes likely depend on their capacity to do so, but some people certainly have more leeway than others. These patterns change with time and conditions and may be subject to great variation in actual practice. The patterns do not actually determine what anyone does but, bearing them in mind, most goings-on seem less surprising. They "fit." Conceptually, even if not morally, they make sense. Generalizations about American culture, then, are better to the extent that they simply make more sense of the place. It is against this background that the symbolic definition of "America" seems particularly fitting.

Nevertheless, within and across disciplines at any point in time, people are apt to use the word "culture" in very different ways. Their senses of the term are particularly tough to parse because the definitions tend themselves to invoke analogy. Consider the most common ones. Think of culture as:

- an onion (with a peel and layers)
- an organism (with stages of life, blood, head, and heart)
- a factory (with raw material, source of power, bosses, and workers)
- a building (with foundation, windows, and façade)
- an ecology (with niches, climates, and food chains)
- a language (with grammar, dialects, and speakers)
- a code (with secrets, transmitters, and receivers)
- a body (with personality, sexuality, upbringing, and occasional disease)
- a system (with inputs, feedback, and outputs)
- a structure (with hierarchy, needs, and objectives)
- a game (with plays, rules, and referees)
- a drama (with roles, script, and audience)
- a city (with streets, sewer lines, and neighborhoods)
- a text (with authors, genres, and readers)
- an ideology (with premises and implications)
- a regime (with a currency, rulers, and rebels)

When unpacked, each of these analogies lends the concept of culture particular qualities. In setting out to understand a culture, it matters a great deal whether you think of it, say, as something you should internalize or peel. Is what you have to do more like conducting an autopsy, cracking a code, or playing along? Some analogies leave a lot of room for you to join in or to imagine malcontents living in peace. Compare, for instance, the height of the hurdle when you think of culture as a language to learn versus a personality to transform. Or compare the implications for understanding a piece of Americana in its "cultural context," a common challenge in American Studies. Must you, in effect, predict the weather, excavate a building, or just look up the rules?

In this manner, every representation of America tends to assume the hue of the conception of culture that it employs. Each theory encourages us to construe understanding—say, the signs that we have arrived at a worthwhile interpretation of America—in its own way. With practice, just by knowing which analogy a scholar favors, you can anticipate how open or closed, orderly or chaotic, complex or simple the place is apt to seem. In a sense, the analogy determines what counts as evidence as much as the facts. This is among the reasons that academic theories of culture are so ubiquitous, elaborate, and controversial. A lot is at stake.

They can also be excruciatingly self-conscious. People's ways of defining their experience is part of the subject itself. The group of people engaged in American Studies presumably have a culture, just like everyone else.

Each of the disciplines with which American Studies trades usually has its own favored route out of this morass. A leading scholar or a textbook simply declares that culture "*really* is X" or "is best considered Y."

In the history of the culture of doing America Studies, however, the usual solution—especially in the United States—has been more eclectic and pragmatic. There is a playfully ambitious, can-do spirit. Back in 1957, Henry Nash Smith, a founder of the field, dubbed it "a kind of principled opportunism." Ever since, Americanists have been willing to face the charge that they are dilettantes, if the compensation includes insights that academic propriety or highfalutin theory impedes.

Interdisciplinary Americanists scour the disciplines, not so much to reduce the number of their options as to increase the chances that they know a good one. They want to be familiar with every concept of culture that will help them recognize and evaluate a pattern when they see it. After all, sometimes or in some ways, patterns of living actually are connected, say, more like gears in a transmission than like organs of the body. America as a symbol might really befit its time more like a word in a sentence than like the output of a system or a coin of the realm. The long list of analogies is designed to suggest some of the options that have proven most useful. Scholars of American Studies engage such interdisciplinary theory to increase the chances that they will use the most effective concepts rather than fall into the service of the one that is merely orthodox or handy.

The best interpretation of the culture is the one that makes the best sense of America—the one that is the most coherent, comprehensive, imaginative, elegant, and incisive in light of the largest possible body of evidence and the curiosity at hand.

Conclusion

American Studies, then, is an interdisciplinary branch of learning. Its subject is "America." Its roots include concepts of place, nation, stereotype, symbol, and culture, and they include various definitions of one particular place—America—that are both related and worth distinguishing. In "doing American Studies," as in deciding how to define America or culture, scholars aim to be responsive to the diversity of peoples they study, their ability to affect and be affected by turns of events, and their own sensibilities. The following selections are designed to help recall some of the most powerful ways that people have done so.

Concerning the Selections

The preceding introduction is probably sufficient for most readers. In the selections that follow, you can judge for yourselves which oxen are saddled, which are gored, and which are ignored. But people who care about such things might also welcome a few justifications, confessions, and warnings.

Even under cushy circumstances—say, for the Heath or Norton anthologies of American literature, with their thousands of pages and deep pockets—tough choices must be made. Some writings, authors, and topics are showcased while others are slighted. Current U.S. sensitivities, especially among academics still reeling from Cold War conservatism, make the process of selection particularly daunting. An editor's need ever to discriminate—to decide what goes in and what does not—has been implicated in more brutal forms of discrimination.

Very few scholars, for instance, still deny that underrepresentation of Native and African-American materials in college texts has been related to underrepresentation of Native and African-American people on U.S. campuses and in the social classes to which graduation eases admission. This is but one reason why progressive academics are rightly suspicious of any exclusive "canon" or "master narrative" of the past. Yet that is exactly what anthologies invoke.

For example, when works of or about a particular group are omitted, members or their defenders are right to protest. Names missing from the table of contents provoke sadness, shame, or anger. What are lost are not just the feelings of a few folks but also everyone's chance to learn from their experience. Among the benefits that their inclusion might afford is insight into the injustice of which the table of contents is at least a symptom. As voices are silenced, generations of wisdom are, in effect, diminished.

Yet all anthologies have to exclude vastly more than they include, and the shallower the pockets (for example, for reprint permissions and pages), the more people who will be offended and the more wisdom lost. What is worse, judging from experience, some glaring under- or overrepresentations will be obvious only in hindsight.

I remain convinced, though, that the potential rewards are worth the risk. Students generally welcome some help in learning from their predecessors and can be trusted to know that no one's version of the past must ever be their own. That expectation is partly a projection of my own upbringing (which proved pretty immune to Cold War indoctrination) but also a presumption necessary for anyone producing—as well as, I hope, reading—an anthology. At this moment, American Studies could use one, flawed though it may be.

Too often, even if understandably, I think, teachers present the field through texts designed for other purposes, particularly for American literature or history courses. "Straight" history or literature is rendered American Studies by seasoning it, say, with a dash of hip commentary and a dollop of pop culture, as if the field were a regular discipline on acid. More than seventy years of experience in awarding university degrees ought to be enough for American Studies professors to advocate curricula that even "straight" deans and students' prospective employers would accredit.

Yet more challenging has been a tendency to deride "traditional" American Studies (versus, say, "cultural studies" or "New American Studies") as a misguided mode of literary interpretation propagated in the United States during the 1950s. Books such as Russell Reising's *The Unusable Past* (1986) and the latest, quasi-official anthology, Lucy Maddox's *Locating American Studies* (1999), encourage the impression that the field is only now shedding its Cold Warrior qualities. Contributors allege that the intellectual sources of American Studies go back only about fifty years, when the field got its name, budgets, and bureaus in U.S. universities. In the shadow of Josephs Stalin and McCarthy, professors supposedly invented and then imposed notions that uniquely suited the conservative tenor of the times:

- The United States is "exceptional" in world history and should be understood on its own "innocent" terms
- The nation has a "mind"—a single, organic, slow-changing, uniform, and shared culture
- America is best revealed in its most critically acclaimed ("high" versus "low") arts
- The citizenry can be adequately understood through the experience of privileged, heterosexual, Protestant men on the European side of the Western frontier

Having so figured the past, many current Americanists congratulate themselves for having surpassed it. Free at last from Cold War ideology, they expose the flaws of the field's founders. Now they/we can recognize that:

- The United States has hardly been an innocent participant in the Earth's history
- American culture should be considered plural ("cultures") and conflicted
- Popular arts (no less than "the best") are socially mediated cultural forces and expressions
- Citizens are and always have been divided into groups separated by socially constructed, hierarchical, mutable boundaries

Of course, I have to agree that the second set of assertions is preferable to the first. But insofar as I have one fat ox to gore, it is this way of plotting progress, particularly the vanity and hypocrisy with which past and present are distinguished. Folk histories of the field imply a self-serving melodrama: rebellious U.S. academics overcome old-fart adversity.

Of course, too, such a hyperbolic rendering of this lore itself borders on the melodramatic. On the contrary, I think it is fair to say that most observers—the large number of people who speak of "America" in the course of ordinary conversation—do not buy the hokum. Most of them are not in U.S. universities and could not care less about shifts in professorial fashion. Moreover, even the most boastful send-ups for "New American Studies" acknowledge a few, albeit beleaguered, right-thinking pioneers of yore. So, I trust we can avoid another turf war. But I also believe that Americanists owe themselves and their predecessors yet more lessons of the best as well as the worst that people who share a curiosity about America have offered.

When more generously read, interpretors of American culture—even academic literary critics in the 1940s and 1950s—were rarely, I think, as dumb (or original) as celebrants of the New American Studies recently allege. Favorite foils such as Leo Marx's *Machine in the Garden* (1964) seem to be reread precisely because they are unusually easy targets.

Exceptions to the stereotype of the bad old days are ample, even in works that are well known and respected, such as W. E. B. DuBois's *Black Reconstruction* (1935, 1966), Zora Neale Hurston's *Mules and Men* (1935, 1969), Constance Rourke's *American Humor* (1931, 1953), or even Henry Nash Smith's *Virgin Land* (1950). Feminist analyses of America were part of training in nursing and home economics well before they turned academic, from the 1870s to the 1920s. Strategies for treating "high" and "low" art and for interrogating racism were intensely debated by "new humanists" (for example, Irving Babbitt, Norman Foerster, Barrett Wendell) and "literary radicals" (for example, Randolph Bourne, Van Wyck Brooks, Waldo Frank, Vernon Parrington) back in the 1910s. In 1958, when Stow Persons published his classic survey (from which intellectual historians lifted lectures for most of the Cold War), its title was not "*The* American *Mind*" but "American *Minds*," and social conflict was at least as important to his interpretation as consensus.

Likely the first textbook explicitly for American Studies—Albrecht Haushofer et al.'s *Handbuch der Amerikakunde* (1931) in the German series *Handbücher der Auslandskunde*—obviously had nothing to do with stateside fads of the 1950s, Dwight Eisenhower, the House Un-American Activities Committee, or "I Love Lucy." It was never translated into English or distributed in the United States. In fact, quite a few professional American Studies activities, including conferences in Asia as well as whole scholarly societies in Europe, pre-date the American Studies Association in the United States.

The first domestic, academic, and comprehensive literary history of the United States—*The Cambridge History of American Literature*—exhibited a mix of qualities that are now supposed to be distinctive of either the 1950s or the 1990s. But the four volumes were copyrighted from 1917 to 1921. Whatever their shortcomings, editors Trent, Erskine, Sherman, and Van Doren deserve credit for including a chapter on Native American literature and criticism by women of letters (for example, Mary Austin). Again "too early" and contrary to the lesson that such inclusions are supposed to require, they flatter this literature for reflecting a spirit of democracy, idealism, and Christian (versus "communistic") sociality that they took to be distinctly American. For that matter, as original as were the arguments of R. W. B. Lewis in *The American Adam* (1955), his supposed contribution to the field's Cold War tradition—"American innocence"—was also central to Barrett Wendell's *A Literary History of America* back in 1900. In these ways, academic history itself fails to fit the chronology or polarity against which New American Studies is often defined.

Since, too, the "new" view of culture (as inclusive, fractured, and dynamic) seems so reasonable (even though also, in some respects, old), I am disappointed when colleagues fail to apply it in accounting for the field. If the culture of American Studies were defined as inclusively as scholars have learned to define America, the "new" culture of American Studies would also seem less exceptional. In particular, when more diverse arts, social and natural sciences, and foreign and nonacademic contributors are included, tales of the field become part of a much larger, more accessible, and instructive conversation. People in American Studies have much to gain in studying their/our diverse antecedents, flaws and all.

The main objective of this anthology, therefore, is broadening the background for discussions in American Studies. While some newly popular sorts of diversity may be left to others (for example, the other volumes in this series, forthcoming ones, or the Maddox anthology), old ones should be recalled and new ones recommended. In particular, I decided that exemplars of American Studies notions would be pursued beyond the current canon (chiefly race, class, ethnicity, sexuality, and gender in twentieth-century U.S. popular arts) in three directions:

- *Outside the United States.* A goal was to illustrate curiosity about America that overflows domestic agendas. At times foreign interpretations have led and at other times followed kindred concerns in the United States. Such traveling notions might help readers internationalize their views.

- *Back in time.* A goal was to highlight, not necessarily the first or most influential of strategies for understanding America, but ones that were widely discussed before the field's institutionalization in the 1950s. Engaged by lots of people, they developed (that is, they figured in discussions or social movements or bore allusions) in ways that might inspire Americanists now.
- *Outside the university.* A goal was to link moments or reframe issues that might be otherwise segregated into hermetic categories, such as "entertaining" versus "academic." As George Lipsitz (following Duke Ellington) has suggested, once Americanists "learn to listen," the wall between raw and interpreted material or between primary and secondary sources becomes more permeable.

So in this volume near and far, traditional and recent, cultivated and vernacular sources are juxtaposed to invite critical comparison.

These general principles still leave a lot to the imagination. In practice, inescapably, I think, selection is an improvisational affair. I did not, for example, begin with a specific list of substantive topics or greatest hits. Sequences evolved as one powerful juxtaposition invited another and created gaps to be filled. Given the recent publication of *Locating American Studies*, there seemed to be no need to revisit the strictly academic history. When faced with tough choices, I took comfort from Michael Frisch's compliment of Warren Susman's contribution to that volume:

> By embracing tensions and contradictions, by reminding us of the inevitable implication of these tendencies to myth and history, utopianism and ideology, in the very nature of perceiving history in the present and in imagining the nature and possibility of change, he places history and historians back where they belong—as part of a broad history-making continuum linking intellectuals and ordinary citizens in the struggle to make sense of their lives, communities, and the world around them.

With such well-tended roots in place, the process of making and, I hope, interpreting choices is more inviting.

I thought that the selections should be notable or provocative enough to serve teachers whose interests differ from mine. Students might feel encouraged to move beyond the approach that the introductions and juxtapositions suggest. Some excerpts were chosen just because it is hard to imagine an American Studies course without them, even though students these days, I gather, rarely encounter the originals. I also reluctantly bypassed many classics (for example, by Gloria Anzaldúa, Martin Luther King Jr., Maxine Hong Kingston, Toni Morrison, Leslie Marmon Silko, Alice Walker) not only because of the high cost of reprint permissions but also because students tell me that they already (via assignments repeated since primary school) know those originals so well. In the case of non-U.S. sources, where the list of omissions must be particularly long, I favored regions (for example, East Asia and Western Europe) where I happen to have a little more experience. Often I was just trying to find pairs of pieces that could be useful in triangulating a response to topics of recent discussion.

The introductions to each selection are designed to open rather than constrain the interpretation of a text. They suggest some ways that an excerpt might be both hitched to its context and carried to other ones. Hence, selections are arrayed less to represent chronology or coverage than to suggest avenues that readers might pursue. Many of the selections are abbreviated with spelling and punctuation standardized to make them more accessible to readers of modern English. Along the way, I try to define some terms and trends that may be useful in yet other reading, listening, watching, agitating, or just getting on with life that includes curiosity about America.

In these ways, I aim to graft roots of hardy, disparate stock. I hope that these selections may help students and teachers to cultivate even better American Studies in the future.

I | America as a New World

Some Guiding Questions

Should America be considered a separate place—
   distinct and distant from other places?
   Which ones?
   What differences are supposed to set it apart?
In what respects is America "new" or "young"?
   When compared to what?
   From whose point of view?
   For better or worse?
How are these qualities—the degree to which
   America is distinct, distant, new—to be gauged?
   What inclines people to ask?
   How is it supposed to matter?
   For example, should the New World be considered
      better (or worse) to the extent that it resembles
      (or fails to resemble) an old one?

How might the answers to such questions depend
on other sorts of relations or presumptions
about them?
The relationship between Europeans and Indians?
Between empires and colonists?
Church and state?
Fact and myth?
Tradition and modernity?

1 How America Was Discovered (c. 1735–1815)

Since the European invasion of North America began in the East, that is also where relations between natives and newcomers have an especially long and complex history. European accounts of contact—British, Dutch, French, German, Italian, Portuguese, Spanish—quickly found their ways into print, but the continent's first nations also had a mix of common and particular experiences. They drew their own lessons about the meaning of Europe's "New World" and insofar as possible passed them on to their descendants, generally through a well-preserved oral tradition.

From the sixteenth through the mid-eighteenth centuries, the territory of the Iroquois came to include most of the nations of eastern North America. About 1720, while European colonists still fought over footholds along the coast, the League of Six Nations—the Mohawk, Onondaga, Cayuga, Oneida, Tuscarora, and Seneca—enjoyed dominion from the Atlantic to the Mississippi and from the Saint Lawrence to the Tennessee Rivers. They were a force to be reckoned with, and for more than a century they masterfully played off alliances with the French and the British. But after the American Revolution (in which the Seneca sided with the Tories), Europeans gained the upper hand, often brutally.

As their losses intensified, the Seneca prophet Handsome Lake inspired a following for his 1799 vision of restoration through resistance to white encroachment, repentance for assimilation, and return to "traditional" ways of life. This Long House Religion, like the Ghost Dance, was one among many nativist movements that sustained Indian peoples and attracted fear and repression from whites. Nevertheless, there are still more than 50,000 Iroquois people in the United States and yet more in Canada. Most of the Seneca remain in and around their ancestral lands in western New York.

The following example of Handsome Lake's teaching comes by way of his half-brother, Chief Edward Cornplanter (Sosondowa). Cornplanter himself had a European father and Seneca mother, and he led raids on the side of the British during the Revolution. He was the one forced to sign the 1784 Treaty of Fort Stanwix, ceding to the United States nearly all Iroquois lands.

This particular version was collected about 1923 by Arthur Caswell Parker, a thoroughly bicultural and multidisciplinary Americanist. Through his father and father's father (a relative of Handsome Lake) he was born Seneca, but since their wives were New England missionaries and since maternity determines descent, he was not officially a member of the Seneca nation. But he grew up on the Cattaraugus Reservation, playing in a patois of Seneca and English. He began grade school on the reservation but finished at White Plains High School. When the time came to choose a profession, he declined an invitation to earn his Ph.D. with Franz Boas, reputedly the founder of U.S. anthropology at Columbia University. Instead, he dedicated himself to an eclectic career of research (archaeology, folklore, history, ethnology), writing, and public education, chiefly with the New York State Museum. He coined the term "museology" to describe his work.

In presenting Seneca folklore, Parker compares his purpose with that of a poet, fiction writer, missionary ("sectarian enthusiast"), or philologist:

> The value of this collection is not a literary one but a scientific one. It reveals the type of tale that held the interest and attention of the Seneca; it reveals certain mental traits and tendencies; it reveals many customs and incidents in native life, and finally, it serves as an index of native psychology. . . .
>
> The student of folklore . . . [seeks] to so present his legend that it will awaken in the mind of his reader sensations similar to those aroused in the mind of the Indian auditor hearing it from the native raconteur. The recorder of the tale seeks to assimilate its characteristics, to become imbued with its spirit, to understand its details, to follow its language—its sentences—one by one, as they follow in sequence, and then he seeks to present it consistently. . . .
>
> The temptation is ever present to tell a good story, and let the legend become the skeleton over which the words are woven. Needless to say, this is not an honest thing to do, and the folklore student resists this temptation, and gives his product a genuine presentation, regardless of what literary critics may think. He strives only to be the medium by which a native tale is transformed from its original language to that of another language. The thought, the form and the sequence of the story, he insists, must remain exactly as it was, though the verbal dress is European and not Indian. . . . Our plan is to smooth out the language, divest it of its awkward arrangement, and allow the thought to flow on.

Parker called the goal "an honestly constructed free translation."

> According to Chief Cornplanter, Handsome Lake taught that America was discovered in the manner here related.

A great queen had among her servants a young minister. Upon a certain occasion she requested him to dust some books that she had hidden in an old chest. Now when the young man reached the bottom of the chest he found a wonderful book which he opened and read. It told that the white men had killed the son of the Creator and it said, moreover, that he had promised to return in three days and then again in forty but that he never did. All his followers then began to despair but some said, "He surely will come again some time." When the young preacher read this book he was worried because he had discovered that he had been deceived and that his Lord was not on earth and had not returned when he promised. So he went to some of the chief preachers and asked them about the matter, and they answered that he had better seek the Lord himself and find if he were not on the earth now. So he prepared to find the Lord, and the next day when he looked out into the river he saw a beautiful island and marveled that he had never noticed it before. As he continued to look he saw a castle built of gold in the midst of the island, and he marveled that he had not seen the castle before. Then he thought that so beautiful a palace on so beautiful an isle must surely be the abode of the son of the Creator. Immediately he went to the wise men and told them what he had seen, and they wondered greatly and answered that it must indeed be the house of the Lord. So together they went to the river, and when they came to it they found that it was spanned by a bridge of gold. Then one of the preachers fell down and prayed a long time and arising to cross the bridge turned back because he was afraid to meet his Lord. Then the other crossed the bridge and knelt down upon the grass and prayed, but he became afraid to go near the house. So the young man went boldly over to attend to the business at hand and walking up to the door knocked. A handsome man welcomed him into a room and bade him be of ease. "I wanted you," he said. "You are a bright young man; those old fools will not suit me for they would be afraid to listen to me. Listen to me, young man, and you will be rich. Across the ocean there is a great country of which you have never heard. The people there are virtuous, they have no evil habits or appetites but are honest and single-minded. A great reward is yours if you enter into my plans and carry them out. Here are five things. Carry them over to the people across the ocean and never shall you want for wealth, position or power. Take these cards, this money, this fiddle, this whiskey and this blood corruption and give them all to the people across the water. The cards will make them gamble away their goods and idle away their time, the money will make them dishonest and covetous, the fiddle will make them dance with women and their lower natures will command them, the whiskey will excite their minds to evil doing and turn their minds, and the blood corruption will eat their strength and rot their bones."

The young man thought this a good bargain and promised to do as the man had commanded him. He left the palace, and when he had stepped over the bridge it was gone, likewise the golden palace and also the island. Now he wondered if he had seen the Lord, but he did not tell the great ministers of his bargain because they might try to forestall him. So he looked about and at length found Columbus to whom he told the whole story. So Columbus fitted out some boats and sailed out into the ocean to find the land on the other side. When he had sailed for many days on the water the sailors said that unless Columbus turned about and went home they would behead him, but he asked for another day, and on that day land was seen and that land was America. Then they turned around and going back reported what they had discovered. Soon a great flock of ships came over the ocean, and white men came swarming into the country bringing with them cards, money, fiddles, whiskey and blood corruption.

Now the man who had appeared in the gold palace was the devil, and when afterward he saw what his words had done, he said that he had made a great mistake, and even he lamented that his evil had been so enormous.

WILLIAM SHAKESPEARE

2 | The Tempest (1611)

One of the bonds between modern professors of American Studies and the first European explorers is the idea of "American exceptionalism." For half a millenium people have engaged (if not shared) an impression that there is (or ought to be) something "new" in lands west of England, Portugal, and Spain (later, east of China, north of Mexico). Differences of opinion have more often centered on the quality of American uniqueness than on the question of its existence. Like scouts and settlers, critics still wonder: Is America distinctly pristine or wild? Pure or dangerous?—as if lands, like other objects of men's desire, must be either blonde or brunette.

In 1607 a London company called the site of Britain's first outpost (the home of about 10,000 members of the Powhatan Confederation) "Virginia," and in 1950 Henry Nash Smith called his dissertation-turned-book (the first canonical contribution to American Studies) *Virgin Land*. As evident in the mocking title of Annette Kolodny's response, *The Lay of the Land* (1975), the image of America as an under- or oversexed maiden has been objectionable for many years. Of course, too, the millions of people who lived in North America for thousands of years hardly needed aliens to discover, invent, or otherwise probe their "innocence." But variants of such exceptionalist notions endure.

One reason is endemic to sociality itself. It is hard to prompt loyalty to a group, much less a polity, without also hyping its distinction. Indian no less than Asian, African, and European sovereigns have consistently asserted that "their" people were special, at least different if not better than citizens of colonies or rival states. Even the Old Testament can be read as a plea for Hebraic exceptionalism, the New Testament for Christians, and the Koran for Muslims. Plato and Herodotus were only among the most famous of ancients to have insisted that their travels put them in touch with fundamentally different grades of humanity.

According to nearly every report, fifteenth- to seventeenth-century European explorers found America awesome. As Miranda, the fair maiden of Shakespeare's *The Tempest*, exclaimed:

7

O, wonder!
How many goodly creatures are there here!
How beauteous mankind is! O brave new world,
That has such people in't!

Explorers provided detailed, though often also outlandish accounts of
"such people." Even the most determinedly scientific reports now seem
radically ethnocentric. They took America to be a relic of Europe's long-lost
past or an omen of its future. The farther west they went, the more they
seemed to assume that natives were like ancestors in a state of racially
arrested development or siblings who had missed the boat to Civilization.
Hence, English settlers such as Thomas Merton, Captain John Smith, and
Roger Williams first depicted Indians by bloating their stereotypes of the
Irish. In fact, many of the British commanders who had lorded over the
conquest of Ireland were the very same people who colonized America,
and they acted accordingly.

Philosophers, scientists, and historians subsequently debated whether
the source of this East/West, Old/New World relation was a sign of God's
design, an accident of racial/cultural history, or a climatic effect. Despite
such disagreements, they generally agreed that the measure of the New
World would be the best and worst inclinations of the Old. As a result, in
their discussions we learn much less about what America was than what it
was not. Witness, for example, the impression that a century of European
exploration left on Michel de Montaigne:

> It is a nation . . . that hath no kind of traffic, no knowledge of letters,
> no intelligence of numbers, no name of magistrate nor of political su-
> periority, no use of service, of riches or of poverty, no contracts, no
> successions, no dividences, no occupation but idle, no respect of kin-
> dred but common, no apparel but natural, no manuring of lands, no
> use of wine, corn or metal. . . .
>
> They have great abundance of fish and flesh that have no resem-
> blance at all with ours, and eat them without any sauces or skill of
> cookery. . . . They rise with the sun and feed for all day. . . . They spend
> the whole day in dancing. . . .
>
> Their wars are noble and generous. . . . They contend not for gain-
> ing of new lands, for to this day they yet enjoy that natural . . . abun-
> dance [that] furnish[es] them with all necessary things. . . . Whatsoever
> is beyond it is to them superfluous. . . .
>
> The aged are esteemed as fathers to all the rest. These leave this
> full possession of goods in common, and without individuity to their
> heirs, without other claim or title but that which nature doth plainly
> impart unto all creatures, even as she brings them into the world.

These passages from Montaigne's essay, "Of Cannibals" (translated into
English by John Florio in 1603), are among the sources that William
Shakespeare consulted in preparing *The Tempest* for its premiere at the
wedding of Princess Elizabeth in 1611. Phrases are lifted verbatim.

Yet more important sources for the play, however, were reports of an
actual tempest just two years before. Since Shakespeare's social circle included several members of the Virginia Company, he surely was among the
many Europeans who heard about the company's encounter with a hurri-
cane off the Virginia coast in 1609. The governor's ship was forced off

course to Bermuda under terrifying circumstances like those with which the play begins.

Subsequent scenes explore familiar Shakespearean themes: statecraft, patriarchy, witchcraft, jealousy, revenge, greed, devotion, love, and death. But *The Tempest* is also very specifically about European colonization of America, especially about the sovereignty of natives and newcomers. In the following excerpt from Act I, the two contend.

Caliban (a play on the word "cannibal") is an aborigine, "a savage and deformed Slave." His attachment to the land is a birthright conveyed through his mother, the witch Sycorax. Prospero, "the right Duke of Milan," is a colonist and the father of the maiden Miranda. He has only just arrived by harrowing happenstance, but he already wields extraordinary power, magic, and science. He is both a "wizard" and a professor of "liberal arts." Caliban and Prospero discuss, among other things, the power of language, nature, art, sex, nativity, and knowledge in the New World.

PROSPERO

> Thou poisonous slave, got by the devil himself
> Upon thy wicked dam, come forth!

[*Enter* CALIBAN]

CALIBAN

> As wicked dew as e'er my mother brush'd
> With raven's feather from unwholesome fen,
> Drop on you both! A southwest blow on ye
> And blister you all o'er!

PROSPERO

> For this, be sure, tonight thou shalt have cramps,
> Side-stitches that shall pen thy breath up; urchins
> Shall, for that vast of night that they may work,
> All exercise on thee; thou shalt be pinch'd
> As thick as honeycomb, each pinch more stinging
> Than bees that made 'em.

CALIBAN

> I must eat my dinner.
> This island's mine, by Sycorax my mother,
> Which thou tak'st from me. When thou camest first,
> Thou strok'dst me and mad'st much of me, wouldst give me
> Water with berries in't, and teach me how
> To name the bigger light, and how the less,
> That burn by day and night; and then I lov'd thee

And show'd thee all the qualities o' th' isle,
The fresh springs, brine-pits, barren place and fertile.
Cursed be I that did so! All the charms
Of Sycorax—toads, beetles, bats light on you!
For I am all the subjects that you have,
Which first was mine own king; and here you sty me
In this hard rock, whiles you do keep from me
The rest o' th' island.

PROSPERO

Thou most lying slave,
Whom stripes may move, not kindness! I have us'd thee,
(Filth as thou art) with humane care, and lodg'd thee
In mine own cell till thou didst seek to violate
The honour of my child.

CALIBAN

O ho, O ho! Would't had been done!
Thou didst prevent me; I had peopled else
This isle with Calibans.

PROSPERO

Abhorred slave,
Which any print of goodness wilt not take,
Being capable of all ill! I pitied thee,
Took pains to make thee speak, taught thee each hour
One thing or other. When thou didst not, savage,
Know thine own meaning, but wouldst gabble like
A thing most brutish, I endow'd thy purposes
With words that made them known. But thy vile race,
Though thou didst learn, had that in't which good natures
Could not abide to be with. Therefore wast thou
Deservedly confin'd into this rock, who hadst
Deserved more than a prison.

CALIBAN

You taught me language; and my profit on't
Is, I know how to curse. The red plague rid you
For learning me your language!

PROSPERO

    Hag-seed, hence!
    Fetch us in fuel; and be quick, thou'rt best,
    To answer other business. Shrug'st thou, malice?
    If thou neglect'st or dost unwillingly
    What I command, I'll rack thee with old cramps,
    Fill all thy bones with aches, make thee roar
    That beasts shall tremble at thy din.

CALIBAN

    No, pray thee.
    [*Aside*] I must obey: his art is of such pow'r
    It would control my dam's god, Setebos,
    and make a vassal of him.

PROSPERO

    So, slave; hence! [*Exit* CALIBAN]

JOHN WINTHROP

3 A Model of Christian Charity (1630)

When considering religion in America, it is hard to find generalizations that leave room for the variety of piety and iniquity in reality. Extremes are obvious even within families (as for cousins "Killer" Jerry Lee Lewis and televangelist Jimmy Swaggart) and among television programs that share prime time (as for CBN and WWF, the Christian Broadcasting Network and the World Wrestling Federation). For that matter, individual pop stars such as Little Richard, Elvis Presley, and Madonna gained allure by swinging from pelvis to pulpit. Nevertheless, Americans are among the most frequent churchgoers on the planet, and there is a common perception, unmistakable in malls before Christmas and Easter, that the United States is "basically a Christian country." The stereotype of the first American is a British Puritan, envisioned as a scowling, Bible-thumping witch-burner in black garb. Works of fiction such as Nathaniel Hawthorne's *The Scarlet Letter* (1850) and Arthur Miller's *The Crucible* (1953) have popularized and perpetuated that impression. Even today, sexual repression and obsessive propriety go by the name of "puritanical."

Of course, there are lots of reasons to resist the stereotype. During the sixteenth and seventeenth centuries, Europeans were a tiny proportion of North America's inhabitants. Even then, the Spanish and French (mainly Catholic rather than Protestant) outnumbered the English, as other nationalities did in the eighteenth, nineteenth, and twentieth centuries. Furthermore, the Puritans were not as puritanical as people assume.

Admittedly, their leadership was stern. The main purpose of the clergy was to guide or, when necessary, force their flock to heed God's will. Gambling and theater were taboo. The Sabbath was a day of mandatory worship, and heresy was suppressed (as it was among other contemporary faiths on both sides of the Atlantic). Suspected witches in their midst (generally women) were, in fact, accused (generally by other women), tried and killed (nearly always by men).

But Puritans also wore brightly colored clothes and enjoyed dancing, music, chess, and beer in moderation. Apparently most couples conceived their first child before rather than after marriage. Since knowing the Bible was a sacred duty, literacy was highly prized. Hence, Puritans frequented bookstores and founded America's first college, Harvard, a mere six years after the Massachusetts Bay Colony itself. In 1647 they mandated the continent's first public schools. The theologian and lawyer John Winthrop (governor of the colony nearly every year from its inception in 1629 till his death in 1649) was also a fan of cutting-edge science. He donated to Harvard the telescope that Thomas Brattle used in contributing to Sir Isaac Newton's *Mathematical Principles of Natural Philosophy* (*Philosophiae naturalis principia mathematica*, 1687). By this short but indirect route, a leading Puritan, Winthrop himself, provided an instrument of the Enlightenment challenge to theocracy.

It is also fair to say that most of the first British settlers shared a deep faith in Protestant principles, albeit at odds with the established church. They insisted on the severity of original sin and predestination but took encouragement from the possibility of salvation for those devoted to it. The most sensitive target of their dissent after 1560 (prior to migration) was the ruling hierarchy of the Church of England, which they considered a corrupt vestige of Catholicism. As the Stuart kings and bishops clung to power, dissenters tried to change the church from within. Unlike other reformed Calvinists (for example, the Pilgrims who in 1620 opted to "separate" via the *Mayflower* to nearby Plymouth), the Puritan strategy was nonseparatist: they would depart from Anglican authority only so far as necessary to blaze a holier path. In 1630, as the British economy worsened and persecution intensified under Charles I, about 700 of them opted to cross the Atlantic aboard a dozen ships, led by John Winthrop's *Arbella*.

Apparently while still at sea, Winthrop sought prophesy in God's words, human history, and the laws of nature. Although the exact time and place of the resulting lay sermon are uncertain, Americanists have long imagined him preaching on *Arbella*'s deck, with New Canaan in view. "A great company of religious people" welcomed a vision of perfection befitting their exodus "from the Island of Great Britain to New England in the North America. *Anno* 1630."

Christian Charity

A Model Hereof

God Almighty in His most holy and wise providence hath so disposed of the condition of mankind, as in all times: some must be rich, some poor; some high and eminent in power and dignity, others mean and in subjection.

The Reason Hereof

First Reason: First, to hold conformity with the rest of His works, being delighted to show forth the glory of His wisdom in the variety and difference of the creatures and the glory of His power, in ordering all these differences for the preservation and good of the whole and the glory of His greatness; that as it is the glory of princes to have many officers, so this great King will have many Stewards, counting Himself more honored in dispensing His gifts to man by man than if He did it by His own immediate hand.

Second Reason: Secondly, that He might have the more occasion to manifest the work of His Spirit: first, upon the wicked in moderating and restraining them, so that the rich and mighty should not eat up the poor, nor the poor and despised rise up against their superiors and shake off their yoke; second, in the regenerate, in exercising His graces in them: as in the great ones, their love, mercy, gentleness, temperance, etc.; in the poor and inferior sort, their faith, patience, obedience, etc.

Third Reason: Thirdly, That every man might have need of other men, and from hence they might be all knit more nearly together in the bond of brotherly affection. From hence it appears plainly that no man is made more honorable than another or more wealthy etc., out of any particular and singular respect to himself but for the glory of his Creator and the common good of the creature, man. Therefore God still reserves the property of these gifts to Himself (as in Ezekiel: 16.17). He there calls wealth *His gold and His silver*, etc. And (in Proverbs: 3.9) He claims their service as His due, *Honor the Lord with thy riches*, etc. All men being thus (by divine providence) ranked into two such sorts: rich and poor. Under the first are comprehended all such as are able to live comfortably by their own means duly improved, and all others are poor according to the former distribution.

There are two rules whereby we are to talk one towards another: JUSTICE and MERCY. These are always distinguished in their act and in their object, yet may they both concur in the same subject in each respect—as sometimes there may be an occasion of showing mercy to a rich man in some sudden danger of distress, and also doing of mere Justice to a poor man in regard of some particular contract, etc. There is likewise a double law by which we are regulated in our conversation, one towards another: In both the former respects, the law of nature and the law of grace, or the moral law or the law of the Gospel (to omit the rule of justice as not properly belonging to this purpose, otherwise then it may fall into consideration in some particular cases). By the first of these laws man, as he was enabled so with all, is commanded to love his neighbor as himself. Upon this ground stands all the precepts of the moral law, which concerns our dealings with men. To apply this to the works of mercy, this law requires two things: First, that every man afford his help to another in every want or distress; Second, that he perform this out of the same affection which makes him careful of his own good according to that of our Saviour (Matthew: 7.12) *Whatsoever ye would that men should do to you.* This was practiced by Abraham and Lot in entertaining the Angels and the old man Gibea.

The law of grace or the Gospel hath some difference from the former, as in these respects. First, the law of nature was given to man in the estate of innocency . . . in the estate of regeneracy. Secondly, the former propounds one man to another, as the same flesh and image of God, this as a brother in Christ also, and in the communion of the same spirit and so teaches us to put a difference between Christians and others. *Do good to all especially to the household of faith.* Upon this ground the Israelites were to put a difference between the brethren of such as were strangers though not of the Canaanites. Thirdly, the law of nature could give no rules for dealing with enemies, for all are to be considered as friends in the estate of innocency, but the Gospel commands love to an enemy. Proof: *If thine Enemy hunger, feed him; Love your enemies, do good to them that hate you* (Matthew: 5.44).

This law of the Gospel propounds likewise a difference of seasons and occasions. There is a time when a Christian must sell all and give to the poor as they did in the Apostles' times. There is a time also when a Christian (though they give not all yet) must give beyond their ability, as they of Macedonia (2 Corinthians: 8.1–4). Likewise, community of perils calls for extraordinary liberality and so doth Community in some special service for the church. Lastly, when there is no other means whereby our Christian brother may be relieved in this distress, we must help him beyond our ability, rather than tempt God, in putting Him upon help by miraculous or extraordinary means.

This duty of mercy is exercised in the kinds, *giving, lending* and *forgiving* . . . .

From hence we may frame these Conclusions.

First, all true Christians are of one body in Christ. (1 Corinthians: 12.12–27) *Ye are the body of Christ and members of their part.* . . .

Second, the ligaments of this body which knit together are love.

Third, no body can be perfect which wants its proper ligaments.

Fourth, all the parts of this body being thus united are made so contiguous in a special relation as they must partake of each other's strength and infirmity, joy, and sorrow, weal and woe. (1 Corinthians: 12.26) *If one member suffers, all suffer with it; if one be in honor, all rejoice in it.*

Fifth, this sensibleness and Sympathy of each other's Conditions will necessarily infuse into each part a native desire and endeavor, to strengthen, defend, preserve, and comfort the other.

To insist a little on this Conclusion being the product of all the former, the truth hereof will appear both by precept and pattern (1 John: 3.10) *Ye ought to lay down your lives for the brethren.* (Galatians: 6.2) *Bear ye one another's burdens and so fulfill the law of Christ. . . .*

It rests now to make some application of this discourse by the present design which gave the occasion of writing of it. Herein are four things to be propounded: First, the persons; second, the work; third, the end; and fourth, the means.

1. For the *persons*, we are a Company professing ourselves fellow members of Christ, in which respects—only though we were absent from each other many miles and had our employments as far distant— yet we ought to account ourselves knit together by this bond of love and live in the exercise of it, if we would have comfort of our being in Christ. This was notorious in the practice of the Christians in former times, as is testified of the Waldenses from the mouth of one of the adversaries Aeneas Sylvius *"mutuo ament pene antequam norunt"*— they used to love any of their own religion even before they were acquainted with them.

2. For the *work* we have in hand, it is by a mutual consent, through a special overruling providence and more than an ordinary approbation of the churches of Christ, to seek out a place of cohabitation and consortship under a due form of government both civil and ecclesiastical. In such cases as this, the care of the public must oversway all private respects, by which not only conscience but mere Civil policy doth bind us; for it is a true rule that particular estates cannot subsist in the ruin of the public.

3. The *end* is to improve our lives to do more service to the Lord, the comfort and increase of the body of Christ whereof we are members, that our selves and posterity may be the better preserved from the common corruptions of this evil world, to serve the Lord and work out our salvation under the power and purity of His holy ordinances.

4. For the *means* whereby this must be effected, they are twofold: a conformity with the work and end we aim at. These we see are extraordinary. Therefore we must not content ourselves with usual ordi-

nary means. Whatsoever we did or ought to have done when we lived in England, the same must we do and more also where we go. That which the most in their churches maintain as a truth in profession only, we must bring into familiar and constant practice; as in this duty of love, we must love brotherly without dissimulation. We must *love one another with a pure heart fervently*. We must *bear one another's burdens*. We must look not only on our own things, but also on the things of our brethren. Neither must we think that the Lord will bear with such failings at our hands as He doth from those among whom we have lived. . . .

Thus stands the cause between God and us. We are entered into covenant with Him for this work. We have taken out a commission. The Lord hath given us leave to draw our own articles. We have professed to enterprise these actions upon these. And these ends we have hereupon besought Him of favor and blessing. Now if the Lord shall please to hear us and bring us in peace to the place we desire, then hath He ratified this covenant and sealed our commission, and will expect a strict performance of the articles contained in it. But if we shall neglect the observation of these articles which are the ends we have propounded and, dissembling with our God, shall fall to embrace this present world and prosecute our carnal intentions, seeking great things for our selves and our posterity, the Lord will surely break out in wrath against us to be revenged of such a perjured people and make us know the price of the breach of such a covenant.

Now the only way to avoid this shipwreck and to provide for our posterity is to follow the counsel of Micah: *to do Justly, to love mercy, to walk humbly with our God*. For this end, we must be knit together in this work as one man. We must entertain each other in brotherly affection. We must be willing to abridge our selves of our superfluities, for the supply of others' necessities. We must uphold a familiar commerce together in all meekness, gentleness, patience, and liberality. We must delight in each other, make others' conditions our own— rejoice together, mourn together, labor and suffer together, always having before our eyes our commission and community in the work, our community as members of the same body. So shall we *keep the unity of the spirit in the bond of peace*. The Lord will be our God and delight to dwell among us, as His own people and will command a blessing upon us in all our ways, so that we shall see much more of His wisdom, power, goodness, and truth than formerly we have been acquainted with. We shall find that the God of Israel is among us, when ten of us shall be able to resist a thousand of our enemies, when He shall make us a praise and glory, that men shall say of succeeding plantations: "The Lord make it like that of NEW ENGLAND." For we must consider that we shall be as a City upon a Hill. The eyes of all people are upon us; so that if we shall deal falsely with our God in this work we have undertaken and so cause Him to withdraw His present help from us, we shall be made a story and a byword through the world. We shall open the mouths of enemies to speak evil of the ways of God and all professors for God's sake. We shall shame the faces of many of God's worthy servants, and cause their prayers to be turned into curses upon us till we be consumed out of the good land whither we are going.

And to shut up this discourse with that exhortation of Moses, that faithful servant of the Lord in his last farewell to Israel (Deuteronomy: 30.15–20): *Beloved, there is now set before us life and good, death and evil, in that we are Commanded this day to love the Lord our God and to love one another, to walk in His ways and to keep His Command-ments and His Ordinances, and His laws,* and the Articles of our Cov-enant with Him that *we may live and multiply, and that the Lord our God may bless us in the land whither we go to possess it. But if our hearts shall turn away so that we will not obey, but shall be seduced and worship other gods,* our pleasures and profits, *and serve them;* it is propounded unto us this day, *we shall surely perish and we shall not prolong our days upon the good land whither we passed over this vast sea to possess it.*

Therefore let us choose life,
that we and our seed
may live; by obeying His
voice, and cleaving to Him,
for He is our life, and
our prosperity.

4 *Engel v. Vitale* (1962)

Early American refugees from European poverty and religious persecution brought with them the contest between church and state. At least since the fourth century, sundry cadres of bishops and nobles had been fighting to consolidate control of divine and earthly turf. In the spirit of the Peace of Augsburg (1555), each state of Christendom was supposed to establish its own religion, but enforcement would be difficult in distant, dissenting colonies. For example, almost immediately after they crossed the Atlantic (1636–1644), a sect resisting the authority of the Puritan government of Massachusetts Bay founded its own Colony of Rhode Island and Providence Plantations. Its colonial charter, penned by the minister and physician John Clarke, was the first both to mandate democratic rule and to bar established religion.

After Independence, largely to avoid just such factionalism, separation of church and state became national law through "the establishment clause" of Article 1 of the Bill of Rights (amended to the U.S. Constitution in 1791):

> Congress shall make no law respecting an establishment of religion, or prohibiting the free exercise thereof; or abridging the freedom of speech, or of the press; or the right of the people peaceably to assemble, and to petition the government for a redress of grievances.

And Article VI, section 3, of the Constitution:

> No religious test shall ever be required as a qualification to any office or public trust under the United States.

Soon thereafter the U.S. Senate (in ratifying a treaty with Tripoli, June 5, 1805) made the point crystal clear: "The government of the United States of America is not in any sense founded on the Christian religion."

Tests of that reading of American history and culture were rarely visible until the 1960s, when there was a string of Supreme Court challenges to state and local laws permitting prayer on government property or upon civic occasions. The issue of prayer in public schools has been returning to legislatures and courts ever since.

The clearest precedent-setter among these cases remains *Engel v. Vitale*, decided June 25, 1962. Even in siding with the liberal majority, Justice William O. Douglas felt compelled to acknowledge that Supreme Court sessions themselves begin with a supplication—"God save the United States and this Honorable Court." Nevertheless, Justice Hugo Black delivered a majority decision that, in light of a broad review of the role of religion in American life, buttressed the barrier between worship and civil affairs.

We think that the constitutional prohibition against law respecting an establishment of religion must at least mean that in this country it is no part of the business of government to compose official prayers for any group of the American people to recite as a part of a religious program carried on by government.

It is a matter of history that this very practice of establishing governmentally composed prayers for religious services was one of the reasons which caused many of our early colonists to leave England and seek religious freedom in America. . . . Powerful groups representing some of the varying religious views of the people struggled among themselves to impress their particular views upon the Government and obtain amendments of the Book more suitable to their respective notions of how religious services should be conducted in order that the official religious establishment would advance their particular religious beliefs. Other groups, lacking the necessary political power to influence the Government on the matter, decided to leave England and its established church and seek freedom in America from England's governmentally ordained and supported religion.

It is an unfortunate fact of history that when some of the very groups which had most strenuously opposed the established Church of England found themselves sufficiently in control of colonial governments in this country to write their own prayers into law, they passed laws making their own religion the official religion of their respective colonies. Indeed, as late as the time of the Revolutionary War, there were established churches in at least eight of the thirteen former colonies and established religions in at least four of the other five. But the successful Revolution against English political domination was shortly followed by intense opposition to the practice of establishing religion by law. . . .

It is a matter of history that this very practice of establishing governmentally composed prayers for religious services was one of the reasons which caused many of our early colonists to leave England and seek religious freedom in America. The *Book of Common Prayer*, which was created under governmental direction and which was approved by Acts of Parliament in 1548 and 1549, set out in minute detail the accepted form and content of prayer and other religious ceremonies to be used in the established, tax-supported Church of England. . . .

By the time of the adoption of the Constitution . . . people knew, some of them from bitter personal experience, that one of the greatest dangers to the freedom of the individual to worship in his own way lay in the Government's placing its official stamp of approval upon one particular kind of prayer or one particular form of religious services. . . . The First Amendment was added to the Constitution to stand as a guarantee that neither the power nor the prestige of the Federal Government would be used to control, support or influence the kinds of prayer the American people can say. . . .

Neither the fact that the prayer may be denominationally neutral nor the fact that its observance on the part of the students is voluntary can serve to free it from the limitations of the Establishment Clause. . . . The Establishment Clause thus stands as an expression of principle on the part of the Founders of our Constitution that religion is too personal, too sacred, too holy, to permit its "unhallowed perversion" by a civil magistrate. . . .

It has been argued that to apply the Constitution in such a way as to prohibit state laws respecting an establishment of religious services in public schools is to indicate a hostility toward religion or toward prayer. Nothing, of course, could be more wrong. The history of man is inseparable from the history of religion. And perhaps it is not too much to say that since the beginning of that history many people have devoutly believed that "More things are wrought by prayer than this world dreams of." It was doubtless largely due to men who believed this that there grew up a sentiment that caused men to leave the crosscurrents of officially established state religions and religious persecution in Europe and come to this country filled with the hope that they could find a place in which they could pray when they pleased to the God of their faith in the language they chose. . . . It is neither sacrilegious nor antireligious to say that each separate government in this country should stay out of the business of writing or sanctioning official prayers and leave that purely religious function to the people themselves and to those the people choose to look to for religious guidance.

J. HECTOR ST. JOHN DE
CRÈVECOEUR

5 | Letter III from an American Farmer (1782)

Probably the most famous single sentence in American Studies is a question: "What then is the American, this new man?" It first appears in the writing of a French aristocrat who, as a British subject, spent the 1770s on a farm in Orange County, New York. With the exception of a half-dozen later years as French consul in New York City, Crèvecoeur's experience was thoroughly European. But his *Letters* had many qualities that subsequent observers found "distinctively American": the notion that citizens are a "new" sort of people; that their environment—a "natural" land of fecundity, liberty, and opportunity—is shaping them, inspiring "dreams" of self-reliance and success; that they are predominantly European, Christian, and enterprising; that in each region, ways of life differ but that the people are also of a uniformly "middling" sort. Diverse nationalities and faiths, he said, might well "melt" into a more peaceful, justice-loving, and prosperous original, and it should be the envy of the world.

All of these observations are, of course, highly contestable. Like other foreign visitors, this newly "American" farmer—who goes by the name of "James"—was first impressed with differences, especially those that might imply criticism of the homeland that he better knew. Like other colonists, he found a center to American life in part by discounting people (also known as "savages") who would confound his generalizations. Like other agents of colonialism, he hyped the positive.

To his credit, he knew that his generalizing trope—the concept of "national genius"—was problematic. At one point, for example, he wonders:

Posterity will look back with avidity and pleasure, to trace, if possible, the era of this or that particular settlement. Pray, what is the reason that the Scots are in general more religious, more faithful, more honest and industrious than the Irish?

But he instantly backpedals:

> I do not mean to insinuate national reflections—God forbid! It ill becomes any man, and much less an American; but as I know men are nothing of themselves, and that they owe all their different modifications either to government or other local circumstances, there must be some powerful causes which constitute this great national difference.

Many rounds of such speculation and backpedaling have followed, and most of them can find precedent in *Letters from an American Farmer* more than two centuries ago.

The variety of connections that readers have found is immense. According to Grantland Rice, "In the two years after its English publication in 1782, *Letters* had been read by European critics as, variously, a portrayal of the exotic, a benign literary hoax, a contribution to the English literary canon, a colonial panegyric, an invective against the Revolution, a Tory panegyric, an immigration tract, a French Catholic deceit, a Rousseauistic conceit, and a true documentary account of the Americas."

A great deal of this variety can be chalked up to a phase in the history of literary genres. *Letters* came into print before the distinctions between fiction and non-fiction, gentleman and author, or witness and fabler were well established. Hence, it remains unclear whether the writer, Crèvecoeur, and the narrator, James, should be taken to be the same person. (Contemporary readers in English-speaking countries tended to say, yes; in German-speaking countries, no.) In any case, it is certainly possible that Crèvecoeur put words in James's hand (such as the starry-eyed "Letter III" below) precisely to ridicule them.

The first edition of *Letters* was dedicated to the Abbé Raynal, a popular radical in pre-Revolutionary France. In best-selling (albeit banned) books that Crèvecoeur praised, Raynal and his collaborators claimed that agrarian individualism was bunk. Slavery, they said, was an adjunct of free enterprise; colonies could provide only temporary asylum; and in America commerce would eventually set classes against each other, as it had in every other empire, revealing the illusion in American dreams. As the first edition of *Letters* unfolds, the role of "Mr. F. B."—the agent whom James addresses—becomes more intrusive. In the end, James is fed up with the rigmarole of professional authorship and the whole yeoman promise that was his subject. He swears off writing and heads to the West to live among Indians.

In subsequent editions (for example, French translations in 1784 and 1787), Crèvecoeur drops the dedication to Raynal, reduces references to Mr. F. B., and reverses the plot. Emphasis shifts from the bogus sweetness of American dreams to the sour effect of a few bad apples. While the first edition might imply that James had to surpass wishful thoughts of American genius, in later editions he fights to uphold them. Crèvecoeur rededicates *Letters* to the Marquis de Lafayette, a key French ally in the American Revolution, a relatively conservative one.

It remains uncertain whether "Letter III" should be read as straightforward observation, caricature, or some hybrid of the two. In the 1780s this ambiguity was certainly convenient for Crèvecoeur. Since revolutionary passions were high on both sides of the Atlantic, it may have been the only strategy nearly as safe as silence. But with benefit of hindsight, James's question—not just what it meant to Crèvecoeur or his contemporaries but also what it should mean to us—invites a clearer response.

What Is an American?

I wish I could be acquainted with the feelings and thoughts which must agitate the heart and present themselves to the mind of an enlightened Englishman, when he first lands on this continent. He must greatly rejoice that he lived at a time to see this fair country discovered and settled; he must necessarily feel a share of national pride, when he views the chain of settlements which embellishes these extended shores. When he says to himself, this is the work of my countrymen, who, when convulsed by factions, afflicted by a variety of miseries and wants, restless and impatient, took refuge here. They brought along with them their national genius, to which they principally owe what liberty they enjoy, and what substance they possess. Here he sees the industry of his native country displayed in a new manner, and traces in their works the embryos of all the arts, sciences, and ingenuity which flourish in Europe. Here he beholds fair cities, substantial villages, extensive fields, an immense country filled with decent houses, good roads, orchards, meadows, and bridges, where an hundred years ago all was wild, woody and uncultivated! . . .

It is not composed, as in Europe, of great lords who possess every thing and of a herd of people who have nothing. Here are no aristocratic families, no courts, no kings, no bishops, no ecclesiastical dominion, no invisible power giving to a few a very visible one; no great manufacturers employing thousands, no great refinements of luxury. The rich and the poor are not so far removed from each other as they are in Europe. Some few towns excepted, we are all tillers of the earth, from Nova Scotia to West Florida. We are a people of cultivators, scattered over an immense territory communicating with each other by means of good roads and navigable rivers, united by the silken bands of mild government, all respecting the laws, without dreading their power, because they are equitable. We are all animated with the spirit of an industry which is unfettered and unrestrained, because each person works for himself. If he travels through our rural districts he views not the hostile castle, and the haughty mansion, contrasted with the clay-built hut and miserable cabin, where cattle and men help to keep each other warm, and dwell in meanness, smoke, and indigence.

A pleasing uniformity of decent competence appears throughout our habitations. The meanest of our log-houses is a dry and comfortable habitation. Lawyer or merchant is the fairest title our towns afford; that of a farmer is the only appellation of the rural inhabitants of our country. It must take some time ere he can reconcile himself to our dictionary, which is but short in words of dignity, and names of honor.

There, on a Sunday, he sees a congregation of respectable farmers and their wives, all clad in neat homespun, well mounted, or riding in their own humble wagons. There is not among them an esquire, saving the unlettered magistrate. There he sees a parson as simple as his flock, a farmer who does not riot on the labor of others. We have no princes, for whom we toil, starve, and bleed: we are the most perfect society now existing in the world. Here man is free, as he ought to be; nor is this pleasing equality so transitory as many others are. Many ages will not see the shores of our great lakes replenished with inland nations, nor the unknown bounds of North America entirely peopled. Who can tell how far it extends? Who can tell the millions of men whom it will feed and contain? For no European foot has as yet travelled half the extent of this mighty continent!

The next wish of this traveler will be to know whence came all these people? They are a mixture of English, Scotch, Irish, French, Dutch, Germans, and Swedes. From this promiscuous breed, that race now called Americans have arisen. The eastern provinces must indeed be excepted, as being the unmixed descendants of Englishmen. I have heard many wish that they had been more intermixed also. For my part, I am no wisher, and think it much better as it has happened. They exhibit a most conspicuous figure in this great and variegated picture; they too enter for a great share in the pleasing perspective displayed in these thirteen provinces. I know it is fashionable to reflect on them, but I respect them for what they have done; for the accuracy and wisdom with which they have settled their territory; for the decency of their manners; for their early love of letters; for their ancient college, the first in this hemisphere; for their industry, which to me who am but a farmer, is the criterion of everything. There never was a people, situated as they are, who with so ungrateful a soil have done more in so short a time. . . .

In this great American asylum, the poor of Europe have by some means met together. . . . To what purpose should they ask one another what countrymen they are? Alas, two thirds of them had no country. Can a wretch who wanders about, who works and starves, whose life is a continual scene of sore affliction or pinching penury; can that man call England or any other kingdom his country? A country that had no bread for him, whose fields procured him no harvest, who met with nothing but the frowns of the rich, the severity of the laws, with jails and punishments; who owned not a single foot of the extensive surface of this planet? No! Urged by a variety of motives, here they came. Everything has tended to regenerate them: new laws, a new mode of living, a new social system; here they are become men: in Europe they were as so many useless plants, wanting vegetative mould and refreshing showers; they withered and were mowed down by want, hunger, and war; but now by the power of transplantation, like all other plants they have taken root and flourished! Formerly they were not numbered in any civil lists of their country, except in those of the poor; here they rank as citizens. . .

What attachment can a poor European emigrant have for a country where he had nothing? The knowledge of the language, the love of a few kindred as poor as himself, were the only cords that tied him. His country is now that which gives him land, bread, protection, and consequence: *Ubi panis ibi patria*, is the motto of all emigrants. What then is the American, this new man? He is either an European, or the descendant of an European, hence that strange mixture of blood, which you will find in no other country. I could point out to you a family whose grandfather was an Englishman, whose wife was Dutch, whose son married a French woman, and whose present four sons have now four wives of different nations. *He* is an American, who leaving behind him all his ancient prejudices and manners, receives new ones from the new mode of life he has embraced, the new government he obeys, and the new rank he holds.

He becomes an American by being received in the broad lap of our great *Alma Mater*. Here individuals of all nations are melted into a new race of men, whose labors and posterity will one day cause great changes in the world. Americans are the western pilgrims, who are carrying along with them that great mass of arts, sciences, vigor, and industry which began long since in the east; they will finish the great circle. The Americans were once scattered all over Europe; here they are incorporated into one of the finest systems of population which has ever appeared, and which will hereafter become distinct by the power of the different climates they inhabit. The American ought therefore to love this country much better than that wherein either he or his forefathers were born. Here the rewards of his industry follow with equal steps the progress of his labor; his labor is founded on the basis of nature, *self-interest*; can it want a stronger allurement? Wives and children, who before in vain demanded of him a morsel of bread, now, fat and frolicsome, gladly help their father to clear those fields whence exuberant crops are to arise to feed and to clothe them all; without any part being claimed, either by a despotic prince, a rich abbot, or a mighty lord. . . . The American is a new man, who acts upon new principles; he must therefore entertain new ideas, and form new opinions. From involuntary idleness, servile dependence, penury, and useless labor, he has passed to toils of a very different nature, rewarded by ample subsistence—This is an American. . . .

He who would wish to see America in its proper light and have a true idea of its feeble beginnings and barbarous rudiments must visit our extended line of frontiers, where the last settlers dwell and where he may see the first labors of the mode of clearing the earth, in their different appearances; where men are wholly left dependent on their native tempers, and on the spur of uncertain industry, which often fails when not sanctified by the efficacy of a few moral rules. There, remote from the power of example and check of shame, many families exhibit the most hideous parts of our society. They are a kind of forlorn hope, preceding by ten or twelve years the most respectable army of veterans which come after them. In that space, prosperity will polish some, vice and the law will drive off the rest, who uniting again with others like themselves will recede still farther; making room for more industrious people, who will finish their improvements, convert the log-house into a convenient habitation, and rejoicing that the first heavy labors are finished, will change in a few years that hitherto barbarous country into a fine fertile, well regulated district. Such is our progress, such is the march of the Europeans toward the interior parts of this continent. . . .

Exclusive of those general characteristics, each province has its own, founded on the government, climate, mode of husbandry, customs, and peculiarity of circumstances. Europeans submit insensibly to these great powers, and become, in the course of a few generations, not only Americans in general, but either Pennsylvanians, Virginians, or provincials under some other name. Whoever traverses the continent must easily observe those strong differences, which will grow more evident in time. The inhabitants of Canada, Massachusetts, the middle provinces, the southern ones will be as different as their climates; their only points of unity will be those of religion and language.

As I have endeavored to show you how Europeans become Americans, it may not be disagreeable to show you likewise how the various Christian sects introduced, wear out, and how religious indifference becomes prevalent. . . . If sectarians are not settled close together, if they are mixed with other denominations, their zeal will cool for want of fuel, and will be extinguished in a little time. Then the Americans become as to religion, what they are as to country, allied to all. In them the name of Englishman, Frenchman, and European is lost, and in like manner, the strict modes of Christianity as practiced in Europe are lost also. This effect will extend itself still farther hereafter. . . . This mixed neighborhood will exhibit a strange religious medley, that will be neither pure Catholicism nor pure Calvinism. A very perceptible indifference, even in the first generation, will become apparent; and it may happen that the daughter of the Catholic will marry the son of the seceder and settle by themselves at a distance from their parents. . . .

Thus all sects are mixed as well as all nations; thus religious indifference is imperceptibly disseminated from one end of the continent to the other; which is at present one of the strongest characteristics of the Americans. Where this will reach no one can tell; perhaps it may leave a vacuum fit to receive other systems. Persecution, religious pride, the love of contradiction, are the food of what the world commonly calls religion. These motives have ceased here: zeal in Europe is confined; here it evaporates in the great distance it has to travel; there it is a grain of powder enclosed; here it burns away in the open air, and consumes without effect. . . .

Thus have I faintly and imperfectly endeavoured to trace our society from the sea to our woods! . . . .

Our difference from Europe, far from diminishing, rather adds to our usefulness and consequence as men and subjects. Had our forefathers remained there, they would only have crowded it and perhaps prolonged those convulsions which had shook it so long. Every industrious European who transports himself here may be compared to a sprout growing at the foot of a great tree; it enjoys and draws but a little portion of sap; wrench it from the parent roots, transplant it, and it will become a tree bearing fruit also. Colonists are therefore entitled to the consideration due to the most useful subjects; a hundred families barely existing in some parts of Scotland, will here in six years, cause an annual exportation of 10,000 bushels of wheat (100 bushels being but a common quantity for an industrious family to sell, if they cultivate good land). It is here then that the idle may be employed, the useless become useful, and the poor become rich; but by riches I do not mean gold and silver—we have but little of those metals—I mean a better sort of wealth, cleared lands, cattle, good houses, good clothes, and an increase of people to enjoy them.

It is no wonder that this country has so many charms. . . . No sooner does an European arrive, no matter of what condition, than his eyes are opened upon the fair prospect; he hears his language spoke, he retraces many of his own country manners. . . . When in England, he was a mere Englishman; here he stands on a larger portion of the globe, not less than its fourth part, and may see the productions of the north, in iron and naval stores; the provisions of Ireland, the grain of Egypt, the indigo, the rice of China. He does not find, as in Europe, a crowded society, where every place is over-stocked; he does not feel that perpetual collision of parties, that difficulty of beginning, that contention which oversets so many.

There is room for everybody in America: Has he any particular talent, or industry? He exerts it in order to procure a livelihood, and it succeeds. Is he a merchant? The avenues of trade are infinite. Is he eminent in any respect? He will be employed and respected. Does he love a country life? Pleasant farms present themselves; he may purchase what he wants, and thereby become an American farmer. Is he a laborer, sober and industrious? He need not go many miles, nor receive many informations before he will be hired, well fed at the table of his employer, and paid four or five times more than he can get in Europe. Does he want uncultivated lands? Thousands of acres present themselves, which he may purchase cheap. Whatever be his talents or inclinations, if they are moderate, he may satisfy them.

I do not mean that everyone who comes will grow rich in a little time; no, but he may procure an easy, decent maintenance, by his industry. Instead of starving he will be fed, instead of being idle he will have employment; and these are riches enough for such men as come over here. The rich stay in Europe, it is only the middling and the poor that emigrate. Would you wish to travel in independent idleness, from north to south, you will find easy access, and the most cheerful reception at every house: society without ostentation, good cheer without pride, and every decent diversion which the country affords, with little expense. It is no wonder that the European who has lived here a few years is desirous to remain; Europe with all its pomp, is not to be compared to this continent, for men of middle stations, or laborers.

An European, when he first arrives, seems limited in his intentions, as well as in his views; but he very suddenly alters his scale; two hundred miles formerly appeared a very great distance; it is now but a trifle. He no sooner breathes our air than he forms schemes, and embarks in designs he never would have thought of in his own country. . . .

Thus Europeans become Americans. . . . From nothing to start into being; from a servant to the rank of a master; from being the slave of some despotic prince, to become a free man, invested with lands, to which every municipal blessing is annexed! What a change indeed! It is in consequence of that change that he becomes an American. This great metamorphosis has a double effect; it extinguishes all his European prejudices, he forgets that mechanism of subordination, that servility of disposition which poverty had taught him. . . .

These reflections constitute him the good man and the good subject. Ye poor Europeans, ye, who sweat, and work for the great—ye, who are obliged to give so many sheaves to the church, so many to your lords, so many to your government, and have hardly any left for yourselves—ye, who are held in less estimation than favorite hunters or useless lap-dogs—ye, who only breathe the air of nature, because it cannot be withheld from you; it is here that ye can conceive the possibility of those feelings I have been describing; . . . It is not every emigrant who succeeds; no, it is only the sober, the honest, and industrious: happy those to whom this transition has served as a powerful spur to labor, to prosperity, and to the good establishment of children, born in the days of their poverty; and who had no other portion to expect but the rags of their parents, had it not been for their happy emigration. . . .

I knew a man who came to this country, in the literal sense of the expression, stark naked; I think he was a Frenchman and a sailor on board an English man-of-war. Being discontented, he had stripped himself and swam ashore; where finding clothes and friends, he settled afterwards at Maraneck, in the county of Chester, in the province of New York. He married and left a good farm to each of his sons. . . .

Where is then the industrious European who ought to despair? After a foreigner from any part of Europe is arrived and become a citizen, let him devoutly listen to the voice of our great parent, which says to him:

Welcome to my shores, distressed European; bless the hour in which thou didst see my verdant fields, my fair navigable rivers, and my green mountains! If thou wilt work, I have bread for thee; if thou wilt be honest, sober, and industrious, I have greater rewards to confer on thee—ease and independence. I will give thee fields to feed and clothe thee, a . . . fireside to sit by, and tell thy children by what means thou hast prospered; and a decent bed to repose on. I shall endow thee besides with the immunities of a freeman; if thou wilt carefully educate thy children, teach them gratitude to God, and reverence to that government, that philanthropic government which has collected here so many men and made them happy. I will also provide for thy progeny; and to every good man this ought to be the most holy, the most Powerful, the most earnest wish he can possibly form, as well as the most consolatory prospect when he dies. Go thou and work and till; thou shalt prosper, provided thou be just, grateful and industrious.

6 | To the United States (1827)

Qualities of collective life are often presumed to range between logical extremes. People wonder, for example, if the United States is "fundamentally" pragmatic or idealistic. Is the place "basically" egalitarian or hierarchical? Friendly or hostile to nature? Male- or female-dominated? Reserved or demonstrative? Individual- or civic-minded? Playful or purposeful? Traditionalist or innovative? Often these questions gain their urgency in figuring a bottom line: Is America now, in these respects, better or worse than cultures in some other time or place?

There has been a particularly long-running debate (at least since the turn of the nineteenth century) between those who calculate the bottom line through measures associated with the Enlightenment versus Romanticism. At the turn of the twenty-first century a comparable divide exists between modernists and postmodernists. In academia, it has helped distinguish the sciences from the arts and humanities.

In the first case (by Enlightenment, modernist, or scientific measures), cultures are supposed to excel to the extent that they shed old prejudices. They progress by welcoming new ideas, ever pursuing the (presumably eternal) true, beautiful, and just. In advancing such universal goods, every society worth its salt (the French *civilisation*) contributes to a more peaceful, orderly, prosperous, and unified humankind.

In the second case (by Romantic, postmodern, or humanistic measures), cultures excel not by idolizing a pan-human system but by preserving their distinctiveness, passion, and creativity. Every society worth its salt (the German *Kultur*) can and should be good in its own way. Even as it changes, a culture properly maintains local traditions that may ill suit utopia but that emotionally as well as materially well suit actual inhabitants.

Romantics themselves, however, usually resist such forced choices. Instead, they look for ways to foster both the head and the heart, the global and the local, progress and change, and science and art. Among the premier examples in U.S. academia might be American Studies itself, but the disposition was much earlier evident in the work of German intellectuals during the Age of Goethe, roughly 1770–1830. Although also remembered for his service to preceding and subsequent movements—*Sturm und Drang* (storm and stress) and *Klassik* (classicism)—Goethe is best remembered for his contributions to *Romantik*. His hometown, Weimar, was at the time the meeting place for idealist intellectuals who led European developments in creative writing, music, science, philosophy, philology, history, and folklore.

Since the Enlightenment seemed to overindulge innovation and specialization, Romantics looked for (and, not surprisingly, found) beauty in old-fashioned forms, even crude Medieval ones. That aesthetic was part of a more general celebration of provincial pastimes that also figured prominently in the varieties of nationalism that spread throughout the West in the early nineteenth century. These alternatives were intended, not to displace science or pure reason, but better to integrate them with creativity and common sense. Goethe, for example, was just as famous for his contributions to the science of morphology (which he named) as he was for poetry. Romantics aimed to balance respect for tradition and hope for a better future, to blend faith and realism, systematic thinking and intuition, spontaneity and reverence. Here, Goethe imagines how those ideas might play on the other side of the Atlantic.

His opening line, "Amerika, du hast es besser" (America, you're better off) might sound like a flag waver's slogan, and it has been appropriated occasionally for that purpose, as if "better" were a simple idea. But through "America" the poem also challenges common visions of history, literature, and culture and the ways in which a citizen might best relate to them.

To the United States

America, you're better off
Than our continent, the old.
You have no fallen castles,
No rocks of basalt.
Your heart is not troubled,
At this lively moment,
By useless remembering
And futile strife.

Use well the present and good luck to you!
And when your children write verse,
Shelter them well
From stories of knights, robbers, and ghosts.

7 Paddy's Lament (ca. 1865)

Most stories about immigration to the United States flatter the destination. Like ocean liner advertisements, immigrants' memoirs and letters to compatriots include stirring, even fanciful promises. Although few people believed that American streets were literally paved with gold, most could believe that life's prospects, particularly material ones, would improve once they moved. What the advertisements, memoirs, and correspondence often left unsaid was the relatively easy act that the United States had to follow. Most immigrants were fleeing poverty, persecution, or warfare (sometimes all three) in their native lands. The push was at least as important as the pull.

Often also left unsaid was how much immigrants missed their homeland. Tens of thousands opted to return or, barring that possibility, considered life in the United States yet another injury in their refugee experience. It is difficult to say how frequently such thoughts leapt to mind, but disappointment with America clearly has as long a history, even among immigrants, as rags-to-riches dreams.

Among the many tellers of such tales were the Irish who were starved and otherwise driven from their homeland by the English. Since the United States had assisted the Irish during the British-facilitated famine of the 1840s and since centuries of seafaring bridged the North Atlantic, America was a ready alternative. Soon after the largest wave of this immigration (about one million people, 1815–1845), when the Civil War broke out, the Irish were ready for duty. Union regiments such as the 69th New York (commanded by General Thomas F. Meagher) and the 28th Massachusetts established the reputation of "Irish Volunteers" as model patriots, fit for leadership in urban politics after Appomattox (1865). Governance in places such as New York City obviously depended on the support of Irish residents, who comprised about one-quarter of the population.

But many of these same immigrants were also embittered by their experience and eager to spread the word. When, for example, the U.S. government began cutting veterans' benefits, they felt betrayed. They wanted compatriots considering migration to bear their bitter lesson in mind.

The following folksong—with lyrics from the United States in the late nineteenth century—used the melody of a traditional Irish air. (According to the old saying, "There are 10,000 Irish songs, but only 100 Irish tunes.") The chorus of one particularly well-known variant, "Happy Land of Erin," featured a rosy image of immigration:

Cheer up, boys, the time will come again
When the sons of old Erin will be steering,
And to the land will go o'er,
They call "Columbia's shore,"
Where there's freedom for the jolly sons of Erin.

In fact, most Irish-American songs of the Civil War are proud, even if pained, tributes to their patriotism. But the variant of the same air that went by the name of "Paddy's Lament" (or "Lamentation") had a darker message.

And it's by the hush, me boys,
I'm sure that's to hold your noise,
And listen to poor Paddy's lamentation.
I was by hunger pressed
And by poverty distressed
When I took a thought I'd leave the Irish nation.

And hear you boys, do take my advice:
To Americay I'll have you not be comin'
For there's nothin' here but war,
Where the murderin' cannons roar,
And I wish I was back home
In dear old Ireland.

So I sold me horse and plow,
Sold me sheep, me pigs and sow,
Me little plot of land and I we parted.
And me sweetheart Biddy Magee
I'm afraid I'll never see,
For I left her there that mornin' brokenhearted.

And hear you boys . . .

So me and a hundred more
To Americay sailed o'er,
Our fortunes to be makin' we were thinkin'.
But when we got to Yankee land,
They stuck a musket in me hands,
Sayin', "Paddy, you must go and fight for Lincoln."

And hear you boys . . .

General Meagher to us said,
"If you get shot, or you lose your head,
Every mother's son of you will get a pension."
Well, meself I lost me leg,
All I got's a wooden peg.
Oh, me boys, it is the truth to you I mention.

And hear you boys . . .

Now, I'd have thought meself in luck
To be fed on Indian buck
And old Ireland is the land that I delight in,
But by the devil I do say:
Curse Americay!
For I'm sure I've had enough of your hard fightin'.

And hear you boys . . .

MAX WEBER

8 | The Spirit of Capitalism (1905)

Most of the terms used in studying America (including, of course, "America" itself) were coined somewhere else. For example, the popular right-versus-left polarity of modern U.S. culture comes from the Parisian arrangement for seating at the Assemblée Nationale of 1789. Foes of the French Revolution sat to the right, and fans (also known as *américanistes*) to the left of the presiding officer. Likewise, many of the academic disciplines—with their distinctive styles, sources, methods, journals, associations, and whatnot—first developed in Europe.

Through the combined effort of American importers and European émigrés around the turn of the twentieth century, Germany had a particularly strong influence on the growth of higher education in the United States. Often a good deal of the original was transformed in transit. As the global traffic in ideas has intensified, origins and adaptations have further blurred. So, it is now easy to imagine, say, a scholar just about anywhere responding to a U.S. (mis)application of a Polish (mis)reading of an English (mis)translation of a German term derived from Mesopotamia or who knows where.

But in the case of "the Protestant ethic" the lineage is quite clear. The expression comes to us from the German sociologist Max Weber in his classic *Die protestantiscche Ethik und der 'Geist' des Kapitalismus* (1905, translated into English as *The Protestant Ethic and the Spirit of Capitalism*, 1930). He used it to identify features of the Reformation—particularly the association of diligence and thrift with salvation—that preconditioned subsequent, otherwise secular, social and economic change.

Weber's immediate family was, in fact, Protestant, which rendered them targets of Catholic bigots. Since they survived persecution largely by adopting the lifeways of the German bourgeoisie, they also had a personal stake in capitalism. But there were profound differences in Weber's thoughts about the two. In general, despite his infamous advocacy of "value-freeness," he preferred to challenge the culture of capitalism from a Protestant point of view far more than the other way around.

Like many contemporary German intellectuals, he was not optimistic about the prospects of either capitalism or communism. Their attempts to find a third way figured prominently in social thought from the mid-nineteenth century through the rise of the Third Reich. Hitler found it easy to co-opt this work, generally to the horror of the scholars who produced and defended it. Although, for example, Weber was very active in these discussions and helped expose the flaws of liberal democracy, he was also a vocal opponent of Bismarck- and then Weimar-era jingoism and racism.

In fact, much of his work can be read as a jeremiad, a warning about the dangers of economic determinism and similarly fashionable ideologies. He had a particularly long-running dispute with the disciples of Karl Marx. Weber challenged the Marxists' bifurcation of ethics ("superstructure") and economy and their penchant for mechanistic analogy. He argued that society could and should be considered a historical assemblage of neither entirely rational nor irrational actors. Their *geist* (spirit) was as important as their class. Although novel for U.S. Americanists as late as the 1960s, Weber's vision of culture as a fluid but whole, historical, and spiritual accretion was pervasive in German scholarship at least since Hegel, if not Kant.

These ideas, embedded as they were in European history and the life of an ambivalently bourgeois German Protestant, may seem to have little to do with the United States. But they found their way to America through several channels. A key link was English translation and celebration, courtesy of leading U.S. social scientists such as C. Wright Mills, Edward Shills, and Talcott Parsons from the late 1920s through the Cold War. With only a bit of suspicious convenience, for example, Parsons found Weber's sociology a worthy precedent for his own organic, "functionalist" variant of the field.

Another link was Weber's personal experience in the United States, which he found surprisingly pleasant. Since, though, his first tour occurred just one year before the publication of *The Protestant Ethic and the Spirit of Capitalism*, it is obvious that there were earlier connections.

Among Weber's most important resources was the European penchant for treating the United States as a "New World." Of course, by 1905 no one could possibly mistake America for a fledgling polity. Most European nations could well be considered younger than the United States. But many writers—especially in France and Germany—still tended to view America as blazing a trail that they might (but usually did not) want to follow. Would, for example, all that is traditional (for example, Protestantism) be supplanted by all that is modern (for example, capitalism)? How? What parts of the old would remain in the new? And with what consequences?

To find out, Weber, like many other Europeans, treated America as if it were Western Civilization on fast-forward. Consider Friedrich Nietzsche, as he began his critique of "Leisure and Idleness" (1882):

> There is an Indian savagery, a savagery peculiar to the Indian blood, in the manner in which the Americans strive after gold; and the breathless hurry of their work—the characteristic vice of the New World— already begins to infect old Europe, and makes it savage also, spreading over it a strange lack of intellectuality. . . . Thinking is done with a stopwatch, as dining is done with the eyes fixed on the financial newspaper; we live like men who are continually "afraid of letting opportunities

slip." "Better do anything whatever, than nothing"—this principle also is a noose with which all culture and all higher taste may be strangled.

About twenty years later, Weber's predictions were less severe, but he still tracked modernity by way of America. His exemplary capitalist was Benjamin Franklin.

> In the title of this study is used the somewhat pretentious phrase, the *spirit* of capitalism. What is to be understood by it? . . .

If any object can be found to which this term can be applied with any understandable meaning, it can only be . . . a complex of elements . . . which we unite into a conceptual whole from the standpoint of their cultural significance. . . . It must be gradually put together out of the individual parts which are taken from historical reality. . . . A provisional description . . . is, however, indispensable. . . . For this purpose we turn to a document of that spirit which contains what we are looking for in almost classical purity, and at the same time has the advantage of being free from all direct relationship to religion, being thus, for our purposes, free of preconceptions.

> Remember, that *time* is money. . . .
>
> Remember, that *credit* is money. . . .
>
> Remember, that money is of the prolific, generating nature. Money can beget money, and its offspring can beget more, and so on. Five shillings turned is six; turned again it is seven and three-pence; and so on, till it becomes a hundred pounds. . . . He that kills a breeding-sow, destroys all her offspring to the thousandth generation. He that murders a crown [five-shilling coin], destroys all that it might have produced, even scores of pounds.
>
> Remember this saying, *The good paymaster is lord of another man's purse*. He that is known to pay punctually and exactly to the time he promises, may at any time, and on any occasion, raise all the money his friends can spare. This is sometimes of great use. After industry and frugality, nothing contributes more to the raising of a young man in the world than punctuality and justice in all his dealings. Therefore never keep borrowed money an hour beyond the time you promised, lest a disappointment shut up your friend's purse for ever.
>
> The most trifling actions that affect a man's credit are to be regarded. The sound of your hammer at 5:00 in the morning or 8:00 at

night, heard by a creditor, makes him easy six months longer; but if he sees you at a billiard table or hears your voice at a tavern, when you should be at work, he sends for his money the next day. . . .

For six pounds a year you may have the use of one hundred pounds, provided you are a man of known prudence and honesty.

He that spends a groat [four-pence coin] a day idly, spends idly above six pounds a year, which is the price for the use of one hundred pounds.

He that wastes idly a groat's worth of his time per day, one day with another, wastes the privilege of using one hundred pounds each day.

He that idly loses five shillings' worth of time, loses five shillings, and might as prudently throw five shillings into the sea.

He that loses five shillings, not only loses that sum, but all the advantage that might be made by turning it in dealing, which by the time that a young man becomes old, will amount to a considerable sum of money.

It is Benjamin Franklin who preaches to us in these sentences, the same which Ferdinand Kürnberger satirizes in his clever and malicious *Picture of American Culture*. . . . "They make tallow out of cattle and money out of men." The peculiarity of this philosophy of avarice appears to be the ideal of the honest man of recognized credit, and above all the idea of a duty of the individual toward the increase of his capital, which is assumed as an end in itself. Truly what is here preached is not simply a means of making one's way in the world, but a peculiar ethic. The infraction of its rules is treated not as foolishness but as forgetfulness of duty. . . . an ethically colored maxim for the conduct of life. The concept of the spirit of capitalism is here used in this specific sense: it is the spirit of modern capitalism. For that we are here dealing only with Western European and American capitalism is obvious from the way in which the problem was stated. Capitalism existed in China, India, Babylon, in the classic world and in the Middle Ages. But in all these cases, as we shall see, this particular ethos was lacking.

Now, all Franklin's moral attitudes are colored with utilitarianism. Honesty is useful because it assures credit; so are punctuality, industry, frugality, and that is the reason they are virtues. . . . According to Franklin, those virtues, like all others, are only virtues insofar as they are actually useful to the individual, and the surrogate of mere appearance is always sufficient when it accomplishes the end in view. It is a conclusion which is inevitable for strict utilitarianism. The impression of many Germans that the virtues professed by Americanism are pure hypocrisy seems to have been confirmed by this striking case. But in fact the matter is not by any means so simple. Benjamin Franklin's own character, as it appears in the really unusual candidness of his autobiography, belies that suspicion. . . . That he ascribes his recognition of the utility of virtue to a divine revelation . . . shows that something more than mere garnishing for purely egocentric motives is involved. . . .

The earning of more and more money, combined with the strict avoidance of all spontaneous enjoyment of life, is . . . thought of so purely as an end in itself, that from the point of view of the happiness of or utility to the single individual, it appears entirely transcendental and absolutely irrational. Man is dominated by the making of money, by acquisition as the ultimate purpose of his life. Economic acquisition is no longer subordinated to man as the means for the satisfaction of his material needs. This reversal of what we should call the natural relationship . . . is foreign to all peoples not under capitalistic influence. At the same time it expresses a type of feeling which is closely connected with certain religious ideas. If we thus ask, why should "money be made out of men?" Benjamin Franklin himself (although he was a colorless deist) answers in his autobiography with a quotation from the Bible, which his strict Calvinistic father drummed into him again and again in his youth: "Seest thou a man diligent in his business? He shall stand before kings" (Prov. xxii. 29). The earning of money within the modern economic order is, so long as it is done legally, the result and the expression of virtue and proficiency in a calling. . . .

And in truth this peculiar idea, so familiar to us today . . . of one's duty in a calling, is what is most characteristic of the social ethic of capitalistic culture and is in a sense the fundamental basis of it. It is an obligation which the individual is supposed to feel and does feel towards the content of his professional activity, no matter in what it consists. . . .

Of course, this conception has not appeared only under capitalistic conditions. On the contrary, we shall later trace its origins back to a time previous to the advent of capitalism. . . . The capitalistic economy of the present day is an immense cosmos into which the individual is born, and which presents itself to him, at least as an individual, as an unalterable order of things in which he must live. It forces the individual, insofar as he is involved in the system of market relationships, to conform to capitalistic rules of action. The manufacturer who in the long run acts counter to these norms will just as inevitably be eliminated from the economic scene as the worker who cannot or will not adapt himself to them will be thrown into the streets without a job.

Thus the capitalism of today, which has come to dominate economic life, educates and selects the economic subjects which it needs through a process of economic survival of the fittest. But here one can easily see the limits of the concept of selection as a means of historical explanation. In order that a manner of life so well adapted to the peculiarities of capitalism could be selected at all (i.e. should come to dominate others) it had to originate somewhere, and not in isolated individuals alone, but as a way of life common to whole groups of men. This origin is what really needs explanation. Concerning the doctrine of the more naive historical materialism—that such ideas originate as a reflection or superstructure of economic situations—we shall speak more in detail below. At this point it will suffice for our purpose to call attention to the fact that without doubt, in the country of Benjamin Franklin's birth, the spirit of capitalism (in the sense we have attached to it) was present before the capitalistic order. There were complaints of a peculiarly calculating sort of profit seeking in New England, as distinguished from other parts of America, as early as 1632. It is further undoubted that capitalism remained far less developed in some of the neighboring colonies (the later Southern States of the United States of America) in spite of the fact that these latter were founded by large capitalists for business motives, while the New England colonies were founded by preachers and seminary graduates, with the help of small bourgeois craftsmen and yeomen, for religious reasons. In this case the causal relation is certainly the reverse of that suggested by the materialistic standpoint.

But the origin and history of such ideas is much more complex than the theorists of the superstructure suppose. The spirit of capitalism, in the sense in which we are using the term, had to fight its way to supremacy against a whole world of hostile forces. A state of mind, such as that expressed in the passages we have quoted from Franklin, and which called forth the applause of a whole people, would both in ancient times and in the Middle Ages have been proscribed as the lowest sort of avarice and as an attitude entirely lacking in self-respect. It is, in fact, still regularly thus looked upon by all those social groups which are least involved in or adapted to modern capitalistic conditions. This is not wholly because the instinct of acquisition was in those times unknown or undeveloped . . . as the illusions of modern romanticists are wont to believe. The difference between the capitalistic and precapitalistic spirits is not to be found at this point. The greed of the Chinese Mandarin, the old Roman aristocrat, or the modern peasant can stand up to any comparison. . . .

At all periods of history, wherever it was possible, there has been ruthless acquisition, bound to no ethical norms whatever. . . . Capitalistic acquisition as an adventure has been at home in all types of economic society. . . . Likewise the inner attitude of the adventurer, which laughs at all ethical limitations, has been universal. Absolute and conscious ruthlessness in acquisition has often stood in the closest connection with the strictest conformity to tradition. . . . And this fact has been treated either as ethically indifferent or as reprehensible but unfortunately unavoidable. . . .

The most important opponent with which the spirit of capitalism . . . has had to struggle was that type of attitude and reaction to new situations which we may designate as traditionalism. . . . We will begin from below, with the laborers.

One of the technical means which the modern employer uses in order to secure the greatest possible amount of work from his men is the device of piece-rates. . . . But a peculiar difficulty has been met with surprising frequency: raising the piece-rates has often had the result that not more but less has been accomplished in the same time, because the worker reacted to the increase not by increasing but by decreasing the amount of his work. . . . He did not ask: "How much can I earn in a day if I do as much work as possible?" But: "How much must I work in order to earn the wage . . . which I earned before and which takes care of my traditional needs?" This is an example of what is here meant by traditionalism. A man does not "by nature" wish to earn more and more money, but simply to live as he is accustomed to live and to earn as much as is necessary for that purpose. Wherever modern capitalism has begun its work of increasing the productivity of human labor by increasing its intensity, it has encountered the immensely stubborn resistance of this leading trait of precapitalistic labor. . . .

Labor must, on the contrary, be performed as if it were an absolute end in itself, a calling. But such an attitude is by no means a product of nature. It cannot be evoked by low wages or high ones alone, but can only be the product of a long and arduous process of education. . . .

What is meant can again best be explained by means of an example. The type of backward traditional form of labor is today very often exemplified by women workers, especially unmarried ones. An almost universal complaint of employers of girls, for instance German girls, is that they are almost entirely unable and unwilling to give up methods of work inherited or once learned in favor of more efficient ones, to adapt themselves to new methods, to learn and to concentrate their intelligence, or even to use it at all. Explanations of the possibility of making work easier, above all more profitable to themselves, generally encounter a complete lack of understanding. Increases of piece-rates are without avail against the stone wall of habit.

In general it is otherwise . . . only with girls having a specifically religious, especially a Pietistic, background. One often hears and statistical investigation confirms it: that by far the best chances of economic education are found among this group. The ability of mental concentration, as well as the absolutely essential feeling of obligation to one's job, are here most often combined with a strict economy which calculates the possibility of high earnings and a cool self-control and frugality which enormously increase performance. This provides the most favorable foundation for the conception of labor as an end in itself, as a calling which is necessary to capitalism: the chances of overcoming traditionalism are greatest on account of the religious upbringing. This observation of present-day capitalism in itself suggests that it is worthwhile to ask how this connection of adaptability to capitalism with religious factors may have come about in the days of the early development of capitalism. . . .

Until about the middle of the past century, the life of a putter-out was, at least in many of the branches of the Continental textile industry, what we should today consider very comfortable. . . . The number of business hours was very moderate, perhaps five to six a day, sometimes considerably less; in the rush season, where there was one, more. Earnings were moderate; enough to lead a respectable life and in good times to put away a little. On the whole, relations among competitors were relatively good, with a large degree of agreement on the fundamentals of business. A long daily visit to the tavern, often with plenty to drink and a congenial circle of friends, made life comfortable and leisurely.

The form of organization was in every respect capitalistic. . . . But it was traditionalistic business, if one considers the spirit which animated the entrepreneur: the traditional manner of life, the traditional rate of profit, the traditional amount of work, the traditional manner of regulating the relationships with labor, and the essentially traditional circle of customers and the manner of attracting new ones. . . .

Now at some time this leisureliness was suddenly destroyed, and often entirely without any essential change in the form of organization, such as the transition to a unified factory, to mechanical weaving, etc. What happened was, on the contrary, often no more than this: some young man from one of the putting-out families went out into the country, carefully chose weavers for his employ, greatly increased the rigor of his supervision of their work, and thus turned them from peasants into laborers. . . . He would begin to change his marketing methods, . . . would take the details into his own hands, would personally solicit customers, . . . and above all would adapt the quality of the product directly to their needs and wishes. At the same time he began to introduce the principle of low prices and large turnover. There was repeated what everywhere and always is the result of such a process of rationalization: those who would not follow suit had to go out of business. The idyllic state collapsed under the pressure of a bitter competitive struggle. . . . The old leisurely and comfortable attitude toward life gave way to a hard frugality. . . .

It was not generally in such cases a stream of new money invested in the industry which brought about this revolution . . . but, above all . . . the development of the spirit of capitalism. Where it appears and is able to work itself out, it produces its own capital and monetary supplies as the means to its ends, but the reverse is not true. Its entry on the scene was not generally peaceful. A flood of mistrust, sometimes of hatred, above all of moral indignation, regularly opposed itself to the first innovator. . . . It is only by virtue of very definite and highly developed ethical qualities that it has been possible for him to command the absolutely indispensable confidence of his customers and workmen. Nothing else could have given him the strength to overcome the innumerable obstacles, above all the infinitely more intensive work that is demanded of the modern entrepreneur. But these are ethical qualities of quite a different sort from those adapted to the traditionalism of the past.

And, as a rule, it has been neither daredevil and unscrupulous speculators (economic adventurers such as we meet at all periods of economic history) nor simply great financiers who have carried through this change. . . . On the contrary, they were men who had grown up in the hard school of life, calculating and daring at the same time, above all temperate and reliable, shrewd and completely devoted to their business, with strictly bourgeois opinions and principles.

One is tempted to think that these personal moral qualities have not the slightest relation to any ethical maxims, to say nothing of religious ideas. . . . The ability to free oneself from the common tradition, a sort of liberal enlightenment, seems likely to be the most suitable basis for such a businessman's success. And today that is generally precisely the case. Any relationship between religious beliefs and conduct is generally absent, and where any exists (at least in Germany) it tends to be of the negative sort. The people filled with the spirit of capitalism today tend to be indifferent, if not hostile, to the Church. The thought of the pious boredom of paradise has little attraction for their active natures; religion appears to them as a means of drawing people away from labor in this world. If you ask them what is the meaning of their restless activity, why they are never satisfied with what they have . . . they would perhaps give the answer, if they know any at all: "To provide for my children and grandchildren." But more often and (since that motive is not peculiar to them, but was just as effective for the traditionalist) more correctly, simply: that business with its continuous work has become a necessary part of their lives. That is in fact the only possible motivation, but it at the same time expresses what is—seen from the viewpoint of personal happiness— so irrational about this sort of life, where a man exists for the sake of his business, instead of the reverse.

Of course, the desire for the power and recognition which the mere fact of wealth brings plays its part. When the imagination of a whole people has once been turned toward purely quantitative bigness (as in the United States) this romanticism of numbers exercises an irresistible appeal to the poets among businessmen. . . .

But it is just that which seems to the precapitalistic man so incomprehensible and mysterious, so unworthy and contemptible. That anyone should be able to make it the sole purpose of his life-work, to sink into the grave weighed down with a great material load of money and goods, seems to him explicable only as the product of a perverse instinct. . . .

Now, how could activity, which was at best ethically tolerated, turn into a calling in the sense of Benjamin Franklin? . . . In the most highly capitalistic center of that time—in Florence of the fourteenth and fifteenth centuries, the money and capital market of all the great political powers—this attitude was considered ethically unjustifiable, or at best to be tolerated. But in the backwoods small-bourgeois circumstances of Pennsylvania in the eighteenth century—where business threatened for simple lack of money to fall back into barter, where there was hardly a sign of large enterprise, where only the earliest beginnings of banking were to be found—the same thing was considered the essence of moral conduct, even commanded in the name of duty. To speak here of a reflection of material conditions in the ideal superstructure would be patent nonsense. What was the background of ideas that could account for the sort of activity—apparently directed toward profit alone—as a calling toward which the individual feels himself to have an ethical obligation? For it was this idea which gave the way of life of the new entrepreneur its ethical foundation and justification. . . .

It is only necessary, for instance, to read Franklin's account of his efforts in the service of civic improvements in Philadelphia clearly to apprehend this obvious truth. And the joy and pride of having given employment to numerous people, of having had a part in the economic progress of his hometown . . . all these things obviously are part of the specific and undoubtedly idealistic satisfactions in life to modern men of business. Similarly it is one of the fundamental characteristics of an individualistic capitalistic economy that it is rationalized on the basis of rigorous calculation, directed with foresight and caution toward the economic success which is sought in sharp contrast to the hand-to-mouth existence of the peasant and to the privileged traditionalism of the guild craftsman and of the adventurer's capitalism, oriented to the exploitation of political opportunities and irrational speculation.

It might thus seem that the development of the spirit of capitalism is best understood as part of the development of rationalism as a whole. . . . In the process Protestantism would only have to be considered insofar as it had formed a stage prior to the development of a purely rationalistic philosophy. But . . . the history of rationalism shows a development which by no means follows parallel lines in the various departments of life. . . . In fact, one may—this simple proposition, which is often forgotten, should be placed at the beginning of every study which essays to deal with rationalism—rationalize life from fundamentally different basic points of view and in very different directions. Rationalism is an historical concept which covers a whole world of different things. It will be our task to find out whose intellectual child the particular concrete form of rational thought was, from which the idea of a calling and the devotion to labor in the calling has grown, which is, as we have seen, so irrational from the standpoint of purely eudaemonistic self-interest, but which has been and still is one of the most characteristic elements of our capitalistic culture. We are here particularly interested in the origin of precisely the irrational element which lies in this, as in every conception of a calling.

H. L. MENCKEN

9 | On Being an American (1922)

Among the most popular of arts in the United States is biting social sarcasm. The more sacred cows that fall, the better. Through the early twentieth century, for example, most American newspapers were organs of political parties, and they defamed their foes with stories that today would count as libelous. Although now less predictably partisan, cartoons on editorial pages remain irreverent. Thanks, for example, to the German-American artist Thomas Nast (1840–1902) of *Harper's Weekly*, political cartoonists still picture the Republican Party as an elephant and the Democratic Party as an ass. Humorists such as Jack Downing (Seba Smith), Mark Twain (Samuel Clemens), Will Rogers, Lenny Bruce, George Carlin, and Whoopi Goldberg also gained celebrity through lampoonery. Mocking U.S. pretensions remains an immensely popular pastime. At home, at least, even patriots ridicule the culture.

But the invention of "objective" reporting—free of affect except "serious"—in the early 1900s also rendered laughter or even imagination an enemy of the front page. Hence, when 1960s columnists rediscovered a literary voice, proponents such as Tom Wolfe (after earning a Yale Ph.D. in American Studies) announced the invention of a "New Journalism." When pressed for precedents, he turned to "realist" novelists such as Dickens and Balzac. But he did not need to range so far nor to limit the relevant strategies to realism (witness Erma Bombeck, Joan Didion, and Hunter Thompson).

Credit for establishing a twentieth-century model of the American critic as a brash but witty, hard-drinking cynic probably belongs to H. L. Mencken. He insisted on that persona in popular Baltimore periodicals—the *Morning Herald*, the *Sun*, *The Smart Set*, and *The American Mercury*—and more than twenty books published from 1899 till his death in 1956. He styled himself both a Prohibition-flouting "Baltimoron" and "an incurable snob," the voice of "the intelligent minority" determined "to stir up the animals." Offending nearly everyone was, in his opinion, a noble calling: "Nature declares that the things I esteem most in this world . . . to wit, truth, liberty, tolerance, and common decency, are kept alive, not by great masses of men, but by small groups of men, most of them very well fed." As usual, he opts for hyperbole, mingling arrogance and populism, that congratulates a reader for being in on the joke. Scholars and moralists beware: "One horse laugh is worth ten thousand syllogisms."

Many readers take Mencken's bigotry for tongue-in-cheek and hence flatter themselves for being wise enough to forgive it. Others assume that his prejudice is justified but that they just so happen to be out of range. In either case, they can laugh along with the iconoclast.

Here he explains how, like many contemporary intellectuals of (in Gertrude Stein's words) the "lost generation," he disdains America, but also why, unlike those contemporaries, he feels no need to seek more worthy civilizations overseas.

1

Apparently there are those who begin to find it disagreeable—nay, impossible. Their anguish fills the Liberal weeklies, and every ship that puts out from New York carries a groaning cargo of them, bound for Paris, London, Munich, Rome and way points—anywhere to escape the great curses and atrocities that make life intolerable for them at home. Let me say at once that I find little to cavil at in their basic complaints. . . . It is, for example, one of my firmest and most sacred beliefs, reached after an inquiry extending over a score of years and supported by incessant prayer and meditation, that the government of the United States, in both its legislative arm and its executive arm, is ignorant, incompetent, corrupt, and disgusting—and from this judgment I except no more than twenty living lawmakers and no more than twenty executioners of their laws. It is a belief no less piously cherished that the administration of justice in the Republic is stupid, dishonest, and against all reason and equity—and from this judgment I except no more than thirty judges, including two upon the bench of the Supreme Court of the United States. It is another that the foreign policy of the United States—its habitual manner of dealing with other nations, whether friend or foe—is hypocritical, disingenuous, knavish, and dishonorable—and from this judgment I consent to no exceptions whatever, either recent or long past. And it is my fourth (and, to avoid too depressing a bill, final) conviction that the American people, taking one with another, constitute the most timorous, sniveling, poltroonish, ignominious mob of serfs and goose-steppers ever gathered under one flag in Christendom since the end of the Middle Ages, and that they grow more timorous, more sniveling, more poltroonish, more ignominious every day. . . .

Yet I remain on the dock, wrapped in the flag, when the Young Intellectuals set sail. Yet here I stand, unshaken and undespairing, a loyal and devoted Americano, even a chauvinist, paying taxes without complaint, obeying all laws that are physiologically obeyable, accepting all the searching duties and responsibilities of citizenship unprotestingly, investing the sparse usufructs of my miserable toil in the obligations of the nation, avoiding all commerce with men sworn to overthrow the government, contributing my mite toward the glory of the national arts and sciences, enriching and embellishing the native language, spurning all lures (and even all invitations) to get out and stay out—here am I, a bachelor of easy means, forty-two years old, unhampered by debts or issue, able to roam wherever I please and to stay as long as I please—here am I, contentedly and even smugly basking beneath the Stars and Stripes, a better citizen, I daresay, and certainly a less murmurous and exigent one, than thousands who put the Hon. Warren Gamaliel Harding beside Friedrich Barbarossa and Charlemagne, and hold the Supreme Court to be directly inspired by the Holy Spirit, and belong ardently to every Rotary Club, Ku Klux Klan, and Anti-Saloon League, and choke with emotion when the band plays "The Star-Spangled Banner," and believe with the faith of little children that one of Our Boys, taken at random, could dispose in a fair fight of ten Englishmen, twenty Germans, thirty Frogs, forty or fifty Japs, or a hundred Bolsheviki.

Well, then, why am I still here? Why am I so complacent (perhaps even to the point of offensiveness), so free from bile, so little fretting and indignant, so curiously happy? Why did I answer only with a few academic "Hear, Hears" when Henry James, Ezra Pound, Harold Stearns and the émigrés of Greenwich Village issued their successive calls to the corn-fed *intelligentsia* to flee the shambles, escape to fairer lands, throw off the curse forever? The answer, of course, is to be sought in the nature of happiness, which tempts to metaphysics. But let me keep upon the ground. To me, at least (and I can only follow my own nose), happiness presents itself in an aspect that is tripartite. To be happy (reducing the thing to its elementals) I must be:

a. Well-fed, unbounded by sordid cares, at ease in Zion.
b. Full of a comfortable feeling of superiority to the masses of my fellowmen.
c. Delicately and unceasingly amused according to my taste.

It is my contention that, if this definition be accepted, there is no country on the face of the earth wherein a man roughly constituted as I am—a man of my general weaknesses, vanities, appetites, prejudices, and aversions—can be so happy, or even one-half so happy, as he can be in these free and independent states. Going further, I lay down the proposition that it is a sheer physical impossibility for such a man to live in These States and *not* be happy—that it is as impossible to him as it would be to a schoolboy to weep over the burning down of his school-house. If he says that he isn't happy here, then he either lies or is insane. . . . Here, more than anywhere else that I know of or have heard of, the daily panorama of human existence, of private and communal folly—the unending procession of governmental extortions and chicaneries, of commercial brigandages and throat-slittings, of theological buffooneries, or aesthetic ribaldries, of legal swindles and harlotries, of miscellaneous rogueries, villainies, imbecilities, grotesqueries, and extravagances—is so inordinately gross and preposterous, so perfectly brought up to the highest conceivable amperage, so steadily enriched with an almost fabulous daring and originality, that only the man who was born with a petrified diaphragm fails to laugh himself to sleep every night, and to awake every morning with all the eager, unflagging expectation of a Sunday-school superintendent touring the Paris peep-shows. . . . The *boobus Americanus* is a bird that knows no closed season. . . .

In the older countries, where competence is far more general and competition is thus more sharp, the thing is often cruelly difficult, and sometimes almost impossible. But in the United States it is absurdly easy, given ordinary luck. Any man with a superior air, the intelligence of a stockbroker, and the resolution of a hat-check girl—in brief, any man who believes in himself enough, and with sufficient cause, to be called a journeyman—can cadge enough money, in this glorious commonwealth of morons, to make life soft for him.

And if a lining for the purse is thus facilely obtainable, given a reasonable prudence and resourcefulness, then balm for the ego is just as unlaboriously got, given ordinary dignity and decency. . . . Here is a country in which all political thought and activity are concentrated upon the scramble for jobs—in which the normal politician, whether he be a President or a village road supervisor, is willing to renounce any principle, however precious to him, and to adopt any lunacy, however offensive to him, in order to keep his place at the trough. . . . Here is a land in which women rule and men are slaves. Train your women to get your slippers for you, and your ill fame will match Galileo's or Darwin's. Once more, here is the Paradise of backslappers, of democrats, of mixers, of go-getters. . . .

2

All of which may be boiled down to this: that the United States is essentially a commonwealth of third-rate men—that distinction is easy here because the general level of culture, of information, of taste and judgment, of ordinary competence is so low. No sane man, employing an American plumber to repair a leaky drain, would expect him to do it at the first trial, and in precisely the same way no sane man, observing an American Secretary of State in negotiation with Englishmen and Japs, would expect him to come off better than second best. Third-rate men, of course, exist in all countries, but it is only here that they are in full control of the state, and with it of all the national standards. The land was peopled, not by the hardy adventurers of legend, but simply by incompetents who could not get on at home, and the lavishness of nature that they found here, the vast ease with which they could get livings, confirmed and augmented their native incompetence. No American colonist, even in the worst days of the Indian wars, ever had to face such hardships as ground down the peasants of Central Europe during the Hundred Years War, nor even such hardships as oppressed the English lower classes during the century before the Reform Bill of 1832. In most of the colonies, indeed, he seldom saw any Indians at all; the one thing that made life difficult for him was his congenital dunderheadedness. The winning of the West, so rhetorically celebrated in American romance, cost the lives of fewer men than the single battle of Tannenberg, and the victory was much easier and surer. The immigrants who have come in since those early days have been, if anything, of even lower grade than their forerunners. The old notion that the United States is peopled by the offspring of brave, idealistic and liberty loving minorities, who revolted against injustice, bigotry and mediaevalism at home—this notion is fast succumbing to the alarmed study that has been given of late to the immigration of recent years. The truth is that the majority of non-Anglo-Saxon immigrants since the Revolution, like the majority of Anglo-Saxon immigrants before the Revolution, have been, not the superior men of their native lands, but the botched and unfit: Irishmen starving to death in Ireland, Germans unable to weather the *Sturm und Drang* of the post-Napoleonic reorganization, Italians weed-grown on exhausted soil, Scandinavians run to all bone and no brain, Jews too incompetent to swindle even the barbarous peasants of Russia, Poland, and Romania. Here and there among the immigrants, of course, there may be a bravo, or even a superman—e.g., the ancestors of Volstead, Ponzi, Jack Dempsey, Schwab, Daugherty, Debs, Pershing—but the average newcomer is, and always has been, simply a poor fish.

Nor is there much soundness in the common assumption, so beloved of professional idealists and wind-machines, that the people of America constitute "the youngest of the great peoples." . . . What gives it a certain specious plausibility is the fact that the American Republic, compared to a few other existing governments, is relatively young. But the American Republic is not necessarily identical with the American people; they might overturn it tomorrow and set up a monarchy, and still remain the same people. The truth is that as a distinct nation, they go back fully three hundred years, and that even their government is older than those of most other nations, e.g., France, Italy, Germany, Russia. Moreover, it is absurd to say that there is anything properly describable as youthfulness in the American outlook. . . . All the characteristics of senescence are in it: a great distrust of ideas, an habitual timorousness, a harsh fidelity to a few fixed beliefs, a touch of mysticism. The average American is a prude and a Methodist under his skin, and the fact is never more evident than when he is trying to disprove it. . . . If you would penetrate the causes thereof, simply go down to Ellis Island and look at the next shipload of immigrants. You will not find the spring of youth in their step; you will find the shuffling of exhausted men. From such exhausted men the American stock has sprung. It was easier for them to survive here than it was where they came from, but that ease, though it made them feel stronger, did not actually strengthen them. It left them what they were when they came: weary peasants, eager only for the comfortable security of a pig in a sty. Out of that eagerness has issued many of the noblest manifestations of American *Kultur*: the national hatred of war, the pervasive suspicion of the aims and intents of all other nations, the short way with heretics and disturbers of the peace, the unshakable belief in devils, the implacable hostility to every novel idea and point of view.

All these ways of thinking are the marks of the peasant. . . . He likes money and knows how to amass property, but his cultural development is but little above that of the domestic animals. He is intensely and cocksurely moral, but his morality and his self-interest are crudely identical. . . . He is a violent nationalist and patriot, but he admires rogues in office and always beats the tax-collector if he can. He has immovable opinions about all the great affairs of state, but nine-tenths of them are sheer imbecilities. He is violently jealous of what he conceives to be his rights, but brutally disregardful of the other fellow's. . . . This man, whether city or country bred, is the normal Americano —the 100 percent. . . . He exists in all countries, but here alone he rules. . . .

The dominance of mob ways of thinking, this pollution of the whole intellectual life of the country by the prejudices and emotions of the rabble, goes unchallenged because the old landed aristocracy of the colonial era has been engulfed and almost obliterated by the rise of the industrial system, and no new aristocracy has arisen to take its place, and discharge its highly necessary functions. An upper class, of course, exists, and of late it has tended to increase in power, but it is culturally almost indistinguishable from the mob. . . . Their culture, like their aspiration, remains that of a pawnshop. . . .

I often wonder, indeed, if there would be any intellectual life at all in the United States if it were not for the steady importation in bulk of ideas from abroad. . . . The average American of the Anglo-Saxon majority, in truth, is simply a second-rate Englishman, and so it is no wonder that he is spontaneously servile, despite all of his democratic denial of superiorities, to what he conceives to be first-rate Englishmen. He corresponds, roughly, to an English Nonconformist of the better-fed variety. . . . This inferior Anglo-Saxon is losing his old dominance in the United States—that is, biologically. But he will keep his cultural primacy for a long, long while, in spite of the overwhelming inrush of men of other races, if only because those newcomers are even more clearly inferior than he is. . . .

3

In rainy weather, when my old wounds ache . . . I often find myself speculating sourly as to the future of the Republic. Native opinion, of course, is to the effect that it will be secure and glorious; the superstition that progress must always be upward and onward will not down; in virulence and popularity it matches the superstition that money can accomplish anything. But this view is not shared by most reflective foreigners. . . . Getting a living here has always been easier than anywhere else in Christendom. . . .

The typical American of today has lost all the love of liberty that his forefathers had, and all their distrust of emotion, any pride in self-reliance. He is led no longer by Davy Crocketts; he is led by cheer leaders, press agents, word-mongers, up-lifters. . . . This very weakness, this very credulity and poverty of spirit, on some easily conceivable tomorrow, may convert him into a rebel of a peculiarly insane kind, and so beset the Republic from within with difficulties quite as formidable as those which threaten to afflict it from without. What Mr. James N. Wood calls the corsair of democracy—that is, the professional mob-master, the merchant of delusions, the pumper-up of popular fears and rages—is still content to work for capitalism, and capitalism knows how to reward him to his taste. . . . On some great day of fate, as yet unrevealed by the gods, such a professor of the central democratic science may throw off his employers and set up business for himself. When that day comes there will be plenty of excuse for black type on the front pages of the newspapers. . . .

The chances are bad today simply because the mob is relatively comfortable—because capitalism has been able to give it relative ease and plenty of food in return for its docility. . . . But the time may come and it may . . . introduce the American people, for the first time in their history, to genuine want—and capital would be unable to relieve them. The day of such disaster will bring the savior foreordained. The slaves will follow him, their eyes fixed ecstatically upon the newest New Jerusalem. Men bred to respond automatically to shibboleths will respond to this worst and most insane one. Bolshevism, said General Foch, is a disease of defeated nations.

But do not misunderstand me: I predict no revolution in the grand manner, no melodramatic collapse of capitalism. . . . Capitalism, in the long run, will win in the United States, if only for the reasons that every American hopes to be a capitalist before he dies. Its roots go down to the deepest, darkest levels of the national soil; in all its characters, and particularly in its antipathy to the dreams of man, it is thoroughly American. . . .

4

All the while I have been forgetting the third of my reasons for remaining so faithful a citizen of the Federation, despite all the lascivious inducements from expatriates to follow them beyond the seas, and all the surly suggestions from patriots that I succumb. It is the reason which grows out of my mediaeval but unashamed taste for the bizarre and indelicate, my congenital weakness for comedy of the grosser varieties. The United States, to my eye, is incomparably the greatest show on earth. It is a show which avoids diligently all the kinds of clowning which tire me most quickly—for example, royal ceremonials, the tedious hocus-pocus of *haut politique*, the taking of politics seriously—and lays chief stress upon the kinds which delight me unceasingly—for example, the ribald combats of demagogues, the exquisitely ingenious operations of master rogues, the pursuit of witches and heretics, the desperate struggles of inferior men to claw their way into Heaven. We have clowns in constant practice among us who are as far above the clowns of any other great state as a Jack Dempsey is above a paralytic—and not a few dozen or score of them, but whole droves and herds. Human enterprises which, in all other Christian countries, are resigned despairingly to an incurable dull-ness—things that seem devoid of exhilarating amusement, by their very nature—are here lifted to such vast heights of buffoonery that contemplating them strains the midriff almost to breaking. I cite an example: the worship of God. Everywhere else on earth it is carried on in a solemn and dispiriting manner; in England, of course, the bishops are obscene, but the average man seldom gets a fair chance to laugh at them and enjoy them. Now come home. Here we not only have bish-ops who are enormously more obscene than even the most gifted of the English bishops; we have also a huge force of lesser specialists in ecclesiastical mountebankery—tin-horn Loyolas, Savonarolas and Xaviers of a hundred fantastic rites, each performing untiringly and each full of a grotesque and illimitable whimsicality. Every American town, however small, has one of its own: a holy clerk with so fine a talent for introducing the arts of jazz into the salvation of the damned that his performance takes on all the gaudiness of a four-ring circus, and the bald announcement that he will raid Hell on such and such a night is enough to empty all the town blind-pigs and bordellos and pack his sanctuary to the doors. And to aid him and inspire him there are travelling experts to whom he stands in the relation of a wart to the Matterhorn—stupendous masters of theological imbecility, contrivers of doctrines utterly preposterous. . . . These are the eminences of the American Sacred College. I delight in them. Their proceedings make me a happier American.

Turn, now, to politics. Consider, for example, a campaign for the Presidency. Would it be possible to imagine anything more uproariously idiotic—a deafening, nerve-wracking battle to the death between Tweedledum and Tweedledee, Harlequin and Sganarelle, Gobbo and Dr. Cook—the unspeakable, with fearful snorts, gradually swallowing the inconceivable? I defy anyone to match it elsewhere on this earth. In other lands, at worst, there are at least intelligible issues, coherent ideas, salient personalities. Somebody says something, and somebody replies. But what did Harding say in 1920, and what did Cox reply? Who was Harding, anyhow, and who was Cox? Here, having perfected democracy, we lift the whole combat to symbolism, to transcendentalism, to metaphysics. Here we load a pair of palpably tin cannon with blank cartridges charged with talcum powder, and so let fly. Here one may howl over the show without any uneasy reminder that it is serious, and that some one may be hurt. I hold that this elevation of politics to the plane of undiluted comedy is peculiarly American, that nowhere else on this disreputable ball has the art of the sham-battle been developed to such fineness. . . .

Mirth is necessary to wisdom, to comfort, above all to happiness. Well, here is the land of mirth, as Germany is the land of metaphysics and France is the land of fornication. Here the buffoonery never stops. What could be more delightful than the endless struggle of the Puritan to make the joy of the minority unlawful and impossible? The effort is itself a greater joy to one standing on the sidelines than any or all of the carnal joys it combats. Always, when I contemplate an uplifter at his hopeless business, I recall a scene in an old-time burlesque show, witnessed for hire in my days as a dramatic critic. A chorus girl executed a fall upon the stage, and Rudolph Krausemeyer, the Swiss comedian, rushed to her aid. As he stooped painfully to succor her, Irving Rabinovitz, the Zionist comedian, fetched him a fearful clout across the cofferdam with a slap-stick. So the uplifter, the soul-saver, the Americanizer, striving to make the Republic fit for YMCA secretaries. He is the eternal American, ever moved by the best of intentions, ever running *à la* Krausemeyer to the rescue of virtue, and ever getting his pantaloons fanned by the Devil. I am naturally sinful, and such spectacles caress me. If the slap-stick were a sash-weight, the show would be cruel, and I'd probably complain to the *Polizei*. As it is, I know that the uplifter is not really hurt, but simply shocked. The blow, in fact, does him good, for it helps get him into Heaven, as exegetes prove from Matthew: 5.11: *Heureux serez-vous, lorsqu'on vous outragera, qu'on vous persécutera*, and so on. As for me, it makes me a more contented man, and hence a better citizen. One man prefers the Republic because it pays better wages than Bulgaria. Another because it has laws to keep him sober and his daughter chaste. Another because the Woolworth Building is higher than the cathedral at Chartres. Another because, living here, he can read the New York *Evening Journal*. Another because there is a warrant out for him somewhere else. Me, I like it because it amuses me to my taste. I never get tired of the show. It is worth every cent it costs.

II | America as an Independent Nation

Some Guiding Questions

Should America be considered a political invention?
In what respects?
What qualities of government are supposed to set
the nation apart?
Ideally, for example, how are individuals and the
government related?
What practices should be considered people's rights
or duties?
Which people? Americans alone or everyone?
Do the same rights properly belong to
immigrants as they do to natives?
Of what social standing? In what capacities?
How are inequalities among groups and nations
to be explained?
How, like or unlike rulers, should citizens respond?
Where, in this respect, do political
responsibilities begin and end?

In what respects should the American people be
   considered "independent"?
   From what?
   From whose point of view?
   Internationally and domestically?
   For better or worse?
How are these qualities—for example, the
   democracy of the government or the
   independence of Americans—to be gauged?
   What inclines people to ask?
How is it supposed to matter?
   For example, should the United States be
      considered better to the extent that its
      government has the support of a
      self-interested citizenry?

10 Declaration of Independence (1776)

The Declaration of Independence has long been revered as a stirring justification of revolution and a founding moment for the United States of America. For far-flung readers it has helped immortalize a distinction between colonialism and self-governance, between tyranny and protections for individual liberty, private property, and equality. Such principles are celebrated every Fourth of July, even though the commemorations and the historical record are a bit at odds.

In fact, colonialism had been repudiated in many places and on many occasions before July 4, 1776. The Continental Congress had itself passed an independence resolution on July 2, the date that even the Declaration's signers originally anticipated commemorations. Contrary to the very first sentence, their endorsement was never "unanimous," and even if it had been, the document had no legal force. For some readers at the time, it was no more than a well-timed, albeit elegantly crafted, bit of propaganda. Through appeals to legal, moral, and natural verity, it reluctantly acknowledged a geopolitical reality, boosted domestic morale, and solicited foreign aid. For at least a couple of decades (until revolutionaries in other parts of the world, rivals in domestic political parties, and elderly Founders had a stake in the legacy), most Americans gave the document and the date little thought. Indeed, most of the ideas—even some of the exact wording—came from other, earlier sources, such as John Locke's *Two Treatises of Government* (1690), Thomas Paine's *Common Sense* (January 1776), and the State of Virginia's *Declaration of Rights* (June 1776). Thomas Jefferson was at least hoarding glory late in life when he asked to be remembered, not as one of many collaborators in a grand, global tradition, but as "Author of the Declaration of Independence." It is among the boasts that he ordered chiseled on his tombstone in 1826.

In the early nineteenth century, as Federalist Anglophilia waned, the document secured its sacred status. Through this document more than any other, the Founding Fathers increasingly gained credit for articulating one nation's highest promise to humanity. Inside as well as outside the United States, wave after wave of reformers drew inspiration directly from it. Abolitionists, in particular, often cited its list of "inalienable rights"—particularly that "all men are created equal"—in opposing slavery, the most brutally routine violation of those rights in the Colonies in 1776 and for nearly a century thereafter. In precedent-setting judgments (notably in Massachusetts, *Commonwealth v. Aves*, 1836), the courts began citing the Declaration to sustain opinions that the institution of slavery violated the national purpose.

Hence, it is especially poignant to note that criticisms of slavery, which had been explicit in early drafts of the Declaration, were among the deletions demanded by Congress before passage. Soon after July 4, 1776, long before he wanted to take such singular credit for the document, Jefferson sent letters to his closest associates protesting these changes. Only about two-thirds of his words had made it through revisions by the other members of the draft Committee of Five (John Adams, Benjamin Franklin, Robert R. Livingston, and Roger Sherman) and then the Congress as a whole. Among the deletions that Jefferson protested most strongly are those in brackets, italicized below.

IN CONGRESS, JULY 4, 1776
THE UNANIMOUS DECLARATION OF THE THIRTEEN
UNITED STATES OF AMERICA

When in the Course of human events, it becomes necessary for one people to dissolve the political bands which have connected them with another, and to assume among the powers of the earth, the separate and equal station to which the Laws of Nature and of Nature's God entitle them, a decent respect to the opinions of mankind requires that they should declare the causes which impel them to the separation.

We hold these truths to be self-evident, that all men are created equal, that they are endowed by their Creator with certain unalienable Rights, that among these are Life, Liberty, and the pursuit of Happiness. That to secure these rights, Governments are instituted among Men, deriving their just powers from the consent of the governed. That whenever any Form of Government becomes destructive of these ends, it is the Right of the People to alter or to abolish it, and to institute new Government, laying its foundation on such principles and organizing its powers in such form, as to them shall seem most likely to effect their Safety and Happiness.

Prudence, indeed, will dictate that Governments long established should not be changed for light and transient causes; and accordingly all experience hath shown, that mankind are more disposed to suffer, while evils are sufferable, than to right themselves by abolishing the forms to which they are accustomed.

But when a long train of abuses and usurpations, pursuing invariably the same object evinces a design to reduce them under absolute Despotism, it is their right, it is their duty, to throw off such Government, and to provide new Guards for their future security.

Such has been the patient sufferance of these Colonies; and such is now the necessity which constrains them to alter their former Systems of Government. The history of the present King of Great Britain [George III] is a history of repeated injuries and usurpations, all having in direct object the establishment of an absolute Tyranny over these States. To prove this, let Facts be submitted to a candid world.

He has refused his Assent to Laws, the most wholesome and necessary for the public good.

He has forbidden his Governors to pass Laws of immediate and pressing importance, unless suspended in their operation till his Assent should be obtained, and when so suspended, he has utterly neglected to attend to them.

He has refused to pass other Laws for the accommodation of large districts of people, unless those people would relinquish the right of Representation in the Legislature, a right inestimable to them and formidable to tyrants only.

He has called together legislative bodies at places unusual, uncomfortable, and distant from the depository of their public Records, for the sole purpose of fatiguing them into compliance with his measures.

He has dissolved Representative Houses repeatedly, for opposing with manly firmness his invasions on the rights of the people.

He has refused for a long time, after such dissolutions, to cause others to be elected; whereby the Legislative powers, incapable of Annihilation, have returned to the People at large for their exercise; the State remaining in the meantime exposed to all the dangers of invasion from without, and convulsions within.

He has endeavored to prevent the population of these States; for that purpose obstructing the Laws for Naturalization of Foreigners; refusing to pass others to encourage their migrations hither, and raising the conditions of new Appropriations of Lands.

He has obstructed the Administration of Justice, by refusing his Assent to Laws for establishing Judiciary powers.

He has made Judges dependent on his Will alone, for the tenure of their offices, and the amount and payment of their salaries.

He has erected a multitude of New Offices, and sent hither swarms of Officers to harass our people, and eat out their substance.

He has kept among us, in times of peace, Standing Armies, without the consent of our legislatures.

He has affected to render the Military independent of and superior to the Civil power.

He has combined with others to subject us to a jurisdiction foreign to our constitution and unacknowledged by our laws; giving his Assent to their Acts of pretended Legislation:

- For quartering large bodies of armed troops among us;
- For protecting them by a mock Trial from punishment for any Murders which they should commit on the Inhabitants of these States;
- For cutting off our Trade with all parts of the world;
- For imposing Taxes on us without our Consent;
- For depriving us in many cases of the benefits of Trial by Jury;
- For transporting us beyond Seas to be tried for pretended offences;
- For abolishing the free System of English Laws in a neighboring Province, establishing therein an Arbitrary government, and enlarging its Boundaries so as to render it at once an example and fit instrument for introducing the same absolute rule into these Colonies;
- For taking away our Charters, abolishing our most valuable Laws and altering fundamentally the Forms of our Governments;
- For suspending our own Legislatures, and declaring themselves invested with power to legislate for us in all cases whatsoever.

He has abdicated Government here, by declaring us out of his Protection and waging War against us.

He has plundered our seas, ravaged our Coasts, burnt our towns, and destroyed the lives of our people.

He is at this time transporting large Armies of foreign Mercenaries to complete the works of death, desolation and tyranny, already begun with circumstances of cruelty and perfidy scarcely paralleled in the most barbarous ages, and totally unworthy the Head of a civilized nation.

He has constrained our fellow Citizens taken Captive on the high Seas to bear Arms against their Country, to become the executioners of their friends and Brethren, or to fall themselves by their Hands.

He has excited domestic insurrections amongst us, and has endeavored to bring on the inhabitants of our frontiers, the merciless Indian Savages, whose known rule of warfare is an undistinguished destruction of all ages, sexes and conditions.

[He has waged cruel war against human nature itself, violating its most sacred rights of life and liberty in the persons of a distant people who never offended him, captivating and carrying them into slavery in another hemisphere, or to incur miserable death in their transportation thither. This piratical warfare, the opprobrium of INFIDEL power, is the warfare of the CHRISTIAN king of Great Britain. Determined to keep open a market where MEN should be bought and sold, he has prostituted his negative for suppressing every legislative attempt to prohibit or to restrain this execrable commerce. And that this assemblage of horrors might want no fact of distinguished die, he is now exciting those very people to rise in arms among us, and to purchase that liberty of which he has deprived them, by murdering the people on whom he also obtruded them: thus paying off former crimes committed against the LIBERTIES of one people, with crimes which he urges them to commit against the LIVES of another.]

In every stage of these Oppressions We have Petitioned for Redress in the most humble terms. Our repeated Petitions have been answered only by repeated injury. A Prince, whose character is thus marked by every act which may define a Tyrant, is unfit to be the ruler of a free people.

Nor have We been wanting in attentions to our British brethren.

We have warned them from time to time of attempts by their legislature to extend an unwarrantable jurisdiction over us.

We have reminded them of the circumstances of our emigration and settlement here.

We have appealed to their native justice and magnanimity, and we have conjured them by the ties of our common kindred to disavow these usurpations, which would inevitably interrupt our connections and correspondence.

They too have been deaf to the voice of justice and of consanguinity. We must, therefore, acquiesce in the necessity, which denounces our Separation, and hold them, as we hold the rest of mankind, Enemies in War, in Peace Friends.

We, therefore, the Representatives of the United States of America, in General Congress, Assembled, appealing to the Supreme Judge of the world for the rectitude of our intentions, do, in the Name, and by the authority of the good People of these Colonies, solemnly publish and declare,

That these United Colonies are, and of Right ought to be, Free and Independent States; that they are Absolved from all Allegiance to the British Crown, and that all political connection between them and the State of Great Britain is and ought to be totally dissolved; and that as Free and Independent States, they have full Power to levy War, conclude Peace, contract Alliances, establish Commerce, and to do all other Acts and Things which Independent States may of right do.

And for the support of this Declaration, with a firm reliance on the protection of Divine Providence, we mutually pledge to each other our Lives, our Fortunes, and our sacred Honor.

[Signers of the Declaration represented the new states as follows:]
   New Hampshire:
Josiah Bartlett, William Whipple, Matthew Thornton
   Massachusetts:
John Hancock, Samuel Adams, John Adams, Robert Treat Paine, Elbridge Gerry
   Rhode Island:
Stephen Hopkins, William Ellery
   Connecticut:
Roger Sherman, Samuel Huntington, William Williams, Oliver Wolcott
   New York:
William Floyd, Philip Livingston, Francis Lewis, Lewis Morris
   New Jersey:
Richard Stockton, John Witherspoon, Francis Hopkinson, John Hart, Abraham Clark
   Pennsylvania:
Robert Morris, Benjamin Rush, Benjamin Franklin, John Morton, George Clymer, James Smith, George Taylor, James Wilson, George Ross
   Delaware:
Caesar Rodney, George Read, Thomas McKean
   Maryland:
Samuel Chase, William Paca, Thomas Stone, Charles Carroll of Carrollton

Virginia:

George Wythe, Richard Henry Lee, Thomas Jefferson, Benjamin Harrison, Thomas Nelson, Jr., Francis Lightfoot Lee, Carter Braxton

North Carolina:

William Hooper, Joseph Hewes, John Penn

South Carolina:

Edward Rutledge, Thomas Heyward, Jr., Thomas Lynch, Jr., Arthur Middleton

Georgia:

Button Gwinnett, Lyman Hall, George Walton

11 Declaration of Sentiments (1848)

With particular fervor during the first half of the nineteenth century, U.S. reformers struggled with the difference between reality and "founding" Republican and Christian principles. An elaborate system of race, gender, and class inequality greatly conditioned the outcome. Various individuals and groups experienced and affected that system in very different ways. But no one could entirely avoid the pre-Civil War barrage of messages touting a new, more intensely gendered regime for American life. The difference between "male" and "female" was widened and institutionalized.

In some ways that regime resembles the one that post-Suffrage ("second-wave") feminists targeted in the 1960s. During the Cold War most women, even those born to privilege, confronted barriers recently built for them. Betty Friedan (one of the founders of NOW, the National Organization for Women) was among those who helped to break the silence in which sexism was shrouded, to "raise consciousness" of "the problem that has no name." In 1963 she published a book that helped give it a name: *The Feminine Mystique.* But gender inequity had many names long before Friedan.

More than a century earlier, according to popular American literature and lore, men and women were supposed to occupy two distinct but complementary "spheres." Insofar as possible (for example, insofar as class and race hierarchy permitted) men rather than women were to wield power over public institutions. Since this responsibility might instill ruthless habits of heart, men as well as the public good also required a wholly "separate sphere" of domestic virtue, a Christian home where men would be comforted, children nurtured, and ideals restored. Maintaining that sphere was to be women's holy calling.

Newspaper columns, mass-marketed fiction, songs, sermons, and political oratory, with remarkable uniformity from about 1815 to 1860, in effect advised women to surrender efficacy in public affairs in exchange for an indirect (and thereby "purer") sort through their efficacy at home. An 1839 magazine explained: "The man bears rule over his wife's person and conduct. She bears rule over his inclinations: he governs by law, she by persuasion. . . . The empire of the woman is an empire of softness." Their weapons were patience, kindness, and tears. Nothing might endanger their position so much as advocating their rights too boldly, especially without male representation.

As Barbara Welter explains, these idealized "true women" were thereby bound by their relations to men—as mothers, sisters, wives, or daughters—and their ability to promote "four cardinal virtues—piety, purity, submissiveness, and domesticity." Even on the eve of the Civil War, while women labored in fields, factories, and public institutions as well as homes, as they organized to advance women's education and civil liberties, poets hyped a crystal vision:

> Her eye of light is the diamond bright,
> Her innocence the pearl,
> And these are ever the bridal gems
> That are worn by the American girl.

Many poets disagreed, and a yet larger number of Americans—particularly women who were poor or of Native, African, Asian, Caribbean, or Latin American descent—were at least partly excepted. Race and class hierarchies often overrode dominant gender ideals. Irish factory operatives and black field hands fit neither gender's sphere. By a strict line of reasoning, any woman who had to or chose to transgress was no longer entirely (or "truly") a woman. She lost or unbound the mixed bag of rights and duties of her "femininity."

Many American women had long pursued that end. As Jan Lewis and Linda Kerber have explained, "Republican Wives and Mothers" were among those who justified and won the American Revolution. Deborah Sampson, for example, was one of the troops who fought for independence, albeit in male drag. (Although twice wounded, she was denied a veteran's pension until 1818.) As early as 1801, a "female advocate" found an alternative model of femininity in the life of a more famous Deborah, the Biblical prophet and judge:

> Behold her wielding the sword with one hand, and the pen of wisdom with the other: her sitting at the council board, and there, by her superior talents, conducting the arduous affairs of military enterprise! Say now, shall woman be forever destined solely to the distaff and the needle, and never expand an idea beyond the walls of her house?

Women were especially active in the struggle to abolish slavery. And in 1840, when several prominent American women were denied seats at the World Anti-Slavery Convention in London, they faced an especially blatant reminder that their ability to act on anyone's behalf required their own emancipation.

Among those snubbed in London was Lucretia Mott. She joined her Quaker colleague Elizabeth Cady Stanton to organize a dignified but bold response. They objected not just to any one injustice but to all disadvantages that law and custom placed on women. The convention at Seneca Falls, New York, drew well over two hundred supporters, including about forty men, among them the famed former slave, abolitionist Frederick Douglass. While they protested in an American mode, their cause was global.

Despite the precedent of many earlier movements for women's rights and despite the obvious inferiority of those rights when compared to the "inalienable" ones named in the Declaration of Independence, the Seneca Falls convention had relatively little direct consequence. As has so often been the case, American women were required to be patient, to sacrifice while other injustices—in this case, slavery—took precedence. More than seventy years passed before the U.S. Constitution was amended to ensure that women had the right to vote in national elections. In the spirit of 1848 and 1776, the struggle for justice and equality continued.

When, in the course of human events, it becomes necessary for one portion of the family of man to assume among the people of the earth a position different from that which they have hitherto occupied, but one to which the laws of nature and of nature's God entitles them, a decent respect to the opinions of mankind requires that they should declare the causes that impel them to such a course.

We hold these truths to be self-evident: that all men and women are created equal; that they are endowed by their Creator with certain inalienable rights; that among these are life, liberty, and the pursuit of happiness; that to secure these rights governments are instituted, deriving their just powers from the consent of the governed. Whenever any form of government becomes destructive of these ends, it is the right of those who suffer from it to refuse allegiance to it, and to insist upon the institution of a new government, laying its foundation on such principles, and organizing its powers in such form, as to them shall seem most likely to effect their safety and happiness. Prudence, indeed, will dictate that governments long established should not be changed for light and transient causes; and accordingly all experience hath shown that mankind are more disposed to suffer, while evils are sufferable, than to right themselves by abolishing the forms to which they were accustomed. But when a long train of abuses and usurpations, pursuing invariably the same object, evinces a design to reduce them under absolute despotism, it is their duty to throw off such government, and to provide new guards for their future security. Such has been the patient sufferance of the women under this government, and such is now the necessity which constrains them to demand the equal station to which they are entitled.

The history of mankind is a history of repeated injuries and usurpations on the part of man toward woman, having in direct object the establishment of an absolute tyranny over her. To prove this, let facts be submitted to a candid world.

He has never permitted her to exercise her inalienable right to the elective franchise.

He has compelled her to submit to laws, in the formation of which she had no voice.

He has withheld from her rights which are given to the most ignorant and degraded men—both natives and foreigners.

Having deprived her of this first right of a citizen, the elective franchise, thereby leaving her without representation in the halls of legislation, he has oppressed her on all sides.

He has made her, if married, in the eyes of the law, civilly dead.

He has taken from her all right in property, even to the wages she earns.

He has made her, morally, an irresponsible being, as she can commit many crimes with impunity, provided they be done in the presence of her husband. In the covenant of marriage, she is compelled to promise obedience to her husband, he becoming, to all intents and purposes, her master—the law giving him power to deprive her of her liberty, and to administer chastisement.

He has so framed the laws of divorce, as to what shall be the proper causes, and in case of separation, to whom the guardianship of the children shall be given, as to be wholly regardless of the happiness of women—the law, in all cases, going upon a false supposition of the supremacy of man, and giving all power into his hands.

After depriving her of all rights as a married woman, if single, and the owner of property, he has taxed her to support a government which recognizes her only when her property can be made profitable to it.

He has monopolized nearly all the profitable employments, and from those she is permitted to follow, she receives but a scanty remuneration. He closes against her all the avenues to wealth and distinction which he considers most honorable to himself. As a teacher of theology, medicine, or law, she is not known.

He has denied her the facilities for obtaining a thorough education, all colleges being closed against her.

He allows her in Church, as well as State, but a subordinate position, claiming Apostolic authority for her exclusion from the ministry, and with some exceptions, from any public participation in the affairs of the Church.

He has created a false public sentiment by giving to the world a different code of morals for men and women, by which moral delinquencies which exclude women from society, are not only tolerated, but demand of little account in man.

He has usurped the prerogative of Jehovah himself, claiming it as his right to assign for her a sphere of action, when that belongs to her conscience and her God.

He has endeavored, in every way that he could, to destroy her confidence in her own powers, to lessen her self-respect, and to make her willing to lead a dependent and abject life.

Now, in view of this entire disfranchisement of one-half the people of this country, their social and religious degradation—in view of the unjust laws above mentioned, and because women do feel themselves aggrieved, oppressed, and fraudulently deprived of their most sacred rights—we insist that they have immediate admission to all the rights and privileges which belong to them as citizens of the United States.

In entering upon the great work before us, we anticipate no small amount of misconception, misrepresentation, and ridicule; but we shall use every instrumentality within our power to effect our object. We shall employ agents, circulate tracts, petition the State and National legislatures, and endeavor to enlist the pulpit and the press in our behalf. We hope this Convention will be followed by a series of Conventions in every part of the country.

WHEREAS, The great precept of nature is conceded to be, that "man shall pursue his own true and substantial happiness." Blackstone in his Commentaries remarks, that his law of Nature being coeval with mankind, and dictated by God himself, is of course superior in obligation to any other. It is binding over all the globe, in all countries and at all times; no human laws are of any validity if contrary to this, and such of them as are valid, derive all their force, and all their validity, and all their authority, mediately and immediately, from this original; therefore,

RESOLVED, That such laws which prevent women from occupying such a station in society as her conscience shall dictate, or which places her in a position inferior to that of man, are contrary to the great precept of nature, and therefore of no force or authority.

RESOLVED, That woman is man's equal—was intended to be so by the Creator, and the highest good of the race demands that she be recognized as such.

RESOLVED, That the women of this country ought to be enlightened in regard to the laws under which they live, that they may no longer publish their degradation by declaring themselves satisfied with their present position, nor their ignorance, by asserting that they have all the rights they want.

RESOLVED, That inasmuch as man, while claiming for himself intellectual superiority, does accord to woman moral superiority, it is pre-eminently his duty to encourage her to speak and teach, as she has an opportunity, in all religious assemblies.

RESOLVED, That the same amount of virtue, delicacy, and refinement of behavior that is required of woman in the social state, should also be required of man, and the same transgressions should be visited with equal severity on both man and woman.

RESOLVED, That the objection of indelicacy and impropriety, which is so often brought against woman when she addresses a public audience comes with a very ill-grace from those who encourage, by their attendance, her appearance on the stage, in the concert, or in feats of the circus.

RESOLVED, That woman has too long rested satisfied in the circumscribed limits which corrupt customs and a perverted application of the Scriptures have marked out for her, and that it is time she should move in the enlarged sphere which her great Creator has assigned her.

RESOLVED, That it is the duty of the women of this country to secure to themselves their sacred right to the elective franchise.

RESOLVED, That the equality of human rights results necessarily from the fact of the identity of the race in capabilities and responsibilities.

RESOLVED, That the speedy success of our cause depends upon the zealous and untiring efforts of both men and women, for the overthrow of the monopoly of the pulpit, and for the securing to women an equal participation with men in the various trades, professions, and commerce.

RESOLVED, THEREFORE, That being invested by the Creator with the same capabilities, and the same consciousness of responsibility for their exercise, it is demonstrably the right and duty of woman, equally with man, to promote every righteous cause by every righteous means; and especially in regard to the great subjects of morals and religion, it is self-evidently her right to participate with her brother in teaching them, both in private and in public, by writing and by speaking, by instrumentalities proper to be used, and in any assemblies proper to be held; and in being a self-evident truth growing out of the divinely implanted principles of human nature, any custom or authority adverse to it, whether modern or wearing the hoary sanction of antiquity, is to be regarded as a self-evident falsehood, and at war with mankind.

12 Independence Day Speech (1854)

As grand sachem of the Stockbridges and confederate of the Mohicans (or Mahicans, an Anglicized Dutch pronunciation of Muh-he-con-new), John Quinney addressed the citizens of Reidsville, New York, on Independence Day, 1854, which was also the first year of his U.S. citizenship. Although born nearly sixty years ago, very near where he spoke, he finally agreed to accept citizenship as the cost of securing title to his home. According to the U.S. Congress, "tribal member" and "property owner" had to be exclusive categories. Although he felt compelled to surrender that point, he still could use the Fourth of July to bear witness to such tortured turns in relations among aborigines and immigrants in North America. Just two years earlier at a memorial ceremony before Congress—the very body that caused him such grief—Quinney declared himself "a true Native American." He thereby coined a new English name for the hundreds of Indian or "Red" nations, tribes, bands, and confederacies of the hemisphere.

Quinney provided most of the context for his own speech, but he generously overlooked particulars in his route to the podium. In order to face his audience, for example, he had to travel from Wisconsin, where his people had purchased refuge, about 1,000 miles to the Hudson and Connecticut River region where he was born and where his ancestors had resided for centuries. Quinney had been among the leaders trying to maintain the Stockbridges by finessing sundry schemes of the U.S. government and by resisting encroachment not only from whites but also from other Native Americans whom they were forced to neighbor.

Although the confederacy had been nearly decimated by the time of this speech and Qunney died just one year later, the Stockbridge legacy survives. Among the most recognizable traces are towns bearing their name along the path of their "removal" (Stockbridges in Massachusetts, New York, and Wisconsin) and the phrase "the last of the Mohicans" (from the 1826 novel by James Fenimore Cooper that Michael Mann transferred to film in

1992). But as Quinney hoped and contrary even to his own prediction, the Stockbridges are also very much alive. Approximately 1,500 members of the Stockbridge-Munsee Band of the Mohican Nation still reside on or near 40,000 acres of reservation land in eastern Wisconsin.

It may appear to those whom I have the honor to address, a singular taste, for me, an Indian, to take an interest in the triumphal days of a people, who occupy, by conquest, or have usurped the possessions of my fathers, and have laid and carefully preserved a train of terrible miseries to end when my race ceased to exist. But thanks to the fortunate circumstances of my life, I have been taught in the schools and been able to read your histories and accounts of Europeans, yourselves and the Red Man; which instruct me that, while your rejoicings today are commemorative of the free birth of this giant nation, they simply convey to my mind the recollection of a transfer of the miserable weakness and dependence of my race from one great power to another.

My friends, I am getting old and have witnessed for many years your increase in wealth and power, while the steady consuming decline of my tribe admonishes me that their extinction is inevitable. They know it themselves, and the reflection teaches them humility and resignation, directing their attention to the existence of those happy hunting grounds which the Great Father has prepared for all his red children.

In this spirit, my friends, as a Muh-he-con-new, and now standing upon the soil which once was and now ought to be the property of this tribe, I have thought for once, and certainly the last time, I would shake you by the hand and ask you to listen for a little while to what I have to say.

In the documentary papers of this state and in the various histories of early events in the settlement of this part of the country by whites, the many traditions of my tribe, which are as firmly believed as written annals by you, inform me that there are many errors. Without, however, intending to refer to and correct those histories, I will give you what those traditions are.

About the year 1645, when King Ben (the last of the hereditary chiefs of the Muh-he-con-new Nation) was in his prime, a Grand Council was convened of the Muh-he-con-new tribe, for the purpose of conveying from the old to the young men, a knowledge of the past. Councils for this object especially had been held. Here, for the space of two moons, the stores of memory were dispensed; corrections and comparisons were made and the results committed to faithful breasts, to be transmitted again to succeeding posterity.

Many years after, another and last Council of this kind was held; and the traditions reduced to writing, by two of our young men who had been taught to read and write in the school of the Rev. John Sargeant of Stockbridge, Massachusetts. They were obtained, in some way, by a white man, for publication, who soon after dying, all trace of them became lost. The traditions of the tribe, however, have mainly been preserved, of which I give you substantially, the following:

A great people from the northwest, crossed over the salt water, and after a long and weary pilgrimage (planting many colonies on their track), took possession of and built their fires upon the Atlantic coast, extending from the Delaware on the south to the Penobscott on the north. They became, in process of time, different tribes and interests; all, however, speaking one common dialect. This great confederacy, comprising Delawares, Munsees, Mohegans, Narragansetts, Pequots, Penobscotts, and many others . . . held its Council fires once a year to deliberate on the general welfare. Patriarchal delegates from each tribe attended, assisted by the priests and the wise men who communicated the will and invoked the blessing of the Great and Good Spirit. The policies and decisions of this council were everywhere respected and inviolably observed. Thus contentment smiled upon their existence, and they were happy. Their religion, communicated by priests and prophets, was simple and true. The manner of worship is imperfectly transmitted; but their reverence for a Great and Good Spirit . . . the observance of feasts each year, the offering of beasts in thanksgiving and for atonement is clearly expressed. They believed the soul to be immortal—in the existence of a happy land beyond the view, inhabited by those whose lives had been blameless: while for the wicked had been reserved a region of misery covered with thorns and thistles, where comfort and pleasure were unknown. Time was divided into years and seasons; twelve moons for a year, a number of years by so many winters.

The tribe, to which your speaker belongs and of which there were many bands, occupied and possessed the country from the seashore at Manhattan to Lake Champlain. Having found the ebb and flow of the tide, they said: "This is Muh-he-con-new"—"Like our waters which are never still." From this expression and by this name they were afterwards known, until their removal to Stockbridge in the year 1730.

Housatonic River Indians, Mohegan, Manhattans, were all names of bands in different localities, but bound together as one family by blood, marriage and descent.

At a remote period, before the advent of the European, their wise men foretold the coming of a strange race from the sunrise, as numerous as the leaves upon the trees, who would eventually crowd them from their fair land possessions. But apprehension was mitigated by the knowledge and belief, at that time entertained, that their original home was not there, and after a period of years they would return to the west from which they had come. And moreover they said, "All the Red Men are sprung from a common ancestor, made by the Great Spirit from red clay, who will unite their strength to avert a common calamity." This tradition is confirmed by the common belief, which prevails in our day with all the Indian tribes; for they recognize one another by their color as brothers and acknowledge one Great Creator.

Two hundred and fifty winters ago, this prophecy was verified, and the Muh-he-con-new for the first time beheld the paleface. Their number was small, but their canoes were big. In the select and exclusive circles of your rich men of the present day, I should encounter the gaze of curiosity, but not such as overwhelmed the senses of the aborigines, my ancestors.

> Our visitors were white and must be sick. They asked for rest and kindness; we gave them both. They were strangers, and we took them in—naked, and we clothed them.

The first impression of astonishment and pity was succeeded by awe and admiration of superior art, intelligence and address. A passion for information and improvement possessed the Indians—a residence was freely offered, territory given, and covenants of friendship exchanged.

Your written accounts of events at this period are familiar to you, my friends. Your children read them every day in their school books; but they do not read—no mind at this time can conceive, and no pen record—the terrible story of recompense for kindness, which for two hundred years has been paid the simple, guileless Muh-he-con-new. I have seen much myself—have been connected with more, and I tell you, I know all. The tradition of the wise men is figuratively true, "that our home at last will be found in the west"; for another tradition informs us, that "far beyond the setting sun, upon the smiling happy lands, we shall be gathered with our Fathers and be at rest.

Promises and professions were freely given and ruthlessly—intentionally—broken. To kindle your fires—to be of and with us—was sought as a privilege; and yet at that moment you were transmitting to your kings, beyond the water, intelligence of your possessions, "by right of discovery," and demanding assistance to assert and maintain your hold.

Where are the 25,000 in number, and the 4,000 warriors, who constituted the power and population of the great Muh-he-con-new Nation in 1604? They have been victims to vice and disease, which the white men imported. The smallpox, measles and "strong waters" have done the work of annihilation.

Divisions and feuds were insidiously promoted between the several bands. They were induced to thin each other's ranks without just cause; and subsequently were defeated and disorganized in detail.

It is curious, the history of my tribe, in its decline, in the last two centuries and a half. Nothing that deserved the name of purchase was ever made. From various causes, they were induced to abandon their territory at intervals and retire farther to the inland. Deeds were given indifferently to the Government or to individuals, for which little or no consideration was paid. The Indian was informed, in many instances, that he was selling one parcel, while the conveyance described other and much larger limits. Should a particular band, for purposes of hunting or fishing, desert for a time its usual place of residence, the land was said to be abandoned, and the Indian claim extinguished. To legalize and confirm titles thus acquired, laws and edicts were subsequently passed, and these laws were said then to be, and are now called, justice! Oh! what mockery! to confound justice with law! Will you look steadily at the intrigues, bargains, corruptions and log-rolling of your present Legislatures, and see any trace of justice? And by what test shall be tried the acts of the old Colonial Courts and Councils?

Let it not surprise you, my friends, when I say that the spot upon which we stand has never been rightly purchased or obtained; and that by justice, human and divine, it is the property now of the remnant of that great people from whom I am descended. They left it in the tortures of starvation and to improve their miserable existence; but a cession was never made, and their title was never extinguished.

The Indian is said to be the ward of the white man, and the negro his slave. Has it ever occurred to you, my friends, that while the slave is increasing and increased by every appliance, the Indian is left to rot and die before the inhumanities of this model *Republic*?! You have your tears and groans and mobs and riots for the individuals of the former, while your indifference of purpose and vacillation of policy is hurrying to extinction whole communities of the latter.

What are the treaties of the general Government? How often and when has its plighted faith been kept? Indian occupation forever is next year, or by the next Commissioner, more wise than his predecessor, re-purchased. One removal follows another, and thus your sympathies and justice are evinced in speedily *fulfilling the terrible destinies of our race.*

My friends, your holy book, the Bible, teaches us that individual offenses are punished in an existence, when time shall be no more. And the annals of the earth are equally instructive, that national wrongs are avenged, and national crimes atoned for in this world to which alone the conformation of existence adapts them.

These events are above our comprehension, and for a wise purpose. For myself and for my tribe I ask for justice—I believe it will sooner or later occur—and may the Great and Good Spirit enable me to die in hope.

FREDERICK JACKSON TURNER

13 The Significance of the Frontier in American History (1893)

Ask just about anyone, just about anywhere, to imagine the quintessential American, and sooner or later they will settle on a cowboy. Even in camp incarnations (for example, among the Village People) he is a virile hero—a statuesque, well-tanned but still presumably "white" guy with six-shooter and Stetson. Atop his trusty steed, the Marlboro Man drives cattle across "the wild West," likely envisioned as Monument Valley, a holy Navajo land where film director John Ford immortalized John Wayne. These are, for example, the images of America featured in Denmark's Legoland as purely as in Disneyworld, reruns of "Bonanza," and Ronald Reagan's greatest hits. When Oscar Wilde, Marilyn Monroe, and Mouseketeers play all-American, they don coarse buckskin and blue jeans. There is supposed to be some chain of cause and effect—a kind of homeopathy—by which rough open spaces account for the roughness of Americans as well as their hunger for regeneration in ever more challenging frontiers.

Even in domesticated or feminized variants, such as Laura Ingalls Wilder's *Little House* books (1930s–1940s), there is something supposedly transformative about a prairie. Life far from government, city, and factory brings out the best in folks. Fostering that interpretation of the American spirit was clearly among supporters' motives in promoting those books during Depression-era debates over the New Deal (and their resuscitation in a television series during the Republican surge of the 1980s). The books and their spin-offs conjure up a simple, virtuous alternative to the welfare state that has been associated with "too much government" and the Democrats since Franklin D. Roosevelt.

Of course, this vision of America as a frontier nation owes as much to stereotypes as to history. For example, the period of open-range cattle ranching was extremely brief, no more than about fifteen years. Cattle drives began about the same time that the Civil War ended (the mid-1860s), when Texas stock were shipped east via Missouri terminals, and declined in the 1870s, when the business was already overdeveloped. Cattle drives were rendered anachronisms as early as 1873, when East-West rail lines reached Texas.

Moreover, even in that short period, a typical cowboy was much more likely to be a descendant of Mexican, African, or Indian peoples than English or Irish. The region beyond the Mississippi River was already populated well before Europeans arrived, and migrants from the East were women and children as well as men, more often in pursuit of a decent family farmstead than virile, solitary adventure.

U.S. expansion from east to west (and from mid-continent to south and north) was hardly accomplished through unfettered entrepreneurship. Government protection and subsidies were essential to the massive theft and transfer of land from Indian to European descendants and railroad conglomerates. By 1900, more than 1.4 million new farms were established in western states and territories, yielding mountains of produce that were transported, processed, and marketed by giant corporations. Technological innovations that eased this growth include barbed-wire fences, wind-powered well pumps, and massive tractors. But daily life in the West through the 1930s generally remained hard, often isolated, far from sources of finished goods, companionship, and medical services, with brutal winters and summers, howling winds, storms, and droughts. Hence, a fair stereotype of folks on the frontier would be not a band of buff horsemen but struggling families in drab, tiny houses.

This is not to say that the frontier played a minor role in U.S. cultural history. Its importance was among the lessons that the Columbian Exposition (also known as the Chicago World's Fair) offered 27 million visitors in 1893. It touted the dynamism of the nation, with an accent on "progress" since 1492, the leadership of the city (risen from ashes in 1871), and the region it represented. Thanks to Western experience, the United States could be more than a poor cousin of the Anglo-Saxon, German, or Teutonic ancestors whom contemporary critics lionized. Among the scholars who advanced this more independent interpretation was University of Wisconsin historian Frederick Jackson Turner. At a meeting of the American Historical Association in Chicago during the Exposition, he made a case for the singular significance of the frontier, a perspective thereafter known as "the Turner thesis." Its catalyst was a new U.S. Census report alleging that the line where America's Eastern civilization met Western wilderness had just become a thing of the past.

Americanists now emphasize that pioneers never, in fact, encountered "free land" or virgin wilderness. There never was a "line" between aborigines and migrants but several wide, complex, dynamic, diverse, and dispersed "contact zones." Many scholars find Turner's interpretation itself an example of the distinctly "American intellect" that he aimed to explain. Nevertheless, even his detractors readily acknowledge their debt to this essay for charting interpretive frontiers and welcoming interdisciplinary adventurers.

In a recent bulletin of the Superintendent of the Census for 1890 appear these significant words:

Up to and including 1880 the country had a frontier of settlement, but at present the unsettled area has been so broken into by isolated bodies of settlement that there can hardly be said to be a frontier line. In the discussion of its extent, its westward movement, etc., it cannot, therefore, any longer have a place in the census reports.

This brief official statement marks the closing of a great historic movement. Up to our own day American history has been in a large degree the history of the colonization of the Great West. The existence of an area of free land, its continuous recession, and the advance of American settlement westward, explain American development. . . .

American social development has been continually beginning over again on the frontier. . . . This fluidity of American life, this expansion westward—with its few opportunities, its continuous touch with the simplicity of primitive society—furnishes the forces dominating American character. The true point of view in the history of this nation is not the Atlantic coast; it is the Great West. Even the slavery struggle . . . occupies its important place in American history because of its relation to westward expansion.

In this advance, the frontier is the outer edge of the wave, the meeting point between savagery and civilization. . . . Our early history is the study of European germs developing in an American environment. Too exclusive attention has been paid by institutional students to the Germanic origins, too little to the American factors. The frontier is the line of most rapid and effective Americanization. The wilderness masters the colonist. It finds him a European in dress, industries, tools, modes of travel, and thought. It takes him from the railroad car and puts him in the birch canoe. It strips off the garments of civilization and arrays him in the hunting shirt and the moccasin. It puts him in the log cabin of the Cherokee and Iroquois and runs an Indian palisade around him. Before long he has gone to planting Indian corn and plowing with a sharp stick; he shouts the war cry and takes the scalp in orthodox Indian fashion. In short, at the frontier the environment is at first too strong for the man. He must accept the conditions which it furnishes, or perish, and so he fits himself into the Indian clearings and follows the Indian trails. Little by little he transforms the wilder-

ness, but the outcome is not the old Europe, not simply the development of Germanic germs, any more than the first phenomenon was a
case of reversion to the Germanic mark. The fact is that here is a new
product that is American. At first, the frontier was the Atlantic coast,
the frontier of Europe in a very real sense. Moving westward, the frontier became more and more American. As successive terminal mo-
raines result from successive glaciations, so each frontier leaves its
traces behind it, and when it becomes a settled area the region still
partakes of the frontier characteristics. Thus the advance of the frontier has meant a steady movement away from the influence of Europe,
a steady growth of independence on American lines. And to study
this advance, the men who grew up under these conditions, and the
political, economic, and social results of it, is to study the really American part of our history. . . .

From decade to decade distinct advances of the frontier occurred.
. . . In these successive frontiers we find natural boundary lines which
have served to mark and to affect the characteristics of the frontiers.
. . . The fall line marked the frontier of the seventeenth century; the
Alleghenies that of the eighteenth; the Mississippi that of the first quarter of the nineteenth; the Missouri that of the middle of this century
(omitting the California movement); and the belt of the Rocky Mountains and the arid tract, the present frontier. Each was won by a series
of Indian wars. . . . Land policy . . . has been a series of experimenta-
tions on successive frontiers. Each tier of new states has found in the
older ones material for its constitutions. . . .

But with all these similarities there are essential differences. Due
to the place element and the time element it is evident that the farming frontier of the Mississippi Valley presents different conditions from
the mining frontier of the Rocky Mountains. The frontier reached by
the Pacific Railroad, surveyed into rectangles, guarded by the United
States Army, and recruited by the daily immigrant ship, moves forward at a swifter pace and in a different way than the frontier reached
by the birch canoe or the pack horse. The geologist traces patiently the
shores of ancient seas, maps their areas, and compares the older and
the newer. It would be a work worth the historian's labors to mark
these various frontiers and in detail compare one with another. Not
only would there result a more adequate conception of American development and characteristics, but invaluable additions would be made
to the history of society.

Loria, the Italian economist, has urged the study of colonial life as an aid in understanding the stages of European development, affirming that colonial settlement is for economic science what the mountain is for geology, bringing to light primitive stratifications. "America," he says, "has the key to the historical enigma which Europe has sought for centuries in vain, and the land which has no history reveals luminously the course of universal history." There is much truth in this. The United States lies like a huge page in the history of society. Line by line as we read this continental page from West to East we find the record of social evolution. It begins with the Indian and the hunter; it goes on to tell of the disintegration of savagery by the entrance of the trader, the pathfinder of civilization; we read the annals of the pastoral stage in ranch life; the exploitation of the soil by the raising of unrotated crops of corn and wheat in sparsely settled farming communities; the intensive culture of the denser farm settlement; and finally the manufacturing organization with city and factory system. This page is familiar to the student of census statistics, but . . . what constitutional historian has made any adequate attempt to interpret political facts by the light of these social areas and changes?

The Atlantic frontier was compounded of fisherman, fur-trader, miner, cattle-raiser, and farmer. Excepting the fisherman, each type of industry was on the march toward the West, impelled by an irresistible attraction. Each passed in successive waves across the continent. Stand at Cumberland Gap and watch the procession of civilization, marching single file—the buffalo following the trail to the salt springs, the Indian, the fur-trader and hunter, the cattle-raiser, the pioneer farmer and the frontier has passed by. Stand at South Pass in the Rockies a century later and see the same procession with wider intervals between. The unequal rate of advance compels us to distinguish the frontier into the trader's frontier, the rancher's frontier, or the miner's frontier, and the farmer's frontier. . . .

The rapidity of this advance is connected with the effects of the trader on the Indian. The trading post left the unarmed tribes at the mercy of those that had purchased firearms, a truth which the Iroquois Indians wrote in blood, and so the remote and unvisited tribes gave eager welcome to the trade. "The savages," wrote La Salle, "take better care of us French than of their own children; from us only can they get guns and goods." This accounts for the trader's power and the rapidity of his advance; thus the disintegrating forces of civilization entered the wilderness. Every river valley and Indian trail became a fissure in Indian society, and so that society became honeycombed. Long before the pioneer farmer appeared on the scene, primitive Indian life had passed away. The farmers met Indians armed with guns. The trading frontier, while steadily undermining Indian power by making the tribes ultimately dependent on the whites, yet, through its sale of guns, gave to the Indian increased power of resistance to the farming frontier. French colonization was dominated by its trading frontier; English colonization by its farming frontier. There was an antagonism between the two frontiers as between the two nations. Said Duquesne to the Iroquois,

> Are you ignorant of the difference between the king of England and the king of France? Go see the forts that our king has established, and you will see that you can still hunt under their very walls. They have been placed for your advantage in places which you frequent. The English, on the contrary, are no sooner in possession of a place than the game is driven away. The forest falls before them as they advance, and the soil is laid bare so that you can scarce find the wherewithal to erect a shelter for the night.

And yet, in spite of this opposition of the interests of the trader and the farmer, the Indian trade pioneered the way for civilization. The buffalo trail became the Indian trail, and this became the trader's "traces"; the trails widened into roads, and the roads into turnpikes, and these in turn were transformed into railroads. The same origin can be shown for the railroads of the South, the Far West, and the Dominion of Canada. The trading posts reached by these trails were on the sites of Indian villages which had been placed in positions suggested by nature; and these trading posts, situated so as to command the water systems of the country, have grown into such cities as Albany, Pittsburgh, Detroit, Chicago, St. Louis, Council Bluffs, and Kansas City. Thus civilization in America has followed the arteries made by geology, pouring an ever richer tide through them, until at last the slender paths of aboriginal intercourse have been broadened and interwoven into the complex mazes of modern commercial lines; the wilderness has been interpenetrated by lines of civilization growing ever more numerous. It is like the steady growth of a complex nervous system for the originally simple, inert continent. If one would understand why we are today one nation, rather than a collection of isolated states, he must study this economic and social consolidation of the country. In this progress from savage conditions lie topics for the evolutionist. . . .

The farmer's advance came in a distinct series of waves. . . . Generally, in all the western settlements, three classes, like the waves of the ocean, have rolled one after the other. First comes the pioneer, who depends for the subsistence of his family chiefly upon the natural growth of vegetation, called the "range," and the proceeds of hunting. . . . It is quite immaterial whether he ever becomes the owner of the soil. He is the occupant for the time being, pays no rent, and feels as independent as the "lord of the manor." With a horse, cow, and one or two breeders of swine, he strikes into the woods with his family, and becomes the founder of a new county, or perhaps state. He builds his cabin, gathers around him a few other families of similar tastes and habits . . . till the range is somewhat subdued, and hunting a little precarious, or, which is more frequently the case, till the neighbors crowd around, roads, bridges, and fields annoy him, and he lacks elbow room. The preemption law enables him to dispose of his cabin and cornfield to the next class of emigrants; and, to employ his own figures, he "breaks for the high timber," "clears out for the New Purchase," or migrates to Arkansas or Texas, to work the same process over.

The next class of emigrants purchase the lands, add field to field, clear out the roads, throw rough bridges over the streams, put up hewn log houses with glass windows and brick or stone chimneys, occasionally plant orchards, build mills, schoolhouses, courthouses, etc., and exhibit the picture and forms of plain, frugal, civilized life.

Another wave rolls on. The men of capital and enterprise come. The settler is ready to sell out and take the advantage of the rise in property, push farther into the interior and become, himself, a man of capital and enterprise in turn. The small village rises to a spacious town or city; substantial edifices of brick, extensive fields, orchards, gardens, colleges, and churches are seen. Broadcloths, silks, leghorns, crapes, and all the refinements, luxuries, elegancies, frivolities, and fashions are in vogue. Thus wave after wave is rolling westward; the real Eldorado is still farther on. . . .

Having now roughly outlined the various kinds of frontiers, and their modes of advance, chiefly from the point of view of the frontier itself, we may next inquire what were the influences on the East and on the Old World. A rapid enumeration of some of the more noteworthy effects is all that I have time for.

First, we note that the frontier promoted the formation of a composite nationality for the American people. The coast was preponderantly English, but the later tides of continental immigration flowed across to the free lands. This was the case from the early colonial days. The Scotch-lrish and the Palatine Germans, or "Pennsylvania Dutch," furnished the dominant element in the stock of the colonial frontier. With these peoples were also the freed indentured servants, or redemptioners, who at the expiration of their time of service passed to the frontier. . . . Very generally these redemptioners were of non-English stock. In the crucible of the frontier the immigrants were Americanized, liberated, and fused into a mixed race, English in neither nationality nor characteristics. The process has gone on from the early days to our own. . . . Such examples teach us to beware of misinterpreting the fact that there is a common English speech in America into a belief that the stock is also English.

In another way the advance of the frontier decreased our dependence on England. . . . As it retreated from the coast it became less and less possible for England to bring her supplies directly to the consumer's wharves and carry away staple crops, and staple crops began to give way to diversified agriculture for a time. The effect of this phase of the frontier action upon the northern section is perceived when we realize how the advance of the frontier aroused seaboard cities like Boston, New York, and Baltimore to engage in rivalry for what Washington called "the extensive and valuable trade of a rising empire. "

The legislation which most developed the powers of the national government, and played the largest part in its activity, was conditioned on the frontier. . . . The purchase of Louisiana was perhaps the constitutional turning point in the history of the Republic, inasmuch as it afforded both a new area for national legislation and the occasion of the downfall of the policy of strict construction. . . . Legislation with regard to land, tariff, and internal improvements—the American system of the nationalizing Whig party—was conditioned on frontier ideas and needs. But it was not merely in legislative action that the frontier worked against the sectionalism of the coast. The economic and social characteristics of the frontier worked against sectionalism. The men of the frontier had closer resemblances to the Middle region than to either of the other sections. . . .

The Middle region, entered by New York harbor, was an open door to all Europe. The tidewater part of the South represented typical Englishmen, modified by a warm climate and servile labor, and living in baronial fashion on great plantations; New England stood for a special English movement—Puritanism. The Middle region was less English than the other sections. It had a wide mixture of nationalities, a varied society, the mixed town and county system of local government, a varied economic life, many religious sects. In short, it was a region mediating between New England and the South, and the East and the West. It represented that composite nationality which the contemporary United States exhibits, that juxtaposition of non-English groups, occupying a valley or a little settlement, and presenting reflections of the map of Europe in their variety. It was democratic and non-sectional, if not national; "easy, tolerant, and contented"; rooted strongly in material prosperity. It was typical of the modern United States. It was least sectional, not only because it lay between North and South, but also because with no barriers to shut out its frontiers from its settled region, and with a system of connecting waterways, the Middle region mediated between East and West as well as between North and South. Thus it became the typically American region. . . .

It was this nationalizing tendency of the West that transformed the democracy of Jefferson into the national republicanism of Monroe and the democracy of Andrew Jackson. . . . Interstate migration went steadily on—a process of cross-fertilization of ideas and institutions. The fierce struggle of the sections over slavery on the western frontier does not diminish the truth of this statement; it proves the truth of it. Slavery was a sectional trait . . . but in the West it could not remain sectional. It was the greatest of frontiersmen [Abraham Lincoln] who declared: "I believe this Government can not endure permanently half slave and half free. It will become all of one thing or all of the other." Nothing works for nationalism like intercourse within the nation. Mobility of population is death to localism, and the western frontier worked irresistibly in unsettling population. The effect reached back from the frontier and affected profoundly the Atlantic coast and even the Old World.

But the most important effect of the frontier has been in the promotion of democracy here and in Europe. . . . The rise of democracy as an effective force in the nation came in with western preponderance under Jackson and William Henry Harrison, and it meant the triumph of the frontier—with all of its good and with all of its evil elements. An interesting illustration of the tone of frontier democracy in 1830 comes from the debates in the Virginia convention. . . . A representative from western Virginia declared:

But, sir, it is not the increase of population in the West which this gentleman ought to fear. It is the energy which the mountain breeze and western habits impart to those emigrants. They are regenerated, politically, I mean, sir. They soon become working politicians; and the difference, sir, between a talking and a working politician is immense. The Old Dominion has long been celebrated for producing great orators; the ablest metaphysicians in policy; men that can split hairs in all abstruse questions of political economy. But at home, or when they return from Congress, they have Negroes to fan them asleep. But a Pennsylvania, a New York, an Ohio, or a western Virginia statesman, though far inferior in logic, metaphysics, and rhetoric to an old Virginia statesman, has this advantage: that when he returns home he takes off his coat and takes hold of the plow. This gives him bone and muscle, sir, and preserves his republican principles pure and uncontaminated.

So long as free land exists, the opportunity for a competency exists, and economic power secures political power. But the democracy born of free land, strong in selfishness and individualism, intolerant of administrative experience and education, and pressing individual liberty beyond its proper bounds, has its dangers as well as its benefits. Individualism in America has allowed a laxity in regard to governmental affairs which has rendered possible the spoils system and all the manifest evils that follow from the lack of a highly developed civic spirit. In this connection may be noted also the influence of frontier conditions in permitting lax business honor, inflated paper currency and wildcat banking. . . . A primitive society can hardly be expected to show the intelligent appreciation of the complexity of business interests in a developed society. The continual recurrence of these areas of paper-money agitation is another evidence that the frontier can be isolated and studied as a factor in American history of the highest importance. The East has always feared the result of an unregulated advance of the frontier, and has tried to check and guide it. The English authorities would have checked settlement at the headwaters of the Atlantic tributaries and allowed the "savages to enjoy their deserts in quiet lest the peltry [fur] trade should decrease." This called out Burke's splendid protest:

> If you stopped your grants, what would be the consequence? The people would occupy without grants. They have already so occupied in many places. You can not station garrisons in every part of these

deserts. If you drive the people from one place, they will carry on their annual tillage and remove with their flocks and herds to another. Many of the people in the back settlements are already little attached to particular situations. . . . Already they have topped the Appalachian Mountains. From thence they behold before them an immense plain, one vast, rich level meadow; a square of five hundred miles. Over this they would wander without a possibility of restraint; they would change their manners with their habits of life; would soon forget a government by which they were disowned; would become hordes of English Tartars; and, pouring down upon your unfortified frontiers a fierce and irresistible cavalry, become masters of your governors and your counselors, your collectors and comptrollers, and of all the slaves that adhered to them. Such would, and in no long time must, be the effect of attempting to forbid as a crime and to suppress as an evil the command and blessing of Providence, "Increase and multiply." Such would be the happy result of an endeavor to keep as a lair of wild beasts that earth which God, by an express charter, has given to the children of men.

But the English Government was not alone in its desire to limit the advance of the frontier and guide its destinies. Tidewater Virginia and South Carolina gerrymandered those colonies to insure the dominance of the coast in their legislatures. . . . Madison went so far as to argue to the French minister that the United States had no interest in seeing population extend itself on the right bank of the Mississippi, but should rather fear it. . . . Even Thomas Benton, the man of widest views of the destiny of the West . . . , declared that along the ridge of the Rocky Mountains "the western limits of the Republic should be drawn, and the statue of the fabled god Terminus should be raised upon its highest peak, never to be thrown down." But the attempts to limit the boundaries, to restrict land sales and settlement, and to deprive the West of its share of political power were all in vain. Steadily the frontier of settlement advanced and carried with it individualism, democracy, and nationalism, and powerfully affected the East and the Old World.

The most effective efforts of the East to regulate the frontier came through its educational and religious activity, exerted by interstate migration and by organized societies. . . . The New England preacher and schoolteacher left their mark on the West. The dread of Western emancipation from New England's political and economic control was paralleled by her fears lest the West cut loose from her religion. . . . Home missions were established and Western colleges were erected. As seaboard cities like Philadelphia, New York, and Baltimore strove for the mastery of Western trade, so the various denominations strove for the possession of the West. . . . The multiplication of rival churches in the little frontier towns had deep and lasting social effects. The religious aspects of the frontier make a chapter in our history which needs study.

From the conditions of frontier life came intellectual traits of profound importance. The works of travelers along each frontier from colonial days onward describe certain common traits, and these traits have, while softening down, still persisted as survivals in the place of their origin, even when a higher social organization succeeded. The result is that to the frontier the American intellect owes its striking characteristics. That coarseness and strength combined with acuteness and inquisitiveness; that practical, inventive turn of mind, quick to find expedients; that masterful grasp of material things, lacking in the artistic but powerful to effect great ends; that restless, nervous energy; that dominant individualism, working for good and for evil, and withal that buoyancy and exuberance which comes with freedom— these are traits of the frontier, or traits called out elsewhere because of the existence of the frontier. Since the days when the fleet of Columbus sailed into the waters of the New World, America has been another name for opportunity, and the people of the United States have taken their tone from the incessant expansion which has not only been open but has even been forced upon them.

He would be a rash prophet who should assert that the expansive character of American life has now entirely ceased. Movement has been its dominant fact, and, unless this training has no effect upon a people, the American energy will continually demand a wider field for its exercise. But never again will such gifts of free land offer themselves. For a moment, at the frontier, the bonds of custom are broken and unrestraint is triumphant. There is no *tabula rasa*. The stubborn American environment is there with its imperious summons to accept its conditions; the inherited ways of doing things are also there; and yet, in spite of environment, and in spite of custom, each frontier did indeed furnish a new field of opportunity, a gate of escape from the bondage of the past; and freshness, and confidence, and scorn of older society, impatience of its restraints and its ideas, and indifference to its lessons, have accompanied the frontier. What the Mediterranean

Sea was to the Greeks, breaking the bond of custom, offering new experiences, calling out new institutions and activities, that, and more, the ever retreating frontier has been to the United States directly, and to the nations of Europe more remotely. And now, four centuries from the discovery of America, at the end of a hundred years of life under the Constitution, the frontier has gone, and with its going has closed the first period of American history. . . .

Now in the way of recapitulation. . . . Most important of all has been the fact that an area of free land has continually lain on the western border of the settled areas of the United States. Whenever social conditions tended to crystallize in the East, whenever capital tended to press upon labor or political restraints to impede the freedom of the masses, there was this gate of escape to the free conditions of the frontier. These free lands promoted individualism, economic equality, freedom to rise, democracy. . . . In a word, then, free lands meant free opportunities. Their existence has differentiated the American democracy from the democracies which have preceded it, because ever, as democracy in the East took the form of highly specialized and complicated industrial society, in the West it kept in touch with primitive conditions, and by action and reaction these two forces shaped our history.

In the next place, these free lands and this treasury of industrial resources have existed over such vast spaces that they have demanded of democracy increasing spaciousness of design and power of execution. Never before in the history of the world has a democracy existed on so vast an area and handled things in the gross with such success, with such largeness of design, and such grasp upon the means of execution. In short, democracy has learned in the West of the United States how to deal with the problem of magnitude. The old historic democracies were but little states with primitive economic conditions.

But the very task of dealing with vast resources, over vast areas, under the conditions of free competition furnished by the West, has produced the rise of those captains of industry whose success in consolidating economic power now raises the question as to whether democracy under such conditions can survive. . . .

The question is imperative, then: What ideals persist from this democratic experience of the West; and have they acquired sufficient momentum to sustain themselves under conditions so radically unlike those in the days of their origin? . . . Is there evolving such a concentration of economic and social power in the hands of a comparatively few men as may make political democracy an appearance rather than a reality? The free lands are gone. The material forces that gave vitality to the Western democracy are passing away. It is to the realm of the spirit, to the domain of ideals and legislation, that we must look.

American Progress, John Gast, 1872

In 1845, as U.S. pressure on Mexico mounted, New York editor John L. O'Sullivan gave expansionism a name that captured the divine, political, and natural elements of its justification—"manifest destiny":

> The sweep of our eagle's wing . . . is no longer to us a mere geographical space—a certain combination of coast, plain, mountain, valley, forest, and stream. She is no longer to us a mere country on the map. She comes within the dear and sacred designation of Our Country. . . . Our manifest destiny [is] to overspread the continent allotted by Providence for the free development of our yearly multiplying millions. . . . All this without agency of our government, without responsibility of our people—in the natural flow of events, the spontaneous working of principles, and the adaptation of tendencies and wants of the human race to the elemental circumstances in the midst of which they find themselves placed.

With Darwinists' help, the social, spiritual, and environmental dimensions of such "adaptation" became more apparent after the Civil War. It can, for example, be detected in many popular arts, as in this print from a painting by John Gast. An American icon hovers in the center of the frame, her draped figure wooing the way westward. She bears a schoolbook in one hand and strings telegraph wire with the other. Albeit in vaguely academic, European style, the alleged stages of American evolution appear in her wake: scouts followed by frontiersmen, farmers, then villagers with rail links to ports, cities, and factories in the East. The mere sight of the "Star of Empire" on her crown sets Indians, buffalo, and wildlife scurrying from view.

The Spirit of the West, Edwin Howland Blashfield, 1910

By the turn of the century, an associate of John Gast, Edwin Blashfield, was reputedly the dean of American mural painters. He applied his training in European academic styles to a host of public buildings, including the domes of state capitols and county courthouses, the Manufacturers and Liberal Arts Building at the Chicago World's Fair, and the rotunda of the Library of Congress. This South Dakota mural, with its sundry aliases, has certainly been his most controversial in that it shows, among other things, pioneers trampling Indians. Indians themselves, particularly Sioux survivors of Wounded Knee I and II, pressed authorities to spare them such a heroic rendering of genocide. In 1971 the mural was covered with a curtain and a substitute painting, *The Great Spirit*, commissioned by the governor. The substitute pleased just about no one; it was removed, and the controversy persisted. In 1993 committees began considering yet more options, including moving the mural to the Cultural Heritage Center, "where it could be viewed in a more historic and artistic context." That alternative proved too expensive and dangerous for the original. "To appropriately reflect the changes in the times and the attitudes of the people" the mural would get yet another name. *The Spirit of the West* (best known as *Progress of South Dakota*) became *Only By Remembering Our Mistakes Can We Learn*. Nevertheless, a 1994 state senate bill declared the mural "offensive and embarrassing to most South Dakotans of all races and creeds . . . inappropriate for display in a place of such dignity, significance, and symbolism"—the governor's reception room in the capitol in Pierre. The mural was treated for preservation and buried behind a false wall.

HO CHI MINH

14 Vietnam's Declaration of Independence (1945)

Among the losses to the nations of Western Europe during World War II was much of their conviction and capacity to rule colonies in Africa and Asia. Once "liberated" from fascist invaders, colonists could hardly be expected to renew subjection to their weakened, one-time confederates. Soon, too, the United States and the U.S.S.R. began competing for allies (or "neo-colonies") among these emerging states. That competition, a key one for international relations in the second half of the twentieth century, has often turned on understandings of what "America" means—in particular, ways in which it represents the best or worst to which a nation might aspire. In that volatile context, leaders of former colonies, no less than Cold War propagandists, studied American materials for an answer. Among the more obvious and ironic examples is the Vietnamese Declaration of Independence. The example is obvious because it tethers its cause explicitly to the "undeniable truth" of an American precursor (1776) and its French cousin (1789).

The declaration was presented in 1945 in Hanoi by Ho Chi Minh ("He Who Enlightens," né Nguyen Sinh Cung), the first president of the Democratic Republic of Vietnam. In experience no less than thought, Ho had strong ties to the victors in World War II. His personal and official connections spanned France, Russia, China, and the United States, including a brief wartime stint with the Office of Strategic Services (the precursor of the CIA). So, part of the irony was quite intentional. He cited Allied sources—among them, a French one—to justify an end to French imperialism and the authority of accommodationists such as Emperor Bao Dai. In this way an alien vision of "inalienable rights" helped to justify the successful waging of the French Indochina War (1946–1954). But there is another, yet more tragic irony that Ho Chi Minh could not have fully anticipated at that war's end.

During World War II the Viet Minh (originally, Viet Nam Doc Lap Dong Minh Hoi, the League for the Independence of Vietnam that Ho organized and led) allied with the United States. It was mainly their army that defeated America's Pacific foe, Japan, in Indochina (French-ruled Vietnam, Laos, and Cambodia) in 1941. This is among the reasons that Ho and the Viet Minh could expect that, once Japan fully surrendered, the United States would support their ultimate mission: in the spirit of 1776 to end eighty years of French control. But instead the United States (which had secretly underwritten the French forces since 1949) took up where the French left off, and then some. Rather than honoring the terms of the French surrender, the United States supported South Vietnam President Ngo Dinh Diem beyond 1956. They refused to hold an election (for which the Viet Minh had fought and won but that Diem would surely lose) for leadership of a unified, independent Vietnam.

During the next round of combat—what Americans call "the Vietnam War" and Vietnamese call "the American War" (ca. 1961–1975)—Washington officials vilified their former ally Ho Chi Minh as a brutal dictator and Soviet or Chinese lackey. In those fifteen years, the United States sent 0.5 million troops to defeat his supporters. About 50,000 Americans and 2 million Vietnamese died. At peak periods, U.S. aircraft dropped more bombs per month on this small, impoverished country than they had in all of World War II. In turn, antiwar activists, even some in the United States, joined the vast majority of Vietnamese people in admiration for the deliverer of the 1945 Declaration. They called him "Uncle Ho." Appealing at once to "American" principles, French revolutionaries, and antiwar activists two centuries later, Ho found support for his brand of Communist nationalism and war against Japanese, French, and U.S. armed forces.

"All men are created equal. They are endowed by their Creator with certain inalienable rights, among these are Life, Liberty, and the pursuit of Happiness."

This immortal statement was made in the Declaration of Independence of the United States of America in 1776. In a broader sense, this means: All the peoples on the earth are equal from birth, all the peoples have a right to live, to be happy and free.

The Declaration of the French Revolution made in 1791 on the Rights of Man and the Citizen also states: "All men are born free and with equal rights, and must always remain free and have equal rights." Those are undeniable truths.

Nevertheless, for more than eighty years, the French imperialists, abusing the standard of Liberty, Equality, and Fraternity, have violated our Fatherland and oppressed our fellow citizens. They have acted contrary to the ideals of humanity and justice. In the field of politics, they have deprived our people of every democratic liberty.

They have enforced inhumane laws; they have set up three distinct political regimes in the North, the Center and the South of Vietnam in order to wreck our national unity and prevent our people from being united.

They have built more prisons than schools. They have mercilessly slain our patriots—they have drowned our uprisings in rivers of blood. They have fettered public opinion; they have practiced obscurantism against our people. To weaken our race they have forced us to use opium and alcohol.

In the fields of economics, they have fleeced us to the backbone, impoverished our people, and devastated our land.

They have robbed us of our rice fields, our mines, our forests, and our raw materials. They have monopolized the issuing of bank notes and the export trade.

They have invented numerous unjustifiable taxes and reduced our people, especially our peasantry, to a state of extreme poverty.

They have hampered the prospering of our national bourgeoisie; they have mercilessly exploited our workers.

In the autumn of 1940, when the Japanese Fascists violated Indochina's territory to establish new bases in their fight against the Allies, the French imperialists went down on their bended knees and handed over our country to them.

Thus, from that date, our people were subjected to the double yoke of the French and the Japanese. Their sufferings and miseries increased. The result was that from the end of last year to the beginning of this year, from Quang Tri province to the North of Vietnam, more than two million of our fellow-citizens died from starvation. On March 9, the French troops were disarmed by the Japanese. The French colonialists either fled or surrendered, showing that not only were they incapable of "protecting" us, but that, in the span of five years, they had twice sold our country to the Japanese.

On several occasions before March 9, the Vietminh League urged the French to ally themselves with it against the Japanese. Instead of agreeing to this proposal, the French colonialists so intensified their terrorist activities against the Vietminh members that before fleeing they massacred a great number of our political prisoners detained at Yen Bay and Cao Bang.

Notwithstanding all this, our fellow citizens have always manifested toward the French a tolerant and humane attitude. Even after the Japanese putsch of March 1945, the Vietminh League helped many

Frenchmen to cross the frontier, rescued some of them from Japanese jails, and protected French lives and property.

From the autumn of 1940, our country had in fact ceased to be a French colony and had become a Japanese possession.

After the Japanese had surrendered to the Allies, our whole people rose to regain our national sovereignty and to found the Democratic Republic of Vietnam.

The truth is that we have wrested our independence from the Japanese and not from the French.

The French have fled, the Japanese have capitulated, Emperor Bao Dai has abdicated. Our people have broken the chains which for nearly a century have fettered them and have won independence for the Fatherland. Our people at the same time have overthrown the monarchic regime that has reigned supreme for dozens of centuries. In its place has been established the present Democratic Republic.

For these reasons, we, members of the Provisional Government, representing the whole Vietnamese people, declare that from now on we break off all relations of a colonial character with France; we repeal all the international obligation that France has so far subscribed to on behalf of Vietnam, and we abolish all the special rights the French have unlawfully acquired in our Fatherland.

The whole Vietnamese people, animated by a common purpose, are determined to fight to the bitter end against any attempt by the French colonialists to reconquer their country.

We are convinced that the Allied nations, which at Tehran and San Francisco have acknowledged the principles of self-determination and equality of nations, will not refuse to acknowledge the independence of Vietnam.

A people who have courageously opposed French domination for more than eighty years, a people who have fought side by side with the Allies against the Fascists during these last years, such a people must be free and independent.

For these reasons, we, members of the Provisional Government of the Democratic Republic of Vietnam, solemnly declare to the world that Vietnam has the right to be a free and independent Country and in fact it is so already. The entire Vietnamese people are determined to mobilize all their physical and mental strength, to sacrifice their lives and property in order to safeguard their independence and liberty.

15 Independence Day (1993)

One of the most important developments in the American country music business in the 1980s and 1990s was the revival of strong female performers such as Loretta Lynn or Dolly Parton and the emergence of coyly, subtly, or even openly feminist newcomers. As "new country music" gained popularity, lyrics featured women whose concerns were no longer confined to home, husband, and baby. They could sing about wage work, affections for other women, and lust as well as disinterest in sex. At least in terms of the politics of gender, if not race and class, country and western music moved to the cultural left.

Martina McBride recorded a particularly striking example in 1993. Although her first album (*The Time Has Come*) won praise for respectful renditions of traditional material, the two singles she subsequently released ("My Baby Loves Me the Way That I Am" and especially Gretchen Peters's composition, "Independence Day") plotted a more assertive course. In case any doubt remained about the sort of "independence" that Peters and McBride had in mind, the video version of "Independence Day" (Country Music Association's Video of the Year) made it abundantly clear: Men are assaulting women, and such assaults can no longer be tolerated. Country classics such as "Stand By Your Man" (Peters's favorite record) would thereafter be in dialogue with accounts of abused women fighting back.

In 1974, Loretta Lynn quipped, "A woman's two-cents worth is worth two cents in the music business." By 1994, she, Peters, and McBride were among those who had helped increase the value of their work and make "independence" an important intimate and domestic, no less than governmental, priority.

Although summary statistics are at best crude measures, by most counts domestic violence (felonious assault or the threat of it, not just verbal abuse) may occur in as many as one out of every four marriages in the United States. In any case, no matter who starts a fight, and no matter the age, class, ethnicity, or legal status of the relationship, about 95 percent of the times when someone gets hurt, it is a woman.

Well, she seemed all right by dawn's early light
Though she looked a little worried and weak
She tried to pretend he wasn't drinkin' again
But Daddy'd left the proof on her cheek
I was only eight years old that summer
And I always seemed to be in the way
So I took myself down to the fair in town
On Independence Day

Well, word gets around in a small, small town
They said he was a dangerous man
Mama was proud, and she stood her ground
But she knew she was on the losin' end
Some folks whispered and some folks talked
But everybody looked the other way
And when time ran out there was no one about
On Independence Day

Chorus
Let freedom ring, let the white dove sing
Let the whole world know that today is a day of reckoning
Let the weak be strong, let the right be wrong
Roll the stone away, let the guilty pay
It's Independence Day

Well, she lit up the sky that Fourth of July
By the time that the firemen come
They just put out the flames and they took down some names
And sent me to the county home
Now I ain't sayin' it's right or it's wrong
But maybe it's the only way
Talk about your revolution
It's Independence Day

Chorus
Roll the stone away
It's Independence Day

16 | What to the Slave Is the Fourth of July? (1852)

Frederick Douglass was born in Tuckahoe, Maryland, in 1817. Although the importation of slaves was outlawed in the United States nearly a decade before his birth, colonial and state laws accumulating since the 1660s assured that he and all of his descendants would ever be owned by someone else. Like tens of thousands of African Americans born into slavery before the Civil War, he risked his life and entrusted it to co-conspirators in efforts to escape. He was among the thousand or so who succeeded in 1837.

By crossing the Mason-Dixon Line, he gained the protection of relatively new and untested northern state laws of abolition (1776–1827). Soon thereafter he joined William Lloyd Garrison in leading the national abolitionist movement and serving as a highly visible agent of the Underground Railroad. Like Garrison, he wrote and spoke with power bordering on the demagogic. As much as anyone, Douglass deserves credit for making the Civil War a struggle not only to preserve the Union but also to end the "peculiar institution" of slavery.

The force of his words—grounded in an appeal to what America represents—is probably nowhere better illustrated than in the Fourth of July address that he delivered in 1852 at the invitation of the Ladies' Anti-Slavery Society in Rochester, New York. True to the occasion, Douglass begins with humble, patriotic platitudes. But they become a launching pad for a jeremiad.

Among his targets is the Fugitive Slave Law, first enacted in 1793, upheld as constitutional by the Supreme Court in 1842, and renewed in 1850. At issue—as stipulated in Article IV, Section 2 of the Constitution—is how one state can be held responsible to "deliver" a person "held to Service or Labour" that is "due to a party" in another state. In other words, how would "free" states be bound to return fugitives to slavery? In responding to that question, Douglass had to feel implicated personally as well as in principle. He had recently returned from two years (1845–1847) in England, in flight yet again, yet farther from home, to evade capture under the terms of the very law to which he here protests. At the time Brazil, Cuba, Puerto Rico, and the United States were the only Western nations that had not yet abolished slavery.

Mr. President, Friends and Fellow Citizens:

He who could address this audience without a quailing sensation, has stronger nerves than I have. I do not remember ever to have appeared as a speaker before any assembly more shrinkingly, nor with greater distrust of my ability, than I do this day. . . . I know that apologies of this sort are generally considered flat and unmeaning. I trust, however, that mine will not be so considered. Should I seem at ease, my appearance would much misrepresent me. The little experience I have had in addressing public meetings, in country school houses, avails me nothing on the present occasion. . . .

The fact is, ladies and gentlemen, the distance between this platform and the slave plantation, from which I escaped, is considerable—and the difficulties to be overcome in getting from the latter to the former, are by no means slight. That I am here today is, to me, a matter of astonishment as well as of gratitude. You will not, therefore, be surprised if in what I have to say I evince no elaborate preparation nor grace my speech with any high sounding exordium. With little experience and with less learning, I have been able to throw my thoughts hastily and imperfectly together; and trusting to your patient and generous indulgence, I will proceed to lay them before you.

This, for the purpose of this celebration, is the Fourth of July. It is the birthday of your National Independence and of your political freedom. This, to you, is what the Passover was to the emancipated people of God. It carries your minds back to the day, and to the act of your great deliverance, and to the signs, and to the wonders associated with that act and that day. This celebration also marks the beginning of another year of your national life and reminds you that the Republic of America is now seventy-six years old.

I am glad, fellow-citizens, that your nation is so young. Seventy-six years, though a good old age for a man, is but a mere speck in the life of a nation. Three score years and ten is the allotted time for individual men; but nations number their years by thousands. According to this fact, you are, even now, only in the beginning of your national career, still lingering in the period of childhood. I repeat: I am glad this is so. There is hope in the thought, and hope is much needed, under the dark clouds which lower above the horizon. . . .

Were the nation older, the patriot's heart might be sadder and the reformer's brow heavier. Its future might be shrouded in gloom, and the hope of its prophets go out in sorrow. There is consolation in the thought that America is young. Great streams are not easily turned from channels, worn deep in the course of ages. They may sometimes rise in quiet and stately majesty and inundate the land, refreshing and fertilizing the earth with their mysterious properties. They may also rise in wrath and fury and bear away, on their angry waves, the accumulated wealth of years of toil and hardship. They, however, gradually flow back to the same old channel, and flow on as serenely as ever. But, while the river may not be turned aside, it may dry up and leave nothing behind but the withered branch and the unsightly rock, to howl in the abyss-sweeping wind, the sad tale of departed glory. As with rivers, so with nations.

Fellow citizens, I shall not presume to dwell at length on the associations that cluster about this day. The simple story of it is that, seventy-six years ago, the people of this country were British subjects. . . . But, your fathers, who had not adopted the fashionable idea of this day, of the infallibility of government and the absolute character of its acts, presumed to differ from the home government in respect to the wisdom and the justice of some of those burdens and restraints. They went so far in their excitement as to pronounce the measures of government unjust, unreasonable, and oppressive, and altogether such as ought not to be quietly submitted to. . . . They saw themselves treated with sovereign indifference, coldness and scorn. Yet they persevered. They were not the men to look back.

As the sheet anchor takes a firmer hold when the ship is tossed by the storm, so did the cause of your fathers grow stronger, as it breasted the chilling blasts of kingly displeasure. . . . But with that blindness which seems to be the unvarying characteristic of tyrants since Pharaoh and his hosts were drowned in the Red Sea, the British Government persisted in the exactions complained of.

The madness of this course, we believe, is admitted now, even by England; but we fear the lesson is wholly lost on our present rulers. . . . The timid and the prudent . . . such people lived then, had lived before, and will probably ever have a place on this planet; and their course, in respect to any great change (no matter how great the good to be attained, or the wrong to be redressed by it) may be calculated with as much precision as can be the course of the stars. They hate all changes, but silver, gold, and copper change! Of this sort of change they are always strongly in favor. . . .

Their opposition to the then dangerous thought was earnest and powerful; but amid all their terror and affrighted vociferations against it, the alarming and revolutionary idea moved on, and the country with it. On the 2nd of July, 1776, the old Continental Congress, to the dismay of the lovers of ease and the worshippers of property, clothed that dreadful idea with all the authority of national sanction. . . .

"Resolved, That these united colonies are, and of right, ought to be free and Independent States; that they are absolved from all allegiance to the British Crown; and that all political connection between them and the State of Great Britain is, and ought to be, dissolved."

Citizens, your fathers made good that resolution. They succeeded; and today you reap the fruits of their success. The freedom gained is yours; and you, therefore, may properly celebrate this anniversary. The Fourth of July is the first great fact in your nation's history—the very ring-bolt in the chain of your yet undeveloped destiny.

Pride and patriotism, not less than gratitude, prompt you to celebrate and to hold it in perpetual remembrance. I have said that the Declaration of Independence is the ring-bolt to the chain of your nation's destiny; so, indeed, I regard it. The principles contained in that instrument are saving principles. Stand by those principles; be true to them on all occasions, in all places, against all foes, and at whatever cost.

From the round top of your ship of state, dark and threatening clouds may be seen. Heavy billows, like mountains in the distance, disclose to the leeward huge forms of flinty rocks! That bolt drawn, that chain broken, and all is lost. Cling to this day—cling to it, and to its principles, with the grasp of a storm-tossed mariner to a spar at midnight. . . .

Fellow citizens, I am not wanting in respect for the fathers of this republic. . . . The point from which I am compelled to view them is not, certainly, the most favorable; and yet I cannot contemplate their great deeds with less than admiration. They were statesmen, patriots and heroes, and for the good they did and the principles they contended for, I will unite with you to honor their memory. . . .

They were peaceful men; but they preferred revolution to peaceful submission to bondage. They were quiet men; but they did not shrink from agitating against oppression. They showed forbearance; but that they knew its limits. They believed in order; but not in the order of tyranny. With them, nothing was "settled" that was not right. With them, justice, liberty and humanity were "final"; not slavery and oppression. You may well cherish the memory of such men. They were great in their day and generation. Their solid manhood stands out the more as we contrast it with these degenerate times. . . .Your fathers, the fathers of this republic, did—most deliberately, under the inspiration of a glorious patriotism, and with a sublime faith in the great principles of justice and freedom—lay deep the cornerstone of the national superstructure, which has risen and still rises in grandeur around you.

Of this fundamental work, this day is the anniversary. . . .

Friends and citizens, I need not enter further into the causes which led to this anniversary. Many of you understand them better than I do. . . . The causes which led to the separation of the colonies from the British crown have never lacked for a tongue. They have all been taught in your common schools, narrated at your firesides, unfolded from your pulpits, and thundered from your legislative halls, and are as familiar to you as household words. They form the staple of your national poetry and eloquence.

I remember, also, that, as a people, Americans are remarkably familiar with all facts which make in their own favor. This is esteemed by some as a national trait—perhaps a national weakness. It is a fact that whatever makes for the wealth or for the reputation of Americans (and can be had cheap!) will be found by Americans. I shall not be charged with slandering Americans, if I say I think the American side of any question may be safely left in American hands.

I leave, therefore, the great deeds of your fathers to other gentlemen whose claim to have been regularly descended will be less likely to be disputed than mine!

My business, if I have any here today, is with the present. The accepted time with God and his cause is the ever-living now.

Trust no future, however pleasant,
Let the dead past bury its dead;
Act, act in the living present,
Heart within, and God overhead.

We have to do with the past only as we can make it useful to the present and to the future. To all inspiring motives, to noble deeds which can be gained from the past, we are welcome. But now is the time, the important time. Your fathers have lived, died, and have done their work, and have done much of it well. You live and must die, and you must do your work. You have no right to enjoy a child's share in the labor of your fathers, unless your children are to be blest by your labors. You have no right to wear out and waste the hard-earned fame of your fathers to cover your indolence. . . .

Fellow citizens, pardon me, allow me to ask: Why am I called upon to speak here today? What have I, or those I represent, to do with your national independence? Are the great principles of political freedom and of natural justice, embodied in that Declaration of Independence, extended to us? And am I, therefore, called upon to bring our humble offering to the national altar, and to confess the benefits and express devout gratitude for the blessings resulting from your independence to us?

Would to God, both for your sakes and ours, that an affirmative answer could be truthfully returned to these questions! Then would my task be light and my burden easy and delightful. For who is there so cold, that a nation's sympathy could not warm him? Who so obdurate and dead to the claims of gratitude, that would not thankfully acknowledge such priceless benefits? Who so stolid and selfish, that would not give his voice to swell the hallelujahs of a nation's jubilee, when the chains of servitude had been torn from his limbs? I am not that man. . . .

I say it with a sad sense of the disparity between us. I am not included within the pale of this glorious anniversary! Your high independence only reveals the immeasurable distance between us. The blessings in which you, this day, rejoice, are not enjoyed in common. The rich inheritance of justice, liberty, prosperity and independence bequeathed by your fathers is shared by you, not by me. The sunlight that brought life and healing to you has brought stripes and death to me. This Fourth of July is yours, not mine.

You may rejoice; I must mourn. To drag a man in fetters into the grand illuminated temple of liberty, and call upon him to join you in joyous anthems, were inhuman mockery and sacrilegious irony. Do you mean, citizens, to mock me, by asking me to speak today? If so, there is a parallel to your conduct. And let me warn you that it is dangerous to copy the example of a nation whose crimes, towering up to heaven, were thrown down by the breath of the Almighty, burying that nation in irrecoverable ruin! I can today take up the plaintive lament of a peeled and woe-smitten people!

> By the rivers of Babylon, there we sat down. Yea! we wept when we remembered Zion. We hanged our harps upon the willows in the midst thereof. For there, they that carried us away captive, required of us a song; and they who wasted us required of us mirth, saying, Sing us one of the songs of Zion. How can we sing the Lord's song in a strange land? If I forget thee, O Jerusalem, let my right hand forget her cunning. If I do not remember thee, let my tongue cleave to the roof of my mouth.

Fellow citizens, above your national, tumultuous joy, I hear the mournful wail of millions! whose chains, heavy and grievous yesterday, are today rendered more intolerable by the jubilee shouts that reach them. If I do forget, if I do not faithfully remember those bleeding children of sorrow this day, "may my right hand forget her cunning, and may my tongue cleave to the roof of my mouth!" To forget them, to pass lightly over their wrongs, and to chime in with the popular theme, would be treason most scandalous and shocking and would make me a reproach before God and the world.

My subject, then, fellow-citizens, is AMERICAN SLAVERY . . . from the slave's point of view. Standing there, identified with the American bondman, making his wrongs mine, I do not hesitate to declare, with all my soul, that the character and conduct of this nation never looked blacker to me than on this Fourth of July!

Whether we turn to the declarations of the past or to the professions of the present, the conduct of the nation seems equally hideous and revolting. America is false to the past, false to the present, and solemnly binds herself to be false to the future. Standing with God and the crushed and bleeding slave on this occasion, I will, in the name of humanity which is outraged, in the name of liberty which is fettered, in the name of the constitution and the Bible, which are disregarded and trampled upon, dare to call in question and to denounce, with all the emphasis I can command, everything that serves to perpetuate slavery—the great sin and shame of America!

"I will not equivocate; I will not excuse"; I will use the severest language I can command; and yet not one word shall escape me that any man, whose judgement is not blinded by prejudice or who is not at heart a slaveholder, shall not confess to be right and just.

But I fancy I hear some one of my audience say, "It is just in this circumstance that you and your brother abolitionists fail to make a favorable impression on the public mind. Would you argue more and denounce less, would you persuade more and rebuke less, your cause would be much more likely to succeed."

But, I submit, where all is plain there is nothing to be argued. What point in the anti-slavery creed would you have me argue? On what branch of the subject do the people of this country need light? Must I undertake to prove that the slave is a man? That point is conceded already. Nobody doubts it.

The slaveholders themselves acknowledge it in the enactment of laws for their government. They acknowledge it when they punish disobedience on the part of the slave. There are seventy-two crimes in the State of Virginia which, if committed by a black man (no matter how ignorant he be), subject him to the punishment of death; while only two of the same crimes will subject a white man to the like punishment.

What is this but the acknowledgement that the slave is a moral, intellectual and responsible being? The manhood of the slave is conceded. It is admitted in the fact that Southern statute books are covered with enactments forbidding, under severe fines and penalties, the teaching of the slave to read or to write.

When you can point to any such laws, in reference to the beasts of the field, then I may consent to argue the manhood of the slave. When the dogs in your streets, when the fowls of the air, when the cattle on your hills, when the fish of the sea, and the reptiles that crawl shall be unable to distinguish the slave from a brute, then will I argue with you that the slave is a man!

For the present, it is enough to affirm the equal manhood of the Negro race. Is it not astonishing that, while we are plowing, planting and reaping, using all kinds of mechanical tools, erecting houses, constructing bridges, building ships, working in metals of brass, iron, copper, silver and gold; that, while we are reading, writing and ciphering, acting as clerks, merchants and secretaries, having among us lawyers, doctors, ministers, poets, authors, editors, orators and teachers; that, while we are engaged in all manner of enterprises common to other men, digging gold in California, capturing the whale in the Pacific, feeding sheep and cattle on the hill-side, living, moving, acting, thinking, planning, living in families as husbands, wives and children, and, above all, confessing and worshipping the Christian's God and looking hopefully for life and immortality beyond the grave, we are called upon to prove that we are men!

Would you have me argue that man is entitled to liberty? That he is the rightful owner of his own body? You have already declared it. Must I argue the wrongfulness of slavery? Is that a question for republicans? Is it to be settled by the rules of logic and argumentation? As a matter beset with great difficulty, involving a doubtful application of the principle of justice, hard to be understood? How should I look today, in the presence of Americans, dividing and subdividing a discourse to show that men have a natural right to freedom? Speaking of it relatively, and positively, negatively, and affirmatively. To do so would be to make myself ridiculous and, lo, offer an insult to your understanding. There is not a man beneath the canopy of heaven that does not know that slavery is wrong for him.

What, am I to argue? That it is wrong to make men brutes, to rob them of their liberty, to work them without wages, to keep them ignorant of their relations to their fellow men, to beat them with sticks, to flay their flesh with the lash, to load their limbs with irons, to hunt them with dogs, to sell them at auction, to sunder their families, to knock out their teeth, to burn their flesh, to starve them into obedience and submission to their masters? Must I argue that a system thus marked with blood, and stained with pollution, is wrong? No! I will not. I have better employments for my time and strength, than such arguments would imply.

What, then, remains to be argued? Is it that slavery is not divine; that God did not establish it; that our doctors of divinity are mistaken? There is blasphemy in the thought. That which is inhuman, cannot be divine! Who can reason on such a proposition? They that can, may; I cannot. The time for such argument is past.

At a time like this, scorching irony, not convincing argument, is needed. Oh, had I the ability and could I reach the nation's ear, I would, today, pour out a fiery stream of biting ridicule, blasting reproach, withering sarcasm, and stern rebuke. For it is not light that is needed, but fire; it is not the gentle shower, but thunder. We need the storm, the whirlwind, and the earthquake. . . .

What, to the American slave, is your Fourth of July? I answer: a day that reveals to him, more than all other days in the year, the gross injustice and cruelty to which he is the constant victim. To him, your celebration is a sham; your boasted liberty, an unholy license; your national greatness, swelling vanity; your sounds of rejoicing are empty and heartless; your denunciations of tyrants, brass fronted impudence; your shouts of liberty and equality, hollow mockery; your prayers and hymns, your sermons and thanksgivings, with all your religious parade, and solemnity, are, to him, mere bombast, fraud, deception, impiety, and hypocrisy—a thin veil to cover up crimes which would disgrace a nation of savages.

There is not a nation on the earth guilty of practices more shocking and bloody than are the people of these United States at this very hour.

Go where you may, search where you will, roam through all the monarchies and despotisms of the old world, travel through South America, search out every abuse, and when you have found the last, lay your facts by the side of the everyday practices of this nation, and you will say with me that, for revolting barbarity and shameless hypocrisy, America reigns without a rival.

Take the American slave-trade which, we are told by the papers, is especially prosperous just now. . . . In several states, this trade is a chief source of wealth. It is called (in contradistinction to the foreign slave-trade) "the internal slave-trade." It is, probably, called so, too, in order to divert from it the horror with which the foreign slave-trade is contemplated. That trade has long since been denounced by this government as piracy. . . . To arrest it, to put an end to it, this nation keeps a squadron, at immense cost, on the coast of Africa. Everywhere in this country it is safe to speak of this foreign slave-trade as a most inhuman traffic, opposed alike to the laws of God and of man.

The duty to extirpate and destroy it is admitted even by our DOCTORS OF DIVINITY. In order to put an end to it, some of these last have consented that their colored brethren (nominally free) should leave this country and establish themselves on the western coast of Africa! It is, however, a notable fact that, while so much execration is poured out by Americans upon those engaged in the foreign slave-trade, the men engaged in the slave-trade between the states pass without condemnation, and their business is deemed honorable.

Behold the practical operation of this internal slave-trade, the American slave-trade, sustained by American politics and American religion. Here you will see men and women reared like swine for the market. You know what is a swine-drover? I will show you a man-drover. They inhabit all our Southern States.

They perambulate the country and crowd the highways of the nation with droves of human stock. You will see one of these human flesh-jobbers, armed with pistol, whip and bowie-knife, driving a company of a hundred men, women, and children, from the Potomac to the slave market at New Orleans. These wretched people are to be sold singly or in lots, to suit purchasers. They are food for the cotton-field and the deadly sugar-mill. Mark the sad procession as it moves wearily along, and the inhuman wretch who drives them.

Hear his savage yells and his blood-chilling oaths, as he hurries on his affrighted captives! There, see the old man with locks thinned and gray. Cast one glance, if you please, upon that young mother, whose shoulders are bare to the scorching sun, her briny tears falling on the brow of the babe in her arms. See, too, that girl of thirteen, weeping—yes! weeping, as she thinks of the mother from whom she has been torn!

The drove moves tardily. Heat and sorrow have nearly consumed their strength; suddenly you hear a quick snap. . . ; your ears are saluted with a scream that seems to have torn its way to the center of your soul! The crack you heard was the sound of the slave-whip; the scream you heard was from the woman you saw with the babe. Her speed had faltered under the weight of her child and her chains! That gash on her shoulder tells her to move on. Follow this drove to New Orleans. Attend the auction; see men examined like horses; see the forms of women rudely and brutally exposed to the shocking gaze of American slave-buyers. See this drove sold and separated forever; and never forget the deep, sad sobs that arose from that scattered multitude. Tell me citizens, WHERE under the sun you can witness a spectacle more fiendish and shocking. Yet this is but a glance at the American slave-trade, as it exists at this moment in the ruling part of the United States.

I was born amid such sights and scenes. To me the American slave-trade is a terrible reality. When a child, my soul was often pierced with a sense of its horrors. I lived on Philpot Street, Fell's Point, Baltimore, and have watched from the wharves the slave ships in the Basin, anchored from the shore with their cargoes of human flesh, waiting for favorable winds to waft them down the Chesapeake.

There was, at that time, a grand slave mart kept at the head of Pratt Street, by Austin Woldfolk. His agents were sent into every town and county in Maryland, announcing their arrival, through the papers, and on flaming "handbills," headed CASH FOR NEGROES. These men were generally well-dressed men and very captivating in their manners—ever ready to drink, to treat, and to gamble. The fate of many a slave has depended upon the turn of a single card. . . .

In the deep still darkness of midnight, I have been often aroused by the dead heavy footsteps, and the piteous cries of the chained gangs that passed our door. The anguish of my boyish heart was intense; and I was often consoled, when speaking to my mistress in the morning, to hear her say that the custom was very wicked; that she hated to hear the rattle of the chains and the heartrending cries. I was glad to find one who sympathized with me in my horror.

Fellow citizens, this murderous traffic is, today, in active operation in this boasted republic. In the solitude of my spirit, I see clouds of dust raised on the highways of the South; I see the bleeding footsteps; I hear the doleful wail of fettered humanity on the way to the slave-markets, where the victims are to be sold like horses, sheep, and swine, knocked off to the highest bidder. There I see the tenderest ties ruthlessly broken to gratify the lust, caprice, and rapacity of the buyers and sellers of men. My soul sickens at the sight.

> Is this the land your Fathers loved,
> The freedom which they toiled to win?
> Is this the earth whereon they moved?
> Are these the graves they slumber in?

But a still more inhuman, disgraceful, and scandalous state of things remains to be presented.

By an act of the American Congress, not yet two years old, slavery has been nationalized in its most horrible and revolting form. By that act, Mason and Dixon's line has been obliterated; New York has become as Virginia; and the power to hold, hunt, and sell men, women, and children as slaves remains no longer a mere state institution, but is now an institution of the whole United States.

The power is co-extensive with the star-spangled banner and American Christianity. Where these go, may also go the merciless slave-hunter. . . . Your lawmakers have commanded all good citizens to engage in this hellish sport.

Your President, your Secretary of State, your lords, nobles, and ecclesiastics enforce, as a duty you owe to your free and glorious country and to your God, that you do this accursed thing. Not fewer than forty Americans have, within the past two years, been hunted down and, without a moment's warning, hurried away in chains and consigned to slavery and excruciating torture. Some of these have had wives and children dependent on them for bread; but of this, no account was made.

The right of the hunter to his prey stands superior to the right of marriage and to all rights in this republic, the rights of God included! For black men there are neither law, justice, humanity, nor religion. The Fugitive Slave Law makes MERCY TO THEM, A CRIME; and bribes the judge who tries them. An American JUDGE GETS TEN DOLLARS FOR EVERY VICTIM HE CONSIGNS to slavery, and five, when he fails to do so.

The oath of any two villains is sufficient, under this hell-black enactment, to send the most pious and exemplary black man into the remorseless jaws of slavery! His own testimony is nothing. He can bring no witnesses for himself. The minister of American justice is bound by the law to hear but one side; and that side is the side of the oppressor. Let this damning fact be perpetually told.

Let it be thundered around the world, that—in tyrant-killing, king-hating, people-loving, democratic, Christian America—the seats of justice are filled with judges who hold their offices under an open and palpable bribe and are bound, in deciding in the case of a man's liberty, to hear only his accusers!

In glaring violation of justice, in shameless disregard of the forms of administering law, in cunning arrangement to entrap the defenseless, and in diabolical intent, this Fugitive Slave Law stands alone in the annals of tyrannical legislation. I doubt if there be another nation on the globe having the brass and the baseness to put such a law on the statute-book. If any man in this assembly thinks differently from me in this matter and feels able to disprove my statements, I will gladly confront him at any suitable time and place he may select.

I take this law to be one of the grossest infringements of Christian Liberty, and if the churches and ministers of our country were not stupidly blind or most wickedly indifferent, they, too, would so regard it. . . . The fact that the church of our country (with fractional exceptions) does not esteem "the Fugitive Slave Law" as a declaration of war against religious liberty implies that that church regards religion simply as a form of worship, an empty ceremony and not a vital principle, requiring active benevolence, justice, love, and good will towards men. . . .

But the church of this country is not only indifferent to the wrongs of the slave, it actually takes sides with the oppressors. . . . Many of its most eloquent Divines, who stand as the very lights of the church, have shamelessly given the sanction of religion and the Bible to the whole slave system. They have taught that man may, properly, be a slave; that the relation of master and slave is ordained of God; that to send back an escaped bondman to his master is clearly the duty of all the followers of the Lord Jesus Christ; and this horrible blasphemy is palmed off upon the world for Christianity.

For my part, I would say, welcome infidelity! Welcome atheism! Welcome anything in preference to the Gospel as preached by those Divines! They convert the very name of religion into an engine of tyranny and barbarous cruelty and serve to confirm more infidels in this age than all the infidel writings of Thomas Paine, Voltaire, and Bolingbroke, put together, have done! These ministers make religion a cold and flinty-hearted thing, having neither principles of right action nor bowels of compassion. . . .

But a religion which favors the rich against the poor; which exalts the proud above the humble; which divides mankind into two classes, tyrants and slaves; which says to the man in chains, "Stay there"; and to the oppressor, "Oppress on"; it is a religion which may be professed and enjoyed by all the robbers and enslavers of mankind; it makes God a respecter of persons, denies His fatherhood of the race, and tramples in the dust the great truth of the brotherhood of man. . . .

In the language of Isaiah, the American church might be well addressed,

> Bring no more vain oblations. . . . When ye spread forth your hands I will hide mine eyes from you. Yea! when ye make many prayers, I will not hear. YOUR HANDS ARE FULL OF BLOOD; cease to do evil, learn to do well; seek judgement; relieve the oppressed; judge for the fatherless; plead for the widow.

The American church is guilty, when viewed in connection with what it is doing to uphold slavery; but it is superlatively guilty when viewed in connection with its ability to abolish slavery. The sin of which it is guilty is one of omission as well as of commission. . . .

Let the religious press, the pulpit, the Sunday school, the conference meeting, the great ecclesiastical, missionary, Bible and tract associations of the land array their immense powers against slavery and slave-holding; and the whole system of crime and blood would be scattered to the winds; and that they do not do this involves them in the most awful responsibility of which the mind can conceive. . . .

In speaking of the American church, however, let it be distinctly understood that I mean the great mass of the religious organizations of our land. There are exceptions, and I thank God that there are. Noble men may be found, scattered all over these Northern States, of whom Henry Ward Beecher of Brooklyn, Samuel J. May of Syracuse, and my esteemed friend on the platform [Rev. R. R. Raymond] are shining examples; and let me say further that upon these men lies the duty to inspire our ranks with high religious faith and zeal and to cheer us on in the great mission of the slave's redemption from his chains.

One is struck with the difference between the attitude of the American church towards the anti-slavery movement, and that occupied by the churches in England towards a similar movement in that country.

There, the church, true to its mission of ameliorating, elevating, and improving the condition of mankind, came forward promptly, bound up the wounds of the West Indian slave, and restored him to his liberty. There, the question of emancipation was a high religious question. It was demanded in the name of humanity and according to the law of the living God. . . .

Americans! your republican politics, not less than your republican religion, are flagrantly inconsistent.

You boast of your love of liberty, your superior civilization, and your pure Christianity, while the whole political power of the nation (as embodied in the two great political parties) is solemnly pledged to support and perpetuate the enslavement of three millions of your countrymen. You hurl your anathemas at the crown-headed tyrants of Russia and Austria and pride yourselves on your Democratic institutions, while you yourselves consent to be the mere tools and bodyguards of the tyrants of Virginia and Carolina.

You invite to your shores fugitives of oppression from abroad, honor them with banquets, greet them with ovations, cheer them, toast them, salute them, protect them, and pour out your money to them like water; but the fugitives from your own land you advertise, hunt, arrest, shoot, and kill. You glory in your refinement and your universal education; yet you maintain a system as barbarous and dreadful as ever stained the character of a nation—a system begun in avarice, supported in pride, and perpetuated in cruelty.

You shed tears over fallen Hungary and make the sad story of her wrongs the theme of your poets, statesmen, and orators, till your gallant sons are ready to fly to arms to vindicate her cause against her oppressors; but in regard to the ten thousand wrongs of the American slave, you would enforce the strictest silence and would hail him as an enemy of the nation who dares to make those wrongs the subject of public discourse!

You are all on fire at the mention of liberty for France or for Ireland; but are as cold as an iceberg at the thought of liberty for the enslaved of America. You discourse eloquently on the dignity of labor; yet you sustain a system which, in its very essence, casts a stigma upon labor. You can bare your bosom to the storm of British artillery to throw off a three-penny tax on tea; and yet wring the last hard-earned farthing from the grasp of the black laborers of your country.

You profess to believe "that, of one blood, God made all nations of men to dwell on the face of all the earth," and hath commanded all men everywhere to love one another; yet you notoriously hate (and glory in your hatred) all men whose skins are not colored like your own.

You declare before the world and are understood by the world to declare that you "hold these truths to be self-evident, that all men are created equal; and are endowed by their Creator with certain inalienable rights; and that, among these are, life, liberty, and the pursuit of happiness"; and yet you hold securely, in a bondage which, according to your own Thomas Jefferson, "is worse than ages of that which your fathers rose in rebellion to oppose," a seventh part of the inhabitants of your country.

Fellow citizens! I will not enlarge further on your national inconsistencies. The existence of slavery in this country brands your republicanism as a sham, your humanity as a base pretence, and your Christianity as a lie. It destroys your moral power abroad; it corrupts your politicians at home. It saps the foundation of religion; it makes your name a hissing, and a byword to a mocking earth. It is the antagonistic force in your government, the only thing that seriously disturbs and endangers your Union.

It fetters your progress; it is the enemy of improvement, the deadly foe of education; it fosters pride; it breeds insolence; it promotes vice; it shelters crime; it is a curse to the earth that supports it; and yet you cling to it, as if it were the sheet anchor of all your hopes. Oh! be warned! be warned! A horrible reptile is coiled up in your nation's bosom; the venomous creature is nursing at the tender breast of your youthful republic; for the love of God, tear away, and fling from you the hideous monster, and let the weight of twenty millions crush and destroy it forever!

But it is answered in reply to all this, that precisely what I have now denounced is, in fact, guaranteed and sanctioned by the Constitution of the United States; that the right to hold and to hunt slaves is a part of that Constitution framed by the illustrious Fathers of this Republic.

Then, I dare to affirm, notwithstanding all I have said before, your fathers . . . instead of being the honest men I have before declared them to be, they were the veriest imposters that ever practiced on mankind. This is the inevitable conclusion, and from it there is no escape. But I differ from those who charge this baseness on the framers of the Constitution of the United States. It is a slander upon their memory, at least so I believe.

There is not time now to argue the constitutional question at length. . . . Interpreted as it ought to be interpreted, the Constitution is a GLORIOUS LIBERTY DOCUMENT. Read its preamble; consider its purposes. Is slavery among them? . . . Take the constitution according to its plain reading, and I defy the presentation of a single pro-slavery clause in it. On the other hand, it will be found to contain principles and purposes entirely hostile to the existence of slavery.

I have detained my audience entirely too long already. At some future period I will gladly avail myself of an opportunity to give this subject a full and fair discussion.

Allow me to say, in conclusion, notwithstanding the dark picture I have this day presented of the state of the nation, I do not despair of this country. There are forces in operation which must inevitably work the downfall of slavery. "The arm of the Lord is not shortened," and the doom of slavery is certain. I, therefore, leave off where I began, with hope. While drawing encouragement from the Declaration of Independence, the great principles it contains, and the genius of American institutions, my spirit is also cheered by the obvious tendencies of the age.

Nations do not now stand in the same relation to each other that they did ages ago. No nation can now shut itself up from the surrounding world, and trot round in the same old path of its fathers without interference. . . . Knowledge was then confined and enjoyed by the privileged few, and the multitude walked on in mental darkness. But a change has now come over the affairs of mankind. Walled cities and empires have become unfashionable.

The arm of commerce has borne away the gates of the strong city. Intelligence is penetrating the darkest corners of the globe. It makes its pathway over and under the sea, as well as on the earth. Wind, steam, and lightning are its chartered agents. Oceans no longer divide, but link nations together. From Boston to London is now a holiday excursion. Space is comparatively annihilated. Thoughts expressed on one side of the Atlantic are distinctly heard on the other. The far-off and almost fabulous Pacific rolls in grandeur at our feet. The Celestial Empire, the mystery of ages, is being solved. The fiat of the Almighty—"Let there be Light"—has not yet spent its force. No abuse, no outrage, whether in taste, sport, or avarice, can now hide itself from the all-pervading light.

The iron shoe and crippled foot of China must be seen in contrast with nature. Africa must rise and put on her yet unwoven garment. "Ethiopia shall stretch out her hand unto God." In the fervent aspirations of William Lloyd Garrison, I say, and let every heart join in saying it:

> God speed the year of jubilee
> The wide world o'er!
> When from their galling chains set free,
> Th' oppress'd shall vilely bend the knee,
> And wear the yoke of tyranny
> Like brutes no more.
> That year will come, and freedom's reign,
> To man his plundered fights again
> Restore.
>
> God speed the day when human blood
> Shall cease to flow!
> In every clime be understood,
> The claims of human brotherhood,
> And each return for evil, good,
> Not blow for blow;
> That day will come all feuds to end
> And change into a faithful friend
> Each foe.

God speed the hour, the glorious hour,
When none on earth
Shall exercise a lordly power,
Nor in a tyrant's presence cower;
But all to manhood's stature tower,
By equal birth!
THAT HOUR WILL COME, to each, to all,
And from his prison-house, the thrall
Go forth.

Until that year, day, hour, arrive,
With head, and heart, and hand I'll strive,
To break the rod, and rend the gyve,
The spoiler of his prey deprive —
 So witness Heaven!
And never from my chosen post,
Whate'er the peril or the cost,
Be driven.

III America as a Place to Belong

Some Guiding Questions

Should America be considered a place where
everybody feels they belong?
If the composition is so diverse and changing, to
what do they actually belong?
Is there something substantive and stable about it?
Or do they share only a determination to be
diverse?
To what other loyalties might diversity be hitched?
Can inclusiveness itself be up for grabs?
How should people be able to tell if they belong?
Is acceptance to be earned or awarded?
What standards might they have to meet?
Are different sorts of people supposed to blend in a
particular way? How?
How might race, gender, nationality, or class
affect their fate?

Is tolerance the key?
Or certain kinds of opportunity?
Or affirmation?
How is being "one-hundred percent American"
supposed to matter?
From whose point of view?
What rights and responsibilities does "the
melting pot" afford or efface?
Why would patriots want to make more or less
fuss about them?

WOODROW WILSON

17 Americanism and the Foreign-Born (1915)

According to the cliché, the United States is a "nation of immigrants." Although more true than false, that fact has debatable significance. A people's country of origin can be among their most fleeting features. As Walter Benjamin once quipped, "Origin is an eddy in the stream of becoming." But most émigrés recall the eddy as a site of misery as well as loves left behind. America, whatever else it might be, has been downstream of an especially large and varied mix of such memories. As the conditions of migration—the specific push and pull—have varied and changed, the distance between homeland and new land or between immigrant and native has been bloated and belittled, cherished and suppressed.

Signal instances leap to mind: British Puritans and Pilgrims, African slaves in shackles, East Asians and West Europeans fleeing war and starvation. In the three decades surrounding the turn of the twentieth century, about twenty million people moved to the United States. By 1920, nearly one-quarter of the nation's permanent residents had been born someplace else. The sheer size and distinctly southern and eastern European quality of the migration made it seem different, more challenging to old-stock citizens. They wondered if the United States could still accommodate the growth.

Among the newcomers were natives of nations that shared enough enmity to be killing each other across the Atlantic at that very moment. U.S. wage earners wondered how they would fare in the competition for jobs. Aliens were ready scapegoats for social unrest or inadequacy in urban infrastructure. Before the Civil War, only the slave trade and Chinese migration were federally barred, but legal limits rapidly expanded after 1880 in the wake of the "New Immigration." Racists, xenophobes, anti-Catholics, and anti-Semites joined forces in support of tighter immigration restriction, particularly of quotas to preserve the Protestant and Anglo-Saxon proportion of the population. In 1924 they succeeded via passage of the Johnson-Reed Immigration Act, but it was over the objections of cosmopolitans who had previously prevailed.

Here President Woodrow Wilson, fighting a losing cause for tolerance at home and peace abroad, exhorts an audience in Philadelphia of immigrants. They have just achieved citizenship—"*become* American"—and Wilson aims to explain what that means. Professors Norman Foerster and William W. Pierson immediately republished his interpretation in *American Ideals* (1917), one of the first sourcebooks in the field that became American Studies.

It warms my heart that you should give me such a reception, but it is not of myself that I wish to think tonight, but of those who have just become citizens of the United States. This is the only country in the world which experiences this constant and repeated rebirth. Other countries depend upon the multiplication of their own native people. This country is constantly drinking strength out of new sources by the voluntary association with it of great bodies of strong men and forward-looking women. And so by the gift of the free will of independent people it is constantly being renewed from generation to generation by the same process by which it was originally created. It is as if humanity had determined to see to it that this great nation, founded for the benefit of humanity, should not lack for the allegiance of the people of the world.

You have just taken an oath of allegiance to the United States. Of allegiance to whom? Of allegiance to no one, unless it be God. Certainly not of allegiance to those who temporarily represent this great Government. You have taken an oath of allegiance to a great ideal, to a great body of principles, to a great hope of the human race. You have said, "We are going to America," not only to earn a living, not only to seek the things which it was more difficult to obtain where you were born, but to help forward the great enterprises of the human spirit—to let man know that everywhere in the world there are men who will cross strange oceans and go where a speech is spoken which is alien to them, knowing that, whatever the speech, there is but one longing and utterance of the human heart, and that is for liberty and justice.

And while you bring all countries with you, you come with a purpose of leaving all other countries behind you—bringing what is best of their spirit, but not looking over your shoulders and seeking to perpetuate what you intended to leave in them. I certainly would not be one even to suggest that a man ceases to love the home of his birth and the nation of his origin—these things are very sacred and ought not to be put out of our hearts—but it is one thing to love the place where you were born and it is another thing to dedicate yourself to the place to which you go. You cannot dedicate yourself to America unless you become in every respect and with every purpose of your will thorough Americans. You cannot become thorough Americans if you think of yourselves in groups. America does not consist of groups. A man who thinks of himself as belonging to a particular national group in America, has not yet become an American, and the man who goes among you to trade upon your nationality is no worthy son to live under the Stars and Stripes.

My urgent advice to you would be not only always to think first of America, but always, also, to think first of humanity . . . for America was created to unite mankind by those passions which lift and not by the passions which separate and debase.

We came to America, either ourselves or in the persons of our ancestors, to better the ideals of men, to make them see finer things than they had seen before, to get rid of things that divide, and to make sure of the things that unite. It was but an historical accident no doubt that this great country was called the "United States," and yet I am very thankful that it has the word "united" in its title; and the man who seeks to divide man from man, group from group, interest from interest, in the United States is striking at its very heart. . . .

No doubt you have been disappointed in some of us; some of us are very disappointing. No doubt you have found that justice in the United States goes only with a pure heart and a right purpose, as it does everywhere else in the world. No doubt what you found here didn't seem touched for you, after all, with the complete beauty of the ideal which you had conceived beforehand.

But remember this, . . . if some of us have forgotten what America believed in, you, at any rate, imported in your own hearts a renewal of the belief. That is the reason that I, for one, make you welcome.

If I have in any degree forgotten what America was intended for, I will thank God if you will remind me.

I was born in America. You dreamed dreams of what America was to be, and I hope you brought the dreams with you. . . .

Just because you brought dreams with you, America is more likely to realize the dreams such as you brought. You are enriching us if you came expecting us to be better than we are.

See, my friends, what that means. It means that America must have a consciousness different from the consciousness of every other nation in the world. I am not saying this with even the slightest thought of criticism of other nations. You know how it is with a family. A family gets centered on itself if it is not careful and is less interested in the neighbors than it is in its own members.

So a nation that is not constantly renewed out of new sources is apt to have the narrowness and prejudice of a family. Whereas, America must have this consciousness, that on all sides it touches elbows and touches hearts with all the nations of mankind.

The example of America must be a special example. The example of America must be the example not merely of peace because it will not fight, but of peace because peace is the healing and elevating influence of the world and strife is not.

There is such a thing as a man being too proud to fight. There is such a thing as a nation being so right that it does not need to convince others by force that it is right.

So, if you come into this great nation as you have come, voluntarily seeking something that we have to give, all that we have to give is this: . . . . We cannot exempt you from work; we cannot exempt you from the strife and the heartbreaking burden of the struggle of the day—that is common to mankind everywhere. We cannot exempt you from the loads you must carry; we can only make them light by the spirit in which they are carried. That is the spirit of hope, it is the spirit of liberty, it is the spirit of justice. . . . great ideals which made America the hope of the world.

ALICE STONE BLACKWELL

18 | Objections Answered (1913)

European and American agitation for the extension of the right to vote was warmed in the rhetoric of the American Revolution. By the early nineteenth century, for example, several states found their original property-holding requirements incompatible with republican virtue. But as they extended voting privileges among men, they also tended to eliminate loopholes by which women might enjoy them, too (for example, as heads of their own households). Such gender inequity was only one among many that drew the attention of feminists on both sides of the Atlantic. It was a particularly popular cause among people with the means, determination, mobility, eloquence, time, and money to advance it, albeit slowly over the subsequent century.

Among the obstacles they faced, especially toward the end of the nineteenth century, was the mounting idealization of "domesticity" within the social sector from which they often came: female, white, urban, and educated. Compared to literal domestics—the largest category of urban female wage earners at the time—suffragists were relatively wealthy with a noble, self-sacrificing, home-spirited sense of public service. Like the Founding Fathers, they tended to be "respectable" folks skilled in maneuvering the strictures of gender, class, and race to advance their cause.

Pamphlets such as the one excerpted below were among the huge number and variety they produced. This one coaches a suffragist point by point through the objections that she should expect from an unsympathetic crowd, even on the eve of the Nineteenth Amendment. Cued responses include detailed findings and citations on the status of women and their significance for the nation.

In hindsight, such manuals might be faulted for sidestepping contemporary topics such as xenophobia, the World War, the suppression of dissent (for example, of the Socialist Party), or racism. It is worth remembering that at the time Indians were worse than disenfranchised (they were not granted U.S. citizenship until 1924) and that the status of African Americans eroded substantially despite constitutional protections like those that

131

the manuals endorsed. But in their strength as their weakness, these activists are also models for American Studies. They adroitly confront, accommodate, and elide diverse social and symbolic relations with the United States.

Why Should Women Vote?

The reasons why women should vote are the same as the reasons why men should vote. . . . Roughly stated, the fundamental principle of a republic is this: In deciding what is to be done, we take everybody's opinion, and then go according to the wish of the majority. . . . Certain classes of persons are passed over, whose opinions for one reason or another are thought not to be worth counting. In most of our states, these classes are children, aliens, idiots, lunatics, criminals and women. There are good and obvious reasons for making all these exceptions but the last. . . . Is there any equally good reason why no account should be taken of the opinions of women? Let us consider the reasons commonly given, and see if they are sound.

Are Women Represented?
Women are represented already by their husbands, fathers and brothers.

This so-called representation bears no proportion to numbers. . . . The only fair and accurate way is for each grown person to have one vote, and cast it to represent himself or herself.

American men are the best in the world, and if it were possible for any men to represent women, through kindness and good will to them, American men would do it. But . . . whatever his good will, he cannot fully put himself in a woman's place, and look at things exactly from her point of view. To say this is no more a reflection upon his mental or moral ability than it would be a reflection upon his musical ability to say that he cannot sing both soprano and bass. Unless men and women should ever become alike (which would be regrettable and monotonous), women must either go unrepresented or represent themselves.

Another proof that women's opinions are not now fully represented is . . . the imperfect legal safe-guarding of the moral, educational and humanitarian interests that women have most at heart. . . .

Is Influence Enough?
If the laws are unjust, they can be corrected by women's indirect influence.

Yes, but the indirect method is needlessly long and hard. If women were forbidden to use the direct route by rail across the continent and complained of the injustice, it would be no answer to tell them that it is possible to get from New York to San Francisco by going around Cape Horn.

The slowness with which some of the worst inequalities in the laws are corrected shows the unsatisfactoriness of the indirect way. In most states, a married mother has literally no legal rights over her own children, so long as she and her husband live together. . . . For more than half a century, the suffragists of the United States have been trying to secure legislation making the father and mother joint guardians of their children by law, as they are by nature; but thus far the equal guardianship law has been obtained in only a minority of the states. . . . In Colorado and in California, after women were given the right to vote, the very next Legislature passed an equal guardianship law.

The Ignorant Vote
It would double the ignorant vote.

Statistics published by the National Bureau of Education show that the high schools of every state in the Union are graduating more girls than boys—some of them twice and three times as many. . . . Equal suffrage would increase the proportion of voters who have received more than a merely elementary education. . . .

The Foreign Vote
It would double the foreign vote.

Less than one-third of the immigrants coming to this country are women. According to the latest census, there are in the United States nearly three times as many native-born women as all the foreign-born men and foreign-born women put together.

The foreign vote is objectionable only so far as it is an ignorant vote. Intelligent foreigners, both men and women, are often very valuable citizens. On the other hand, the ignorant foreign immigrants who come here are fully imbued, both men and women, with all the Old World ideas as to the inferiority and subjection of women. It is not until they have become pretty thoroughly Americanized that they can tolerate the idea of women's voting. The husbands are not willing that their wives should vote, and the wives ridicule the suggestion. . . . And, after they have become Americanized, why should they not vote, as well as anyone else?

The Criminal Vote
To the vote of every criminal man, you would add the vote of a criminal woman.

The vicious and criminal class is comparatively small among women. . . . Equal suffrage would increase the moral and law-abiding vote very largely, while increasing the vicious and criminal vote very little. This is a matter not of conjecture but of statistics.

The Bad Women's Vote
The bad women would outvote the good ones.

In America the bad women are so few, compared with the good ones, that their votes could have little influence. . . .

Don't Understand Business . . .
Men, by the nature of their occupations, know more about business than women, and hence are better fitted to run a city or a state.

Women have a vote in every other corporation in which they are shareholders. . . .

A man's business, at best, gives him special knowledge only in regard to one or two departments of city affairs. Women's business, as mothers and housekeepers, also gives them special knowledge in regard to some important departments of public work, those relating to children, schools, playgrounds, the protection of the weak and young, morals, the care of the poor, etc. For what lies outside the scope of their own experience, men and women alike must rely upon experts. All they need, as voters, is sense enough and conscience enough to elect honest and capable persons to have charge of these things. . . .

Would Lose Their Influence
Women would lose their influence.

What gives a woman influence? Beauty, goodness, tact, talent, pleasant manners, money, social position, etc. . . . A woman after enfranchisement would have all the personal influence she has now, and political influence in addition. One thing is certain. Every vicious interest in this country, to which women are hostile, would rather continue to contend with women's "indirect influence" than try to cope with women's vote.

Would Cease to Be Respected
Women would cease to be respected.

. . . . Mrs. K. A. Shepard, president of the New Zealand Council of Women, says: "Since women have become electors, their views have become important and command respect. . . . A young New Zealander in his teens no longer regards his mother as belonging to a sex that must be kept within a prescribed sphere, but as a human being, clothed with the dignity of all those rights and powers which he hopes to enjoy within a few years. That the lads and young men of a democracy should have their whole conception of the rights of humanity broadened and measured by truer standards is in itself an incalculable benefit."

Mrs. A. Watson Lister, secretary of the Woman's National Council of Australia, says: "One striking result of equal suffrage is that members of Parliament now consult us as to their bills, when these bear upon the interests of women. The author of the new divorce bill asked all the women's organizations to come together and hear him read it and to make criticisms and suggestions. I do not remember any such thing happening before. . . ."

Would Make Women Partisans
Women can do more good now than if they had a vote, because now they are nonpartisan. If they became voters, their nonpartisan influence would be lost.

Women continue to be nonpartisan after they have the ballot, and it gives them more power to secure the good things which the women of all parties want.

Prof. Henry E. Kelly, formerly of the Iowa State University, now practicing law in Denver, says in an open letter to State Senator A. H. Gale, of Iowa, that he went to Colorado opposed to equal suffrage, but has been converted by what he has seen of it. Prof. Kelly adds:

"Experience clearly shows that women's interests cannot be aroused in mere partisan strife. Their interests center around questions affecting education, public cleanliness, public morality, civic beauty, charities and correction, public health, public libraries and such subjects as more intimately affect home life and conduce to the prosperity of the family. Men lose sight of these important considerations in the scramble of partisan warfare for office, but women will not see them obscured by anything. . . ."

Opposition of Women
Women in large numbers are organizing against suffrage. The majority are opposed to it and the majority ought to rule.

The organized opposition among women to suffrage is very small compared with the organized movement of women in its favor. Out of forty-eight states only twenty-two have anti-suffrage organizations of any kind. There are suffrage associations in forty-seven. . . .

In every state where petitions for suffrage and remonstrances against it have been sent to the Legislature, the petitioners have always outnumbered the remonstrants, and have generally outnumbered them 50 or 100 to one. . . . In the country at large, despite urgent and widely published appeals from the Antis, only about one per cent of the women have ever expressed any objection to suffrage. Why should the one per cent who protest claim to carry any more weight than the 99 per cent who either want the ballot or do not object to it?

Already Over-Burdened
Women are already over-burdened. A woman would not have time to perform her political duties without neglecting higher duties.

Mrs. Alice Freeman Palmer wrote: "How much time must she spend on her political duties? . . . It cannot be shown that there are any large number of women in this country who have not the necessary time to vote intelligently, and it can be argued that study of the vital questions of our government would make them better comrades to their husbands and friends, better guides to their sons, and more interesting and valuable members of society. Women of every class have more leisure than men, are less tied to hours of routine; they have had more years of school training than men. All this makes simple the combination of public and higher duties."

Women and Office-Holding
If women vote, they must hold office.

When we say that women would be eligible to hold office, what do we mean? Simply that if a majority of the people in any place would rather have a woman to hold a certain position than any one else, and if she is willing to serve, they shall be allowed to elect her. . . . Suffrage does not involve office-holding by the majority of women, but only by a few; and there are always some women of character and ability who could give the necessary time. Women, as a class, have more leisure than men.

In the enfranchised states there has been no rush of women into office, and the offices that women do hold are mainly educational and charitable.

Ballots and Bullets

If women vote, they ought to fight and do police duty.

If no men were allowed to vote except those who were able and willing to do military and police duty, women might consistently be debarred for that reason. But so long as the old, the infirm, the halt, the lame and the blind are freely admitted to the ballot box, some better reason must be found for excluding women than the fact that they do not fight. All men over forty-five are exempt from military service, yet they vote.

Col. T. W. Higginson says: ". . . Grave divines are horrified at the thought of admitting women to vote when they cannot fight, although not one in twenty of their own number is fit for military duty, if he volunteered. Of the editors who denounce woman suffrage, only about one in four could himself carry a musket; while, of the lawyers who fill Congress, the majority could not be defenders of their country, but could only be defended."

Lucy Stone said, "Some woman risks her life whenever a soldier is born into the world. Later she does picket duty over his cradle, and for years she is his quartermaster, and gathers his rations. And when that boy grows to a man, shall he say to his mother, 'If you want to vote, you must first go and kill somebody'? It is a coward's argument!" . . .

Will It Increase Divorce?

It will lead to family quarrels and increase divorce.

. . . . "An ounce of experiment is worth a ton of theory."

Rev. Francis Miner Moody, Secretary of the California Commission working to secure a uniform divorce law throughout the United States, published in the *Woman Voter* of February, 1913, an article showing by actual statistics that every state which has had equal suffrage for a considerable number of years has declined markedly in its divorce rate as compared with the rest of the country. He points out that in Colorado the drop was so great as to be "astonishing.". . .

A father sometimes turns his son out of doors for voting the wrong ticket, but among American men this is rare. Where such a case does arise, it is to be met by educating the domestic despot, not by disfranchising all the members of the family but one. . . .

The Question of Chivalry
It will destroy chivalry.

Justice would be worth more to women than chivalry, if they could not have both. A working girl put the case in a nutshell when she said: "I would gladly stand for twenty minutes in the street car going home if by doing so I could get the same pay that a man would have had for doing my day's work." But . . . justice and chivalry are not in the least incompatible. Women have more freedom and equality in America than in Europe, yet American men are the most chivalrous in the world. . . .

Too Emotional
Women are too emotional and sentimental to be trusted with the ballot.

Mrs. E. T. Brown, at a meeting of the Georgia State Federation of Women's Clubs, read a paper, in which she said:

". . . it is very true of women that they are largely controlled by sentiment, and as a matter of fact, men are largely controlled by sentiment also, in spite of their protesting blushes. Was it logic that swept like a wave over this country and sent our army to protect the Cubans when their suffering grew too intense to be endured even in the hearing? Is it shrewd business calculation that sends thousands of dollars out of this country to feed a starving people during the ever-recurring famines in unhappy India? Was it hard common sense that sent thousands of American soldiers into what looked like the death-trap of China in the almost baseless hope of rescuing a few hundred American citizens? Do not men like Washington, Lincoln, Jefferson and Lee live in the hearts of American men, not alone for what they did, but still more for what they dreamed of? The man who is not controlled by sentiment betrays his friend, sells his vote, is a traitor to his country, or wrecks himself, body and soul, with immoralities; for nothing but sentiment prevents any of these things. The sense of honor is pure sentiment. The sentiment of loyalty is the only thing that makes truth and honesty desirable, or a vote a non-salable commodity.

"Government would be a poor affair without sentiment, and is not likely to be damaged by a slightly increased supply."

What Is the Unit?
The political unit is the family.

The childless widower, the unmarried boy of 21, and the confirmed old bachelor of 80 have votes; the widow with minor children has none. Under our laws the political unit is not the family, but the male individual. The unequal number of grown persons in different families would make it impossible to treat the family as the political unit. . . .

The Test of Experiment
It works badly in practice.

Women in this country now have the full ballot in Wyoming, Colorado, Idaho, Utah, Washington, California, Kansas, Oregon, Arizona, Nevada and Montana and in the territory of Alaska, while in Illinois they can vote for all municipal officers, some county and some state officers, and Presidential electors. Abroad, they have full Parliamentary suffrage in New Zealand, Australia, Finland, Iceland, and Norway; while in the Isle of Man and in Bosnia, women property owners can vote for members of the local Parliament. They have municipal suffrage throughout England, Scotland, Ireland, Wales, nine of the provinces of Canada, Sweden and Denmark, and even in Burma and some parts of India. In some of these countries they have had it for generations.

In all these places put together, the opponents thus far have not found a dozen respectable men who assert over their own names and addresses that it has had any bad results. . . .

Doubling the Vote
It would only double the vote without changing the result.

. . . . If women were exactly like men, equal suffrage would merely double the vote. But women are different from men. . . . This is recognized even by opponents, when they express the fear that equal suffrage would lead to "sentimental legislation." . . . The points of weakness in American politics at present are precisely the points where women are strong. There is no lack in our politics of business ability, executive talent, or "smartness" of any kind. There is a dangerous lack of conscience and humanity. The business interests, which appeal more especially to men, are well and shrewdly looked after; the moral and humanitarian interests, which appeal more especially to women, are apt to be neglected. . . .

Too Many Voters
We have too many voters already.

This only means that we have too many voters of the wrong kind. . . . It is often said that we have . . . too many immigrants of an undesirable kind. We all rejoice when we hear of a large influx from Finland or some other country whose people are considered especially desirable immigrants. We want them to offset those of less virtuous and law-abiding races. The governor of one of the enfranchised states writes of woman suffrage: "The effect of this increase in the vote is the same as if a large and eminently respectable class of citizens had immigrated here."

Would Unsex Women
It will turn women into men.

The differences between men and women are natural; they are not the result of disfranchisement. . . . The women of England, Scotland, Ireland, Australia, New Zealand, the Scandinavian countries and our own equal suffrage states are not perceptibly different in looks or manners from women elsewhere, although they have been voting for years.

All Socialists Are Suffragists, and Suffrage Means Socialism

All Socialists are believers in international peace and arbitration, but it does not follow that all non-Socialists ought to fight the peace societies. If it is meant that equal suffrage will hasten the coming of Socialism, the Socialists themselves do not think so, and the results in the enfranchised States do not bear out the belief.

Between the presidential elections of 1908 and 1912, the Socialist vote increased in every State of the Union. In Wyoming, Colorado, Utah and Idaho—the only States that have had equal suffrage long enough to compare presidential election with presidential election— the rate of increase was below the average. . . . All Socialists have a woman suffrage plank in their theoretical platform, but many say that they do not want woman suffrage to come until Socialism arrives, for fear that the greater conservatism of women will delay the advent of Socialism.

Women Do Not Want It
Whenever the majority of women ask for suffrage, they will get it.

Every improvement in the condition of women thus far has been secured not by a general demand from the majority of women, but by the arguments, entreaties and "continual coming" of a persistent few. In each case the advocates of progress have had to contend not merely with the conservatism of men, but with the indifference of women, and often with active opposition from some of them. . . . It is a matter of history with what ridicule and opposition Mary Lyon's first efforts for the higher education of women were received, not only by the mass of men, but by the mass of women as well.

In eastern countries, where women are shut up in zenanas and forbidden to walk the streets unveiled, the women themselves are often the strongest upholders of these traditional restrictions, which they have been taught to think add to their dignity. The Chinese lady is as proud of her small feet as any American anti-suffragist is of her political disabilities. Pundita Ramabai tells us that the idea of education for girls is so unpopular with the majority of Hindoo women that when a progressive Hindoo proposes to educate his little daughter, it is not uncommon for the women of his family to threaten to drown themselves.

All this merely shows that human nature is conservative, and that it is fully as conservative in women as in men. The persons who take a strong interest in any reform are generally few, whether among men or women, and they are habitually regarded with disfavor, even by those whom the proposed reform is to benefit.

Many changes for the better have been made during the last half century in the laws, written and unwritten, relating to women. Everybody approves of these changes now, because they have become accomplished facts. But not one of them would have been made to this day, if it had been necessary to wait till the majority of women asked for it. The change now under discussion is to be judged on its merits. In the light of history, the indifference of most women and the opposition of a few must be taken as a matter of course. It has no more rational significance now than it has had in regard to each previous step of women's progress.

19 Ain't I a Woman? (1851)

The question, "What does it mean to live in America?" has often been foreclosed with an angry, rhetorical, "Who wants to know?" If the person could be considered alien—by race, gender, sexuality, nationality, or creed—the implied answer might be, "No one." Often, those "no ones" have demanded to be heard. They speak truth to power.

Among the most successful was a slave born "Isabella" about 1797 in New York. With the help of Quakers she escaped to freedom in 1826, a status secured by the state's abolition of slavery in 1828. Equipped with a Bible committed to memory, she became a powerful street-corner preacher on behalf of emancipation. In 1843 she took the name "Sojourner" to indicate that she traveled the Earth in the service of God. Since He is "Truth," she would ever be known as "Sojourner Truth." She soon added other sorts of "no ones" to her liberation ministry.

The occasion of her most famous address was a convention in Akron, Ohio, in May 1851. Most of those in attendance were Protestant ministers (Baptist, Episcopal, Methodist, Presbyterian, and Universalist) who had come to consider resolutions in support of women's rights. The presiding officer, Frances Dana Gage, recalled that the first speakers rose in strident opposition: "One claimed superior rights and privileges for man, on the ground of 'superior intellect'; another, because of the 'manhood of Christ. . . .' Another gave us a theological view of the 'sin of our first mother.' "

They were, Gage said, "getting the better of us," especially because women were not supposed to speak at all. The mere presence of Truth incited worries, even among those in favor of the resolutions, that she might taint their cause. "Women's rights and niggers!" Gage heard someone mutter. Then:

> Slowly from her seat in the corner rose Sojourner Truth, who, till now, had scarcely lifted her head. "Don't let her speak!" gasped half a dozen in my ear. She moved slowly and solemnly to the front, laid her old bonnet at her feet, and turned her great speaking eyes to me. There was a hissing sound of disapprobation above and below. I rose and

announced "Sojourner Truth," and begged the audience to keep silence for a few moments.

The tumult subsided at once, and every eye was fixed on this almost Amazon form, which stood nearly six feet high, head erect, and eyes piercing the upper air like one in a dream. At her first word there was a profound hush. She spoke in deep tones, which, though not loud, reached every ear in the house, and away through the throng at the doors and windows.

Among the items that Gage may have misremembered, though, are the words that Truth actually spoke. There was no "original" text or transcript. All that survives of that moment in Akron are recollections of it, most of them written years later, widely varied, and suspiciously suited to the agenda of the recollector. The first print versions of Truth's address were more humble and Biblical; then they became more sentimental, and then more strident. Abolitionists and white feminists conjured an ever more assertive, but plainspoken and dignified, black and female endorsement. According to Nell Painter, it may, in fact, have been Gage rather than Truth who coined the "Ain't I a woman?" refrain. Nevertheless, Elizabeth Cady Stanton and Susan B. Anthony immortalized Gage's version of Truth's truth in their stirring documentary history of the American women's movement.

Well, children, where there is so much racket there must be something out of kilter. I think that between the niggers of the South and the women at the North, all talking about rights, the white men will be in a fix pretty soon. But what's all this here talking about?

That man over there say that women needs to be helped into carriages, and lifted over ditches, and to have the best place everywhere. Nobody ever helps me into carriages, or over mud-puddles, or gives me any best place! . . . And ain't I a woman?

Look at me! Look at my arm! I have ploughed, and planted, and gathered into barns, and no man could head me! And ain't I a woman?

I could work as much and eat as much as a man—when I could get it—and bear the lash as well! And ain't I a woman?

I have borne thirteen children, and seen most of them sold off to slavery, and when I cried out with my mother's grief, none but Jesus heard me. And ain't I a woman?

Then they talks about this thing in their head; what's this they call it? ("Intellect," someone whispers near.) That's it, honey. What's that got to do with women's rights or niggers' rights? If my cup won't hold but a pint, and yours holds a quart, wouldn't you be mean not to let me have my little half-measure full? (. . . and the cheering was long and loud.)

Then that little man in black there, he say women can't have as much rights as men, because Christ wasn't a woman! Where did your Christ come from? . . . Where did your Christ come from? From God and a woman! Men had nothing to do with Him. . . .

If the first woman God ever made was strong enough to turn the world upside down all alone, these women together . . . ought to be able to turn it back, and get it right side up again! And now that they are asking to do it, the men better let them! (Long, continuous cheering greets this.)

Obliged to you for hearing me, and now old Sojourner has got nothing more to say.

RANDOLPH BOURNE

20 Trans-National America (1916)

At the turn of the twentieth century, a cadre of genteel, proudly Anglo-Saxon and Protestant men still
lorded over civil, religious, and educational institutions in the United States. They acted as guardians of
a fledgling "civilization." But with the rise of corporate capitalism and a giant wave of New Immigrants,
Americans were becoming more "hyphenated," more
surely diverse in origin as well as blue-collar and urban. Brahmin intellectuals were uncomfortable with
these people and their greenhorn ways—strange languages, strong food and drink, raucous amusements
and ambitions.

As early as 1782, Crèvecoeur's "James" had predicted that aliens would effortlessly "melt" into a familiar alloy of the dominant culture. But a century later, prospects were
less cheery. In 1909, for example, a British-born socialist-internationalist,
Israel Zangwill, drew large crowds in New York to his play that featured
Americans pursuing romance across ethnic and religious bounds. The protagonists contemplated marriage as both an act of love and a way to erase
the hyphens that complicated their condition. Wedding just might make
them and their offspring more harmonious, generic citizens of the United
States and the globe. But in the end they felt compelled to refuse. They
were tragic heroes of an imperative to find peace while preserving diversity. Melting was not a viable option. Nevertheless, the title of Zangwill's
play—*The Melting Pot*—soon lost its ironic edge and gained popularity. With
the promotional support of powerful bigots such as Henry Ford, the "melting pot" was transformed into a vision of self-generating, bland "pluralism"
that for much of U.S. history seemed both possible and good.

Viewed from the best brownstones in Boston, newcomers were not
melting according to plan, and America required protection. Hence, for
example, in the 1920s "the best" institutions such as Harvard University
introduced quotas (maximums rather than minimums, as the term was later
used for Affirmative Action) to limit the number of Jews who might be
admitted and thereby challenge patrician dominion. In such ways, albeit
for different reasons, working-class nativists and aristocratic men of letters

146

allied to prevent the New World from becoming too much like the Old World of their imagination.

A younger generation of urban intellectuals, however, saw vitality in the very same changes. In small magazines, lectures, and syndicated columns they advocated an alternative conception of the United States, a way to think better of its inability to meet the standards of respectability touted by an older elite. They welcomed the notion that America might never be "civilized" in a stereotypically European mold: orderly, elegant, dignified. Modernity, for these people, had its dangers, but the best way to respond was not to resurrect Anglo-Saxon formality but to reject formalism altogether. The best future of the human soul could be found precisely in the diversity and dynamism of the city.

It was a decidedly optimistic view, one that would not stand up well to the challenge of World War I or the growth of different sorts of modernism. Likewise, it did not very well engage the experience of women. But for the moment, young intellectuals in the United States as well as Europe announced that time was on their side. In Paris, Moscow, and New York, popular writers celebrated the rise of a cosmopolitan spirit as well as, of course, their own good sense in recognizing it.

Among the most influential of them was Randolph Bourne. Although raised in an old-stock Anglo-Saxon family in New Jersey, he studied at Columbia University in New York City. There his guides included not only anti-formalist philosophers such as John Dewey and new social scientists such as Mary Ritter and Charles Beard but also new-immigrant writers (including Mary Antin through her popular 1912 autobiography, *The Promised Land*) and children on the Lower East Side. They were among those who helped him promote the expository essay as a form of middlebrow literary and cultural criticism. Some obvious chauvinism remained—an anti-rural, anti-Southern, European, and bookish bias. He had stereotypically genteel worries about the nouveaux riches and mass-marketed pleasures. He also, though, had high hopes for modernity and invited readers to see its best promise in America.

No reverberatory effect of the great war has caused American public opinion more solicitude than the failure of the "melting pot." The discovery of diverse nationalistic feelings among our great alien population has come to most people as an intense shock. It has brought out the unpleasant inconsistencies of our traditional beliefs. We have had to watch hard-hearted old Brahmins virtuously indignant at the spectacle of the immigrant refusing to be melted, while they jeer at patriots like Mary Antin who write about our "forefathers." We have had to listen to publicists who express themselves as stunned by the evidence of vigorous traditionalistic and cultural movements in this country among Germans, Scandinavians, Bohemians and Poles, while in the same breath they insist that the alien shall be forcibly assimilated to that Anglo-Saxon tradition which they unquestionably label "American."

As the unpleasant truth has come upon us that assimilation in this country was proceeding on lines very different from those we had marked out for it, we found ourselves inclined to blame those who were thwarting our prophecies. The truth became culpable. We blamed the war, we blamed the Germans. And then we discovered with a moral shock that these movements had been making great headway even before the war even began. We found that the tendency, reprehensible and paradoxical as it might be, has been for the national clusters of immigrants, as they became more and more firmly established and more and more prosperous, to cultivate more and more assiduously the literatures and cultural traditions of their homelands. Assimilation, in other words, instead of washing out the memories of Europe, made them more and more intensely real. Just as these clusters became more and more objectively American, did they become more and more German or Scandinavian or Bohemian or Polish.

To face the fact that our aliens are already strong enough to take a share in the direction of their own destiny, and that the strong cultural movements represented by the foreign press, schools, and colonies are a challenge to our facile attempts, is not, however, to admit the failure of Americanization. It is not to fear the failure of democracy. It is rather to urge us to an investigation of what Americanism may rightly mean. It is to ask ourselves whether our ideal has been broad or narrow—whether perhaps the time has not come to assert a higher ideal than the "melting pot." Surely we cannot be certain of our spiritual democracy when, claiming to melt the nations within us to a comprehension of our free and democratic institutions, we fly into panic at the first sign of their own will and tendency. We act as if we wanted Americanization to take place only on our own terms, and not by the consent of the governed. All our elaborate machinery of settlement and school and union, of social and political naturalization, however, will move with friction just insofar as it neglects to take into account this strong and virile insistence that America shall be what the immigrant will have a hand in making it, and not what a ruling class, descendant of those British stocks which were the first permanent immigrants, decide that America shall be made. This is the condition which confronts us, and which demands a clear and general readjustment of our attitude and our ideal.

Mary Antin is right when she looks upon our foreign-born as the people who missed the *Mayflower* and came over on the first boat they could find. But she forgets that when they did come it was not upon other *Mayflowers*, but upon a "Maiblume," a "Fleur de Mai," a "Fior di Maggio," a "Majblomst." These people were not mere arrivals from the same family, to be welcomed as understood and long-loved, but strangers to the neighborhood, with whom a long process of settling down had to take place. For they brought with them their national and racial characters, and each new national quota had to wear slowly away the contempt with which its mere alienness got itself greeted. Each had to make its way slowly from the lowest strata of unskilled labor up to a level where it satisfied the accredited norms of social success.

We are all foreign-born or the descendants of foreign-born, and if distinctions are to be made between us they should rightly be on some other ground than indigenousness. The early colonists came over with motives no less colonial than the later. They did not come to be assimilated in an American melting pot. They did not come to adopt the culture of the American Indian. They had not the smallest intention of "giving themselves without reservation" to the new country. They came to get freedom to live as they wanted. They came to escape from the stifling air and chaos of the old world; they came to make their fortune in a new land. . . . Tightly concentrated on a hostile frontier, they were conservative beyond belief. Their pioneer daring was reserved for the objective conquest of material resources. In their folkways, in their social and political institutions, they were, like every colonial people, slavishly imitative of the mother country. So that, in spite of the "Revolution," our whole legal and political system remained more English than the English, petrified and unchanging, while in England law developed to meet the needs of the changing times.

It is just this English-American conservatism that has been our chief obstacle to social advance. We have needed the new peoples— the order of the German and Scandinavian, the turbulence of the Slav and Hun—to save us from our own stagnation. I do not mean that the illiterate Slav is now the equal of the New Englander of pure descent. He is raw material to be educated, not into a New Englander, but into a socialized American along such lines as those thirty nationalities are being educated in the amazing schools of Gary. I do not believe that this process is to be one of decades of evolution. The spectacle of Japan's sudden jump from mediaevalism to post-modernism should have destroyed that superstition. We are not dealing with individuals who are to "evolve." We are dealing with their children, who, with that education we are about to have, will start level with all of us. Let us cease to think of ideals like democracy as magical qualities inherent in certain peoples. Let us speak, not of inferior races, but of inferior civilizations. We are all to educate and to be educated. These peoples in America are in a common enterprise. It is not what we are now that concerns us, but what this plastic next generation may become in the light of a new cosmopolitan ideal. . . .

To think of earlier nationalities as culturally assimilated to America, while we picture the later as a sodden and resistive mass, makes only for bitterness and misunderstanding. There may be a difference between these earlier and these later stocks, but it lies neither in motive for coming nor in strength of cultural allegiance to the homeland. The truth is that no more tenacious cultural allegiance to the mother country has been shown by any alien nation than by the ruling class of Anglo-Saxon descendants in these American States. English snobberies, English religion, English literary styles, English literary reverences and canons, English ethics, English superiorities, have been the cultural food that we have drunk in from our mothers' breasts. The distinctively American-spirit pioneer, as distinguished from the reminiscently English that appears in Whitman and Emerson and James, has had to exist on sufferance alongside of this other cult, unconsciously belittled by our cultural makers of opinion. No country has perhaps had so great an indigenous genius which had so little influence on the country's traditions and expressions. The unpopular and dreaded German-American of the present day is a beginning amateur in comparison with those foolish Anglophiles of Boston and New York and Philadelphia whose reversion to cultural type sees uncritically in England's cause the cause of Civilization, and, under the guise of ethical independence of thought, carries along European traditions which are no more American than the German categories themselves.

It speaks well for German-American innocence of heart or else for its lack of imagination that it has not turned the hyphen stigma into a "Tu quoque!" If there were to be any hyphens scattered about, clearly they should be affixed to those English descendants who had had centuries of time to be made American where the Germans had had only half a century. Most significantly has the war brought out of them this alien virus, showing them still loving English things, owing allegiance to the English Kultur, moved by English shibboleths and prejudice. It is only because it has been the ruling class in this country that bestowed the epithets that we have not heard copiously and scornfully of "hyphenated English-Americans." But even our quarrels with England have had the bad temper, the extravagance, of family quarrels. The Englishman of today nags us and dislikes us in that personal, peculiarly intimate way in which he dislikes the Australian, or as we may dislike our younger brothers. He still thinks of us incorrigibly as "colonials." America—official, controlling, literary, political America—is still, as a writer recently expressed it, "culturally speaking, a self-governing dominion of the British Empire."

The non-English American can scarcely be blamed if he sometimes thinks of the Anglo-Saxon predominance in America as little more than a predominance of priority. . . . What has been offered the newcomer has been the chance to learn English, to become a citizen, to salute the flag. And those elements of our ruling classes who are responsible for the public schools, the settlements, all the organizations for amelioration in the cities, have every reason to be proud of the care and labor which they have devoted to absorbing the immigrant. His opportunities the immigrant has taken to gladly, with almost a pathetic eagerness to make his way in the new land without friction or disturbance. The common language has made not only for the necessary communication, but for all the amenities of life.

If freedom means the right to do pretty much as one pleases, so long as one does not interfere with others, the immigrant has found freedom, and the ruling element has been singularly liberal in its treatment of the invading hordes. But if freedom means a democratic cooperation in determining the ideals and purposes and industrial and social institutions of a country, then the immigrant has not been free, and the Anglo-Saxon element is guilty of just what every dominant race is guilty of in every European country: the imposition of its own culture upon the minority peoples. The fact that this imposition has been so mild and, indeed, semi-conscious does not alter its quality. And the war has brought out just the degree to which that purpose of "Americanizing," that is, "Anglo-Saxonizing," the immigrant has failed.

For the Anglo-Saxon now in his bitterness to turn upon the other peoples, talk about their "arrogance," scold them for not being melted in a pot which never existed, is to betray the unconscious purpose which lay at the bottom of his heart. It betrays too the possession of a racial jealousy similar to that of which he is now accusing the so-called "hyphenates." Let the Anglo-Saxon be proud enough of the heroic toil and heroic sacrifices which moulded the nation. But let him ask himself, if he had had to depend on the English descendants, where he would have been living today. To those of us who see in the exploitation of unskilled labor the strident red *leit-motif* of our civilization, the settling of the country presents a great social drama as the waves of immigration broke over it.

Let the Anglo-Saxon ask himself where he would have been if these races had not come? Let those who feel the inferiority of the non-Anglo-Saxon immigrant contemplate that region of the States which has remained the most distinctively "American," the South. Let him ask himself whether he would really like to see the foreign hordes Americanized into such an Americanization. Let him ask himself how superior this native civilization is to the great "alien" states of Wisconsin and Minnesota, where Scandinavians, Poles, and Germans have self-consciously labored to preserve their traditional culture, while being outwardly and satisfactorily American. . . . The South, in fact, while this vast Northern development has gone on, still remains an English colony, stagnant and complacent, having progressed scarcely beyond the early Victorian era. It is culturally sterile because it has had no advantage of cross-fertilization like the Northern states. What has happened in states such as Wisconsin and Minnesota is that strong foreign cultures have struck root in a new and fertile soil. America has meant liberation, and German and Scandinavian political ideas and social energies have expanded to a new potency. The process has not been at all the fancied "assimilation" of the Scandinavian or Teuton. Rather has it been a process of their assimilation of us—I speak as an Anglo-Saxon. The foreign cultures have not been melted down or run together, made into some homogeneous Americanism, but have remained distinct but cooperating to the greater glory and benefit, not only of themselves but of all the native "Americanism" around them.

What we emphatically do not want is that these distinctive qualities should be washed out into a tasteless, colorless fluid of uniformity. Already we have far too much of this insipidity, masses of people who are cultural half-breeds, neither assimilated Anglo-Saxons nor nationals of another culture. Each national colony in this country seems to retain in its foreign press, its vernacular literature, its schools, its intellectual and patriotic leaders, a central cultural nucleus. From this nucleus the colony extends out by imperceptible gradations to a fringe where national characteristics are all but lost. Our cities are filled with these half-breeds who retain their foreign names but have lost the foreign savor. This does not mean that they have actually been changed into New Englanders or Middle Westerners. It does not mean that they have been really Americanized. It means that, letting slip from them whatever native culture they had, they have substituted for it only the most rudimentary American—the American culture of the cheap newspaper, the "movies," the popular song, the ubiquitous automobile. The unthinking who survey this class call them assimilated, Americanized. The great American public school has done its work. With these people our institutions are safe. We may thrill with dread at the aggressive hyphenate, but this tame flabbiness is accepted as Americanization. The same moulders of opinion whose ideal is to melt the different races into Anglo-Saxon gold hail this poor product as the satisfying result of their alchemy.

Yet a truer cultural sense would have told us that it is not the self-conscious cultural nuclei that sap at our American life, but these fringes. It is not the Jew who sticks proudly to the faith of his fathers and boasts of that venerable culture of his who is dangerous to America, but the Jew who has lost the Jewish fire and become a mere elementary grasping animal. It is not the Bohemian who supports the Bohemian schools in Chicago whose influence is sinister, but the Bohemian who has made money and has got into ward politics. Just so surely as we tend to disintegrate these nuclei of nationalistic culture do we tend to create hordes of men and women without a spiritual country, cultural outlaws, without taste, without standards but those of the mob. ... Those who came to find liberty achieve only license. They become the flotsam and jetsam of American life, the downward undertow of our civilization with its leering cheapness and falseness of taste and spiritual outlook, the absence of mind and sincere feeling which we see in our slovenly towns, our vapid moving pictures, our popular novels, and in the vacuous faces of the crowds on the city street. This is the cultural wreckage of our time, and it is from the fringes of the Anglo-Saxons as well as the other stocks that it falls. America has as yet no impelling integrating force. It makes too easily for this detritus of cultures. In our loose, free country, no constraining national purpose, no tenacious folk tradition and folk style hold the people to a line.

The war has shown us that not in any magical formula will this purpose be found. No intense nationalism of the European plan can be ours. But do we not begin to see a new and more adventurous ideal? Do we not see how the national colonies in America, deriving power from the deep cultural heart of Europe and yet living here in mutual toleration, freed from the age-long tangles of races, creeds, and dynasties, may work out a federated ideal? America is transplanted Europe, but a Europe that has not been disintegrated and scattered in the transplanting as in some Dispersion. Its colonies live here inextricably mingled, yet not homogeneous. They merge but they do not fuse.

America is a unique sociological fabric, and it bespeaks poverty of imagination not to be thrilled at the incalculable potentialities of so novel a union of men. To seek no other goal than the weary old nationalism, belligerent, exclusive, inbreeding, the poison of which we are witnessing now in Europe, is to make patriotism a hollow sham, and to declare that, in spite of our boastings, America must ever be a follower and not a leader of nations.

———

If we come to find this point of view plausible, we shall have to give up the search for our native "American" culture. With the exception of the South and that New England which, like the Red Indian, seems to be passing into solemn oblivion, there is no distinctively American culture. It is apparently our lot rather to be a federation of cultures. This we have been for half a century, and the war has made it ever more evident that this is what we are destined to remain. This will not mean, however, that there are not expressions of indigenous genius that could not have sprung from any other soil. Music, poetry, philosophy, have been singularly fertile and new. Strangely enough, American genius has flared forth just in those directions which are least of the people. . . . Our drama and our fiction, the peculiar fields for the expression of action and objectivity, are somehow exactly the fields of the spirit which remain poor and mediocre. American materialism is in some way inhibited from getting into impressive artistic form its own energy with which it bursts. Nor is it any better in architecture, the least romantic and subjective of all the arts. We are inarticulate of the very values which we profess to idealize. But in the finer forms— music, verse, the essay, philosophy—the American genius puts forth work equal to any of its contemporaries. Just insofar as our American genius has expressed the pioneer spirit, the adventurous, forward-looking drive of a colonial empire, is it representative of that whole— America of the many races and peoples, and not of any partial or traditional enthusiasm. And only as that pioneer note is sounded can we really speak of the American culture. As long as we thought of Americanism in terms of the "melting pot," our American cultural tradition lay in the past. It was something to which the new Americans were to be moulded. In the light of our changing ideal of Americanism, we must perpetrate the paradox that our American cultural tradition lies in the future. It will be what we all together make out of this incomparable opportunity of attacking the future with a new key.

Whatever American nationalism turns out to be, it is certain to become something utterly different from the nationalisms of twentieth-century Europe. . . . We must give new edges to our pride. We must be content to avoid the unnumbered woes that national patriotism has brought in Europe, and that fiercely heightened pride and self-consciousness. Alluring as this is, we must allow our imaginations to transcend this scarcely veiled belligerency. We can be serenely too proud to fight if our pride embraces the creative forces of civilization which armed contest nullifies. We can be too proud to fight if our code of honor transcends that of the schoolboy on the playground surrounded by his jeering mates. Our honor must be positive and creative, and not the mere jealous and negative protectiveness against metaphysical violations of our technical rights. . . .

We should hold our gaze to what America has done, not what mediaeval codes of dueling she has failed to observe. We have transplanted European modernity to our soil, without the spirit that inflames it and turns all its energy into mutual destruction. Out of these foreign peoples there has somehow been squeezed the poison. An America "hyphenated" to bitterness is somehow non-explosive. For, even if we all hark back in sympathy to a European nation, even if the war has set every one vibrating to some emotional string twanged on the other side of the Atlantic, the effect has been one of almost dramatic harmlessness.

What we have really been witnessing, however unappreciatively, in this country has been a thrilling and bloodless battle of Kulturs. In that arena of friction which has been the most dramatic—between the hyphenated German-American and the hyphenated English-American—there have emerged rivalries of philosophies which show up deep traditional attitudes, points of view which accurately reflect the gigantic issues of the war. America has mirrored the spiritual issues. The vicarious struggle has been played out peacefully here in the mind. We have seen the stout resistiveness of the old moral interpretation of history on which Victorian England thrived and made itself great in its own esteem. The clean and immensely satisfying vision of the war as a contest between right and wrong; the enthusiastic support of the Allies as the incarnation of virtue on a rampage; the fierce envisaging of their selfish national purposes as the ideals of justice, freedom and democracy—all this has been thrown with intensest force against the German realistic interpretations in terms of the struggle for power and the virility of the integrated State. America has been the intellectual battleground of the nations.

————

The failure of the melting pot, far from closing the great American democratic experiment, means that it has only just begun. Whatever American nationalism turns out to be, we see already that it will have color richer and more exciting than our ideal has hitherto encompassed. In a world which has dreamed of internationalism, we find that we have all unawares been building up the first international nation. The voices which have cried for a tight and jealous nationalism of the European pattern are failing. From that ideal, however valiantly and disinterestedly it has been set for us, time and tendency have moved us further and further away. What we have achieved has been rather a cosmopolitan federation of national colonies, of foreign cultures, from whom the sting of devastating competition has been removed. America is already the world-federation in miniature, the continent where for the first time in history has been achieved that miracle of hope, the peaceful living side by side, with character substantially preserved, of the most heterogeneous peoples under the sun. Nowhere else has such contiguity been anything but the breeder of misery. Here, notwithstanding our tragic failures of adjustment, the outlines are already too clear not to give us a new vision and a new orientation of the American mind in the world.

It is for the American of the younger generation to accept this cosmopolitanism, and carry it along with self-conscious and fruitful purpose. In his colleges, he is already getting, with the study of modern history and politics, the modern literatures, economic geography, the privilege of a cosmopolitan outlook such as the people of no other nation of today in Europe can possibly secure. If he is still a colonial, he is no longer the colonial of one partial culture, but of many. He is a colonial of the world. Colonialism has grown into cosmopolitanism, and his motherland is no one nation, but all who have anything life enhancing to offer to the spirit. That vague sympathy which the France of ten years ago was feeling for the world—a sympathy which was drowned in the terrible reality of war—may be the modern American's, and that in a positive and aggressive sense. If the American is parochial, it is in sheer wantonness or cowardice. His provincialism is the measure of his fear of bogies or the defect of his imagination.

Indeed, it is not uncommon for the eager Anglo-Saxon who goes to a vivid American university today to find his true friends not among his own race but among the acclimatized German or Austrian, the acclimatized Jew, the acclimatized Scandinavian or Italian. In them he finds the cosmopolitan note. In these youths, foreign-born or the children of foreign-born parents, he is likely to find many of his old inbred morbid problems washed away. These friends are oblivious to the repressions of that tight little society in which he so provincially grew up. He has a pleasurable sense of liberation from the stale and familiar attitudes of those whose ingrowing culture has scarcely created anything vital for his America of today. He breathes a larger air. In his new enthusiasms for continental literature, for unplumbed Russian depths, for French clarity of thought, for Teuton philosophies of power, he feels himself the citizen of a larger world. He may be absurdly superficial, his outward-reaching wonder may ignore all the stiller and homelier virtues of his Anglo-Saxon home, but he has at least found the clue to that international mind which will be essential to all men and women of goodwill if they are ever to save this Western world of ours from suicide. His new friends have gone through a similar revolution. America has burned most of the baser metal also from them. Meeting now with this common American background, all of them may yet retain that distinctiveness of their native cultures and their national spiritual slants. They are more valuable and interesting to each other for being different, yet that difference could not be creative were it not for this new cosmopolitan outlook which America has given them and which they all equally possess.

A college where such a spirit is possible even to the smallest degree, has within itself already the seeds of this international intellectual world of the future. It suggests that the contribution of America will be an intellectual internationalism which goes far beyond the mere exchange of scientific ideas and discoveries and the cold recording of facts. It will be an intellectual sympathy which is not satisfied until it has got at the heart of the different cultural expressions, and felt as they feel. It may have immense preferences, but it will make understanding and not indignation its end. Such a sympathy will unite and not divide. Against the thinly disguised panic which calls itself "patriotism" and the thinly disguised militarism which calls itself "preparedness" the cosmopolitan ideal is set. This does not mean that those who hold it are for a policy of drift. They, too, long passionately for an integrated and disciplined America. But they do not want one which is integrated only for domestic economic exploitation of the workers or for predatory economic imperialism among the weaker peoples. They do not want one that is integrated by coercion or militarism, or for the truculent assertion of a mediaeval code of honor and of doubtful rights. They believe that the most effective integration will be one which coordinates the diverse elements and turns them consciously toward working out together the place of America in the world situation. They demand for integration a genuine integrity, a wholeness and soundness of enthusiasm and purpose which can only come when no national colony within our America feels that it is being discriminated against or that its cultural case is being prejudged. This strength of cooperation, this feeling that all who are here may have a hand in the destiny of America, will make for a finer spirit of integration than any narrow "Americanism" or forced chauvinism. In this effort we may have to accept some form of that dual citizenship which meets with so much articulate horror among us. Dual citizenship we may have to recognize as the rudimentary form of that international citizenship to which, if our words mean anything, we aspire. We have assumed unquestioningly that mere participation in the political life of the United States must cut the new citizen off from all sympathy with his old allegiance. Anything but a bodily transfer of devotion from one sovereignty to another has been viewed as a sort of moral treason against the Republic. We have insisted that the immigrant whom we welcomed escaping from the very exclusive nationalism of his European home shall forthwith adopt a nationalism just as exclusive, just as narrow, and even less legitimate because it is founded on no warm traditions of his own. Yet a nation like France is said to permit a formal and legal dual citizenship even at the present time. Though a citizen of hers may pretend to cast off his allegiance in favor of some other sovereignty, he is still subject to her laws when he returns. Once a citizen, always a citizen, no matter how many new citizenships he may embrace. And such a dual citizenship seems to us sound and right. . . .

Indeed, does not the cultivated American who goes to Europe practice a dual citizenship, which, if not formal, is no less real? The American who lives abroad may be the least expatriate of men. If he falls in love with French ways and French thinking and French democracy and seeks to saturate himself with the new spirit, he is guilty of at least a dual spiritual citizenship. He may be still American, yet he feels himself through sympathy also a Frenchman. And he finds that this expansion involves no shameful conflict within him, no surrender of his native attitude. He has rather for the first time caught a glimpse of the cosmopolitan spirit. And after wandering about through many races and civilizations he may return to America to find them all here living vividly and crudely, seeking the same adjustment that he made. He sees the new peoples here with a new vision. They are no longer masses of aliens, waiting to be "assimilated," waiting to be melted down into the indistinguishable dough of Anglo-Saxonism. They are rather threads of living and potent cultures, blindly striving to weave themselves into a novel international nation, the first the world has seen. In an Austria-Hungary or a Prussia the stronger of these cultures would be moving almost instinctively to subjugate the weaker. But in America those wills-to-power are turned in a different direction into learning how to live together.

Along with dual citizenship we shall have to accept, I think, that free and mobile passage of the immigrant between America and his native land again which now arouses so much prejudice among us. We shall have to accept the immigrant's return for the same reason that we consider justified our own flitting about the earth. To stigmatize the alien who works in America for a few years and returns to his own land, only perhaps to seek American fortune again, is to think in narrow nationalistic terms. It is to ignore the cosmopolitan significance of this migration. It is to ignore the fact that the returning immigrant is often a missionary to an inferior civilization.

This migratory habit has been especially common with the unskilled laborers who have been pouring into the United States in the last dozen years from every country in southeastern Europe. Many of them return to spend their earnings in their own country or to serve their country in war. But they return with an entirely new critical outlook, and a sense of the superiority of American organization to the primitive living around them. This continued passage to and fro has already raised the material standard of living in many regions of these backward countries. For these regions are thus endowed with exactly what they need, the capital for the exploitation of their natural resources, and the spirit of enterprise. America is thus educating these laggard peoples from the very bottom of society up, awakening vast masses to a newborn hope for the future. In the migratory Greek, therefore, we have not the parasitic alien, the doubtful American asset, but a symbol of that cosmopolitan interchange which is coming, in spite of all war and national exclusiveness.

Only America, by reason of the unique liberty of opportunity and traditional isolation for which she seems to stand, can lead in this cosmopolitan enterprise. Only the American—and in this category I include the migratory alien who has lived with us and caught the pioneer "spirit" and a sense of new social vistas—has the chance to become that citizen of the world. America is coming to be, not a nationality but a trans-nationality, a weaving back and forth, with the other lands, of many threads of all sizes and colors. Any movement which attempts to thwart this weaving, or to dye the fabric any one color, or disentangle the threads of the strands, is false to this cosmopolitan vision. I do not mean that we shall necessarily glut ourselves with the raw product of humanity. It would be folly to absorb the nations faster than we could weave them. We have no duty either to admit or reject. It is purely a question of expediency. What concerns us is the fact that the strands are here. We must have a policy and an ideal for an actual situation. Our question is: What shall we do with our America? How are we likely to get the more creative America by confining our imaginations to the ideal of the melting pot, or broadening them to some such cosmopolitan conception as I have been vaguely sketching?

The war has shown America to be unable, though isolated geographically and politically from a European world situation, to remain aloof and irresponsible. She is a wandering star in a sky dominated by two colossal constellations of states. Can she not work out some position of her own, some life of being in, yet not quite of, this seething and embroiled European world? This is her only hope and promise. A trans-nationality of all the nations, it is spiritually impossible for her to pass into the orbit of any one. It will be folly to hurry herself into a premature and sentimental nationalism, or to emulate Europe and play fast and loose with the forces that drag into war. No Americanization will fulfill this vision which does not recognize the uniqueness of this trans-nationalism of ours. The Anglo-Saxon attempt to fuse will only create enmity and distrust. The crusade against "hyphenates" will only inflame the partial patriotism of trans-nationals, and cause them to assert their European traditions in strident and unwholesome ways. But the attempt to weave a wholly novel international nation out of our chaotic America will liberate and harmonize the creative power of all these peoples and give them the new spiritual citizenship, as so many individuals have already been given, of a world.

Is it a wild hope that the undertow of opposition to metaphysics in international relations, opposition to militarism, is less a cowardly provincialism than a groping for this higher cosmopolitan ideal? One can understand the irritated restlessness with which our proud pro-British colonists contemplate a heroic conflict across the seas in which they have no part. It was inevitable that our necessary inaction should evolve in their minds into the bogey of national shame and dishonor. But let us be careful about accepting their sensitiveness as final arbiter. Let us look at our reluctance rather as the first crude beginnings of assertion on the part of certain strands in our nationality that they have a right to a voice in the construction of the American ideal. Let us face realistically the America we have around us. Let us work with the forces that are at work. Let us make something of this transnational spirit instead of outlawing it. Already we are living in this cosmopolitan America. What we need is everywhere a vivid consciousness of the new ideal. Deliberate headway must be made against the survivals of the melting-pot ideal for the promise of American life.

We cannot Americanize America worthily by sentimentalizing and moralizing history. When the best schools are expressly renouncing the questionable duty of teaching patriotism by means of history, it is not the time to force shibboleth upon the immigrant. This form of Americanization has been heard because it appealed to the vestiges of our old sentimentalized and moralized patriotism. This has so far held the field as the expression of the new American's new devotion. The inflections of other voices have been drowned. They must be heard. We must see if the lesson of the war has not been for hundreds of these later Americans a vivid realization of their trans-nationality, a new consciousness of what America meant to them as a citizenship in the world. It is the vague historic idealisms which have provided the fuel for the European flame. Our American ideal can make no progress until we do away with this romantic gilding of the past.

All our idealisms must be those of future social goals in which all can participate, the good life of personality lived in the environment of the Beloved Community. No mere doubtful triumphs of the past, which redound to the glory of only one of our trans-nationalities, can satisfy us. It must be a future America, on which all can unite, which pulls us irresistibly toward it, as we understand each other more warmly.

To make real this striving amid dangers and apathies is work for a younger intelligentsia of America. Here is an enterprise of integration into which we can all pour ourselves, of a spiritual welding which should make us, if the final menace ever came, not weaker, but infinitely strong.

21 | Americanism (1919)

At least since the Revolution, patriots have touted moral ideals as if they were a uniquely American responsibility. Since perfection is supposed to be so close—just out of reach but well within everyone's view— imperfection is greeted with exasperation: "If we can put a man on the moon, why can't we. . . ?" Hence, Americans can be cocksure both that their country is great and that it is terribly flawed. By such reasoning, patriotism requires emphasis on the negative no less than on the positive. Griping can be considered a civic duty; exposé, a national pastime. Hence, too, leaders can find it tough to muzzle their critics unless there is a war going on.

Nevertheless, there also have been demands for a more straightforward sort of patriotism, one that would promote loyalty to a uniform, rosy rendering of the national tried-and-true. The United States is one of only a couple of countries on Earth where millions of schoolchildren begin each day chanting a "Pledge of Allegiance" to the flag and "the Republic for which it stands." Such routines have a strikingly short history that touches both the political left and right.

For example, standards for displaying the flag did not pass Congress until 1942. The flag became a fixture in public schools only about a century ago. Credit for placing it there belongs mainly to the salesmanship of a popular Boston weekly (*Youths' Companion*) in league with some liberal businessmen (James Upham and Daniel Ford), a Christian socialist (Francis Bellamy, cousin of Edward Bellamy, the author of *Looking Backward*), and the National Education Association. At the time (c. 1890) Francis Bellamy was both an activist and a minister whose sermons included titles such as "Jesus, the Socialist." Soon after his Baptist congregation decided that he was too radical for the pulpit, he wrote the "Pledge of Allegiance" for the 400th Columbus Day in 1892.

Subsequently, however, these symbols took a shift to the right. For example, the initial mode of honoring the flag, an uplifted right-arm salute, took a giant step in that direction (inspiring a change) when it was also adopted by the Third Reich. During the Cold War (1954) the U.S. Congress added the words "under God" to the Pledge, in keeping with the recently discovered/invented "Judeo-Christian ethic" that the Rev. Mr. Bellamy had mysteriously neglected. The Knights of Columbus had promoted the change to make it yet clearer that the Lord was on the U.S. side in fighting "godless communism."

Although the nativist variety of patriotism is often associated with the 1950s, an earlier strain dates from the 1910s, between World War I and II. It went by the name of "America First" or "Americanism" (usually with the intensifier, "one-hundred percent"). Like many positives, this one implied many negatives: anti-immigrant, anti-Semite, anti-Catholic, anti-union, anti-radical (anti-socialist, -anarchist, -internationalist, et al.) It was as bigoted and fearful as it was patriotic. Among the first to embrace the slogan was the Ku Klux Klan (KKK) during its 1920s revival. "Americanism" signaled a shift in the KKK from its original Reconstruction-era agenda (maintaining oppression of blacks in the South) to a more generic white supremacy (Protestant, xenophobic, and right-wing) that would also extend its appeal in the North and Midwest.

But "Americanism" also has a more respectable pedigree. Among its first and still greatest champions is the American Legion, a fraternal organization of military veterans. The name is supposed to "tie the whole together for truth, remembrance, constancy, honor, service, veterans affairs and rehabilitation, children and youth, loyalty, and Americanism." The organization now boasts about 3 million members (Legionnaires) affiliated with about fifteen thousand centers (Posts) scattered across the United States. Posts are popular gathering places and symbols of civic pride.

The American Legion was initiated by a caucus of the American Expeditionary Forces in Paris one year after the Treaty of Versailles. Its original purpose was to support U.S. troops overseas and to help ensure that they would remain uncorrupted by foreign influence. It was a practical answer to the question posed in the hit song (by Sam Lewis, Paul Young, and Walter Donaldson, also in 1919), "How 'ya gonna keep 'em down on the farm, after they've seen Paree?" Given persistent anxieties about the vast number of recent immigrants, nativists worried that international experience might divide veterans' loyalties, too. Hence, for example, the Legion's standing Americanism Commission also included a Counter Subversive Activities Committee.

Legionnaires have proudly volunteered for social as well as ideological service. They helped author the GI Bill of 1944 that expanded benefits for veterans and dramatically advanced higher education in the United States as a whole. Theirs was the first veterans' group to identify Gulf War syndrome after the 1991 "Operation Desert Storm" in Kuwait and Iraq. They annually sponsor marksmanship and baseball competitions in thousands of communities and claim to donate more blood to the Red Cross than any other organization.

The following Preamble to the Constitution of the American Legion (adopted in St. Louis in 1919) is mounted on the wall of every Post and recited at every official gathering.

For God and Country, we associate ourselves together for the following purposes:

- to uphold and defend the Constitution of the United States of America;
- to maintain law and order;
- to foster and perpetuate a one hundred percent Americanism;
- to preserve the memories and incidents of our associations in the great wars;
- to inculcate a sense of individual obligation to the community, state and nation;
- to combat the autocracy of both the classes and the masses;
- to make right the master of might;
- to promote peace and goodwill on earth;
- to safeguard and transmit to posterity the principles of justice, freedom and democracy;
- to consecrate and sanctify our comradeship by our devotion to mutual helpfulness.

Statue of Liberty, Frédéric-Auguste Bartholdi, 1886

In 1875, French workers, led by sculptor Frédéric-Auguste Bartholdi and engineer Alexandre Gustave Eiffel (of Eiffel Tower fame), began building a massive gift for the United States. Ten years later, "Liberty Enlightening the World" was finished, then disassembled, crated, and shipped from Rouen to New York Harbor. It was re-erected on Bedloe's Island, across from Ellis Island, where in the next few decades about 20 million emigrants would become immigrants. Emma Lazarus provided the inscription:

The New Colossus

Not like the brazen giant of Greek fame,
With conquering limbs astride from land to land;
Here at our sea-washed, sunset gates shall stand
A mighty woman with a torch, whose flame
Is the imprisoned lightning, and her name
Mother of Exiles. From her beacon-hand
Glows world-wide welcome; her mild eyes command
The air-bridged harbor that twin cities frame.
"Keep, ancient lands, your storied pomp!" cries she
With silent lips. "Give me your tired, your poor,
Your huddled masses yearning to breathe free,
The wretched refuse of your teeming shore.
Send these, the homeless, tempest-tos't to me.
I lift my lamp beside the golden door!"

Americans All!, Howard Chandler Christy, 1919

World War I inspired the first self-conscious efforts of the U.S. government to advertise itself. Outfits such as the Creel Committee were supposed to manage public information and thereby frustrate the "brainwashing" projects of Pavlovian foes. Among the records of wartime propaganda are posters such as this one by Howard Chandler Christy. Its main purpose was to sell bonds that would help finance the war. But it also featured an appeal to national unity that has become standard fare. As when casting films, ads, and radio and television shows, honor is extended through an assemblage of old- and new-stock names so diverse that they would rarely meet in the real world: Du Bois, Smith, O'Brien, Cejka, Haucke, Pappandrikopolous, Andrassi, Villotto, Levy, Turovich, Kowalski, Chriczanevicz, Knutson, and Gonzales. On the other hand, the object of their loyalty appears to be a conspicuously pure, "old-stock" Lady Liberty. Minorities are expected to rally around the fair, slight, and sensuous all-American girl, not the mighty figure of the Statue of Liberty (for which the sculptor's Alsatian mother posed) nor some broad-hipped, swarthy foreigner.

The Melting Pot, postcard from the Fourth of July parade in Wethersfield, Connecticut, 1913

Goddess of Democracy under Construction with Foreign Correspondents in View, The Central Academy of Fine Arts, Beijing, photo by Zhou Yan, 1989

Goddess of Democracy Faces Mao, Tiananmen Square, Beijing, 1989

Chinese Protest Belgrade Bombing, 1999

In 1999, in line with the NATO-endorsed mission of halting Yugoslav forces in Kosovo, U.S. aircraft began "precision bombing" of Belgrade. On the night of May 7–8, the Chinese embassy was struck. Three occupants were killed and twenty-five wounded. President Clinton insisted that it was a regretted, singular mistake, but next to no one in China heard or believed him. So, very near the tenth anniversary of a comparably stirring "incident," this time with government encouragement, hundreds of thousands of protesters took to the streets, and U.S. diplomatic facilities were heavily damaged. Among those Chinese who joined officials in explaining their outrage were families of the victims:

Letter for the daddy of Chelsea, U.S. President Clinton:

I am Chinese. . . . Today I went to see the dead bodies of my eldest daughter Zhu Ying (a photographer) and my son-in-law Xu Xinghu (a correspondent for the Guangmong daily newspaper), killed in the NATO bombing of the Chinese embassy in Belgrade.

I see the tragedy of these dead people with grief and desperation. My family was very happy; my daughter and son-in-law loved their parents. They were married in the autumn of 1997; their house was full of joy. I am sure your home is also filled with joy when you are with your wife and daughter. You are happy as we were. But now I have only two corpses who cannot smile at me or speak to me or embrace me.

My daughter was only 27. What did she and my son-in-law do to you? . . . No one thought that a diplomatic place such as the Chinese embassy would be an objective of the bombing carried out by you and your NATO. . . .

At home in Beijing my wife cries day and night. The mother of my son-in-law is a peasant living in Jaingsu rural area. When she heard the tragic news she fainted. In a moment a happy life had been destroyed; the sky fell to earth. You caused this tragedy. What do you say, as a father, a human being, a defender of human rights?

I hope you receive this letter and that it will be translated into English in American newspapers. I hope you understand that the Chinese people are like the American people: We also have the right to live; we also want to be happy. We Chinese say: "Blood when shed is never wasted: the Chinese people will not let anyone step on them."

I hope you and your wife and daughter live a happy and united life.

—Zhu Fulai, Belgrade, May 10, 1999

FRED LEWIS PATTEE

22 Century Readings (1919)

Between about 1900 and 1920 there was a changing of
the guard of American literature. Throughout the nineteenth century the guardians had been chiefly men of
letters, genteel nonacademics (such as William Dean
Howells) in the tradition of Ralph Waldo Emerson.
Their membership and mode were decidedly Anglo-
American, male, Northeastern, and Protestant, but their
avowed interest was the totality of contemporary writing and society. They aimed to improve them both.

In the first decades of the new century, though,
their labor was divided. Criticism of contemporary
writing became more the province of professional journalists. Reviewers in
newspapers and small magazines advised an expanding audience how and
what to read. They helped consumers navigate through the torrent of fresh
sources of inspiration, self-improvement, and pleasure.

In universities, modern literature was still considered too accessible
to qualify as a subject of serious study. Academic reading had less to do
with engaging "sentiment" (maligned as superficial and "feminine") than
with tending a respectable (long and hardy) legacy. Hence, classical, pon-
derous texts were preferred. Philology was only gradually supplanted by
literary history in the 1920s. Once sorted by authors and regions, texts
were re-sorted into periods or movements in national development.

The first academic efforts to find an American literary heritage mainly
lamented the shortage of worthy sources. When viewed with Anglo-Saxon
vanity, American tradition seemed barely worth the bother. But scholars
soon invented or discovered one and began celebrating it. Very few universities offered surveys of American literature in 1920; by 1940, 95 percent
of them did.

Among their inspirations was contemporary social unrest—the same
domestic and international turbulence that troubled supporters of the
American Legion. Professors aimed to find a literary haven for "Americanism" in distress.

Yet, close to home, they were also responding to the German-inspired
professionalization of their workplace. To qualify for university appoint-
ment in the United States after about 1910, a generalist A.M. or D.D. degree

would no longer do. Professors were increasingly expected to hold a Ph.D. (ideally from Germany) in a discipline that was bureaucratically and intellectually distinct.

Literature professors organized in part merely to match competition within the university from newly established social sciences. Since those competitors seemed to feed on urban and industrial development, discovering literary Americanism presented English professors with a chance at once to pursue their curiosity, legitimate their profession, and rescue their civilization.

Many of these scholarly trends could be traced through the career of a few closely connected individuals: Edwin David Sanborn, for example, who initiated the first American literature lectures for men at Dartmouth in the 1860s; his daughter Kate Sanborn, who delivered the first such lectures for women at Smith in the 1880s; or Edwin's student Charles Francis Richardson, who with Moses Coit Tyler published the first academic surveys of the subject before 1880. They were among the scholars who helped establish the field's professional organization, the Modern Language Association (MLA) in 1883.

Consider the career of another Sanborn understudy, Fred Lewis Pattee. After graduate training in Germany, Pattee took a position at Pennsylvania State University where he became one of the first persons ever to hold the title "Professor of American Literature." A tireless and effective promoter of the field, he helped found the MLA's American Literature Group and helped produce its first collaborative, authoritative survey, *The Cambridge History of American Literature*, in 1917

Much earlier he had published an anthology of his own, *A History of American Literature* (1896). Its conceptualization strikingly foreshadows founding and persistent principles of American Studies. He begins with the assertion that "the literature of a nation is closely entwined with its history." Hence, he can invite students through reading "to follow the development of the American spirit and of thought under the agencies of race, environment, epoch, and personality."

The following excerpt from a 1919 edition yet more boldly states Pattee's reasoning and its connection to contemporary circumstances. The anthology itself includes works that later became part of a fickle, ragtag canon: great stories, poems, historic documents, speeches, and "patriotic songs . . . with notes explaining their origin and their early use."

The recent manifestations of American patriotism, the new discovery by Europe of the soul of America, and the new insistence upon the teaching of Americanism in our schools and colleges, especially in those that for a time were under government control, has brought the study of American literature into the foreground as never before. More and more clearly is it seen now that the American soul, the American conception of democracy—Americanism—should be made prominent in our school curriculums as a guard against the rising spirit of experimental lawlessness which has followed the great war, and as a guide to the generation now molding for the future. For courses in literature, as literature is now taught, handbooks are necessary. The insistence now is not upon facts *about* the authors and masterpieces, but upon the masterpieces themselves. The pupil must read wisely and intensively from the best work of the authors included in the course, and with the equipment of the average school or college library this is impossible. Each member of a large class cannot go to the library and draw the Poems of Longfellow when Longfellow is under consideration, or the writings of Poe or Lowell or Whitman or Burroughs when those authors are up for consideration, and the ordinary student is not able to buy for himself separate editions of the various classics comprehended in the course. The only solution is a book of selections copious enough to illustrate the message and the style and the significance of each of the major authors and of each of the great phases of our literature.

The present handbook attempts to furnish such material for teachers and students of American literature. It has been thought best to begin with the first genuinely American authors like Franklin and Freneau, men of the new Republic, and to go quickly to the major figures of Irving, Cooper, and Bryant. The selections have been made from three standpoints: first, literary excellence and originality; second, style and individuality of the author; and, third, light thrown upon the period of the author and upon the growth of the American spirit. The last of these has been kept constantly in mind, for it has been considered by no means the least important of the three. The book is not only a handbook illustrating American literary art and its gradual evolution during more than a century: it is, if the compiler has done what he considers his duty, a handbook in Americanism, an interpretation of the American spirit by those who have been our spiritual leaders and our Voices.

RALPH LINTON

23 The One-Hundred Percent American (1937)

From the 1920s through the 1960s, U.S. social and psychological scientists became more distrustful of common sense, enamored of measurement, and defensive of their professionalism. They paled before the celebrity of natural science, medicine, and engineering. While many in their number (for example, Chicago and Frankfurt "schools") continued to engage a general audience and express left-wing sympathies, the cutting edge increasingly eschewed sentiment of any sort as if it were superstition. Just as women such as Ruth Benedict, Zora Neale Hurston, and Margaret Mead were establishing reputations and new subfields, other influential social scientists (at times, Mead herself) were insisting that a traditionally "male" demeanor—dispassionate, detached, disinterested—was essential.

When such a flat tone is turned on three-dimensional, living subjects—actual human beings—the result can be a zinger, cutting understatement, or comic irony. A bit of jargon or just a single, unadorned fact (for example, "The Balinese don't do it that way," or "93.2 percent of the population has a threshold XYZ score") can slay a sacred cow. No one need even wrinkle a lab coat.

So, it has always been a very short distance from serious social science to parody, and many have enjoyed the trip. Probably the most frequently reprinted example is Horace Miner's 1956 article in the *American Anthropologist*, "Body Ritual Among the Nacirema" ("America," spelt backwards). With cool affect, he at once ridicules Americans and high-serious ethnographers. For example:

> Mention must be made of certain practices which have their base in native esthetics but which depend upon the pervasive aversion to the natural body and its functions. There are ritual fasts to make fat people thin and ceremonial feasts to make thin people fat. Still other rites are used to make women's breasts larger if they are small, and smaller if they are large. General dissatisfaction with breast shape is symbolized

in the fact that the ideal form is virtually outside the range of human variation. A few women afflicted with almost inhuman hypermammary development are so idolized that they make a handsome living by simply going from village to village and permitting the natives to stare at them for a fee.

In the following essay, the anthropologist Ralph Linton uses a similar strategy to skewer "one-hundred percent Americanism," the slogan around which many anti-immigrant, anti-radical, anti-labor, anti-Catholic, anti-Semite, isolationist, and white supremacist groups rallied between the world wars. His dull monotone works like an axe. In the process he also clears ground for the contemporary cause of common, albeit eclectic destiny. Pluralism was both a long-standing hallmark of his field and a new, urgent priority of national leaders.

At the time (1937) the United States was among the nations suffering through a great depression. Labor and civil rights uprisings were frequent and intense enough to warrant concerns about the viability of basic, national political and economic structures. Judging from the rise of despots and war in Europe, prospects were bleak. If those structures were to survive, the effort to distinguish "pure" and "hyphenated" Americans would have to stop. Linton offers a passionately dispassionate brief to that effect.

There can be no question about the average American's Americanism or his desire to preserve this precious heritage at all costs. Nevertheless, some insidious foreign ideas have already wormed their way into his civilization without his realizing what was going on. Thus dawn finds the unsuspecting patriot garbed in pajamas, a garment of East Indian origin; and lying in a bed built on a pattern which originated in either Persia or Asia Minor. He is muffled to the ears in un-American materials: cotton, first domesticated in India; linen, domesticated in the Near East; wool from an animal native to Asia Minor; or silk whose uses were first discovered by the Chinese. All these substances have been transformed into cloth by a method invented in Southwestern Asia. If the weather is cold enough he may even be sleeping under an eiderdown quilt invented in Scandinavia.

On awakening he glances at the clock, a medieval European invention, uses one potent Latin word in abbreviated form, rises in haste, and goes to the bathroom. Here, if he stops to think about it, he must feel himself in the presence of a great American institution; he will have heard stories of both the quality and frequency of foreign plumbing and will know that in no other country does the average man perform his ablutions in the midst of such splendor. But the invidious foreign influences pursue him even here. Glass was invented by the ancient Egyptians, the use of glazed tiles for floors and walls in the

Near East, porcelain in China, and the art of enameling on metal by Mediterranean artisans of the Bronze Age. Even his bathtub and toilet are but slightly modified copies of Roman originals. The only purely American contribution to the ensemble is the steam radiator.

In this bathroom the American washes with soap invented by the ancient Gauls. Next he cleans his teeth, a subversive European practice which did not invade America until the latter part of the eighteenth century. He then shaves, a masochistic rite first developed by the heathen priests of ancient Egypt and Sumer. The process is made less of a penance by the fact that his razor is of steel, an iron-carbon alloy discovered in either India or Turkestan. Lastly, he dries himself on a Turkish towel.

Returning to the bedroom, the unconscious victim of un-American practices removes his clothes from a chair, invented in the Near East, and proceeds to dress. He puts on close-fitting tailored garments whose form derives from the skin clothing of the ancient nomads of the Asiatic steppes and fastens them with buttons whose prototypes appeared in Europe at the close of the Stone Age. This costume is appropriate enough for outdoor exercise in a cold climate, but is quite unsuited to American summers, steam-heated houses, and Pullmans. Nevertheless, foreign ideas and habits hold the unfortunate man in thrall even when common sense tells him that the authentically American costume of gee string and moccasins would be far more comfortable. He puts on his feet stiff coverings made from hide prepared by a process invented in ancient Egypt and cut to a pattern which can be traced back to ancient Greece, and makes sure they are properly polished, also a Greek idea. Lastly, he ties about his neck a strip of bright-colored cloth which is a vestigial survival of the shoulder shawls worn by seventeenth-century Croats. He gives himself a final appraisal in the mirror, an old Mediterranean invention, and goes down-stairs to breakfast.

Here a whole new series of foreign things confronts him. His food and drink are placed before him in pottery vessels, the popular name of which—china—is sufficient evidence of their origin. His fork is a medieval Italian invention and his spoon a copy of a Roman original. He will usually begin the meal with coffee, an Abyssinian plant first discovered by the Arabs. He will follow this with a bowl of cereal made from grain domesticated in the Near East and prepared by methods also invented there. From this he will go on to waffles, a Scandinavian invention, with plenty of butter, originally a Near-Eastern cosmetic.

Breakfast over, he places upon his head a molded piece of felt, invented by the nomads of Eastern Asia, and if it looks like rain, puts on outer shoes of rubber, discovered by the ancient Mexicans, and takes an umbrella, invented in India. He then sprints for his train—the train, not the sprinting, being an English invention. At the station he pauses for a moment to buy a newspaper, paying for it with coins invented in ancient Lydia. Once on board he settles back to inhale the fumes of a cigarette invented in Mexico, or a cigar invented in Brazil. Meanwhile, he reads the news of the day, imprinted in characters invented by the ancient Semites by a process invented in Germany upon a material invented in China. As he scans the latest editorial pointing out the dire results to our institutions of accepting foreign ideas, he will not fail to thank a Hebrew God in an Indo-European language that he is a one-hundred percent (decimal system invented by the Greeks) American (from Americus Vespucci, Italian geographer).

TOM LEHRER

24 | National Brotherhood Week (1965)

Tom Lehrer grew up during the Great Depression and spent most of his life studying and teaching mathematics in the sedate, ivied halls of Cambridge, Massachusetts. But in the 1950s—after a tour of military duty, just as the Cold War began to thaw but before the 1960s heated up—he began writing satirical songs that were just bawdy and biting enough to titillate the bohemians he befriended. By the late 1950s his performances were in demand around Harvard and then on the nascent, campus-oriented club circuit that was developing for the likes of George Carlin and the Kingston Trio. By the mid-1960s his audience had become national. The main vehicles for his celebrity were LP recordings (the large, long-playing platters that displaced 78s and preceded CDs) and a role on the NBC television series, "That Was the Week That Was." These were among the first of many popular amusements to engage Cold War–weary Baby Boomers with "hip" or "with it" (fashionably avant-garde) social sarcasm.

His cultural criticism was both outlandish and thoughtful but hardly radical. He was an educator and entertainer. His melodies came from pop charts, and his allusions from the mainstream press. But his lyrics were, by the standards of his time and social class, daringly cynical if not "leftist": anti-nuclear, anti-imperialist, egalitarian, cosmopolitan. In 1968 he lent his support to Senator Eugene McCarthy, the candidate for president who represented voters opposed to the U.S. military mission in Vietnam.

But Lehrer also lampooned the vanity of earnest liberals, particularly those staffing the contemporary folk revival. In Lehrer's lyrics, the scene was good-hearted but also shallow and bourgeois. He dubbed this vanguard of the 1960s counterculture "the folk song army." As a coy reminder of the limitations of satire and conscientious art in general, Lehrer parodied their (and, by implication, his own) ambition: "Ready, aim, sing!"

Here, from a 1965 recording of a performance at San Francisco's "hungry i," he parodies a matched set of American traditions: bigotry and lame liberality. Following a brief introduction, he breaks out in a melody that resembles a catchy show tune.

One week of every year is designated National Brotherhood Week. This is just one of many such weeks honoring various worthy causes. (One of my favorites is National Make-Fun-of-the-Handicapped Week, which Frank Fontaine and Jerry Lewis are in charge of, as you know.) During National Brotherhood Week various special events are arranged to drive home the message of brotherhood—this year, for example, on the first day of the week, Malcolm X was killed, which gives you an idea of how effective the whole thing is.

I'm sure we all agree that we ought to love one another, and I know there are people in the world who do not love their fellow human beings, and I *hate* people like that!

Here's a song about National Brotherhood Week:

Oh, the white folks hate the black folks,
And the black folks hate the white folks.
To hate all but the right folks
Is an old established rule.

But during National Brotherhood Week, National Brotherhood Week,
Lena Horne and Sheriff Clark are dancing cheek to cheek.
It's fun to eulogize
The people you despise,
As long as you don't let 'em in your school.

Oh, the poor folks hate the rich folks,
And the rich folks hate the poor folks.
All of my folks hate all of your folks;
It's American as apple pie.

But during National Brotherhood Week, National Brotherhood Week,
New Yorkers love the Puerto Ricans 'cause it's very chic.
Step up and shake the hand
Of someone you can't stand.
You can tolerate him if you try!

Oh, the Protestants hate the Catholics,
And the Catholics hate the Protestants,
And the Hindus hate the Moslems,
And everybody hates the Jews.

But during National Brotherhood Week, National Brotherhood Week,
It's National Everyone-Smile-at-One-Anotherhood Week.
Be nice to people who
Are inferior to you.
It's only for a week, so have no fear;
Be grateful that it doesn't last all year!

25 America (1953)

After the Civil War, African America faced both the promise of greater civil rights and experience with harsher racism. Decisions in U.S. courts such as *Plessy v. Ferguson* (1896) and Jim Crow laws in the states made it plain that segregation would continue to serve white supremacy. From the 1890s through the 1920s lynch mobs provided regular, brutal reminders of the failure of the Fourteenth Amendment by murdering an average of 50 to 100 African Americans per year.

But during the same period many former slaves and their children gained a formal education, organized for pride and self-defense, and moved to the city and out of the old Confederacy. Between 1910 and 1930, approximately one of every ten African Americans moved to the North, in all well over a million people. Particularly in the riot-filled years of 1919 to 1921, they faced both better employment opportunities and violent backlash. But they also found new strength in their struggle, their color, faith, family, art, music, and neighborhoods. In increasing numbers, they resisted European dreams and Southern nostalgia. They claimed a better place for the sorts of folks who they felt they really were: hustlers as well as scholars, prudes and prostitutes, idlers and athletes, and voices of the stoop and stage, the Gospels, blues, and jazz. In 1925 these were the people whom Howard University professor Alain Locke dubbed "the New Negro."

Among their most celebrated representatives was Claude McKay. His popular, proud, and angry poem "If We Must Die" (1922) became the unofficial anthem of the associated cultural and artistic movement, the Harlem Renaissance. In some ways, though, he was an unlikely spokesman.

Festus Claudius McKay was, in fact, born in Jamaica, not Harlem, and he did not set foot in the United States until 1914, when he was twenty-five years old. His first couple of years were spent not on Lenox Street corners, but studying at the Tuskegee Institute and then Kansas State. Although he never returned to the island, it was the setting for the bulk of his writing as well as his citizenship papers until 1940. In 1977, Jamaican authorities declared him *their* national poet.

As brief as was his time in Harlem, it was also frequently interrupted. Like many North American artists of "the lost generation," he spent most of the 1920s on the east side of the Atlantic. In 1919 he headed for Europe and North Africa and did not resettle in the United States until 1934. For two of those years (1921–1923), he was a guest of the Soviet government, befriended Leon Trotsky, and announced his support for communism (which he later denied), anti-colonialism, women's rights, trade unionists, and Negro liberation. His classic *The Negroes in America* (1923) was originally published in Russian.

So it seems fitting that he be remembered as a writer of the world as well as of America. But Harlem—the look, sound, and feel of the place—left a strong mark on McKay's work, one that continued to occupy his writing, even after World War II, when Soviet communism seemed a less appealing alternative.

His most powerful prose and poetry dramatize the clash of nationality, gender, ideology, and race. Sometimes the site of that struggle is Harlem; at others, Chicago, the small-town South, Kingston, Tangier, or Marseilles. At yet others, it plays out in the interaction of "a book fellah" and a "razor-flashing nigger" such as Ray and Zeddy in *Home to Harlem* (1928) or in the body of a heroine such as Bita in *Banana Bottom* (1933). Here he simply calls it/him/her "America."

> Although she feeds me bread of bitterness,
> And sinks into my throat her tiger's tooth,
> Stealing my breath of life, I will confess
> I love this cultured hell that tests my youth!
> Her vigor flows like tides into my blood,
> Giving me strength erect against her hate.
> Her bigness sweeps my being like a flood.
> Yet as a rebel fronts a king in state,
> I stand within her walls with not a shred
> Of terror, malice, not a word of jeer.
> Darkly I gaze into the days ahead,
> And see her might and granite wonders there,
> Beneath the touch of Time's unerring hand,
> Like priceless treasures sinking in the sand.

26 This Land Is Your Land (1940)

Woody Guthrie is probably best known as a folk singer and songwriter, an early comrade of the revivalist and activist Pete Seeger, a model for 1960s rebels such as Bob Dylan, and the father of Arlo Guthrie. His namesake was a genteel, turn-of-the-century liberal (Woodrow Wilson), but his music was adamantly grounded in the Great Depression of the 1930s. He drew inspiration from and directed attention to the downtrodden and dispossessed—farm and factory workers with no work to do, hoboes riding the rails, tenants fighting with their landlords and strikers with their bosses. He also wrote and performed joyous children's music, but he helped establish the popular persona of the American folk singer as progressive cultural critic and proletarian balladeer.

It is consequently more than a little ironic that many Americans treat his 1940 composition, "This Land Is Your Land," as if it were a simple and direct expression of nationalist pride. The first couple of stanzas and the chorus (a common abbreviation) might be confused with an anthem such as Irving Berlin's "God Bless America," which Kate Smith belted out to jubilant and misty-eyed throngs from the late 1930s through the 1970s. In fact, Guthrie later claimed that he changed the last line of the chorus from "God blessed America for me" to "This land was made for you and me" precisely to gain distance from Smith's tiresome jingoism. At least that is the correction that appears in a manuscript version dated February 23, 1940. Guthrie's name appears over the salutation: "All you can write is what you can see."

This land is your land, this land is my land
From California, to the New York island;
From the redwood forest, to the Gulf Stream waters
This land was made for you and me.

As I was walking that ribbon of highway
I saw above me that endless skyway.
I saw below me that golden valley:
This land was made for you and me.

This land is your land, . . .

I've roamed and rambled and I followed my footsteps
To the sparkling sands of her diamond deserts;
And all around me a voice was sounding:
This land was made for you and me.

This land is your land, . . .

When the sun came shining and I was strolling,
And the wheat fields waving and the dust clouds rolling,
As the fog was lifting, a voice was chanting:
This land was made for you and me.

This land is your land, . . .

As I was walking, I saw a sign there,
And on the sign it said "No Trespassing"
But on the other side it didn't say nothing:
That side was made for you and me.

This land is your land, . . .

In the shadow of the steeple I saw my people,
By the relief office I seen my people;
As they stood there hungry, I stood there asking,
Is this land made for you and me?

This land is your land, . . .

IV | America as a Land of the Free

Some Guiding Questions

When people speak of "freedom" in America, what
   do they have in mind?
   What elements of experience do they tend to
      emphasize or slight?
   How, for example, is the capacity positive or
      negative?
      A freedom *to* or *from* something?
      What things?
   What might an individual be expected to gain with
      freedom or lose without it?
      How about the groups to which they do or do not
         belong?
   In what respects should America be considered
      freer than other places?
      How, for example, is it a condition that
         governments afford and troops protect?

Or that ordinary citizens achieve?
How might it be related to wealth or a group's
social standing?
Do Americans as a whole have a responsibility to
"exercise" their freedoms?
Should they push for greater liberties?
If so, which ones, and with what justification?
What good or bad might be expected from
pushing against limits?
How, for example, might the push affect qualities
of life inside, outside, and on the borders of
the United States?

ABRAHAM LINCOLN

27 Gettysburg Address (1863)

Relatively few veterans have ever engaged directly in combat, but the mere thought of it touches extremes of patriotism and peril. The armed forces require risking "the ultimate sacrifice"—your own or an enemy's life—on behalf of compatriots. Whatever their specific memory of active duty or its aftermath, U.S. veterans (now more than 10 percent of the population) and their kin have particularly strong feelings for casualties of war. Hence, ceremonies and sites of commemoration can evoke powerful sentiments of condolence for survivors, respect for the dead, and—at least by implication—the nation, policies, and regimes that occasioned their loss.

President Abraham Lincoln provided a prominent example at the dedication of the Gettysburg National Cemetery on November 19, 1863. At that site, early that July, more than 150,000 Union and Confederate troops fought a battle that in the end turned the Civil War in the Union's favor. The number of soldiers missing and dead after just three days totalled more than 20,000 on each side. The strategies of Generals Meade and Lee, the futility of Pickett's charge, even the cause for which they supposedly fought, paled before the indescribable carnage.

Four months later, thousands of mourners gathered at the site. The challenge of delivering an adequate eulogy fell on the able shoulders of Edward Everett—a former governor of Massachusetts, congressman, senator, secretary of state, ambassador to Great Britain, and president of Harvard University. Although Everett's keynote speech earned the bulk of immediate attention, the brief remarks of Lincoln proved to be the more memorable. On the day after the dedication, Everett wrote to Lincoln: "I should be glad if I could flatter myself that I came as near to the central idea of the occasion in two hours as you did in two minutes."

Four-score and seven years ago, our fathers brought forth on this continent a new nation, conceived in liberty, and dedicated to the proposition that all men are created equal.

Now we are engaged in a great civil war, testing whether that nation, or any nation so conceived and so dedicated, can long endure. We are met on a great battlefield of that war. We have come to dedicate a portion of that field, as a final resting place for those who here gave their lives that that nation might live. It is altogether fitting and proper that we should do this.

But, in a larger sense, we can not dedicate—we can not consecrate—we can not hallow—this ground. The brave men, living and dead, who struggled here, have consecrated it, far above our poor power to add or detract. The world will little note, nor long remember, what we say here, but it can never forget what they did here. It is for us the living, rather, to be here dedicated to the unfinished work which they who fought here have thus far so nobly advanced. It is rather for us to be here dedicated to the great task remaining before us—that from these honored dead we take increased devotion to that cause for which they gave the last full measure of devotion—that we here highly resolve that these dead shall not have died in vain—that this nation, under God, shall have a new birth of freedom—and that government of the people, by the people, for the people, shall not perish from the earth.

Flag Raising on Iwo Jima, Joe Rosenthal and Felix DeWeldon, 1945 and 1954

World War II (1939–1945) occasioned some of the worst horrors that anyone can remember. The Holocaust remains the global measure of "man's inhumanity to man." Pictures of Hiroshima, pulverized into a mushroom cloud (August 6, 1945), still figure in fears of new technology. But probably the most widely circulated vision of the war came by way of the Pulitzer Prize-winning photograph that Joe Rosenthal snapped atop Mount Suribachi on Iwo Jima (Sulfur Island) on February 23,1945. The Allies' thirty-six-day assault on the Japanese-held island in the Pacific was brutal. About 7,000 Americans and 21,000 Japanese died. Of approximately 70,000 U.S. Marines and Naval Corpsmen who were engaged, more than one-third suffered casualties. Three of the six men shown planting the flag were killed on Iwo Jima after the Suribachi victory. Experience in the Navy and admiration of Rosenthal's photograph inspired sculptor Felix DeWeldon to craft a massive, privately funded, cast-bronze version that eventually became the Marine Corps War Memorial in Arlington, Virginia. President Eisenhower dedicated the monument on the 179th birthday of the Corps in 1954. Through the assault, the flag raising, the photo, the sculpture, their precedents, and their spin-offs, a moment on a Japanese battlefield became an icon of triumphant patriotism in the United States.

Manzanar Relocation Center, Dorothea Lange, 1942

Americans generally associate concentration camps and racial roundups with "the other side" in World War II. In fact, while at war the United States incarcerated relatively few political prisoners. The vast majority of resident aliens or citizens of German and Italian descent were free to roam, as were Japanese as close to the front as Hawaii. But in 1942, at the urging of California Attorney General Earl Warren, President Roosevelt issued Executive Order 9066, requiring the internment of all Japanese living on the West Coast. Although few of them were aliens and not one of them was ever convicted of treason, they were all deemed a security risk. Armed military police rounded up about 110,000 "Japanese" people (70 percent of whom were U.S. citizens by birth), forced them onto buses and trains, and confined them in War Relocation Authority camps—remote tar-paper barracks—for up to three years. In *Korematsu v. United States* (1944) even the Supreme Court upheld the constitutionality of the WRA. Japanese-American losses during confinement included $400 million in personal property. As her many WRA photos attest, Dorothea Lange (unlike her counterpart, Ansel Adams) used her position as an outsider to document life in the camps and to publicize the outrages she saw. After many years of protest, the U.S. government authorized compensation for surviving internees ($38.5 million in 1959 and $20,000 apiece in 1988). In 1983 a congressional committee admitted that "racial prejudice, war hysteria, and failure of political leadership" were to blame for a "grave injustice" against these Americans of Japanese descent. These two Lange photographs depict a California WRA camp, first in the midst of a windstorm and then, she wrote, when "the dust has settled."

HERBERT HOOVER

28 The American System (1928)

Probably the most famous feature of the United States is the individualism of its people. In knowing right from wrong, Americans seem more ready to consult the "self"—how does it affect me?—than society, philosophy, or history. Compared, say, to modern Africans or Asians, Americans can come across as downright selfish. Of course, the trait is neither an invention nor a monopoly of the United States. The German philosophers Karl Marx and Friedrich Engels, for example, pitched *The Communist Manifesto* (1848) to appeal to readers' (presumably, European workers') sense of their singularity. They argued that individualism was inherently both a privilege of bourgeois society and its prey.

Nevertheless, whatever its origin and generality, individualism is supposed to be distinctly American. Echoes of Walt Whitman's "Song of Myself" (1855) can still be heard when lounge lizards sing-along "I Gotta Be Me" or pop therapists prescribe "self-actualization" as the cure-all. Despite their differences in space and time, U.S. liberal academics (such as Robert Bellah et al. in *Habits of the Heart*, 1985, 1996) and alien aristocrats (such as Alexis de Tocqueville in *Democracy in America*, 1835–1840) could agree: Many of the fulfilling as well as foolish and frustrating features of America can be related to the varieties of individualism that predominate. It is also evident within the U.S. practice of American Studies itself. With few exceptions (notably, *Habits of the Heart*), insight is credited to solitary, independent-minded critics.

Among the toughest dynamics to explain are the ways that these people link self-reliance and altruism. In principle the two ought to conflict, but Americans often assume that in practice they normally or properly do not. Politicians for most of U.S. history have debated exactly how or why that should be so. Although associated with liberals in the early Republic, in the twentieth century it was conservatives who championed individualism as the means to collective ends. In 1849, for example, Henry David Thoreau asserted that the conscientious individual was "a higher and independent authority" than the state—particularly a state that would

191

maintain slavery and the Mexican War. In his famous defense of civil dis-obedience, he coined the phrase: "That government is best which governs least." In 1972, for very different ends, future president Ronald Reagan appealed to a similar sentiment: "Government does not solve problems; it subsidizes them."

Here, Republican candidate for president Herbert Hoover elaborates by way of a campaign speech in New York City just a couple of weeks be-fore the election. Hoover's opponent is Democratic governor of New York ("the Happy Warrior") Al Smith. A progressive reformer, Smith was advocat-ing greater government intervention in a troubled economy. As a distin-guished veteran of relief work in Europe after World War I, Hoover could shrug off accusations of callousness or provincialism. But he also never lacked faith in "voluntary cooperation" among capitalists nor enmity to-ward socialism as a salve for human suffering.

In November 1928 he won a landslide victory. Almost exactly one year later, the stock market crashed, and Hoover, as well as voluntarism and capitalism, lost luster. A mere two years later, Hoover himself was advocat-ing remedies akin to those he had campaigned against. He thereby took the first, reluctant steps toward building the welfare state more often associ-ated with his rival and successor, President Franklin Delano Roosevelt (1933–1945).

This campaign now draws near to a close. The plat-forms of the two parties defining principles and offering solutions of various national problems have been presented and are being earnestly considered by our people. . . .

Tonight, I will not deal with the multitude of issues which have been already well canvassed. I propose rather to discuss some of those more fundamental principles and ideals upon which I believe the Government of the United States should be conducted. . . .

Yearly the relation of Government to national prosperity becomes more and more intimate. It was only by keen large vision and coopera-tion by the Government that stability in business and stability in em-ployment have been maintained during this past seven and a half years. Never has there been a period when the Federal Government has given such aid and impulse to the progress of our people, not alone to eco-nomic progress but to development of those agencies which make for moral and spiritual progress.

But in addition to this great record of contributions of the Repub-lican Party to progress, there has been a further fundamental contribu-tion—a contribution perhaps more important than all the others—and that is the resistance of the Republican Party to every attempt to inject the Government into business in competition with its citizens.

After the war, when the Republican Party assumed administration of the country, we were faced with the problem of determination of the very nature of our national life. Over 150 years we have builded up a form of self-government, and we had builded up a social system which is peculiarly our own. It differs fundamentally from all others in the world. It is the American system. It is just as definite and positive a political and social system as has ever been developed on earth. It is founded upon the conception that self-government can be preserved only by decentralization of Government in the State and by fixing local responsibility; but further than this, it is founded upon the social conception that, only through ordered liberty, freedom and equal opportunity to the individual will his initiative and enterprise drive the march of progress.

During the war we necessarily turned to the Government to solve every difficult economic problem. . . . For the preservation of the State the Government became a centralized despotism which undertook responsibilities, assumed powers, exercised rights, and took over the business of citizens. To a large degree we regimented our whole people temporarily into a socialistic state. However justified it was in time of war, if continued in peace time it would destroy not only our system but progress and freedom in our own country and throughout the world. When the war closed, the most vital of all issues was whether the Government should continue war ownership and operation of many instrumentalities of production and distribution. We were challenged with the choice of the American system or the choice of a European system of diametrically opposed doctrines—doctrines of paternalism and state socialism. The acceptance of these ideas meant the destruction of self-government through centralization of government; it meant the undermining of initiative and enterprise upon which our people have grown to unparalleled greatness.

The Democratic administration cooperated with the Republican Party to demobilize many of her activities, and the Republican Party from the beginning of its period of power resolutely turned its face away from these ideas and these war practices, back to our fundamental conception of the State and the rights and responsibilities of the individual. Thereby it restored confidence and hope in the American people, it freed and stimulated enterprise, it restored the Government to its position as an umpire instead of a player in the economic game. For these reasons the American people have gone forward in progress while the rest of the world is halting and some countries have even gone backwards.

If anyone will study the causes which retarded the recuperation of Europe, he will find much of it due to the stifling of private initiative on one hand, and overloading of the Government with business on the other. I regret, however, to say that there has been revived in this campaign a proposal which would be a long step to the abandonment of our American system, to turn to the idea of government in business. Because we are faced with difficulty and doubt over certain national problems with which we are faced—that is, prohibition, farm relief and electrical power—our opponents propose that we must to some degree thrust government into these businesses and in effect adopt state socialism as a solution. There is, therefore, submitted to the American people the question—Shall we depart from the American system and start upon a new road? And I wish to emphasize this question on this occasion. I wish to make clear my position on the principles involved, for they go to the very roots of American life in every act of our Government. . . .

Business requires centralization; self-government requires decentralization. Our government to succeed in business must become in effect a despotism. There is thus at once an insidious destruction of self-government. Moreover there is a limit to human capacity in administration. Particularly is there a limit to the capacity of legislative bodies to supervise governmental activities. Every time the Federal Government goes into business 530 Senators and Congressmen become the Board of Directors of that business. Every time a state government goes into business 100 or 200 state senators and assemblymen become directors of that business. Even if they were supermen, no bodies of such numbers can competently direct that type of human activity which requires instant decision and action. No such body can deal adequately with all sections of the country. And yet if we would preserve government by the people, we must preserve the authority of our legislators over the activities of our Government. . . .

The effect upon our economic progress would be even worse. Business progressiveness is dependent on competition. New methods and new ideas are the outgrowth of the spirit of adventure of individual initiative and of individual enterprise. Without adventure there is no progress. No government administration can rightly speculate and take risks with taxpayers' money. But even more important than this—leadership in business must be through the sheer rise of ability and character. That rise can take place only in the free atmosphere of competition. Competition is closed by bureaucracy. Certainly political choice is a feeble basis for choice of leaders to conduct a business. There is no better example of the practical incompetence of government to conduct business than the history of our railways. . . .

But we can examine this question from the point of view of the person who gets a Government job and is admitted into the new bureaucracy. Upon that subject let me quote from a speech of that great leader of labor, Samuel Gompers, delivered in Montreal in 1920, a few years before his death. He said:

> I believe there is no man to whom I would take second position in my loyalty to the Republic of the United States, and yet I would not give it more power over the individual citizenship of our country. . . . It is a question of whether it shall be Government ownership or private ownership under control. . . . If I were in the minority of one in this convention, I would want to cast my vote so that the men of labor shall not willingly enslave themselves to Government authority in their industrial effort for freedom. . . .

I would amplify Mr. Gompers' statement. These great bodies of Government employees would either comprise political machines at the disposal of the party in power, or alternatively, to prevent this, the Government by stringent civil-service rules must debar its employees from their full rights. . . .

Bureaucracy does not spread the spirit of independence; it spreads the spirit of submission into our daily life, penetrates the temper of our people; not with the habit of powerful resistance to wrong, but with the habit of timid acceptance of the irresistible might. Bureaucracy is ever desirous of spreading its influence and its power. You cannot give to a government the mastery of the daily working life of a people without at the same time giving it mastery of the people's souls and thoughts. . . . Free speech does not live many hours after free industry and free commerce die. It is false liberalism that inserts itself into the Government operation of business. The bureaucratization of our country would poison the very roots of liberalism that is free speech, free assembly, free press, political equality and equality of opportunity. It is the road, not to more liberty, but to less liberty. Liberalism should be found not striving to spread bureaucracy, but striving to set bounds to it. True liberalism seeks freedom first in the confident belief that without freedom the pursuit of all other blessings and benefits is vain. That belief is the foundation of all American progress, political as well as economic.

Liberalism is a force truly of the spirit, a force proceeding from the deep realization that economic freedom cannot be sacrificed if political freedom is to be preserved. Even if governmental conduct of business could give us more efficiency instead of giving us decreased efficiency, the fundamental objection to it would remain unaltered and unabated. It would destroy political equality. It would cramp and cripple the mental and spiritual energies of our people. It would dry up the spirit of liberty and progress. It would extinguish equality of opportunity, and for these reasons fundamentally and primarily it must be resisted. For a hundred and fifty years liberalism has found its true spirit in the American system, not in the European systems.

I do not wish to be misunderstood in this statement. I am defining a general policy! It does not mean that our government is to part with one iota of its national resources without complete protection to the public interest. I have already stated that where the Government is engaged in public works for purposes of flood control, of navigation, of irrigation, of scientific research or national defense, or in pioneering a new art, it will at times necessarily produce power or commodities as a by-product. But they must be by-products, not the major purpose.

Nor do I wish to be misinterpreted as believing that the United States is free-for-all and the devil-take-the-hindmost. The very essence of equality of opportunity is that there shall be no domination by any group or trust or combination in this republic, whether it be business or political. It demands economic justice as well as political and social justice. It is no system to laissez-faire.

There is but one consideration in testing these proposals—that is, public interest. I do not doubt the sincerity of those who advocate these methods of solving our problems. I believe they will give equal credit to our honesty. If I believed that the adoption of such proposals would decrease taxes, would cure abuses or corruption, would produce better service, would decrease rates or benefit employees; if I believed they would bring economic equality, would stimulate endeavor, would encourage invention and support individual initiative, would provide equality of opportunity; if I believed that these proposals would not wreck our democracy but would strengthen the foundations of social and spiritual progress in America—or if they would do a few of these things—then I would not hesitate to accept these proposals, stupendous as they are. . . . But it is not true that such benefits would result to the public. The contrary would be true.

I feel deeply on this subject because during the war I had some practical experience with governmental operation and control. I have witnessed not only at home but abroad the many failures of government in business. I have seen its tyrannies, its injustices, its undermining of the very instincts which carry our people forward to progress. I have witnessed the lack of advance, the lowered standards of living, the depressed spirits of people working under such a system. My objection is based not upon theory or upon a failure to recognize wrongs or abuses but because I know that the adoption of such methods would strike at the very roots of American life and would destroy the very basis of American progress.

Our people have the right to know whether we can continue to solve our great problems without abandonment of our American system. I know we can. We have demonstrated that our system is responsive enough to meet any new and intricate development in our economic and business life. We have demonstrated that we can maintain our democracy as master in its own house and that we can preserve equality of opportunity and individual freedom.

In the last fifty years we have discovered that mass production will produce articles for us at half the cost that obtained previously. We have seen the resultant growth of large units of production and distribution. This is big business. Business must be bigger for our tools are bigger, our country is bigger. . . .

Our great problem is to make certain that while we maintain the fullest use of the large units of business yet that they shall be held subordinate to the public interest. The American people from bitter experience have a rightful fear that these great units might be used to dominate our industrial life and by illegal and unethical practices destroy equality of opportunity. Years ago the Republican Administration established the principle that such evils could be corrected by regulation. It developed methods by which abuses could be prevented and yet the full value of economic advance retained for the public. . . .

No system is perfect. We have had abuses in the conduct of business that every good citizen resents. But I insist that the results show our system better than any other and retains the essentials of freedom.

As a result of our distinctly American system our country has become the land of opportunity to those born without inheritance, not merely because of the wealth of its resources and industry, but because of this freedom of initiative and enterprise. Russia has natural resources equal to ours. Her people are equally industrious, but she has not had the blessings of 150 years of our form of government and of our social system. The wisdom of our forefathers in their conception that progress must be the sum of the progress of free individuals has been reinforced by all of the great leaders of the country since that day. Jackson, Lincoln, Cleveland, McKinley, Roosevelt, Wilson, and Coolidge have stood unalterably for these principles. By adherence to the principles of decentralization, self-government, ordered liberty, and opportunity and freedom to the individual, our American experiment has yielded a degree of well-being unparalleled in all the world. It has come nearer to the abolition of poverty, to the abolition of fear, of want, than humanity has ever reached before. Progress of the past seven years is the proof of it. It furnishes an answer to those who would ask us to abandon the system by which this has been accomplished. There is a still further road to progress which is consonant with our American system—a method that reinforces our individualism by reducing, not increasing, Government interference in business. . . . Much abuse has been and can be cured by inspiration and cooperation, rather than by regulation of the Government. . . .

I wish to say something more on what I believe is the outstanding ideal in our whole political, economic and social system—that is, equality of opportunity. We have carried this ideal farther into our life than has any other nation in the world. Equality of opportunity is the right of every American, rich or poor, foreign or native born, without respect to race or faith or color, to attain that position in life to which his ability and character entitle him. We must carry this ideal further than to economic and political fields alone. . . .

In these past few years some groups in our country have lagged behind others in the march of progress. They have not had the same opportunity. . . . I know you will cooperate gladly in the faith that in the common prosperity of our country lies its future.

29 | The Four Freedoms (1941)

Americans were for the most part deeply disillusioned with the outcome of World War I. The suffering that was supposed to spread democracy and guarantee peace obviously did neither. After the war, Americans focused on domestic life, which seemed to be as troubled as the economy since the mid-1920s. They vowed in the future better to resist international alliances and fighting words. So, when in the 1930s invasions became an Asian, African, and European commonplace, many Americans prized their isolation. Despite pleas from far-flung victims of Japanese, Italian, and German aggression, politicians clung—at least in public—to neutrality. A small but influential assemblage of pacifists, xenophobes, and left- and right-wingers rallied around the slogan, "America First."

In 1939 and 1940, however, the obvious question was: "America next?" Hitler's offensive was spreading from east to west and Hirohito's from west to east. Enough people shared a fear of fascists, hope for the New Deal, and distaste for Republicans to secure the reelection of President Franklin Delano Roosevelt to a third, unprecedented term. In his 1941 State of the Union address, he framed the moment in the larger context of American history and posited point-by-point implications.

His history was biased, to say the least. It is perhaps unforgivable but also understandable that he would neglect examples of America's own violations of other sovereigns, brutality toward Indian nations, collusion with European colonizers in Asia, and a recent rash of Latin American and Caribbean invasions. Selective memory, highlighting more principled and defensive operations, would more readily distinguish the United States from the Third Reich.

The principles themselves seem unassailable. In stating them so clearly, he took a giant step toward committing the United States to join in World War II. He also helped conjure what became known as the "free world." Rather than a specific terrain, it was to be a limitless arena of virtue with America—tender-hearted but tough-minded and well armed—at its center.

Roosevelt was a master of the media, particularly radio, which carried his January 6 address to Congress. His key concept—"the four freedoms"—was firmly immortalized when sentimentalized and serialized by the *Saturday Evening Post* illustrator, Norman Rockwell.

Mr. Speaker, members of the 77th Congress:

I address you, the members of this new Congress, at a moment unprecedented in the history of the union. I use the word "unprecedented" because at no previous time has American security been as seriously threatened from without as it is today.

Since the permanent formation of our government under the Constitution in 1789, most of the periods of crisis in our history have related to our domestic affairs. And, fortunately, only one of these—the four-year war between the States—ever threatened our national unity. Today, thank God, 130,000,000 Americans in forty-eight States have forgotten points of the compass in our national unity. . . .

What I seek to convey is the historic truth that the United States as a nation has at all times maintained opposition—clear, definite opposition—to any attempt to lock us in behind an ancient Chinese wall while the procession of civilization went past. Today, thinking of our children and of their children, we oppose enforced isolation for ourselves or for any other part of the Americas. . . .

Even when the World War broke out in 1941 it seemed to contain only a small threat of danger to our own American future. . . . I suppose that every realist knows that the democratic way of life is at this moment being directly assailed in every part of the world—assailed either by arms or by secret spreading of poisonous propaganda by those who seek to destroy unity and promote discord in nations that are still at peace.

During sixteen long months this assault has blotted out the whole pattern of democratic life in an appalling number of independent nations, great and small. And the assailants are still on the march, threatening other nations, great and small.

Therefore, as your President, performing my constitutional duty to "give to the Congress information of the state of the union," I find it unhappily necessary to report that the future and the safety of our country and of our democracy are overwhelmingly involved in events far beyond our borders.

Armed defense of democratic existence is now being gallantly waged in four continents. If that defense fails, all the population and all the resources of Europe and Asia, Africa and Australia will be dominated by conquerors. And let us remember that the total of those populations in those four continents, the total of those populations and their resources greatly exceeds the sum total of the populations and the resources of the whole of the Western Hemisphere —yes, many times over. . . .

As a nation we may take pride in the fact that we are soft-hearted; but we cannot afford to be soft-headed. We must always be wary of those who with sounding brass and a tinkling cymbal preach the ism of appeasement. We must especially beware of that small group of selfish men who would clip the wings of the American eagle in order to feather their own nests.

I have recently pointed out how quickly the tempo of modern warfare could bring into our very midst the physical attack which we must eventually expect if the dictator nations win this war.

There is much loose talk of our immunity from immediate and direct invasion from across the seas. Obviously, as long as the British Navy retains its power, no such danger exists. Even if there were no British Navy, it is not probable that any enemy would be stupid enough to attack us by landing troops in the United States from across thousands of miles of ocean, until it had acquired strategic bases from which to operate. But we learn much from the lessons of the past years in Europe—particularly the lesson of Norway, whose essential seaports were captured by treachery and surprise built up over a series of years.

The first phase of the invasion of this hemisphere would not be the landing of regular troops. The necessary strategic points would be occupied by secret agents and by their dupes—and great numbers of them are already here and in Latin America.

As long as the aggressor nations maintain the offensive they, not we, will choose the time and the place and the method of their attack. And that is why the future of all the American Republics is today in serious danger. That is why this annual message to the Congress is unique. . . .

The need of the moment is that our actions and our policy should be devoted primarily—almost exclusively—to meeting this foreign peril. For all our domestic problems are now a part of the great emergency. Just as our national policy in internal affairs has been based upon a decent respect for the rights and the dignity of all of our fellow men within our gates, so our national policy in foreign affairs has been based on a decent respect for the rights and the dignity of all nations, large and small. And the justice of morality must and will win in the end.

Our national policy is this: First, by an impressive expression of the public will and without regard to partisanship, we are committed to all-inclusive national defense.

Second, by an impressive expression of the public will and without regard to partisanship, we are committed to full support of all those resolute people everywhere who are resisting aggression and are thereby keeping war away from our hemisphere. By this support we express our determination that the democratic cause shall prevail, and we strengthen the defense and the security of our own nation.

Third, by an impressive expression of the public will and without regard to partisanship, we are committed to the proposition that the principle of morality and considerations for our own security will never permit us to acquiesce in a peace dictated by aggressors and sponsored by appeasers. We know that enduring peace cannot be bought at the cost of other people's freedom. . . .

To change a whole nation from a basis of peacetime production of implements of peace to a basis of wartime production of implements of war is no small task. The greatest difficulty comes at the beginning of the program, when new tools, new plant facilities, new assembly lines, new shipways must first be constructed before the actual material begins to flow steadily and speedily from them. . . . I shall ask this Congress for greatly increased new appropriations and authorization to carry on what we have begun.

I also ask this Congress for authority and for funds sufficient to manufacture additional munitions and war supplies of many kinds, to be turned over to those nations which are now in actual war with aggressor nations. Our most useful and immediate role is to act as an arsenal for them as well as for ourselves. They do not need manpower, but they do need billions of dollars' worth of the weapons of defense. . . . I recommend that we make it possible for those nations to continue to obtain war materials in the United States, fitting their orders into our own program. And nearly all of their material would, if the time ever came, be useful in our own defense. . . .

Let us say to the democracies: "We Americans are vitally concerned in your defense of freedom. We are putting forth our energies, our resources and our organizing powers to give you the strength to regain and maintain a free world. We shall send you in ever-increasing numbers, ships, planes, tanks, guns. That is our purpose and our pledge. . . ." Such aid is not an act of war, even if a dictator should unilaterally proclaim it so to be. . . . The happiness of future generations of Americans may well depend on how effective and how immediate we can make our aid felt. . . . A free nation has the right to expect full cooperation from all groups. . . .

The best way of dealing with the few slackers or trouble-makers in our midst is, first, to shame them by patriotic example, and if that fails, to use the sovereignty of government to save government. . . .

The nation takes great satisfaction and much strength from the things which have been done to make its people conscious of their individual stake in the preservation of democratic life in America. Those things have toughened the fiber of our people, have renewed their faith and strengthened their devotion to the institutions we make ready to protect.

Certainly this is no time for any of us to stop thinking about the social and economic problems which are the root cause of the social revolution which is today a supreme factor in the world. For there is nothing mysterious about the foundations of a healthy and strong democracy.

The basic things expected by our people of their political and economic systems are simple. They are:

- Equality of opportunity for youth and for others
- Jobs for those who can work
- Security for those who need it
- The ending of special privilege for the few
- The preservation of civil liberties for all
- The enjoyment of the fruits of scientific progress in a wider and constantly rising standard of living

These are the simple, the basic things that must never be lost sight of in the turmoil and unbelievable complexity of our modern world. The inner and abiding strength of our economic and political systems is dependent upon the degree to which they fulfill these expectations.

Many subjects connected with our social economy call for immediate improvement. . . . I have called for personal sacrifice, and I am assured of the willingness of almost all Americans to respond to that call. A part of the sacrifice means the payment of more money in taxes.

. . . No person should try, or be allowed, to get rich out of the program, and the principle of tax payments in accordance with ability to pay should be constantly before our eyes to guide our legislation.

If the Congress maintains these principles the voters, putting patriotism ahead of pocketbooks, will give you their applause.

In the future days which we seek to make secure, we look forward to a world founded upon four essential human freedoms.

- The first is freedom of speech and expression—everywhere in the world.
- The second is freedom of every person to worship God in his own way—everywhere in the world.
- The third is freedom from want, which, translated into world terms, means economic understandings which will secure to every nation a healthy peaceful life for its inhabitants—everywhere in the world.
- The fourth is freedom from fear, which, translated into world terms, means a world-wide reduction of armaments to such a point and in such a thorough fashion that no nation will be in a position to commit an act of physical aggression against any neighbor—anywhere in the world.

That is no vision of a distant millennium. It is a definite basis for a kind of world attainable in our own time and generation. That kind of world is the very antithesis of the so-called "new order" of tyranny which the dictators seek to create with the crash of a bomb. To that new order we oppose the greater conception—the moral order. A good society is able to face schemes of world domination and foreign revolutions alike without fear. Since the beginning of our American history we have been engaged in change, in a perpetual, peaceful revolution, a revolution which goes on steadily, quietly, adjusting itself to changing conditions without the concentration camp or the quicklime in the ditch. The world order which we seek is the cooperation of free countries, working together in a friendly, civilized society.

This nation has placed its destiny in the hands, heads and hearts of its millions of free men and women, and its faith in freedom under the guidance of God. Freedom means the supremacy of human rights everywhere. Our support goes to those who struggle to gain those rights and keep them. Our strength is our unity of purpose.

To that high concept there can be no end save victory.

Freedom from Want, Norman Rockwell, 1943

This print is probably the most popular of the four in which illustrator Norman Rockwell envisioned the freedoms that President Roosevelt named. The series was reproduced in the *Saturday Evening Post* and featured in posters for the Office of War Information (the precursor of the United States Information Agency). More than $130 million in war bonds were sold in traveling exhibitions.

30

Bowers v. Hardwick (1986)

Loosely speaking, social life in the United States is governed by law. Whenever a freedom is restricted or a responsibility shirked, an American is apt to protest: "There ought to be a law. . . ." It is a disposition that, among other things, keeps attorneys busy. Hence, too, observers searching for evidence of American values are apt to credit the codes that are there in force. For example, when statutes better protect the owners and sellers than the victims of firearms, critics can claim to have found proof that the United States condones gunslinging. Again, loosely speaking, that may be true, but priorities in ordinary, practical circumstances are seldom so plain.

Legislation is advanced by some interests and violated, opposed, or ignored by others. Through extended campaigns and negotiations—often entailing great expense, trade in tangential favors, bluster, face-saving, etc.—the actual statute that gets on the books is likely to be not only tolerable to many citizens (at least the powerful ones) but also representative of just about no one's ideal. Depending on yet other contingencies, it may or may not be implemented in anything like the spirit of its passage, the "legislative intent." Furthermore, all of the above—the purpose and process of enactment and enforcement— may or may not be judged befitting higher constitutional principles that are themselves subject to contest.

American conceptions of freedom, for example, can be tracked through the courts where individuals, groups, corporations, and various levels and agencies of government vie for authority. From the mid-1940s through the 1960s, for example, the civil rights movement was visible at schools, lunch counters, churches, and rallies across the country as well as in national news media, films, paintings, and creative writing. But it was also powerfully present in a series of anti-segregation decisions of the U.S. Supreme Court under the leadership of Chief Justice Earl Warren.

For example, in *Loving v. Virginia* the Court in effect struck down all codes that then (1967) barred interracial marriage in sixteen states. In this case, Virginia aimed to defend its Jim Crow laws enacted between World

Wars I and II. The state claimed its right and responsibility "to preserve the racial integrity" and "racial pride" of its citizens by barring the "corruption of blood" that "a mongrel breed of citizens" would produce. Section 20-57 of the Virginia code declared: "All marriages between a white person and a colored person shall be absolutely void." Interracial marriage was not just a crime but a felony requiring at least one and maybe as many as five years of imprisonment. Through the 1960s the code defined the racial categories that the criminal justice system was to maintain:

> For the purpose of this chapter, the term "white person" shall apply only to such person as has no trace whatever of any blood other than Caucasian; but persons who have one-sixteenth or less of the blood of the American Indian and have no other non-Caucasic blood shall be deemed to be white persons.

The particularly bizarre exception for slightly mixed-blood Indians apparently was designed to render "white" the descendants of Pocahontas and John Rolfe. (The descendants of Thomas Jefferson and his slave Sally Hemings had no such privilege.)

The plaintiffs in this case, Richard Loving ("white") and Mildred Jeter ("colored"), were legally married in the District of Columbia in 1958. Their crime came in returning to Virginia, daring to live as husband and wife in their Caroline County home. In 1959 they were arrested, pled guilty, and were sentenced to a year in jail, but the sentence was suspended on the condition that they leave the state and stay out of it for at least twenty-five years. In upholding that ruling, the Circuit Court judge hitched Virginia's legislative intent to a higher authority:

> Almighty God created the races white, black, yellow, malay and red, and He placed them on separate continents. . . . The fact that He separated the races shows that He did not intend for the races to mix.

The Supreme Court, though, found the Circuit Court's decision a violation of the Equal Protection and Due Process Clauses (Section 1) of the Fourteenth Amendment to the U.S. Constitution:

> No State shall make or enforce any law which shall abridge the privileges or immunities of citizens of the United States; nor shall any State deprive any person of life, liberty, or property, without due process of law; or deny to any person within its jurisdiction the equal protection of the laws.

The decision in *Loving v. Virginia* made it boldly evident that antimiscegenation codes were unconstitutional by their very nature. While acknowledging that marriage was properly a state rather than federal concern, the Court insisted that constitutional protections of equality and liberty must prevail—especially the right of citizens to be protected from bigotry ("arbitrary and invidious discrimination") in the intimacy of their own homes:

> The freedom to marry has long been recognized as one of the vital personal rights essential to the orderly pursuit of happiness by free men. Marriage is one of the "basic civil rights of man," fundamental to our very existence and survival.

Subsequently, however, U.S. courts upheld laws barring intimacy across other social divides, particularly those distinguishing hetero- and homosexual union. As the following excerpt from the decision in *Bowers v. Hardwick* makes clear, after 1969 (when President Nixon appointed Warren Burger to succeed the liberal Earl Warren as Chief Justice) the Supreme Court was more inclined to promote judicial restraint. Despite precedents such as *Loving v. Virginia* or *Roe v. Wade* (the 1973 decision overturning restrictions of abortion that violate a "right to privacy"), in *Bowers v. Hardwick* the Court upheld anti-sodomy law even when it plainly discriminated against homosexuals. Dissenting justices (the predictable 4 in 5–4 decisions) protested that homophobia was just as arbitrary and invidious as racism. Briefs in support of the dissent came from the states of New York and California, the American Jewish Congress, the New York City Bar Association, the National Organization for Women, the U.S. Presbyterian Church, the Lesbian Rights Project, the National Gay Rights Advocates, and the American Public Health Association as well as the American Psychological Association, which had recently removed homosexuality from its list of "diseases." In a footnote, the minority protested, "The parallel between *Loving* and this case is almost uncanny."

> *Abstract of decision delivered by Justice Byron White, joined by Justices Burger, O'Connor, Powell, and Rehnquist, June 30, 1986.*

After being charged with violating the Georgia statute criminalizing sodomy by committing that act with another adult male in the bedroom of his home, respondent Hardwick (respondent) brought suit in Federal District Court, challenging the constitutionality of the statute insofar as it criminalized consensual sodomy. The court granted the defendant's motion to dismiss for failure to state a claim. The Court of Appeals reversed and remanded, holding that the Georgia statute violated respondent's fundamental rights.

Held: The Georgia statute is constitutional.

(a) The Constitution does not confer a fundamental right upon homosexuals to engage in sodomy. None of the fundamental rights announced in this Court's prior cases involving family relationships, marriage, or procreation bear any resemblance to the right asserted in this case. And any claim that those cases stand for the proposition that any kind of private sexual conduct between consenting adults is constitutionally insulated from state proscription is unsupportable.

(b) Against a background in which many States have criminalized sodomy and still do, to claim that a right to engage in such conduct is "deeply rooted in this Nation's history and tradition" or "implicit in the concept of ordered liberty" is, at best, facetious.

(c) There should be great resistance to expand the reach of the Due Process Clauses to cover new fundamental rights. Otherwise, the

Judiciary necessarily would take upon itself further authority to govern the country without constitutional authority. The claimed right in this case falls far short of overcoming this resistance.

(d) The fact that homosexual conduct occurs in the privacy of the home does not affect the result. *Stanley v. Georgia*, distinguished.

(e) Sodomy laws should not be invalidated on the asserted basis that majority belief that sodomy is immoral is an inadequate rationale to support the laws.

Chief Justice Burger, concurring:

I join the Court's opinion, but I write separately to underscore my view that in constitutional terms there is no such thing as a fundamental right to commit homosexual sodomy.

As the Court notes . . . the proscriptions against sodomy have very "ancient roots." Decisions of individuals relating to homosexual conduct have been subject to state intervention throughout the history of Western civilization. Condemnation of those practices is firmly rooted in Judeo-Christian moral and ethical standards. . . . To hold that the act of homosexual sodomy is somehow protected as a fundamental right would be to cast aside millennia of moral teaching.

This is essentially not a question of personal "preferences" but rather of the legislative authority of the State. I find nothing in the Constitution depriving a State of the power to enact the statute challenged here.

Justice Blackmun, with Justices Brennan, Marshall, and Stevens, dissenting:

I.

This case is no more about "a fundamental right to engage in homosexual sodomy," as the Court purports to declare, than *Stanley v. Georgia* (1969) was about a fundamental right to watch obscene movies or *Katz v. United States* (1967) was about a fundamental right to place interstate bets from a telephone booth. Rather, this case is about "the most comprehensive of rights and the right most valued by civilized men," namely, "the right to be let alone." *Olmstead v. United States* (1928).

The statute at issue, *Ga. Code Ann.* 16-6-2 (1984), denies individuals the right to decide for themselves whether to engage in particular forms of private, consensual sexual activity. The Court concludes that 16-6-2 is valid essentially because "the laws of . . . many States

. . . still make such conduct illegal and have done so for a very long time." But the fact that the moral judgments expressed by statutes like 16-6-2 may be " 'natural and familiar . . . ought not to conclude our judgment upon the question whether statutes embodying them conflict with the Constitution of the United States.' " *Roe v. Wade* (1973), quoting *Lochner v. New York* (1905) (Holmes, J., dissenting). Like Justice Holmes, I believe that "it is revolting to have no better reason for a rule of law than that so it was laid down in the time of Henry IV. It is still more revolting if the grounds upon which it was laid down have vanished long since, and the rule simply persists from blind imitation of the past." Holmes, *The Path of the Law* (1897). I believe we must analyze respondent Hardwick's claim in the light of the values that underlie the constitutional right to privacy. If that right means anything, it means that, before Georgia can prosecute its citizens for making choices about the most intimate aspects of their lives, it must do more than assert that the choice they have made is an " 'abominable crime not fit to be named among Christians.' " *Herring v. State* (1904).

In its haste to reverse the Court of Appeals and hold that the Constitution does not "confer a fundamental right upon homosexuals to engage in sodomy," the Court relegates the actual statute being challenged to a footnote and ignores the procedural posture of the case before it. A fair reading of the statute and of the complaint clearly reveals that the majority has distorted the question this case presents.

First, the Court's almost obsessive focus on homosexual activity is particularly hard to justify in light of the broad language Georgia has used. Unlike the Court, the Georgia Legislature has not proceeded on the assumption that homosexuals are so different from other citizens that their lives may be controlled in a way that would not be tolerated if it limited the choices of those other citizens. Rather, Georgia has provided that "a person commits the offense of sodomy when he performs or submits to any sexual act involving the sex organs of one person and the mouth or anus of another." *Ga. Code Ann.* 16-6-2(a) (1984). The sex or status of the persons who engage in the act is irrelevant as a matter of state law. In fact, to the extent I can discern a legislative purpose for Georgia's 1968 enactment of 16-6-2, that purpose seems to have been to broaden the coverage of the law to reach heterosexual as well as homosexual activity. . . . Michael Hardwick's standing may rest in significant part on Georgia's apparent willingness to enforce against homosexuals a law it seems not to have any desire to enforce against heterosexuals. But his claim that 16-6-2 involves an unconstitutional intrusion into his privacy and his right of intimate association does not depend in any way on his sexual orientation.

Second, I disagree with the Court's refusal to consider whether 16-6-2 runs afoul of the Eighth or Ninth Amendments or the Equal Protection Clause of the Fourteenth Amendment. . . . It is a well-settled principle of law that "a complaint should not be dismissed merely because a plaintiff's allegations do not support the particular legal theory he advances, for the court is under a duty to examine the complaint to determine if the allegations provide for relief on any possible theory." Thus, even if respondent did not advance claims based on the Eighth or Ninth Amendments, or on the Equal Protection Clause, his complaint should not be dismissed if any of those provisions could entitle him to relief. . . . The Court's cramped reading of the issue before it makes for a short opinion, but it does little to make for a persuasive one.

II.

"Our cases long have recognized that the Constitution embodies a promise that a certain private sphere of individual liberty will be kept largely beyond the reach of government." *Thornburgh v. American College of Obstetricians & Gynecologists* (1986). In construing the right to privacy, the Court has proceeded along two somewhat distinct, albeit complementary, lines. First, it has recognized a privacy interest with reference to certain decisions that are properly for the individual to make. E.g., *Roe v. Wade* (1973); *Pierce v. Society of Sisters* (1925). Second, it has recognized a privacy interest with reference to certain places without regard for the particular activities in which the individuals who occupy them are engaged. E.g., *United States v. Karo* (1984); *Payton v. New York* (1980); *Rios v. United States* (1960). The case before us implicates both the decisional and the spatial aspects of the right to privacy.

A. The Court concludes today that none of our prior cases dealing with various decisions that individuals are entitled to make free of governmental interference "bears any resemblance to the claimed constitutional right of homosexuals to engage in acts of sodomy that is asserted in this case." While it is true that these cases may be characterized by their connection to protection of the family, the Court's conclusion that they extend no further than this boundary ignores the warning in *Moore v. East Cleveland* (1977), against "closing our eyes to the basic reasons why certain rights associated with the family have been accorded shelter under the Fourteenth Amendment's Due Process Clause." We protect those rights not because they contribute, in some direct and material way, to the general public welfare, but because they form so central a part of an individual's life. "The concept of privacy embodies the 'moral fact that a person belongs to himself and not others nor to society as a whole.' " *Thornburgh v. American College of Obstetricians & Gynecologists*. And so we protect the decision whether to marry precisely because marriage "is an association that promotes a way of life, not causes; a harmony in living, not political faiths; a bilateral loyalty, not commercial or social projects." *Griswold v. Connecticut*. We protect the decision whether to have a child because parenthood alters so dramatically an individual's self-definition, not because of demographic considerations or the Bible's command to be fruitful and multiply. And we protect the family because it contributes so powerfully to the happiness of individuals, not because of a preference for stereotypical households. The Court recognized in *Roberts*, that the "ability independently to define one's identity that is central to any concept of liberty" cannot truly be exercised in a vacuum; we all depend on the "emotional enrichment from close ties with others."

Only the most willful blindness could obscure the fact that sexual intimacy is "a sensitive, key relationship of human existence, central to family life, community welfare, and the development of human personality," *Paris Adult Theatre I v. Slaton* (1973); see also *Carey v. Population Services International* (1977). The fact that individuals define themselves in a significant way through their intimate sexual relationships with others suggests, in a Nation as diverse as ours, that there may be many "right" ways of conducting those relationships, and that much of the richness of a relationship will come from the freedom an individual has to choose the form and nature of these intensely personal bonds.

In a variety of circumstances we have recognized that a necessary corollary of giving individuals freedom to choose how to conduct their lives is acceptance of the fact that different individuals will make different choices. For example, in holding that the clearly important state interest in public education should give way to a competing claim by the Amish to the effect that extended formal schooling threatened their way of life, the Court declared: "There can be no assumption that today's majority is 'right' and the Amish and others like them are 'wrong.' A way of life that is odd or even erratic but interferes with no rights or interests of others is not to be condemned because it is different." *Wisconsin v. Yoder* (1972). The Court claims that its decision today merely refuses to recognize a fundamental right to engage in homosexual sodomy; what the Court really has refused to recognize is the fundamental interest all individuals have in controlling the nature of their intimate associations with others.

B. The behavior for which Hardwick faces prosecution occurred in his own home, a place to which the Fourth Amendment attaches special significance. The Court's treatment of this aspect of the case is symptomatic of its overall refusal to consider the broad principles that have informed our treatment of privacy in specific cases. Just as the right to privacy is more than the mere aggregation of a number of entitlements to engage in specific behavior, so, too, protecting the physical integrity of the home is more than merely a means of protecting specific activities that often take place there. Even when our understanding of the contours of the right to privacy depends on "reference to a 'place,' " *Katz v. United States*, "the essence of a Fourth Amendment violation is 'not the breaking of doors and the rummaging of his drawers,' but rather is 'the invasion of his indefensible right of personal security, personal liberty and private property.' " *California v. Ciraolo* (1986) quoting *Boyd v. United States* (1886).

The Court's interpretation of the pivotal case of *Stanley v. Georgia* (1969), is entirely unconvincing. *Stanley* held that Georgia's undoubted power to punish the public distribution of constitutionally unprotected, obscene material did not permit the State to punish the private possession of such material. According to the majority here, *Stanley* relied entirely on the First Amendment, and thus, it is claimed, sheds no light on cases not involving printed materials. But that is not what *Stanley* said. Rather, the *Stanley* Court anchored its holding in the Fourth Amendment's special protection for the individual in his home:

> "The makers of our Constitution undertook to secure conditions favorable to the pursuit of happiness. They recognized the significance of man's spiritual nature, of his feelings and of his intellect. They knew that only a part of the pain, pleasure and satisfactions of life are to be found in material things. They sought to protect Americans in their beliefs, their thoughts, their emotions and their sensations." [quoting *Olmstead v. United States*] . . . .

These are the rights that appellant is asserting in the case before us. He is asserting the right to read or observe what he pleases—the right to satisfy his intellectual and emotional needs in the privacy of his own home.

The central place that *Stanley* gives Justice Brandeis' dissent in *Olmstead*, a case raising no First Amendment claim, shows that *Stanley* rested as much on the Court's understanding of the Fourth Amendment as it did on the First. Indeed, in *Paris Adult Theatre I v. Slaton* (1973), the Court suggested that . . . "The right of the people to be secure in their . . . houses," expressly guaranteed by the Fourth Amendment, is perhaps the most "textual" of the various constitutional provisions that inform our understanding of the right to privacy, and thus I cannot agree with the Court's statement that "the right pressed upon us here has no . . . support in the text of the Constitution." Indeed, the right of an individual to conduct intimate relationships in the intimacy of his or her own home seems to me to be the heart of the Constitution's protection of privacy.

III.

The Court's failure to comprehend the magnitude of the liberty interests at stake in this case leads it to slight the question whether petitioner, on behalf of the State, has justified Georgia's infringement on these interests. I believe that neither of the two general justifications for 16-6-2 that petitioner has advanced warrants dismissing respondent's challenge for failure to state a claim.

First, petitioner asserts that the acts made criminal by the statute may have serious adverse consequences for "the general public health and welfare," such as spreading communicable diseases or fostering other criminal activity. Inasmuch as this case was dismissed by the District Court on the pleading, it is not surprising that the record before us is barren of any evidence to support petitioner's claim. In light of the state of the record, I see no justification for the Court's attempt to equate the private, consensual sexual activity at issue here with the "possession in the home of drugs, firearms, or stolen goods," to which *Stanley* refused to extend its protection. None of the behavior so mentioned in *Stanley* can properly be viewed as "victimless." Drugs and weapons are inherently dangerous, see, *McLaughlin v. United States* (1986), and for property to be "stolen," someone must have been wrongfully deprived of it. Nothing in the record before the Court provides any justification for finding the activity forbidden by 16-6-2 to be physically dangerous, either to the persons engaged in it or to others.

The core of petitioner's defense of 16-6-2, however, is that respondent and others who engage in the conduct prohibited by 16-6-2 interfere with Georgia's exercise of the " 'right of the Nation and of the States to maintain a decent society,' " *Paris Adult Theatre I v. Slaton*, quoting *Jacobellis v. Ohio* (1964). Essentially, petitioner argues, and the Court agrees, that the fact that the acts described in 16-6-2 "for hundreds of years, if not thousands, have been uniformly condemned as immoral" is a sufficient reason to permit a State to ban them today.

I cannot agree that either the length of time a majority has held its convictions or the passions with which it defends them can withdraw legislation from this Court's security. See, e.g., *Roe v. Wade* (1973); *Loving v. Virginia* (1967); *Brown v. Board of Education* (1954). As Justice Jackson wrote so eloquently for the Court in *West Virginia Board of Education v. Barnette* (1943), "we apply the limitations of the Constitution with no fear that freedom to be intellectually and spiritually diverse or even contrary will disintegrate the social organization. . . . Freedom to differ is not limited to things that do not matter much. That would be a mere shadow of freedom. The test of its substance is the right to differ as to things that touch the heart of the existing order." It is precisely because the issue raised by this case touches the heart of what makes individuals what they are that we should be especially sensitive to the rights of those whose choices upset the majority.

The assertion that "traditional Judeo-Christian values proscribe" the conduct involved, cannot provide an adequate justification for 16-6-2. That certain, but by no means all, religious groups condemn the behavior at issue gives the State no license to impose their judgments on the entire citizenry. The legitimacy of secular legislation depends instead on whether the State can advance some justification for its law beyond its conformity to religious doctrine. See, e.g., *McGowan v. Maryland* (1961); *Stone v. Graham* (1980). Thus, far from buttressing his case, petitioner's invocation of Leviticus, Romans, Saint Thomas Aquinas, and sodomy's heretical status during the Middle Ages undermines his suggestion that 16-6-2 represents a legitimate use of secular coercive power. A State can no more punish private behavior because of religious intolerance than it can punish such behavior because of racial animus. "The Constitution cannot control such prejudices, but neither can it tolerate them. Private biases may be outside the reach of the law, but the law cannot, directly or indirectly, give them effect." *Palmore v. Sidoti* (1984). No matter how uncomfortable a certain group may make the majority of this Court, we have held that "mere public intolerance or animosity cannot constitutionally justify the deprivation of a person's physical liberty." *O'Connor v. Donaldson* (1975).

Nor can 16-6-2 be justified as a "morally neutral" exercise of Georgia's power to "protect the public environment," *Paris Adult Theatre I*. Certainly, some private behavior can affect the fabric of society as a whole. Reasonable people may differ about whether particular sexual acts are moral or immoral, but "we have ample evidence for believing that people will not abandon morality, will not think any better of murder, cruelty and dishonesty, merely because some private sexual practice which they abominate is not punished by the law." H. L. A. Hart, *Immorality and Treason*, reprinted in *The Law as Literature* (1961). Petitioner and the Court fail to see the difference between laws that protect public sensibilities and those that enforce private morality. Statutes banning public sexual activity are entirely consistent with protecting the individual's liberty interest in decisions concerning sexual relations: the same recognition that those decisions are intensely private which justifies protecting them from governmental interference can justify protecting individuals from unwilling exposure to the sexual activities of others. But the mere fact that intimate behavior may be punished when it takes place in public cannot dictate how States can regulate intimate behavior that occurs in intimate places. . . .

This case involves no real interference with the rights of others, for the mere knowledge that other individuals do not adhere to one's value system cannot be a legally cognizable interest, cf. *Diamond v. Charles* (1986), let alone an interest that can justify invading the houses, hearts, and minds of citizens who choose to live their lives differently.

IV.

It took but three years for the Court to see the error in its analysis in *Minersville School District v. Gobitis* (1940), and to recognize that the threat to national cohesion posed by a refusal to salute the flag was vastly outweighed by the threat to those same values posed by compelling such a salute. See *West Virginia Board of Education v. Barnette* (1943). I can only hope that here, too, the Court soon will reconsider its analysis and conclude that depriving individuals of the right to choose for themselves how to conduct their intimate relationships poses a far greater threat to the values most deeply rooted in our Nation's history than tolerance of nonconformity could ever do. Because I think the Court today betrays those values, I dissent.

31 Puerto Ricans (1961)

Born in 1902 and raised in the Midwest, Langston Hughes moved to New York in 1920 to study at Columbia University. So it was in Harlem that he, like many other African-American artists, developed enduring, effective portraits of everyday life as well as the human condition. After a couple of years in West Africa and Europe (1922–1924), he returned to the United States determined to advance the social and artistic independence of African peoples. Although he well recognized common foibles, he parted company with an older generation by advocating pride in black reality over the promise of eventual "uplift." He was among the very first to extol the point through a modern idiom: "Why should I want to be white? I am a Negro and beautiful."

In service of that vision, he traveled yet more widely and worked in many genres—poetry, autobiography, drama, jazz, blues, short stories, essays, lectures, and editorials. The volume and variety as well as the depth and accessibility of his work help account for his high position in the canon of the Harlem Renaissance. He is often remembered as a voice of the 1920s and 1930s, but he was productive through the 1960s.

Among his most popular creations was the character Jesse B. Semple (also known as "Simple"), a Harlem jokester whom he introduced in 1943 in his column in the *Chicago Defender*, the most influential black newspaper of the first half of the twentieth century. A Southerner-come-North, Simple's plainspoken humor bespoke the incessant injustices that white Americans impose and black Americans endure. His stoop-mate straight man was a sophisticate named Boyd, who would invariably find a more circumspect and hopeful view of the same events. For more than twenty years, the back-and-forth between Simple and Boyd amused millions of readers, speaking powerfully to and of them. It was only in 1965 that Hughes decided that the civil rights movement had rendered such folksy wit obsolete. Here, in a bit taken from one of the five "Best of" collections, Simple identifies a fault that crosses contours of race, language, class, and nationality in the United States.

Neither racism nor the more general conception of "natural" hierarchy, of course, is distinctly American. Credit or blame for the idea can be traced in the West at least back to Aristotle, who imagined that nature assigned each creature to an appropriate rung on the ladder of life. Near the bottom are the archaic and crude (primitive) forms; near the top, the new and refined ones, with humans occupying the very top rung. As Arthur O. Lovejoy observed in his 1936 classic, proponents of "the great chain of being" have periodically added (and then subtracted) yet higher rungs for God, angels, and apostles as well as "lower" and "higher" sorts of humanity. Charles Darwin, his contemporaries, and their descendants made a science out of elaborating the process. In such ways Western peoples have revised and mobilized social hierarchies for myriad purposes. Here, Simple riffs on some American ones.

I was rushing past the newsstand at 125th and Lenox on the way to work this morning when I bought a comic book to read in the subway. When I got on the train and opened it, that book were in some kind of foreign language. I said to the guy beside me, "What's this?"

He said, "*Español!*"

I said, "What?"

He said, "Spanish—for Puerto Ricans."

I said, "Puerto Ricans? Are you one?"

He said, "Sí, are you one, too?"

I said, "I am not! I am just plain old American."

He said, "You—*Negro* American."

I said, "You look just like me, don't you? Who's the darkest, me or you?"

He said, "You, darkest."

I said, "I admit I have an edge on almost anybody. But you are colored, too, daddy-o, don't forget, Puerto Rican or not."

He said, "In my country, no."

"In *my* country, yes," I said. "Here in the U.S.A. you, me—all *colored* folks—are colored."

He said, "*No entiendo.* Don't understand."

I said, "I don't blame you. I wouldn't understand color either if I could talk Spanish. Here, take this comic book in your language which, me—*no entiendo.*"

So I gave him my comic book and went on to work. On the way I kept thinking about what a difference a foreign language makes. Just speak something else and you don't have to be colored in this here

U.S.A.—at least, not as colored as me, born and raised here, and 102 percent American. The Puerto Ricans come up here from the islands and start living all over New York, Chicago, anywhere, where an ordinary American-speaking Negro can't get a foothold, much less a room or an apartment—and the last place a Puerto Rican wants to live is Harlem, because that is colored. So they live uptown, downtown, all around town, the Bronx, Brooklyn, anywhere but with me, unless they can't help it. And do I blame them? I do not! Nobody loves Jim Crow but an idiot, and I am Jim Crowed.

Español! Now that is a language which, if you speak it, will take *some* of the black off of you if you are colored. Just say, *Sí*, and folks will think you are a foreigner, instead of only a plain old ordinary colored American Negro. Don't you remember a few years ago reading about that Negro who put on a turban and went all over the South speaking pig Latin and staying at the best hotels? They thought he was an A-rab, and he wasn't nothing but a Negro. Why does a language, be it pig Latin or Spanish, make all that much difference?

I have been in this country speaking English all my life, daddy-o, yet and still if I walk in some of them rich restaurants downtown, they look at me like I was a varmint. But let somebody darker than me come in there speaking Spanish or French or Afangulo and the head-waiter will bow plumb down to the ground. I wonder why my mama did not bear me in Cuba instead of in Virginia? Had she did so, I would walk right up to the White Sulphur Springs Hotel now and engage me a room, dark though I be, and there would not be a white man in Dixie say a word. But just let *me* enter and say in English, "I would like a reservation."

The desk clerk would say to me, "Negro, are you crazy?"

I would say, "No, I am not crazy. I am just American."

He would say, "American though you be, you will never sleep in here. This hotel is for white folks."

Then I would say, "You ought to be ashamed of yourself, drawing the color line in Virginia where Thomas Jefferson was born, in this day and age of such great democracy."

Whereupon he would call the manager, who would say, "You better get out of here before I have you arrested for disturbing the peace."

I would say, "What kind of peace are you talking about? That is the trouble with you white folks, always wanting peace, and I ain't got no privileges. You are always keeping the best of everything for yourself. All the peace is on your side."

Then the old head desk clerk would say, "Get out of here before I call the law." And the manager would reach for the phone.

Whereupon I would pull my Spanish on him. I would say, "*No entiendo.*"

Then they would both get all red in the face and say, "Oh, I beg your pardon! Are you Spanish?"

But by that time I would be mad, so I would say, "I will not accept a room here." And walk stalking out. I would say, "Where I cannot spend my money if I speak American, I will *not* if I speak Spanish. You white folks act right simple. Good-by!" I would leave them with their mouths wide open. "*Adios!*"

Then, if I was an artist, I would put all that into a comic book. I wonder why somebody don't make comic books out of the funny way white folks in America behave—talking democracy out of one side of their mouth and, "Negro, stay in your place," out of the other. I wish I could draw, I would make me such a book. I would start a whole series of comics which I bet would sell a million copies—*Jess Simple's Jim Crow Jive*, would be the title. I would make my books in both English and Spanish so the Puerto Ricans could laugh, too. Because it must tickle them to see what a little foreignness will do. Just be foreign— then you don't have to be colored.

ANA LYDIA VEGA

32 Wrestling with the Hard One (1994)

Many people in the United States got their first glimpse of Puerto Ricans as "the Sharks" in the movie, *West Side Story* (1961). They were "misunderstood" members of a street gang (plus "chicks") who would now and then break out in Spanglish song and dance for Leonard Bernstein's orchestra. The film was actually set in New York, not the Caribbean. It was adapted from a Broadway musical (1959) that was based on Shakespeare's *Romeo and Juliet*, set in an Italian city ("fair Verona") three hundred years ago. Many of the New York street scenes were actually shot on a sound stage. Anglos played most Latino roles (for example, Natalie Wood—née Natasha Nikolaevna Gurdin—as María) with bogus accents and in bizarre clothes. Hence, it is a little surprising that mainstream critics touted the film's realism. It is a judgment that makes sense only in light of Cold War television fables such as *Leave It to Beaver* (1957–1963). When the film (*Don't Leave It to Bernardo?*) reached San Juan, residents picketed their local theaters.

In hindsight, at least, the movie turns surreal even at its forthright best. In a song-and-dance number, for example, twenty-five-year-old *niñas* and *niños* spar in rhyme:

Anita: Puerto Rico, my heart's devotion—let it sink back in the ocean.
... I like the island of Manhattan, smoke on your pipe and put that in!
Girls: I like to be in America, OK by me in America. . . .
Anita: Life can be bright in America
Boys: If you can fight in America
Girls: Life is all right in America

Boys:	If you're all white in America
Girls:	Here you are free and you have pride
Boys:	Long as you stay on your own side
Girls:	Free to be anything you choose
Boys:	Free to wait tables and shine shoes

The girls, fans of assimilation, gain credibility through their leader, Anita. She is masterfully played by Rita Moreno, who was born Rosa Dolores Alverio in Humacao, Puerto Rico. Granted, she was better known for posing as Mexican or Indian, or even as a Thai princess in *The King and I* (1956). The boys, defenders of Puerto Rico, however, follow a leader (Bernardo) played by George Chakiris, whose real-life migrations began in Ohio and whose parents were Greek. And everyone begs the more fundamental question: Isn't Puerto Rico *in* "America," anyway?

The United States gained sovereignty over Puerto Rico by invading it in the Spanish-American War. The Paris Treaty of 1898 rescinded the right to self-rule that the islands had just won from Spain. By the Jones Act (1917, later amended), Puerto Rico became a U.S. territory ("organized but unincorporated," in other words, a colony), which it remained until becoming a commonwealth with its own constitution in 1952. So, Puerto Ricans have been Americans for at least a century but—per *Balzac v. Porto Rico* (1922)—an act of Congress rather than the Constitution is the source of their civil rights.

Hence, too, Puerto Ricans are second-class citizens. They have been exempted, for instance, from U.S. minimum-wage, health, and safety protections. They cannot vote in U.S. presidential elections, nor can their representatives vote in Congress. Their governor was only first elected (versus appointed) in 1948. Among the privileges gained earliest by islanders was the capacity to risk their lives for the U.S. Army. Hundreds rallied to reject the offer, but thousands served under U.S. command during World War I. Nevertheless, U.S. citizenship was officially downplayed until 1940, when Puerto Ricans as well as U.S. bases on Culebra and Vieques were needed for another world war. Puerto Ricans have consistently objected to the environmental and public health fallout of the Navy's practice assaults on their land. Of course, islanders might also welcome their freedom from the Internal Revenue Service, but most also resent their limited ability to affect the national government that they otherwise serve.

Movements for independence—first from Spain and then the United States—date from the beginning of the nineteenth century. After the U.S. invasion, the Partido Unionista and other major political parties featured self-rule planks. Bold protests and brutal repression ensued (for example, massacres at Rio Piedras and Ponce in the 1930s) that made martyrs of such nationalists as Elias Beauchamp, Pedro Albizu Campos, Juan Antonio Corretjer, Hiram Rosado, and Clemente Soto Vélez. Subsequent drives for greater autonomy or for statehood have intensified. But since the mid-1980s, voters—albeit in nonbinding plebiscites, by ever-slimmer margins, bloated by dependence—have consistently clung to their commonwealth status.

Plainly, in the bulk of its institutions and sentiments, Puerto Rico is as "American" as New York City, and millions of people literally belong to both. Large migrations from one to the other began in the mid-1940s and peaked in the 1950s. Well before *West Side Story* premiered, migrants had reared an entire generation whose connections to the islands were often both more intense and more abstract than their own. For example, many of them knew the Caribbean either as a mythical homeland, a paradise of the imagination, or through once-a-year visits rather than residence. Some of these migrants began to feel more comfortable in English than Spanish and estranged from everyday life on the islands. There are now almost as many people of Puerto Rican origin living on the mainland (about 3 million) as there are in Puerto Rico itself (4 million), and there are more than twice as many residing in New York City as in San Juan.

Given such long experience with colonialism and migration, it is tough to fix Puerto Rican relations to America precisely. Here professor and award-winning writer Ana Lydia Vega explores childhood moments of contact and separation.

In 1952, the lone-star flag of Puerto Rico, which until that moment had been the symbol of a clandestine independence movement, flew up into the sky for the official celebration of our brand-new neo-colonial status. It did not, of course, fly alone. Right beside it was its inevitable companion since the beginning of the twentieth century: Old Glory, the American flag, better known in the island as "la pecosa" (the freckled one) because of its many stars.

That was also the year I went to school for the first time. Like many couples who had migrated from the country to San Juan, the capital of Puerto Rico, my parents worked very hard so as to be able to send their children to an American Catholic school. Their goal was not so much to put us on the way to salvation through a religious education as to save us from the fatality of underdevelopment by having us learn English most religiously. That is how I finally found myself one day sitting in the middle of a stern-looking classroom in my shamrock-green uniform and my little white blouse.

The nuns, mostly of Irish-American descent, set themselves to the ungrateful task of converting us into nice little American citizens. Each morning, we piously sang the O-say-can-you-see gospel song and we pledged allegiance to the freckled flag of the Union, hand over heart and all. English was, naturally, the language our classes were conducted in. We had to speak it at all times, even to seek permission to go to the rest rooms or else face ridicule by wetting our pants in public. Is it then surprising that we, the spoiled children of colonialism, developed from childhood to adolescence a passionate and conflictive love/hate relationship with the language our people have christened, in fearful and reverent awe, "el difícil," the hard one?

When third grade came around, we had already mastered the Pavlovian reflexes of basic English that would help us survive the nuns' dictatorship. Imported textbooks and attitudes were rapidly creating in our little heads an alien world distinctly separate from the one we lived in at home. In my family's wooden Santurce house, my father, a self-taught country bard, improvised verses in Spanish and would not even let us call him "Papi" because it sounded too much like English to his purist ear. At school, on the other hand, it was absolutely forbidden to lapse into Spanish when some elusive English word escaped our memory. Little by little, English was gaining in our eyes the prestige of a code that stood for progress and modernity while Spanish was more and more relegated to the spheres of the domestic and the outdated. All the technical, scientific and literary vocabulary referring to the most diverse aspects of knowledge, we naturally learned in English. I clearly remember that when I was admitted to the University of Puerto Rico, very often I had to run to the dictionary in search of math and science terms or the names of some historical figure or exotic country, for all of which I did not know the Spanish word.

The lexical gaps were embarrassing enough but they were not the worst part of it. The most insidious thing was rather the double standard that had been subtly infiltrated into our circulatory system. We were profoundly, and, of course, unconsciously convinced that English would give us access to the Great Conquests of Western Civilization while Spanish tied us irremediably to backwardness and vulgarity. It was an intimate conviction like that of the existence of God which was never questioned or even put into words. English was, like the Catholic religion that was also hammered into our heads from childhood, a password to Heaven.

So greetings for any special occasion had to be in English. Sending someone you loved a melodramatic poem in the language of Latin soap-operas was definitely not the same as expressing your feelings through a brief, discreet and sophisticated message in the language of Perry Como. And even more so if the Spanish words' blatant sentimentalism was accompanied by a strident display of bleeding hearts over violet velvet flowers. Even American kitsch had more savoir-faire than Spanish chic. Hallmark had surreptitiously established its gentle monopoly over our newborn Puerto Rican middle-class sensibility.

The same was true of our movie preferences. Those Mexican films starring Chachita and Pedro Armendáriz we watched every afternoon on television were, to our colonized eyes, the absolute incarnation of Latin vulgarity. And while we secretly cried our eyes out with Pedro Infante and Dolores del Río's tragic love affairs or laughed to death before the hilarious adventures of Cantinflas or Tintán, we would never confess such degrading faux-pas to our school friends who, undoubtedly, shared our sinful delights and also kept quiet.

My generation's role models were Elvis Presley, Pat Boone and Gidget. Rock and roll turned us away from the traditional bolero songs soaked in the Latin American ideology of passionate love. My older sister, who went to a Puerto Rican public school and whose childhood was less subjected to the process of Americanization, sighed over singers like Tito Lara and Edmundo Disdier, all of which left me dry-eyed and skeptical for I was only moved to tears by Ricky Nelson, Neil Sedaka or Paul Anka.

The most picturesque part of all this was the code-switching which made us leap, in one phrase, from the cultural universe of our daily lives to the trans-cultural universe of our education. The word grafts we had to create responded in most cases to a desperate search for concepts that would reflect the changing reality of our new habits and tastes and the vertiginous modernity of our aspirations. Saying "my date" sounded, for instance, freer and more modern than saying "mi novio" (my fiancé), a word that reeked of chaperones and engagement rings. And when we had to tackle thorny subjects like sex, it was much more civilized to speak of a "French kiss" than to use the Spanish expression "beso de lengua" (tongue-kiss), which sounded so very gross. And who would not prefer to be called a square or a nerd than to be forever offended by such a strong insult as our own "pendejo"? Yes, it was evident that the times of the Spanish empire in which our parents still seemed to live were now a thing of the past.

There were, of course, small crevasses in the process of linguistic and cultural colonization we were undergoing. Even those fervent missionaries of American civilization that were the Dominican nuns in my school could not control every single detail. Their Irish-American nationalism would unexpectedly barge in, unrestrained, on the 17th day of March each year, when they would make us wear shamrocks and sing the whole repertory of patriotic Irish ballads in the style of "Galway Bay," "Oh Danny Boy" and "When Irish Eyes Are Smiling." And although they did everything they possibly could to smother our own Puerto Rican nationalism, they also made us vibrate with anti-British passion while we sang with tears in our eyes:

And the strangers came and tried to teach us their ways
And scorned us just for being what we are,
But they might as well go chasing after moonbeams
Or light a penny-candle from a star.

Time and experience have led me to understand, after so many years, that we private American Catholic school students in Puerto Rico were the avant-garde guinea pigs of a quietly violent de-Puertoricanization process. We suffered the concentrated and accelerated effects of the deformation our country would be gradually going through. We were being prepared for a great destiny: after our college studies, which would most likely take place in the United States, we were to become a part of the ruling pro-American elite of Puerto Rico that would defend against all odds the USA's economical interests in Latin America. In many cases, as was to be expected, the project was a complete success. In others, by producing a deep-seated sense of rebellion, it failed almost miraculously.

"Well," says my mother sternly whenever I broach that rather risqué subject during family reunions, "at least you learned some English!"

ANDY WARHOL

33 POPism (1975)

Since its inception, America seemed distinctly prone to cross commercialism. Regardless of education or rank, anybody supposedly could buy almost anything. Given also the association of refinement with aristocracy, republicans could be expected to rush headlong only toward mediocrity. With the advance of mass marketing, the guardians of culture had yet more reason to worry: How could the fine arts survive?

Through the 1940s this fear of a mind-numbing, common-denominating "mass culture" was equally at home on the left and on the right. Whether the problem was supply or demand—rules rigged by corporate moguls or the pathetic tastes of the great unwashed—the cultural consequence would be the same, and it would be ugly.

But in the 1950s, as the United States mounted a strident self-defense, the arts seemed refreshingly free of central (Soviet-style) control. America's mass culture was "democratic." Among the scholars who best articulated this view was Daniel Bell. In *The End of Ideology* (1960) he prophesied the flowering of a freer and more diverse public culture—at least in the heart and mind of each beholder, even if it seemed tacky to almost everyone else.

At about the same moment, British, Continental, and, especially, American artists themselves began to find great potential in mass-market schlock. The champion of that movement was Andy Warhol (1937–1987), who began his career as a commercial designer and called his studio "the factory." The movement might best be appreciated as a healthy correction to the earnest indulgences of its predecessor, Abstract Expressionism. But it was also part of a kinky love affair with America.

Traveling cross-country around 1960, Warhol had a realization:

The farther west we drove, the more Pop everything looked on the highways. Suddenly we all felt like insiders because even though Pop was everywhere—that was the thing about it, most people still took it for granted, whereas we were dazzled by it—to us, it was the new Art. Once you "got" Pop, you could never see a sign the same way again. And once you thought Pop, you could never see America the same way again.

Unlike conventional art, Pop was anything but "serious," subtle, universal, original, or inspiring. Instead, Warhol and his contemporaries (such as

Jasper Johns, Roy Lichtenstein, Claes Oldenburg, James Rosenquist, and Tom Wesselmann) made copies—literal, unadorned representations—of "vacant and vacuous" objects in flat, primary colors. Among their first creations were immense blow-ups of banal cartoons. But they quickly shifted focus to more ubiquitous and commercial icons: brand-name foods, movie stars, billboards. Reproductions of Warhol's "Campbell's Soup Can" (1965) became almost as common as the cans themselves.

Such work seemed to invite a viewer to stare blankly, as if free of affect or, in perfectly equal measures, horrified and amused. The feeling was intensified through the repetition of images (as in "192 One-dollar Bills" or "210 Coca-Cola Bottles") whereby the print might itself resemble a heap of commodities. Pop Art performers staged "happenings" that were proudly devoid of honesty, coherence, and meaning. Mockery and self-mockery became so densely entangled that the movement soon seemed as mannerist as its snooty detractors.

By the time the Museum of Modern Art paid about $10 million for "200 Soup Cans," it became hard to distinguish the parodies from their subjects. Patrons began to prize Pop images, not as new or insightful, but as nostalgic kitsch in their own right. As early as the mid-1970s, Pop Art was becoming passé in America, but the layers of irony continued to multiply in the aisles of Wal-Mart and outside the United States.

The following is a bit of Pop philosophy in the offhand manner that Warhol helped popularize. As he justifies his sense of wonder in America, he ridicules both mass-culture anxiety and democratic sanctimony.

What's great about this country is that America started the tradition where the richest consumers buy essentially the same things as the poorest. You can be watching TV and see Coca-Cola, and you can know that the President drinks Coke, Liz Taylor drinks Coke, and just think, you can drink Coke, too. A Coke is a Coke and no amount of money can get you a better Coke than the one the bum on the corner is drinking. All the Cokes are the same and all the Cokes are good. Liz Taylor knows it, the President knows it, the bum knows it, and you know it.

In Europe the royalty and the aristocracy used to eat a lot better than the peasants—they weren't eating the same things at all. It was either partridge or porridge, and each class stuck to its own food. But when Queen Elizabeth came here and President Eisenhower bought her a hot dog, I'm sure he felt confident that she couldn't have had delivered to Buckingham Palace a better hot dog than that one he bought her for maybe twenty cents at the ballpark. Because there *is* no better hot dog than a ballpark hot dog. Not for a dollar, not for ten dollars, not for a hundred thousand dollars could she get a better hot dog. She could get one for twenty cents and so could anybody else.

Sometimes you fantasize that people who are really up-there and rich and living it up have something you don't have, that their things must be better than your things because they have more money than you. But they drink the same Cokes and eat the same hot dogs and wear the same ILGWU clothes and see the same TV shows and the same movies. Rich people can't see a sillier version of *Truth or Consequences* or a scarier version of *The Exorcist*. You can get just as revolted as they can—you can have the same nightmares. All of this is really American.

Five Coke Bottles, Andy Warhol, 1962

"Give and Take," Say I, and *"Cheers,"* Haddon Sundblom, 1937 and 1944.

The United States has been the world's top promoter of Christmas commerce. But trade in images of Saint Nicholas, the "father" of the holiday, can also be traced back to the Christ child himself (*Christkindl*, the German root of the English "Kris Kringle"). For centuries Western stories, poems, and pictures depicted *Père Noël* variously as a phantom or visitor in disguise, tiny or tall, gaunt or plump, a source of fright or delight. The most popular variant came from Asia Minor (home of the Bishop of Myra, né Nicholas in 270) through the Port of New York/New Amsterdam, a millennium and a half later. English speakers dubbed that figure—the Dutch *Sinterklaas*—"Santa Claus." He gained most of his trademark accouterments in U.S. commerce after the Civil War: his white whiskers, red suit and cheeks, sleigh, reindeer, Mrs. Claus and the elves, and a North Pole facility as well as a fondness for chimneys, stockings, and "Ho, Ho, Ho!" His appearance was finally standardized through the artistry of The Coca-Cola Company, particularly their illustrator Haddon Sundblom, whose "friendlier and more human" images of Santa began gracing Coke ads and paraphernalia in 1931. His inspirations included Clement Clarke Moore's 1822 poem, "A Visit from Saint Nicholas" (" 'Twas the night before Christmas . . . ") and a globeful of newfound markets.

Publicity Poster for *A Great Wall: An American Comedy Made in China*, 1986

In 1949, after more than a century of interaction, the peoples of the world's most populous and prosperous nations, China and the United States, stopped communicating. Mistrust was intense. It peaked during the Korean War (1950–1953) and has yet fully to recover. But in 1972 representatives of the two governments (including Richard Nixon, Henry Kissinger, Deng Xiaoping, and Zhou Enlai) agreed to some tentative exchanges. They began in soft media (for example, sports, which provided the strategy's name, "Ping-Pong diplomacy") and a few commodities (for example, pandas and Coca-Cola). A Beijing-born director, Peter Wang, and a San Franciscan producer, Shirley Sun, were the first to respond through a feature-length fiction film. It was shot on location in the two countries with English and Mandarin dialogue. The plot follows a reunion between Chinese and their Chinese-American kin, exploring the differences that America presumably made. Appropriately enough, the climax features a Ping-Pong match between rival suitors for a Chinese girl's affections. (This bit of artistic license helps account for the suppression of the film in China, where such fraternization was illegal.) The Chinese-American suitor (Paul) is beefy and spoiled, albeit with some of the charm recognizable among China's first-born sons. Beijingers could hope he was educable. His unhyphenated counterpart (Liu) is the unflappable underdog, slight in build and a bit dull of mind, though sharp enough to be able to recite "The Gettysburg Address" in Chinglish. A viewer's first sight of the newly "open" Beijing comes as Liu chugs an oversweet and overpriced but oh-so-chic bottle of Coke.

Great Castigation Series: Coca-Cola, Wang Guangyi, 1993

Chinese artist Wang Guangyi was born in the remote northern city of Harbin in 1956, when contact with the West was nearly nil. He came of age during the Cultural Revolution (1966–1976), when even vaguely alien vestiges were purged. But Wang now lives and works in Beijing, a vibrant capital for intellectuals, government, and business representatives around the world. This image from his "Great Castigation Series" is a premier example of a style sometimes called "Political Pop Art." Works in this mode date from the 1980s, when foreign influence and domestic self-criticism were on the rise. They juxtapose political and commercial imagery with a result that differs markedly from Western precedent but that remains accessible within as well as outside China.

34 | An Okie from Muskogee (1969)

Modern country and western music in America, as likely as not, is composed by a team of conservatory graduates in New York City, recorded by engineers in Nashville, and distributed by a Japanese company with the help of Los Angeles MBAs. But its history, themes, and tones recall an old or at least acoustic, rural South. Before World War II, the Grand Ole Opry, synthesizers, and radio mass marketing, it was called hillbilly music. The instrumentation and lyrics were simple and direct. Its performers plied a distinctly local circuit and they evoked scenes and sentiments of everyday life: hope and despair, hard work and play, love and loneliness among just plain, generally white, rural or small-town folks. In "new country music," references to eighteen-wheelers or pick-ups outnumber anything horse-drawn and protagonists no longer hoe cotton, but the pedigree remains easy to detect.

Since the mid-1950s, and especially since the 1980s, country and western performers' ham-handed humility, sequined costumes, and schmaltzy productions have had predictable effects. Their music has become accessible to more people and easier to dismiss because of its accessibility.

To jazz fans eager for improvisation, folkies who idealize authenticity, or rockers who await some "edge," the music sounds pat and flat. Such real or anticipated snubs, with their ready class and race allusions, can actually lend allure to the music for proudly working-class whites. Yet other fans can join in to express solidarity with them and opposition to a prissy, artsy, liberal or leftist urban bourgeoisie. In this way, country and western music has long been a popular front in battles over the promise of American life.

Merle Haggard launched one of the most blatant of such skirmishes in the heyday of the 1960s. To the yahoos of concert and radio fans, "Okie from Muskogee" neatly opposed the accouterment of the counterculture and small-town patriots. In 1969 it earned Academy of Country Music awards for single and song of the year. It also became the battle hymn of the cultural right.

Almost immediately, bands of the cultural left launched mocking counters (for example, the Youngbloods in "Hippie from Olema"). But others found it effective to take a self-confident, self-mocking higher ground. One of the most famous performances of "Okie from Muskogee" was not by Merle Haggard down at the courthouse, but by the Grateful Dead, live at the Fillmore East in New York City, on April 27, 1971. With a sense of humor, the same battle hymn could serve either side.

Generally forgotten in this subcultural scuffle is the fact that Muskogee's first courthouse was Indian. The Oklahoma town got its name from the confederation of Creek peoples (whom European settlers dubbed "Muscogee"). They were "livin' right" in the southeastern quarter of North America for at least four hundred years before hippies and Haggard's drinking buddies were born.

We don't smoke marijuana in Muskogee;
We don't take our trips on LSD;
We don't burn our draft cards down on Main Street;
We like livin' right, and bein' free.

We don't make a party out of lovin';
We like holdin' hands and pitchin' woo;
We don't let our hair grow long and shaggy,
Like the hippies out in San Francisco do.

I'm proud to be an Okie from Muskogee,
A place where even squares can have a ball.
We still wave Old Glory down at the courthouse,
And white lightnin's still the biggest thrill of all.

Leather boots are still in style for manly footwear;
Beads and Roman sandals won't be seen.
Football's still the roughest thing on campus,
And the kids here still respect the college dean.

And I'm proud to be an Okie from Muskogee,
A place where even squares can have a ball.
We still wave Old Glory down at the courthouse,
And white lightnin's still the biggest thrill of all.

We still wave Old Glory down at the courthouse,
In Muskogee, Oklahoma, USA.

IRIS DeMENT

35 Wasteland of the Free (1996)

Iris DeMent was among the singer/songwriters whose music overflowed the categories of studios, producers, distributors, and charts in the 1990s. Her origins were solidly "country." In 1961 she was the last of fourteen children born to a God-fearing Arkansas family. Although pushed first from farm to factory town and then to college and the city, her music remained hitched to rural, Southern gospel tradition. But her early sound—personal, simple, and spare—soon shifted to accommodate rock influences. Her lyrics became political and fierce enough to scare "country radio." "Wasteland of the Free" was even a bit hot for such liberal, urbane venues as National Public Radio (NPR). That song was, for example, on the "inappropriate" play list that Rep. John Grant cited in his initiative to withhold Florida funding for the NPR affiliate, WMNF.

Among DeMent's allusions here are fund-raising scandals of President Clinton's 1996 reelection campaign, televangelists of the Christian right, the 1990 U.S. war against Iraq, World War II, and the 1922 poem, "The Waste Land," by the Missouri-born British poet, T. S. Eliot.

We got preachers dealing in politics and diamond mines,
And their speech is growing increasingly unkind.
They say they are Christ's disciples,
But they don't look like Jesus to me.
And it feels like I am living in the wasteland of the free.

We got politicians running races on corporate cash.
Now don't tell me they don't turn around and
    kiss them peoples' ass.
You may call me old-fashioned,

But that don't fit my picture of a true democracy.
And it feels like I am living in the wasteland of the free.

We got CEOs making two hundred times the workers' pay,
But they'll fight like hell against raising the minimum wage.
And if you don't like it, mister, they'll ship your job
To some third-world country 'cross the sea.
And it feels like I am living in the wasteland of the free.

Living in the wasteland of the free,
Where the poor have now become the enemy.
"Let's blame our troubles on the weak ones"—
Sounds like some kind of Hitler remedy.
Living in the wasteland of the free.

We got little kids with guns fighting inner city wars.
So what do we do? We put these little kids behind prison doors.
And we call ourselves the advanced civilization.
That sounds like crap to me.
And it feels like I am living in the wasteland of the free.

We got high-school kids running 'round in Calvin Klein and
Guess
Who cannot pass a sixth-grade reading test.
But if you ask them, they can tell you
The name of every crotch on MTV.
And it feels like I am living in the wasteland of the free.

We kill for oil; then we throw a party when we win.
Some guy refuses to fight, and we call that the sin.
But he's standing up for what he believes in,
And that seems pretty damned American to me.
And it feels like I am living in the wasteland of the free.

Living in the wasteland of the free,
Where the poor have now become the enemy.
"Let's blame our troubles on the weak ones"—
Sounds like some kind of Hitler remedy.
Living in the wasteland of the free.

While we sit gloating in our greatness,
Justice is sinking to the bottom of the sea.
Living in the wasteland of the free,
Living in the wasteland of the free,
Living in the wasteland of the free.

W. E. B. DuBois

36 Of Our Spiritual Strivings (1903)

In an era of strict racial segregation and lynching of "people like him," W. E. B. DuBois gained credentials from two of the top universities in the nation, one black (Fisk, B.A., 1888) and the other white (Harvard, Ph.D., 1895). His work thereafter spanned many conventional divides—between social science and the humanities, monograph and verse, commentary and advocacy, elite and populist, and, maybe most of all, African and American.

His doctoral dissertation and first book, *The Suppression of the African Slave Trade to the United States of America, 1638–1870*, can be easily categorized as "history," but the departments in which he was a professor (chiefly at Atlanta University) were also named "economics" and "sociology." Scholars from a larger number of disciplines join in praise of his second monograph, *The Philadelphia Negro* (1899), one of the first works to unite documentary and field research via case study and the very first on a black community in America. His most popular book, *The Souls of Black Folk*, seems to defy disciplinary categories altogether.

Outside of academia, he was better known as a leader of the Niagara Movement, which promoted racial integration in the United States. He was among the founders of its chief organization, the National Association for the Advancement of Colored People (NAACP) in 1909. As its director of research and editor of publications (including *Horizon*, later *Crisis*) for several decades, DuBois came to represent a strong, largely middle-class and biracial alternative to the more accommodationist policies of Booker T. Washington.

The bitter disagreement between DuBois and Washington remains infamous. Through the 1910s and 1920s, for example, DuBois insisted that integration was a necessary means of achieving equality, while Washington more often considered it a consequence. For leadership in that effort, DuBois advocated an elite squad of agitators ("the talented tenth"), while Washington credited a battalion of bootstrapping workers. Their difference is well symbolized by the pair of black schools with which they were associated:

the liberal-arts-oriented Fisk University, where DuBois first experienced the South, versus the more vocation-oriented Tuskegee Institute, where Washington was a founder and the first president. The difference is also obvious in their contemporary classics, particularly Washington's *Up from Slavery* (1901) versus DuBois's *Souls of Black Folk* (1903).

These examples, though, probably overstate the difference. They obviously allied in opposition to racism and shared a commitment to public service and formal education. Both took sustenance from what they took to be the distinct spiritual strength of African-American peoples. In flexing it to fight white supremacy, they in effect collaborated. As Houston Baker explains, their disputes helped establish a broad strain of "Afro-American modernism," Baker's term for their common aim and mode. Their dispute was more a matter of strategy, the particular way they turned forms of subjection into instruments of resistance. Washington worked through "mastery of the form" (like a trickster, coyly turning strength back on oppressors); DuBois, through "the deformation of mastery" (like a rebel, changing the rules of engagement). Both of them deserve credit for developing and popularizing a matched set of modernist moves.

Furthermore, over the course of his career DuBois was hardly single-minded. For example, while advancing a U.S.-centered, integrationist agenda, he was also pioneering Pan-Africanism, a movement for global solidarity among African peoples. He helped organize the first Pan-African Conference in London in 1900 as well as subsequent congresses through the 1920s. By the 1930s, contrary to the "anti-Washington" scenario, his commitment to varieties of separatist, proletarian self-determination—black nationalism, black enterprise, and socialism—had so intensified that he joined those who bashed the NAACP for neglecting "the black masses." From 1934 to 1944 he felt compelled to leave the organization and returned only briefly (1944–1948) before he again decided that it was too bourgeois. When persecuted for pro-Soviet, Communist sympathies in the 1950s, DuBois defended himself as a loyal American. For example, he was indicted as an unregistered alien agent but fought for and won an acquittal in 1951. Nevertheless, DuBois eventually renounced his U.S. citizenship and moved to Ghana, where he legally "became African" just before his death in 1963. In light of this long, complex career and his thousands of political and editorial decisions, DuBois should hardly be defined by his rivalry with another African American.

Probably the one idea of his that is most familiar to modern Americanists is the one that goes by the name of "double-consciousness." That term, too, has gone through some twists and turns. For example, some Americanists now use it to refer to a wide range of thoughts that are hitched to an even wider array of "subaltern" experiences: occasioned by race, gender, sexuality, ethnicity, class, body type, age, faith, ideology, region, etc. Some argue that "double-consciousness" is a privileged sort of epistemology, a "standpoint" for seeing social reality more clearly. While it is a credit to DuBois's work that his ideas should be so extended, it is also worth trying to preserve some of the subtlety and specificity of his original. The consciousness of which he wrote, for example, was both "double" and "veiled," powerful but not necessarily empowering. Moreover, he insisted that these ideas were grounded in very particular black American experiences, including his own.

O water, voice of my heart, crying in the sand,
 All night long crying with a mournful cry,
 As I lie and listen, and cannot understand
 The voice of my heart in my side or the voice of the sea,
 O water, crying for rest, is it I, is it I?
 All night long the water is crying to me.

Unresting water, there shall never be rest
 Till the last moon droop and the last tide fail,
 And the fire of the end begin to burn in the west;
 And the heart shall be weary and wonder and cry like the sea,
 All life long crying without avail,
 As the water all night long is crying to me.

—Arthur Symons

Between me and the other world there is ever an unasked question: unasked by some through feelings of delicacy, by others through the difficulty of rightly framing it. All, nevertheless, flutter round it. They approach me in a half-hesitant sort of way, eye me curiously or compassionately, and then, instead of saying directly, How does it feel to be a problem? they say, I know an excellent colored man in my town; or, I fought at Mechanicsville; or, Do not these Southern outrages make your blood boil? At these I smile, or am interested, or reduce the boiling to a simmer, as the occasion may require. To the real question, How does it feel to be a problem? I answer seldom a word.

And yet, being a problem is a strange experience—peculiar even for one who has never been anything else, save perhaps in babyhood and in Europe. It is in the early days of rollicking boyhood that the revelation first bursts upon one, all in a day, as it were. I remember well when the shadow swept across me. I was a little thing, away up in the hills of New England, where the dark Housatonic winds between Hoosac and Taghkanic to the sea. In a wee wooden schoolhouse, something put it into the boys' and girls' heads to buy gorgeous visiting cards—ten cents a package—and exchange. The exchange was merry, till one girl, a tall newcomer, refused my card—refused it peremptorily, with a glance. Then it dawned upon me with a certain suddenness that I was different from the others; or like, mayhap, in heart and life and longing, but shut out from their world by a vast veil. I had thereafter no desire to tear down that veil, to creep through; I held all beyond it in common contempt, and lived above it in a region of blue sky and great wandering shadows. That sky was bluest when I could beat my mates at examination-time, or beat them at a foot race, or even beat their stringy heads. Alas, with the years all this fine contempt began to fade; for the words I longed for, and all their dazzling opportunities, were theirs, not mine. But they should not keep these prizes, I said; some, all, I would wrest from them. Just how I would do it I could never decide: by reading law, by healing the sick, by telling the wonderful tales that swam in my head—some way. With other black boys the strife was not so fiercely sunny: their youth shrunk into tasteless sycophancy, or into silent hatred of the pale world about them and mocking distrust of everything white; or wasted itself in a bitter cry, Why did God make me an outcast and a stranger in mine own house? The shades of the prison house closed round about us all: walls strait and stubborn to the whitest, but relentlessly narrow, tall, and unscalable to sons of night who must plod darkly on in resignation, or beat unavailing palms against the stone, or steadily, half hopelessly, watch the streak of blue above.

After the Egyptian and Indian, the Greek and Roman, the Teuton and Mongolian, the Negro is a sort of seventh son, born with a veil, and gifted with second-sight in this American world—a world which yields him no true self-consciousness, but only lets him see himself through the revelation of the other world. It is a peculiar sensation, this double-consciousness, this sense of always looking at one's self through the eyes of others, of measuring one's soul by the tape of a world that looks on in amused contempt and pity. One ever feels his twoness—an American, a Negro; two souls, two thoughts, two unreconciled strivings; two warring ideals in one dark body, whose dogged strength alone keeps it from being torn asunder.

The history of the American Negro is the history of this strife—this longing to attain self-conscious manhood, to merge his double self into a better and truer self. In this merging he wishes neither of the older selves to be lost. He would not Africanize America, for America has too much to teach the world and Africa. He would not bleach his Negro soul in a flood of white Americanism, for he knows that Negro blood has a message for the world. He simply wishes to make it possible for a man to be both a Negro and an American, without being cursed and spit upon by his fellows, without having the doors of Opportunity closed roughly in his face.

This, then, is the end of his striving: to be a co-worker in the kingdom of culture, to escape both death and isolation, to husband and use his best powers and his latent genius. These powers of body and mind have in the past been strangely wasted, dispersed, or forgotten. The shadow of a mighty Negro past flits through the tale of Ethiopia the Shadowy and of Egypt the Sphinx. Through history, the powers of single black men flash here and there like falling stars, and die sometimes before the world has rightly gauged their brightness. Here in America, in the few days since Emancipation, the black man's turning hither and thither in hesitant and doubtful striving has often made his very strength to lose effectiveness, to seem like absence of power, like weakness. And yet it is not weakness—it is the contradiction of double aims. The double-aimed struggle of the black artisan—on the one hand to escape white contempt for a nation of mere hewers of wood and drawers of water, and on the other hand to plough and nail and dig for a poverty-stricken horde—could only result in making him a poor craftsman, for he had but half a heart in either cause. By the poverty and ignorance of his people, the Negro minister or doctor was tempted toward quackery and demagogy; and by the criticism of the other world, toward ideals that made him ashamed of his lowly tasks. The would-be black savant was confronted by the paradox that the knowledge his people needed was a twice-told tale to his white neighbors, while the knowledge which would teach the white world was Greek to his own flesh and blood. The innate love of harmony and beauty that set the ruder souls of his people a-dancing and a-singing raised but confusion and doubt in the soul of the black artist; for the beauty revealed to him was the soul-beauty of a race which his larger audience despised, and he could not articulate the message of another people. This waste of double aims, this seeking to satisfy two unreconciled ideals, has wrought sad havoc with the courage and faith and deeds of ten thousand people—has sent them often wooing false gods and invoking false means of salvation, and at times has even seemed about to make them ashamed of themselves.

Away back in the days of bondage they thought to see in one divine event the end of all doubt and disappointment; few men ever worshipped Freedom with half such unquestioning faith as did the American Negro for two centuries. To him, so far as he thought and dreamed, slavery was indeed the sum of all villainies, the cause of all sorrow, the root of all prejudice; Emancipation was the key to a promised land of sweeter beauty than ever stretched before the eyes of wearied Israelites. In song and exhortation swelled one refrain—Liberty; in his tears and curses the God he implored had Freedom in his right hand. At last it came—suddenly, fearfully, like a dream. With one wild carnival of blood and passion came the message in his own plaintive cadences:

"Shout, O children! Shout, you're free! For God has bought your liberty!"

Years have passed away since then—ten, twenty, forty; forty years of national life, forty years of renewal and development, and yet the swarthy specter sits in its accustomed seat at the Nation's feast. In vain do we cry to this our vastest social problem:

"Take any shape but that, and my firm nerves shall never tremble!"

The Nation has not yet found peace from its sins; the freedman has not yet found in freedom his promised land. Whatever of good may have come in these years of change, the shadow of a deep disappointment rests upon the Negro people—a disappointment all the more bitter because the unattained ideal was unbounded save by the simple ignorance of a lowly people.

The first decade was merely a prolongation of the vain search for freedom, the boon that seemed ever barely to elude their grasp—like a tantalizing will-o'-the-wisp, maddening and misleading the headless host. The holocaust of war, the terrors of the Ku Klux Klan, the lies of carpetbaggers, the disorganization of industry, and the contradictory advice of friends and foes left the bewildered serf with no new watchword beyond the old cry for freedom. As the time flew, however, he began to grasp a new idea. The ideal of liberty demanded for its attainment powerful means, and these the Fifteenth Amendment gave him. The ballot, which before he had looked upon as a visible sign of freedom, he now regarded as the chief means of gaining and perfecting the liberty with which war had partially endowed him. And why not? Had not votes made war and emancipated millions? Had not votes enfranchised the freedmen? Was anything impossible to a power that had done all this? A million black men started with renewed zeal to vote themselves into the kingdom. So the decade flew away, the revolution of 1876 came, and left the half-free serf weary, wondering, but still inspired. Slowly but steadily, in the following years, a new vision began gradually to replace the dream of political power—a powerful movement, the rise of another ideal to guide the unguided, another pillar of fire by night after a clouded day. It was the ideal of "book-learning"; the curiosity, born of compulsory ignorance, to know and test the power of the cabalistic letters of the white man, the longing to know. Here at last seemed to have been discovered the mountain path to Canaan; longer than the highway of Emancipation and law, steep and rugged, but straight, leading to heights high enough to overlook life.

Up the new path the advance guard toiled, slowly, heavily, doggedly; only those who have watched and guided the faltering feet, the misty minds, the dull understandings, of the dark pupils of these schools know how faithfully, how piteously, this people strove to learn. It was weary work. The cold statistician wrote down the inches of progress here and there, noted also where here and there a foot had slipped or some one had fallen. To the tired climbers, the horizon was ever dark, the mists were often cold, Canaan was always dim and far away. If, however, the vistas disclosed as yet no goal, no resting-place, little but flattery and criticism, the journey at least gave leisure for reflection and self-examination; it changed the child of Emancipation to the youth with dawning self-consciousness, self-realization, self-respect. In those somber forests of his striving his own soul rose before him, and he saw himself—darkly as through a veil; and yet he saw in himself some faint revelation of his power, of his mission. He began to have a dim feeling that, to attain his place in the world, he must be himself, and not another. For the first time he sought to analyze the burden he bore upon his back, that deadweight of social degradation partially masked behind a half-named Negro problem. He felt his poverty; without a cent, without a home, without land, tools, or savings, he had entered into competition with rich, landed, skilled neighbors. To be a poor man is hard, but to be a poor race in a land of dollars is the very bottom of hardships. He felt the weight of his ignorance—not simply of letters, but of life, of business, of the humanities; the accumulated sloth and shirking and awkwardness of decades and centuries shackled his hands and feet. Nor was his burden all poverty and ignorance. The red stain of bastardy, which two centuries of systematic legal defilement of Negro women had stamped upon his race, meant not only the loss of ancient African chastity, but also the hereditary weight of a mass of corruption from white adulterers, threatening almost the obliteration of the Negro home.

A people thus handicapped ought not to be asked to race with the world, but rather allowed to give all its time and thought to its own social problems. But alas! while sociologists gleefully count his bastards and his prostitutes, the very soul of the toiling, sweating black man is darkened by the shadow of a vast despair. Men call the shadow prejudice, and learnedly explain it as the natural defense of culture against barbarism, learning against ignorance, purity against crime, the "higher" against the "lower" races. To which the Negro cries, Amen! and swears that to so much of this strange prejudice as is founded on just homage to civilization, culture, righteousness, and progress, he humbly bows and meekly does obeisance. But before that nameless prejudice that leaps beyond all this he stands helpless, dismayed, and well-nigh speechless; before that personal disrespect and mockery, the ridicule and systematic humiliation, the distortion of fact and wanton license of fancy, the cynical ignoring of the better and the boisterous welcoming of the worse, the all-pervading desire to inculcate disdain for everything black, from Toussaint [L'Ouverture] to the devil —before this there rises a sickening despair that would disarm and discourage any nation save that black host to whom "discouragement" is an unwritten word.

But the facing of so vast a prejudice could not but bring the inevitable self-questioning, self-disparagement, and lowering of ideals which ever accompany repression and breed in an atmosphere of contempt and hate. Whisperings and portents came home upon the four winds: Lo! we are diseased and dying, cried the dark hosts; we cannot write, our voting is vain; what need of education, since we must always cook and serve? And the Nation echoed and enforced this self-criticism, saying: Be content to be servants, and nothing more; what need of higher culture for half-men? Away with the black man's ballot, by force or fraud—and behold the suicide of a race! Nevertheless, out of the evil came something of good—the more careful adjustment of education to real life, the clearer perception of the Negroes' social responsibilities, and the sobering realization of the meaning of progress.

So dawned the time of *Sturm und Drang*: storm and stress today rocks our little boat on the mad waters of the world-sea; there is within and without the sound of conflict, the burning of body and rending of soul; inspiration strives with doubt, and faith with vain questionings. The bright ideals of the past—physical freedom, political power, the training of brains and the training of hands—all these in turn have waxed and waned, until even the last grows dim and overcast. Are they all wrong—all false? No, not that, but each alone was over-simple and incomplete—the dreams of a credulous race-childhood, or the fond imaginings of the other world which does not know and does not want to know our power. To be really true, all these ideals must be melted and welded into one. The training of the schools we need today more than ever—the training of deft hands, quick eyes and ears, and above all the broader, deeper, higher culture of gifted minds and pure hearts. The power of the ballot we need in sheer self-defense—else what shall save us from a second slavery? Freedom, too, the long-sought, we still seek—the freedom of life and limb, the freedom to work and think, the freedom to love and aspire. Work, culture, liberty—all these we need, not singly but together, not successively but together, each growing and aiding each, and all striving toward that vaster ideal that swims before the Negro people, the ideal of human brotherhood, gained through the unifying ideal of Race; the ideal of fostering and developing the traits and talents of the Negro, not in opposition to or contempt for other races, but rather in large conformity to the greater ideals of the American Republic, in order that some day on American soil two world-races may give each to each those characteristics both so sadly lack. We the darker ones come even now not altogether empty-handed: there are today no truer exponents of the pure human spirit of the Declaration of Independence than the American Negroes; there is no true American music but the wild sweet melodies of the Negro slave; the American fairy tales and folklore are Indian and African; and, all in all, we black men seem the sole oasis of simple faith and reverence in a dusty desert of dollars and smartness. Will America be poorer if she replace her brutal dyspeptic blundering with light-hearted but determined Negro humility? or her coarse and cruel wit with loving jovial good humor? or her vulgar music with the soul of the Sorrow Songs?

Merely a concrete test of the underlying principles of the great republic is the Negro Problem, and the spiritual striving of the freedmen's sons is the travail of souls whose burden is almost beyond the measure of their strength, but who bear it in the name of an historic race, in the name of this the land of their fathers' fathers, and in the name of human opportunity.

V | America as an Empire

Some Guiding Questions
How should the power and influence of the United States be understood? Where does its jurisdiction properly begin and end? With what justifications and consequences? How is such reasoning uniquely American or better credited to other sources? Racism? Wealth? Geography? How has U.S. expansionism been justified and resisted? For example, in what respects should the impetus be considered offensive or defensive? How might Americans be distinctly insensitive to other peoples? What are the stakes? For whom? In what respects should America be considered imperialist or anti-imperialist?

37

The Utility of the Union (1787)

The Federalist Papers have become the authoritative rationale for one side—the winning one—in the late-eighteenth-century debate over the proper size and shape of the U.S. government. Their authors concluded that it should be more powerful and united. Their route to that conclusion was by way of a carefully reasoned review of the history, geography, economy, institutions, and predispositions of the American people—in other words, a sort of American Studies. Their goal was overtly political: to justify the shift from a Confederation (per the Articles of 1781) to a more unified sovereign under the newly drafted Constitution. Hence, Alexander Hamilton, James Madison, and John Jay (sharing the alias "Publius") urged readers of New York newspapers to welcome the change. Over a period of seven months, 1787–1788, their eighty-five essays refuted Anti-Federalists point by point.

In *The Federalist Papers* Number 3, for example, John Jay argued that a more centralized government would be better able to resist furies of the sort that turned past grievances into wars:

Such violences are more frequently caused by the passions and interests of a part than of the whole; of one or two States than of the Union. Not a single Indian war has yet been occasioned by aggressions of the present federal government, feeble as it is; but there are several instances of Indian hostilities having been provoked by the improper conduct of individual States, who, either unable or unwilling to restrain or punish offenses, have given occasion to the slaughter of many innocent inhabitants. . . .

The pride of states, as well as of men, naturally disposes them to justify all their actions, and opposes their acknowledging, correcting, or repairing their errors and offenses. The national government, in such cases, will not be affected by this pride, but will proceed with moderation and candor to consider and decide on the means most proper to extricate them from the difficulties which threaten them.

In the following excerpt from Number 11 of *The Federalist Papers*, Alexander Hamilton extends Jay's vision of greater peace through a more powerful union. In doing so, he joins other Founders, including Anti-Federalists such as Thomas Jefferson, in disputing contemporary European science. Continental naturalists (such as Georges Louis Leclerc, comte de Buffon) compiled what they took to be proof that life forms literally degenerate in the New World. Hamilton rejoined that Americans are, in fact, helping to regenerate the world. Since imperialism was a distinctly European malady, a militarily and commercially assertive U.S. government could be the cure.

To the People of the State of New York:

The importance of the Union, in a commercial light, is one of those points about which there is least room to entertain a difference of opinion, and which has, in fact, commanded the most general assent of men who have any acquaintance with the subject. This applies as well to our intercourse with foreign countries as with each other.

There are appearances to authorize a supposition that the adventurous spirit, which distinguishes the commercial character of America, has already excited uneasy sensations in several of the maritime powers of Europe. They seem to be apprehensive of our too great interference in that carrying trade, which is the support of their navigation and the foundation of their naval strength. Those of them which have colonies in America look forward to what this country is capable of becoming, with painful solicitude. They foresee the dangers that may threaten their American dominions from the neighborhood of States, which have all the dispositions, and would possess all the means, requisite to the creation of a powerful marine. Impressions of this kind will naturally indicate the policy of fostering divisions among us, and of depriving us, as far as possible, of an ACTIVE COMMERCE in our own bottoms [ships]. This would answer the threefold purpose of preventing our interference in their navigation, of monopolizing the profits of our trade, and of clipping the wings by which we might soar to a dangerous greatness. . . .

If we continue united, we may counteract a policy so unfriendly to our prosperity in a variety of ways. By prohibitory regulations, extending, at the same time, throughout the States, we may oblige foreign countries to bid against each other, for the privileges of our markets. This assertion will not appear chimerical to those who are able to appreciate the importance of the markets of three millions of people—increasing in rapid progression, for the most part exclusively addicted to agriculture, and likely from local circumstances to remain so—to any manufacturing nation; and the immense difference there would be to the trade and navigation of such a nation, between a direct communication in its own ships, and an indirect conveyance of its products and returns, to and from America, in the ships of another country. . . .

A further resource for influencing the conduct of European nations toward us, in this respect, would arise from the establishment of a federal navy. There can be no doubt that the continuance of the Union under an efficient government would put it in our power, at a period not very distant, to create a navy which, if it could not vie with those of the great maritime powers, would at least be of respectable weight if thrown onto the scale of either of two contending parties. This would be more peculiarly the case in relation to operations in the West Indies. A few ships of the line, sent opportunely to the reinforcement of either side, would often be sufficient to decide the fate of a campaign, on the event of which interests of the greatest magnitude were suspended. . . . A price would be set not only upon our friendship, but upon our neutrality. By a steady adherence to the Union we may hope, ere long, to become the arbiter of Europe in America, and to be able to incline the balance of European competitions in this part of the world as our interest may dictate.

But in the reverse of this eligible situation, we shall discover that the rivalships of the parts would make them checks upon each other, and would frustrate all the tempting advantages which nature has kindly placed within our reach. In a state so insignificant our commerce would be a prey to the wanton intermeddlings of all nations at war with each other; who, having nothing to fear from us, would with little scruple or remorse, supply their wants by depredations on our property as often as it fell in their way. The rights of neutrality will only be respected when they are defended by an adequate power. A nation, despicable by its weakness, forfeits even the privilege of being neutral.

Under a vigorous national government, the natural strength and resources of the country, directed to a common interest, would baffle all the combinations of European jealousy to restrain our growth. This situation would even take away the motive to such combinations, by inducing an impracticability of success. An active commerce, an extensive navigation, and a flourishing marine would then be the offspring of moral and physical necessity. We might defy the little arts of the little politicians to control or vary the irresistible and unchangeable course of nature.

But in a state of disunion, these combinations might exist and might operate with success. It would be in the power of the maritime nations, availing themselves of our universal impotence, to prescribe the conditions of our political existence; and as they have a common interest in being our carriers, and still more in preventing our becoming theirs, they would in all probability combine to embarrass our navigation in such a manner as would in effect destroy it, and confine us to a PASSIVE COMMERCE. We should then be compelled to content ourselves with the first price of our commodities, and to see the profits of our trade snatched from us to enrich our enemies and persecutors. That unequaled spirit of enterprise, which signalizes the genius of the American merchants and navigators, and which is in itself an inexhaustible mine of national wealth, would be stifled and lost, and poverty and disgrace would overspread a country which, with wisdom, might make herself the admiration and envy of the world.

There are rights of great moment to the trade of America which are rights of the Union—I allude to the fisheries, to the navigation of the Western lakes, and to that of the Mississippi. The dissolution of the Confederacy would give room for delicate questions concerning the future existence of these rights; which the interest of more powerful partners would hardly fail to solve to our disadvantage. . . . As a nursery of seamen, it now is, or, when time shall have more nearly assimilated the principles of navigation in the several States, will become, a universal resource. To the establishment of a navy, it must be indispensable.

To this great national object, a NAVY, union will contribute in various ways. Every institution will grow and flourish in proportion to the quantity and extent of the means concentrated towards its formation and support. A navy of the United States, as it would embrace the resources of all, is object far less remote than a navy of any single State or partial confederacy, which would only embrace the resources of a single part. It happens, indeed, that different portions of confederated America possess each some peculiar advantage for this essential establishment. The more southern States furnish in greater abundance certain kinds of naval stores—tar, pitch, and turpentine. Their wood for the construction of ships is also of a more solid and lasting texture. . . . Some of the Southern and of the Middle States yield a greater plenty of iron, and of better quality. Seamen must chiefly be drawn from the Northern hive. . . .

An unrestrained intercourse between the States themselves will advance the trade of each by an interchange of their respective productions, not only for the supply of reciprocal wants at home, but for exportation to foreign markets. The veins of commerce in every part will be replenished, and will acquire additional motion and vigor from a free circulation of the commodities of every part. Commercial enterprise will have much greater scope, from the diversity in the productions of different States. When the staple of one fails from a bad harvest or unproductive crop, it can call to its aid the staple of another. The variety, not less than the value, of products for exportation contributes to the activity of foreign commerce. . . . The speculative trader will at once perceive the force of these observations, and will acknowledge that the aggregate balance of the commerce of the United States would bid fair to be much more favorable than that of the thirteen States without union or with partial unions. . . . A unity of commercial, as well as political, interests, can only result from a unity of government.

There are other points of view in which this subject might be placed, of a striking and animating kind. But they would lead us too far into the regions of futurity, and would involve topics not proper for a newspaper discussion. I shall briefly observe, that our situation invites and our interests prompt us to aim at an ascendant in the system of American affairs. The world may politically, as well as geographically, be divided into four parts, each having a distinct set of interests. Unhappily for the other three, Europe, by her arms and by her negotiations, by force and by fraud, has, in different degrees, extended her dominion over them all. Africa, Asia, and America, have successively felt her domination. The superiority she has long maintained has tempted her to plume herself as the Mistress of the World, and to consider the rest of mankind as created for her benefit. Men admired as profound philosophers have, in direct terms, attributed to her inhabitants a physical superiority, and have gravely asserted that all animals, and with them the human species, degenerate in America— that even dogs cease to bark after having breathed awhile in our atmosphere. Facts have too long supported these arrogant pretensions of the Europeans. It belongs to us to vindicate the honor of the human race, and to teach that assuming brother, moderation. Union will enable us to do it. Disunion will add another victim to his triumphs. Let Americans disdain to be the instruments of European greatness! Let the thirteen States, bound together in a strict and indissoluble Union, concur in erecting one great American system, superior to the control of all transatlantic force or influence, and able to dictate the terms of the connection between the old and the new world!

38 The Monroe Doctrine (1823)

When President James Monroe delivered his 1823 message to Congress, the nations of the Americas were barely in a position to defend their own territories, much less those of anyone else. Russia and Great Britain, for example, were vigorously contesting the northern boundaries of the United States, while Portugal and Spain clung to colonies to the south. Hence, when Monroe insisted that his administration would, in effect, consider the entire Western Hemisphere its independent protectorate, the claim had little force. It was mainly a gesture of solidarity with newly independent states and against intercontinental aggression.

It was also timed to attract a welcome. Followers of Simón Bolívar, Francisco de Miranda, Bernardo O'Higgins, José de San Martín, and Miguel Hidalgo had long pressed for such encouragement. Their governments valued U.S. diplomatic recognition (for example, won just the prior year by Argentina, Chile, Colombia, Mexico, and Peru), especially as they faced menacing news from the so-called Holy Alliance. Prussian, Russian, and Austrian officials were plotting with the French to return former colonies to Christian monarchies, including Spain and Portugal. Britain, which had a significant naval capacity and a stake in the South Atlantic trade, vowed to resist the Alliance and pressured Monroe for diplomatic support. So, by announcing kindred sympathies, the United States went on record in favor of the status quo. The "occasion" to which Monroe referred was a new threat to continental self-determination and international peace.

However, in the 1840s, Presidents John Tyler and James Polk cited the Monroe Doctrine to justify expansionist ventures in Mexican territory, Texas, then California and Oregon. President Theodore Roosevelt used the same source to legitimate ever more aggressive Latin American and Caribbean interventions. His "Corollary" to the Doctrine (1904) in effect authorized U.S. incursion just about anywhere in the hemisphere if threats to American interests were in the offing—a condition that U.S. officials would define on their own. After a brief respite between the wars, the "big stick"—the Monroe Doctrine rendered a blunt instrument—was again ready for wielding wherever communism was detected or contrived.

In such ways the policy has been complicit in both anti-imperialism and colonialism. It put the United States on the side of independent states but also corralled them in "America's backyard," ever vulnerable to "help" via U.S. invasion. The contradiction is all the more remarkable because Monroe claimed only to reason from brute realities in a judicious, generous spirit.

The occasion has been judged proper for asserting, as a principle in which the rights and interests of the United States are involved, that the American continents, by the free and independent condition which they have assumed and maintain, are henceforth not to be considered as subjects for future colonization by any European power. . . .

Of events in that quarter of the globe, with which we have so much intercourse and from which we derive our origin, we have always been anxious and interested spectators. The citizens of the United States cherish sentiments the most friendly in favor of the liberty and happiness of their fellow men on that side of the Atlantic. In the wars of the European powers in matters relating to themselves we have never taken any part, nor does it comport with our policy to do so.

It is only when our rights are invaded or seriously menaced that we resent injuries or make preparations for our defense. With the movements in this hemisphere we are of necessity more immediately connected, and by causes which must be obvious to all enlightened and impartial observers.

The political system of the allied powers is essentially different in this respect from that of America. This difference proceeds from that which exists in their respective Governments; and to the defense of our own, which has been achieved by the loss of so much blood and treasure, and matured by the wisdom of their most enlightened citizens, and under which we have enjoyed unexampled felicity. . . .

We owe it, therefore, to candor and to the amicable relations existing between the United States and those powers to declare that we should consider any attempt on their part to extend their system to any portion of this hemisphere as dangerous to our peace and safety. With the existing colonies or dependencies of any European power we have not interfered and shall not interfere. But with the Governments who have declared their independence and maintain it, and whose independence we have, on great consideration and on just principles, acknowledged, we could not view any interposition for the purpose of oppressing them, or controlling in any other manner their destiny, by any European power in any other light than as the manifestation of an unfriendly disposition toward the United States. . . .

Our policy in regard to Europe . . . nevertheless remains the same, . . . to cultivate friendly relations with it, and to preserve those relations by a frank, firm, and manly policy, meeting in all instances the just claims of every power, submitting to injuries from none.

But . . . it is impossible that the allied powers should extend their political system to any portion of either continent without endangering our peace and happiness; nor can anyone believe that our southern brethren, if left to themselves, would adopt it of their own accord. It is equally impossible, therefore, that we should behold such interposition in any form with indifference. If we look to the comparative strength and resources of Spain and those new Governments, and their distance from each other, it must be obvious that she can never subdue them.

It is still the true policy of the United States to leave the parties to themselves, in hope that other powers will pursue the same course.

ARTHUR DE GOBINEAU

39 The European Colonizations of America (1855)

Regard for family—people bound by birth and law or ceremony—is apparently universal. Anyone who has tried to raise better beans or goats also knows the significance of heredity. Within a few generations, parents, siblings, and offspring are considered "blood" relations, close enough even to look alike. They constitute a sort of breed, a taxon smaller and less specialized than a species but still unique: Acorns don't fall far from the tree. Such sentiment, enhanced with globetrotting experience, suggests that humanity "naturally" includes folks from different lands with different ancestors who pass down "native" traits. And it is a short hop from there to the idea of "race."

It is much tougher to figure out how race matters. Since the age of exploration, when the term entered the English language, Western theologians, explorers, philosophers, and scientists have debated the point. Imperialism greatly conditioned the discussion. From the 1500s through the 1800s, races were distinguished by criteria at once social, geographic, and political. Europeans were "we," near, familiar, the empire; non-Europeans were "they," far, different, the colonies.

By the mid-nineteenth century, even distant bloodlines were obviously mixed, and Europeans lost the ability to govern their colonies directly, but they maintained indirect dominion and were eager to understand or justify that advantage. In this neocolonial context, distance and difference became "racial." No one could doubt that race mattered a lot. It had something to do with human diversity, inequality, history, nature, maybe also God's design. But precisely how were they related?

This is the puzzle that the French count, diplomat, creative writer, and critic Arthur de Gobineau aimed to solve in four volumes that he published between 1853 and 1855. His *Essai sur l'inégalité des races humaines* was nothing if not ambitious. A Philadelphia company immediately produced an abridged translation under a fitting title: *The Moral and Intellectual Diversity of Races, With Particular Reference to Their Respective Influence in the Civil and Political History of Mankind.* The source of Gobineau's solution, then, was the totality of human experience. In one form or another, *Essai* gained a huge following on both sides of the Atlantic.

The main issue that Gobineau first had to finesse was religious. Discussions of human inequality at the time seemed always to begin with an article of faith: God's design in Creation. Was the variety of Adam and Eve's descendants (for example, Chinese versus Carthaginian) determined in Eden? Does Genesis divine diversity? Or is it a consequence of conditions for which mortals are responsible? Are racial differences, then, deep and fixed or shallow and transient? By implication, should inequality (as in neocolonial relations) be accepted as a fact of life? Gobineau aimed to answer that final question while evading the theological preliminaries:

> I do not wish to run counter to even literal interpretations of the text [the Bible], if they are generally accepted. I will merely point out that we might, perhaps, doubt their value, without going beyond the limits imposed by the Church. . . . I will simply ask whether, independent of any question of an original unity or multiplicity, there may not exist the most radical and far-reaching differences, both physical and moral, between human races.

Gobineau's answer was yes: "In spite of climate and lapse of time, mankind is no less completely and definitely split into separate parts than it would be if specific differences were due to a real divergence of origin." Racial characteristics, he argued, are "absolutely fixed, hereditary, and *permanent.*"

At first, especially within the emerging science of culture (ethnology or anthropology), readers enthusiastically welcomed this approach. Among those crediting it were such prominent intellectuals as the philosopher Friedrich Nietzsche, the composer Richard Wagner and his son-in-law, the racist and naturalized German, Houston Stewart Chamberlain, who inspired Kaiser Wilhelm II and then Adolf Hitler. It was Gobineau who first identified an "Aryan" race destined to exceed all others. The combination of that discovery/invention and the power of *Essai*'s readers accounts for Gobineau's more recent reputation as "a prophet of evil" and "the father of racism" in the Western world.

Gobineau himself, though, was hardly an advocate of any particular regime (most certainly not a German one). He aimed for disinterested science. But he also showed respect for human diversity. He felt compelled, for example, to master Asian languages and literatures. Although he found in Aryans a uniquely elevated destiny, he also claimed that every race has its talents and moments. Most of them have at one time or another produced a worthy civilization. But all of the great ones have suffered a common fate: decline occasioned by the introduction of racial impurities. Degeneracy, he concluded, is the inevitable result of miscegenation.

Since bloods are apt to mix in proportion to a civilization's reach, Gobineau, unlike many of his fans, opposed imperialism. He emphasized the risk to dominant no less than to subjugated peoples:

> Intolerance is one of the chief notes of European civilization. . . . As it sees obstacles to its own progress in everything that is different from itself, it is apt to demand a complete change in its subjects' point of

view. . . . [But] enlightened nations cannot set up institutions unsuited to the character of their subjects. . . . Since the 16th Century, when Europe first turned her face towards the East, we cannot find the least trace of any moral influence exerted by her, even in the case of the peoples she has completely conquered. . . . The order has gone forth to abolish existing customs, and put in their place others which the masters knew to be good and useful. Has the attempt ever succeeded?

America provides us with the richest field for gathering answers to this question.

The editor of the first English translation (1856) explained why *Essai*'s American studies should also appeal to general readers in the United States:

In this country, it is peculiarly interesting and important, for not only is our immense territory the abode of the three best defined varieties of human species—the white, the Negro, and the Indian—to which the extensive immigration of the Chinese on our Pacific coast is rapidly adding a fourth, but the fusion of diverse nationalities is nowhere more rapid and complete; nowhere is the great problem of man's perfectibility being solved on a grander scale, or in a more decisive manner.

None of the English editions to date, though, include the following section from *Essai*. It comes from a final chapter of the 1855 original, the one that surveys the lessons of Euro-American experience. Gobineau actually counsels little faith in "perfectibility."

Since the discovery of 1495, relations between the indigenous Americans and the European nations have varied substantially, as determined in part by the primitive genealogy of the groups present. To speak of a kinship between the nations of the New World and the navigators of the Old will seem at first accidental. With sustained reflection, one will realize that nothing is more real, and one will confront its effects.

The colonists who have most affected the Indians are the Spanish, the Portuguese, the French, and the English.

From the very beginning, the subjects of the Catholic kings have been intimately associated with the country's people. Without a doubt they have pillaged, beaten, and very often massacred them. Such events are inseparable from any conquest and even of all domination. It is no less true that the Spanish paid homage to the political organization of their subjects and respected ways that would not conflict with their supremacy. . . . They readily accepted Incan daughters as their wives. . . . This facility of morals came, no doubt, from points of attraction that the composition of the respective races allowed between masters and subjects. . . .

For the French, it was about the same, although not entirely. In Canada, our immigrants have frequently accepted an alliance with natives that was quite rare for Anglo-Saxon colonizers. They often and easily adopted the lifestyle of the parents of their aboriginal wives. . . .

The Anglo-Saxons of British origin represent the shade farthest from the blood of both aborigines and African Negroes. It is not that one could not find in their essence some Finnish traces; but they are counter-balanced by a Germanic nature, in truth (albeit a bit faded and shed of grandeur) still rigid and vigorous in nature. They, therefore, represent a crossbreed of the two great inferior varieties of the species, irreconcilable antagonists. That is the situation in their own land. With regard to the other independent regions of America, they account for strong state-to-state antagonism. Instead of opposing the American Union, . . . they possess only anarchy in all degrees. And what anarchy, since it reunites the American incongruities with those of Romanized Europe!

The Anglo-Saxon seed existing in the United States therefore can be readily recognized as the hardy element of the new continent. . . . The Anglo-Saxons act as masters of the inferior nations . . . so it is useful to take advantage of this occasion to study the relations between strong and weak in detail. Remote times and obscure annals have not always afforded a vision as precise as the picture that is now before us.

The Anglo-Saxon remnant in North America forms a group that does not doubt for a single instant its innate superiority over the rest of the human species and the rights of birth that this superiority confers upon them. . . . They invented terms, theories, rhetoric to exonerate their behavior. . . .

In relations with the Negroes, they showed themselves to be as imperious as the natives. They skinned them to the bone. . . . They were so crude as to imagine foisting on their subjects or on foreign nations the use of liquors or other pernicious things. This is a modern idea. . . . Our civilization is the only one that has possessed this instinct, and at the same time, this homicidal power. It is the only one that without anger, without irritation—believing itself, on the contrary, mild and compassionate to excess, proclaiming the most unlimited tolerance—works ceaselessly to surround itself with a horizon of tombs.

Representing conquerors faithful to this mode of culture, Anglo-Americans have conformed to its laws. They are not reprehensible. It is without hypocrisy that they believed themselves right to join in the eighteenth-century concert of complaint against all manner of political oppression, against Negro slavery in particular. The parties and the nations enjoyed, like women, the advantage of illogic, endorsing intellectual and moral incongruities without surprise or insincerity. In their passionate pleas for the emancipation of the black species, fellow citizens of Washington felt no obligation to provide evidence. . . .

The Anglo-Saxons of America are sincerely religious. This trait has remained rather well imprinted from the noble part of their origin. However, they accepted neither the terrors nor the despotism of their faith. . . . Possessed by the thirst to reign, to command, to possess, to take and to stretch forth always, the Anglo-Saxons of America are primitive farmers and warriors (I say "warriors," and not "soldiers"—their need for independence demands it). . . .

This republican people bear witness to two sentiments that cut across all the natural tendencies of all democracies grown out of such excessive mixture. First, there is the taste for tradition, for things ancient, for (to use a judicial term) precedents. This bias is so pronounced in the order of affections that it prompts defensiveness even of England when challenged. In America, institutions are ever being changed, but among the descendants of the Anglo-Saxons there is a marked repugnance to radical and sudden transformations. . . . Second, Americans are worried about any individual who boasts social distinction; everyone wants it. The name "citizen" is less popular among them than the chivalrous title "*squire*," and this instinctive preoccupation with personal position was brought by colonists of the same stock to Canada, where it has effected the same result. One can well read in an announcement page of a newspaper in Montreal that "Mr. ***, grocer, *gentleman*" holds thus and such commodity for public sale.

This is not an indifferent usage of terms. It indicates among democrats of the New World a disposition to treasure that which distinguishes them from the revolutionaries of old. . . .

The Anglo-Saxon group on this side of the Atlantic cannot be represented, properly speaking, by the word *democracy*. It is rather a majorstate without troops. They are men suited to domination who would not exercise this faculty on their equals but who would on their supposed inferiors. . . .

This situation is not without precedent. When the armies of Semitic Rome conquered the kingdoms of Asia Minor, the Romans and the Hellenists found themselves acquiring their style of culture from the same sources. . . .

The same perspective has been legitimated among the Anglo-Saxon group. Whether by conquest or by influence, North Americans seem destined to master the entire social surface of the New World. Who would stop them? . . .

Assessing the intensity of the effect of the people of the United States on the other groups of the New World has not so far been a question of the race that founded the nation. Purely by supposition, I have treated their race now as if it preserved its distinct, original value and persisted indefinitely. But nothing could be further from the truth. On the contrary, among the countries of the world since the beginning of the century and especially in the last years, the American union represents the one that has seen abound on its land the largest mass of heterogeneity. It is a new condition that could, if not change, at least modify gravely the conclusions presented above. . . .

Anglo-Saxon descendants of the ancient English colonists no longer comprise the majority of the region's inhabitants. Although persisting for a while, as hundreds of thousands of Irish and Germans annually move to American soil, much of the national race will disappear before the end of the century. Among the remainder there will be the profound weakness of mixtures. For some time it will certainly continue to appear vital; then this appearance will be erased, and the empire will fall completely in the hands of a mixed family, where the Anglo-Saxon element will have only the most subordinate role. I note, incidentally, that already the bulk of the primitive variety is uprooting from the seacoast and digging in the West, where the style of life is better suited to its taste for action and courageous adventure.

But the newly arrived—what are they? They represent the most varied remnants of old Europe, races from whom there is less to expect. They are the detritus of all times: Irish, Germans so many times cross-bred, survivals of the French who are otherwise extinct, Italians who surpass them all. The union of all these types of degenerates gives and will necessarily give birth to new ethnic disorders. These disorders are nothing unexpected, nothing new; they will not produce any hybrid that has not already been realized or could not be on our continent. No prolific element could avoid it. . . . The products of an indefinite series of combinations—German, Irish, Italian, French, and Anglo-Saxon—will increase and amalgamate in the south with blood composed of the essence of Indians, Negroes, Spanish, and Portuguese who live there. There is no way to imagine what horrible confusion will come with this incoherent assemblage of most degraded beings.

I follow with interest—as well as with some sympathy, I swear—
the great movements that utilitarian instincts are developing in
America. I don't recognize their manifest power; but by best estimates,
what can result from this unknown? And how does it really resemble
an original? Is something happening there that would be fundamentally foreign to European concepts? Is there a determining pattern that
would revive hope of future triumphs for a young humanity yet to be
born? Let one weigh maturely the pros and cons, and one will not
doubt the futility of such hopes. The United States of America is not
the first commercial state in the world. Those who have preceded it
have produced nothing resembling a regeneration of the race from
which they came. . . .

All past experience uniformly proves that the amalgamation of
exhausted ethnic principles cannot produce a new vitality in combination. There is already a lot to foresee, a lot to reconcile, in suppos-
ing that the republic of the New World can conquer the countries that
surround it. Even with such great success, which would give to them
a certain right to compare themselves to Semitic Rome, . . . it would
probably go bankrupt. As for the renewal of human society, as for the
creation of a superior or at least different civilization . . . it always
comes back to the same thing: . . . such phenomena are only produced
in the presence of a relatively pure and young race. This condition
does not exist in America. All of the country's labors can only exagger-
ate certain aspects of European culture (and not necessarily the finest), to ape some, and to miss the rest. This people who is said to be
"young" is the oldest people of Europe, less constrained by the most
obliging laws and no better inspired. In the long and sad voyage that
casts immigrants to a new country, the air of the Ocean does not transform them. As they left, so they arrive. The simple transfer from one
point to another will not regenerate races that are more than half
exhausted.

RUDYARD KIPLING

40 The White Man's Burden (1899)

Given its unhappy experience with European colonialism, the United States tends to downplay its own imperial record. Americans prefer to consider themselves ever on the side of underdogs. They aim less to advance than to defend national interests. Only under duress will they wield or share advantages that Americans "just so happen" to have. Their relative reluctance to do so—when compared, say, with the Japanese, Spanish, or British empires—is a matter of some pride as well as delusion, at least in light of Native, African, East Asian, Caribbean, and Latin American history.

The conflict between U.S. imperialists and anti-imperialists became particularly heated during the Spanish-American War (1898). U.S. objectives in the war were widely debated: Could the bloodshed and expense be justified? If Spanish forces could be defeated in Cuba, the Philippines, Puerto Rico, and Guam, what sort of surrender would the McKinley administration require? In whose interests? What sort of nation would the United States thereby become?

As the Senate considered the treaty that would end the war (in fact, just two days prior to its ratification), the bard of British imperialism, India-born Rudyard Kipling, piped in with stereotypically Victorian advice. To the mass of readers of the popular American magazine *McClure's*, his verse effused: keep a stiff upper lip.

Judging from responses published at the time, relatively few Americans appreciated the message. U.S. periodicals featured lampoons and parodies galore. Advocates of independence bemoaned the poem's blatant chauvinism. The black press targeted its bigotry and hypocrisy. Nearly everyone could agree that avarice was considerably more at issue than generosity, duty, race, or masculinity.

Nevertheless, the United States ratified the Treaty of Paris in 1899, gaining control of Cuba, Puerto Rico, and Guam as well as the capacity to "purchase" the Philippines for $20 million. However hesitant Americans might have been to accept Kipling's advice, they were even more reluctant to allow their charges self-determination. It would take another half-century before the U.S. government would "grant" them citizenship, much less sovereignty.

It did not take long, however, for Kipling's words to find their way into bloated estimates of America's place in the world. On the Fourth of July 1906, for example, U.S. presidential candidate and populist William Jennings Bryan appealed to a London audience by quoting directly from *McClure's* in 1899. Descendants of friends as well as foes of the Founding Fathers could embrace a common destiny required by "the superiority of Western over Eastern civilization." With Kipling's help, the sort of paternalism that had been reserved for genteel defenders of slavery and of Native American "relocation" was now cast across Asia and the Pacific:

> No one can travel among the dark-skinned races of the Orient without feeling that the white man occupies an especially favored position among the children of men, and the recognition of this fact is accompanied by the conviction that there is a duty inseparably connected with the advantages enjoyed. There is a white man's burden—a burden which the white man should not shirk even if he could, a burden which he could not shirk even if he would.

In contrast with such variants, Kipling's poem might seem restrained.

Take up the White Man's burden—
Send forth the best ye breed—
Go bind your sons to exile
To serve your captives' need;
To wait in heavy harness,
On fluttered folk and wild—
Your new-caught, sullen peoples,
Half-devil and half-child.

Take up the White Man's burden—
In patience to abide,
To veil the threat of terror
And check the show of pride;
By open speech and simple,
An hundred times made plain,
To seek another's profit,
And work another's gain.

Take up the White Man's burden—
The savage wars of peace—
Fill full the mouth of Famine
And bid the sickness cease;
And when your goal is nearest
The end for others sought,
Watch Sloth and heathen Folly
Bring all your hope to nought.

Take up the White Man's burden—
No tawdry rule of kings,
But toil of serf and sweeper—
The tale of common things.
The ports ye shall not enter,
The roads ye shall not tread,
Go make them with your living,
And mark them with your dead.

Take up the White Man's burden—
And reap his old reward:
The blame of those ye better,
The hate of those ye guard—
The cry of hosts ye humour
(Ah, slowly!) toward the light:—
"Why brought ye us from bondage,
Our loved Egyptian night?"

Take up the White Man's burden—
Ye dare not stoop to less—
Nor call too loud on Freedom
To cloak your weariness;
By all ye cry or whisper,
By all ye leave or do,
The silent sullen peoples
Shall weigh your Gods and you.

Take up the White Man's burden—
Have done with childish days—
The lightly proffered laurel,
The easy, ungrudged praise,
Comes now, to search your manhood
Through all the thankless years,
Cold, edged with dear-bought wisdom,
The judgment of your peers!

MAO TSE-TUNG

41 Cast Away Illusions, Prepare for Struggle (1949)

In the spirit of the Truman Doctrine (1947), U.S. government authorities styled themselves the good guys of the Cold War. Unlike the Soviets, U.S. foreign relations were supposed to promote liberty, justice, and democracy. But as early as the summer of 1949, they had to acknowledge that their chosen side in the Chinese civil war was both unpopular and overwhelmed. Instead of governing a huge nation, as it had from 1928 to 1947, the Nationalist Party (the Kuomintang) under Commander Chiang Kai-shek fled in disgrace to the island of Taiwan. For hundreds of millions of people the Chinese Communist Party (CCP) and Chairman Mao Tse-tung were the heroes, and alliance with the United States only helped discredit the vanquished. Thereafter, despite a record of subverting as well as defending colonialism, America would find its name more frequently linked to imperialism.

It is an association that Mao had previously finessed. Just five years earlier, for example, when aiming to convince U.S. diplomats to route anti-Japanese armaments through the CCP instead of the Kuomintang and to reduce his dependence on the Soviets, Mao stated: "America does not need to fear. . . . We must have American help. This is why it is important to us Communists to know what you Americans are thinking and planning. We cannot risk crossing you—cannot risk conflict with you." A clear, popular Communist victory in China and the U.S. refusal to acknowledge it (at least officially for thirty years) rendered such discretion unnecessary.

Secretary of State Dean Acheson and U.S. Ambassador to China Leighton Stuart began issuing public responses to the change. Rippling recriminations—"Who lost China?"—shocked right-wing patriots such as Senator

Joseph McCarthy and fueled much of the subsequent Red Scare. But outside the United States, colonies and neo-colonies found it easier to name their oppressor "American," and Mao aimed to help.

It is no accident that the U.S. State Department's White Paper on China-U.S. Relations and Secretary of State Acheson's Letter of Transmittal to President Truman have been released at this time. The publication of these documents [August 5, 1949] reflects the victory of the Chinese people and the defeat of imperialism. . . . The imperialist system is riddled with insuperable internal contradictions, and therefore the imperialists are plunged into deep gloom. . . .

The latest war of aggression against the Chinese people . . . has gone on for three years, waged to all appearances by Chiang Kai-shek, but in reality by the United States. As stated in Acheson's Letter . . . it is a war in which the United States supplies the money and guns, and Chiang Kai-shek supplies the men to fight for the United States and slaughter the Chinese people. All these wars of aggression, together with political, economic and cultural . . . oppression, have caused the Chinese to hate imperialism, made them stop and think, "What is all this about?" and compelled them to bring their revolutionary spirit into full play and become united through struggle. . . .

Imperialist aggression stimulated China's social economy, brought about changes in it and created the opposites of imperialism. . . . To serve the needs of its aggression, imperialism ruined the Chinese peasants by exploiting them through the exchange of unequal values and thereby created great masses of poor peasants, numbering hundreds of millions and comprising 70 percent of China's rural population. To serve the needs of its aggression, imperialism created for China millions of big and small intellectuals of a new type, differing from the old type of *literatus* or scholar-bureaucrat. But imperialism and its running dogs, the reactionary governments of China, could control only a part of these intellectuals. . . . All the rest got out of control and turned against them. . . . The Communist Party is the party of the poor and . . . has won the support of several hundred million people, including the majority of the intellectuals, and especially the student youth.

Part of the intellectuals still want to wait and see. . . . They are the very people who have illusions about the United States. They are unwilling to draw a distinction between the U.S. imperialists, who are in power, and the American people, who are not. They are easily duped by the honeyed words of the U.S. imperialists, as though these imperialists would deal with People's China on the basis of equality and mutual benefit without a stern, long struggle. . . . They are the middle-of-the-roaders or the right-wingers in People's China. They are the supporters of what Acheson calls "democratic individualism." The deceptive maneuvers of Acheson's still have a flimsy social base in China.

Acheson's White Paper admits that the U.S. imperialists are at a complete loss as to what to do. . . . Acheson says in his Letter of Transmittal:

> The unfortunate but inescapable fact is that the ominous result of the civil war in China was beyond the control of the government of the United States. Nothing that this country did or could have done within the reasonable limits of its capabilities could have changed that result; nothing that was left undone by this country has contributed to it. It was the product of internal Chinese forces, forces which this country tried to influence but could not.

According to logic, Acheson . . . should treat People's China on the basis of equality and mutual benefit and stop making trouble. But no, says Acheson. Troublemaking will continue, and indefinitely so. Will there be any result? There will, says he. On what group of people will he rely? On the supporters of "democratic individualism." Says Acheson:

> . . . . Ultimately the profound civilization and the democratic individualism of China will reassert themselves and she will throw off the foreign yoke. I consider that we should encourage all developments in China which now and in the future work toward this end.

How different is the logic of the imperialists from that of the people! Make trouble, fail, make trouble again, fail again . . . till their doom; that is the logic of the imperialists and all reactionaries the world over in dealing with the people's cause, and they will never go against this logic. This is a Marxist law. . . .

Fight, fail, fight again, fail again, fight again . . . till their victory; that is the logic of the people, and they too will never go against this logic. This is another Marxist law. The Russian people's revolution followed this law, and so has the Chinese people's revolution.

Classes struggle; some classes triumph; others are eliminated. Such is history, such is the history of civilization for thousands of years. To interpret history from this viewpoint is historical materialism; standing in opposition to this viewpoint is historical idealism. . . .

The only course is to organize forces and struggle against them. . . . Only then will there be any hope of dealing with imperialist foreign countries on the basis of equality and mutual benefit. Only then will there be any hope that those landlords, bureaucrat-capitalists, members of the reactionary Kuomintang clique and their accomplices, who have laid down their arms and surrendered, can be given education for transforming the bad into the good and be transformed, as far as possible, into good people. . . .

It is the duty of progressives—the Communists, members of the democratic parties, politically conscious workers, the student youth and progressive intellectuals—to unite with the intermediate strata, middle-of-the-roaders and backward elements of various strata, with all those in People's China who are still wavering; . . . give them sincere help, criticize their wavering character, educate them, win them over to the side of the masses, prevent the imperialists from pulling them over and tell them to cast away illusions and prepare for struggle. . . .

The slogan, "Prepare for struggle," is addressed to those who still cherish certain illusions. . . . Their minds are still not made up . . . because they still have illusions about the United States. There is still a very wide, or fairly wide, gap between these people and ourselves on this question.

The publication of the U.S. White Paper and Acheson's Letter of Transmittal is worthy of celebration, because it is a bucket of cold water and a loss of face for those who have ideas of the old type of democracy or democratic individualism, who do not approve of . . . people's democracy, or democratic collectivism, or democratic centralism, or collective heroism, or patriotism based on internationalism—but who still have patriotic feelings and are not Kuomintang reactionaries. It is a bucket of cold water particularly for those who believe that everything American is good and hope that China will model herself on the United States.

Acheson openly declares that the Chinese democratic individualists will be "encouraged" to throw off the so-called "foreign yoke." That is to say, he calls for the overthrow of Marxism-Leninism and the people's democratic dictatorship led by the Communist Party of China.

This "ism" and this system, it is alleged, are "foreign," with no roots in China, imposed on the Chinese by the German, Karl Marx (who died sixty-six years ago), and the Russian, Lenin (who died twenty-five years ago) and Stalin (who is still alive). This "ism" and this system, moreover, are downright bad, because they advocate the class struggle, the overthrow of imperialism, etc.; hence they must be got rid of. In this connection, it is alleged, "the democratic individualism of China will reassert itself" with the "encouragement" of President Truman, the backstage Commander-in-Chief Marshall, Secretary of State Acheson (the charming foreign mandarin responsible for the publication of the White Paper) and Ambassador Leighton Stuart, who has scampered off. Acheson and his like think they are giving "encouragement." But for those Chinese democratic individualists who still have patriotic feelings (even though they believe in the United States) this might be a bucket of cold water thrown on them and a loss of face. Instead of dealing with the authorities of the Chinese people's democratic dictatorship in the proper way, Acheson and his like are doing this filthy work, and what is more, they have openly published it. What a loss of face! What a loss of face! To those who are patriotic, Acheson's statement is not "encouragement" but an insult.

China is in the midst of a great revolution. All China is seething with enthusiasm. The conditions are favorable for winning over and uniting with all those who do not have a bitter and deep-seated hatred for the cause of the people's revolution, even though they have mistaken ideas. Progressives should use the White Paper to persuade all these persons.

42 U.S. and Mexican Pastimes (1946)

In 1946 three strong-willed parties—the commissioner of American major league baseball (A. B. "Happy" Chandler), a promoter of Mexican baseball (Jorge Pasquel), and a fledgling players' union (the American Baseball Guild)—competed for control of the sport that many ordinary U.S. citizens considered *their* pastime. The realm in question was "just a game," but play can incite serious passions. Even now, after countless rounds of scandals, strikes, and lockouts, and despite internationalist, multicultural bluster, *Esquire* magazine could still declare baseball "the last thing left in America to believe in."

There is good reason to doubt that the game was ever all that distinctly "American," anyway. Its rules have a lot in common with older sports, particularly the British game of rounders. For at least a century it has been popular—some would say more popular and better played—in places such as Cuba, the Dominican Republic, Nicaragua, Venezuela, and Mexico. Since the 1890s, Japanese amateurs have been daring the nearest Yanks to prove that their best could prevail in a truly "World" series. U.S. expatriates on Honshu, for example, made a habit of laughing off repeated challenges from a Tokyo high school (Ichiko) best known for grooming members of the Japanese elite. But when the dare was accepted in 1896, despite home-field advantage at their own private club and some ringer sailors added last-minute to the roster, the Americans were trounced by the Japanese preppies, three games out of four.

Nevertheless, many people have long clung to the belief that there is something not only distinctly but also proudly American, manly, and (until Jackie Robinson broke the color barrier in 1947) Anglo-Saxon about baseball. So as the game became more modern in the 1940s—more routinized and hierarchical with huge investments at stake—the forces of nativism as well as finance, race, and gender were visibly entwined.

These strands of American nationalism may have been most obvious in the contemporary dispute over rights to make and break baseball contracts. While players were rallying for free agency (a player's right to decide for whom he plays) and while Chandler defended team owners' prerogatives, Pasquel offered large bonuses to U.S. major leaguers if they would come south and sign on with the Liga Mexicana. Appreciation of Pasquel's bravado as well as sympathy for underpaid players actually seems to have thrilled people (certainly the press) on both sides of the border. But Chandler held his ground. He threatened to bar from U.S. games any player who even talked to Pasquel. He appealed to the courts and the State Department as well as xenophobia and racism to bar "bandit raids" on "the American game." Those appeals were generally unsuccessful, but in responding to the brouhaha, people on both sides of the border struggled to figure out exactly what might or might not be "American" in the dispute.

In this Associated Press report, for example, a member of the Mexican diplomatic corps embraces baseball and its alleged virtues to challenge the nationality of the game.

WASHINGTON, April 6 (AP)—The boys at the Mexican Embassy got into the hubbub today over the Mexican League signing up some American baseball players.

With a quick oral delivery, a person close to Ambassador Antonio Espinosa de los Monteros suggested that big league owners were missing the international pitch of a lifetime.

Asserting the Ambassador is "very interested and sympathetic" toward baseball—he "played it as a kid" and "kept up with it while a student at Gettysburg and Harvard"—this Mexican official asked:

"Why all this fuss over some American players going to Mexico? It looks like a rare opportunity for baseball to go to bat in furthering the exchange of international ideals.

"Here we are with the United Nations meeting in New York and baseball finds in its lap this rare opportunity for a practical demonstration of spreading ideas from one country to another.

"Sportsmanship is a wonderful medium for learning about democracy," this official continued. "Both of our countries feel that athletics are vitally important in this respect. They could be used to tighten relationships between peoples, perhaps more effectually even than governments.

"We exchange students, professors, artists and workers and so on, so why not ball players? After all, we learned baseball from Americans.

"We even borrowed American coaches to teach our youngsters to play your game. Now that we're coming of age in the sport, are we to be cut off from this relationship?

"In the past Mexican players have played in American leagues, so why not the other way around?

"Come to think of it, it's too bad you don't have bull-fighting, Mexico's national sport. Then we could reciprocate by sending you some of our big-league toreadors in exchange for some of your guys who make the kill with the bases loaded."

43 Ugly American Sightings (2000)

Among the most familiar of stereotypes around the world is "the ugly American." In 1878, well before the term was coined, Henry James got the gist of the idea:

A very large proportion of the Americans who annually scatter themselves over Europe are by no means flattering to the national vanity. Their merits, whatever they are, are not of a sort that strike the eye— still less the ear. They are ill-made, ill-mannered, ill-dressed.

The term itself, though, comes from the 1958 novel by William J. Lederer and Eugene Burdick. Set in war-torn "Sarkhan," *The Ugly American* is a thinly disguised censure of Cold Warriors' bumbling designs on developing nations (particularly Indochina, where French forces were supported and eventually supplanted by the United States in Vietnam). In the late 1940s and early 1950s, there was an extraordinarily large number of comparable clashes in colonies and former colonies around the world. Westerners were eager to know how better to respond.

The characters in the novel present basically two choices. One option is a prototype for the Peace Corps volunteer—generous, sympathetic, learning how to help by toiling shoulder-to-shoulder with the natives. The other is a stereotypical expatriate—well educated, ambitious but scotch-impaired, gleefully out of touch with local reality. A Philippine official explains:

The simple fact is, Mr. Ambassador, that average Americans, in their natural state, if you will excuse the phrase, are the best ambassadors a country can have. . . . But something happens to most Americans when they go abroad. Many of them are . . . second-raters. Many of them, against their own judgement, feel that they must live up to their commissaries and big cars and cocktail parties. But get an unaffected American, sir, and you have an asset. And if you get one, treasure him—keep him out of the cocktail circuit, away from bureaucrats, and let him work in his own way.

In the novel, readers may be surprised to find, "the ugly American" is actually the name that the "natural, unaffected" variety self-mockingly assumes. Homer Atkins is a volunteer with proudly "ugly" hands, calloused from engineering U.S. roads and dams. He is appalled at the well-manicured but ill-mannered incompetence of Western officials in Asia, especially when compared to their Maoist rivals. The Russians and Chinese engage peasants' hearts and minds. Given the choice, who could blame those peasants for "going Communist"? Homer fumes:

> You people do not understand such things. But men that work with their hands and muscles understand one another. . . . Don't give me statistics; don't tell me about national aspirations. Just answer me: have you been out in the boondocks?

So, ugly Americans Homer and Emma Atkins engage Sarkhan native ingenuity. They promote what would later be called "appropriate technologies." With "Mid-western practicality," they harness cheap, locally renewable resources to produce contraptions that ease daily life and thereby, they assume, reduce revolutionary passion.

Given their attack on U.S. policy and pride, it is not surprising that the authors (both veterans—Burdick, a Berkeley political scientist, and Lederer, a retired naval commander) attracted passionate, diverse responses. Serialized in the *Saturday Evening Post*, topping best-seller lists, and selected by the Book-of-the-Month Club, *The Ugly American* was read by millions. Some—especially Cold War liberals—found the book's paternalism attractive, at least when compared to the darker moral of Graham Greene's *The Quiet American* (1955). Some—especially leftists—suspected that the book's charges of U.S. incompetence would encourage nativists to cut foreign aid or right-wingers to resume "witch hunts" in the manner of Senator Joseph McCarthy or HUAC (House Un-American Activities Committee) earlier in the 1950s. Yet others—especially on the right—used the book as an occasion for patriotic bravado, to defend the State Department, or to advocate more aggressive anti-communism.

The modern popular sense of the term "ugly American" seems flat by comparison. But it is also a ready, almost unavoidable referent for U.S. tourists and their hosts abroad. It is an understanding of America that mediates their relations and that sets nerves on edge. Here is a sample of "ugly American sightings" posted to Rick Steves's Internet bulletin board for "European Back Door Travelers" (EBDT) in 2000.

Ugly American Sightings. Of course, back door travelers [BDT] are beautiful Americans overseas. But sooner or later you bump into an American who makes you want to wear a Canadian flag. Tell us your most horrifying Ugly American story.

Please Note: This is not a forum for debate on cultural differences and values. We want to hear about your encounters with travelers in Europe who "just don't get it."

Moderator Rick, U.S.A.

[Editor: Posts are here abbreviated and rearranged.]

Nothing in my opinion equals the statement I overheard on the Champs Elysées in 1966, from two aging American ladies with blue hair: "I never, Mabel—ya come all the way to France and all ya hear is French!"

Steve P, Mililani, HI USA 01/24/99

I was living in England and was in London for a day. While waiting to cross the street at Piccadilly Circus, there were two loud American men in front of me. They kept saying (loudly), "These f***ing English, they don't know how to drive. They're on the wrong side of the f***ing road." Needless to say, I was ashamed to be American at that moment and just kept my head down, crossing the street quickly.

Staci USA 11/08/98

After having traveled to Europe on a continual basis for the last fifteen years, my wife and I have come to the main conclusion that there is a segment of the U.S. public that has absolutely no business traveling to Europe or even to Las Vegas for that matter. These UAs are found everywhere. They expect to be entertained at every turn of the road; they appreciate only the manufactured computer-age gimmicks and have absolutely no common sense or street smarts. The best thing for this segment is to stay home and let the true adventure-seeking segment enjoy the finer things without their constant whining and complaining. They make us all look bad. We are judged by their rudeness.

Dennis R, Perry, IA USA 11/13/99

My most common encounter with Ugly Americans is usually people who are inappropriately dressed for the religion, ethics, or local mores. I can't say how many times I've seen halter tops and microminis on women in Third-World countries where even the prostitutes don't dress like that. In most countries, T-shirts and shorts are only worn by small children and mentally defective people. To them, you look like you are travelling in your underwear. After a while, I have to agree—you can spot the tourist in the crowd by the enormous amount of exposed flesh.

Ellen J, Reno, NV USA 04/25/99

Don't worry about cameras and Hawaiian shirts advertising you as a tourist. The natives recognize tourists instantly, no matter what you do. I would recommend, though, avoiding the classic "American tourist" look: blue jeans, white socks, white sneakers. Even though any Parisian will know in an instant that I am American, when they see me wearing brown socks and shoes with jeans, they know that I know. Sounds ridiculous, but my Parisian friends have confirmed this.

Bob L, Derby UK 11/29/98

I hate it when Americans in Europe want to talk to every other American they come across about idiotic things "back in the States." I didn't go to Europe to listen to someone gab on and on about the Pittsburgh Steelers or the problem Buffy is having with her cheerleading chores in Iowa. Anytime I am speaking English in public with my wife and an American marches up and says, "How nice it is to hear English again . . . Where are you from? I'm from Ohio. . ." I want to run, screaming.

Quentin USA 10/25/99

I am Dutch. First of all, there are ugly people from all countries, but I believe we tend to pay more attention to our own folks. I often find ugly Dutch on my trips. . . . Just a question to you Americans: I often overhear conversations between Americans in the train (I live close to Amsterdam). Why do so many people travel all the way to Europe to discuss Margie's divorce, Peter's new girlfriend, or their own terrible new neighbors??

Sjoerd, Amsterdam NL 02/03/99

Boy, we have a lot of Ugly American sightings in Rome. I have one, too: I was absolutely mortified when a woman (from my home-town, Chicago, actually) was yelling at a waiter in a restaurant in Rome. The waiter spoke a scant amount of English; she spoke no Italian. She was, literally, yelling at him, "Can't you put some cheese on this pizza?!" And then with her pasta order, "Don't you have Alfredo sauce, AL-FRAY-DOH sauce, you know, like in the United States?!" The waiter just kept saying, "Ah, no comprende." That just made her louder. We wanted to absolutely lay down and die, we were so embarrassed.

Sabrina, Miami, FL USA 08/22/99

Many descriptions here do indeed fit what I would call an "Ugly American," but others just seem to point to rudeness or lack of preparation, not necessarily attitude based on being an American. My own definition of an Ugly American is pretty specific: someone who does not appreciate cultural differences, but instead judges other cultures based on what it is like in the U.S.; almost always thinks the U.S. way is better without thinking about why it may or may not be; and expects others to accommodate them by preferential treatment or by speaking English to them. Two of my most detested "Ugly American" statements are: "Why don't they speak English?" and "The French seem to forget we saved them during the war."

Dan W, Durham, NC USA 01/26/99

Why do so many people around the world hate Americans? Is this some kind of universal rule?

LA, CA USA 07/08/99

LA, CA: I don't think "people around the world hate Americans" exactly. It's more of a "love/hate relationship." We've been the world's dominant culture for the past fifty years, and that's bound to breed resentment. Imagine how we'd react if we were farther down the pecking order of nations and, say, the Swiss were the world's dominant culture. We'd be saying: "What? 'Heidi' is on TV again?! And what's with this stupid cheese? I'm tired of the Swiss!" We're also the loudest and most materialistic people on earth, and generally have a lack of perspective on history (mainly because ours is so short). On the other hand, we've been the world's torchbearers for democracy for two centuries. Though we sometimes handle this role in a bumbling, heavy-handed way, the net result has been very positive for the world. I think most people in the world recognize this and are grateful to us. I think they also admire our positive, enthusiastic approach to everything, our ability to get things done, and our great love of personal freedom. So . . . I don't think you can say "people around the world hate Americans"—they hate us and love us and resent us and admire us, all at once.

Jim C, Boulder, CO USA 07/11/99

The fear of being the ugly American seems to make some travelers bashful to the point of being stepped on. . . . I doubt that there are many Europeans who hate Americans in person, even if they hate Americans as a nation. If American, be American. Just be cool about it.

Chris B, Santa Monica, CA USA 01/06/99

Anyone want to join me in becoming a citizen of Mexico?

Brian and Cheri B, London UK 05/18/99

Hey, EBDTers . . . be proud and wear your American good nature all over Europe, and maybe we can shame the idiots into invisibleness through a fun-loving, educated and respectful way of travel. I refuse to walk on eggshells in fear that I might get labeled an Ug Am. I am an Am and proud I am. Amen.

Sistah K, HI USA 06/04/99

I saw several similar incidents in Ireland. Visiting American rugby players were in rather upscale bars and kept demanding obscure American "shots" like the purple hooter, as well as liquors like tequila and jagermeister, which aren't really commonly found in such places in Ireland. The bartender kept saying, "How about a whiskey? Maybe you'd like a Guinness?" and generally acting very courteous. They kept complaining how no decent college bar (oxymoron) in the States would be without their novelty liquors. Finally the bartender—who had many other polite patrons to whom to attend—said, "Then perhaps I can offer you the door?" and in one swift motion came out from behind the door, took the most obstreperous of the bunch by the collar, and unceremoniously dumped him out. When he returned, lightly wiping his hands with his Harp bar towel, he asked the lad's friends, "And what can I get you gentlemen?" "Guinness, please," was the almost universal reply of the former rowdies.

Chris, St. Louis, MO USA 11/18/99

I work for a music school that has a growing Irish music program. On our recent trip to Ireland, we shot a lot of videotape of Irish musicians to share with the students back home. At the Cliffs of Moher we came across a young man playing his accordion along the pathway. As my husband taped his performance, we overhead an American lady saying, "Isn't it terrible the way that people take pictures of those poor beggars!" We chatted with the accordionist afterwards, who turned out to be from Boston and was "just hanging around Ireland for a while to learn more about Irish music" and made some extra cash by "busking" at the Cliffs. What you see isn't always what you expect!

Samantha T USA 12/02/98

As a Spaniard living in Japan I fear the nice weather which brings tourists with it. The LOUD voices of venerable American ladies would scare anyone. . . .

As a European (yes, we Spanish are European too, as I've tried to explain many times) from Barcelona, we generalize a lot about all foreigners. We call them "guiris," which could be described as "sneakers or sandals, cheap T-shirt, shorts, funny hats, camera, RED from the sun." Yes, it is negative but implies the funny side, too.

Europeans are not so keen on each other, either.

I'd like to introduce a new type of UA (or ugly English-speaker in general): the pseudo-intellectual. He or she has been working as an English teacher for some time in a European/Asian country. This entitles him or her to deeply criticize the country/culture/women's rights/ smoking habits/food. They do that while getting drunker and drunker or having a funny smoke, demonstrating how cool or brave he is. Avoid them completely.

Be polite, don't shout, eat your food and happy travelling!

Ricardo R SPAIN 06/11/99

I've also met Europeans in the United States who were shocked (and a little disappointed) that everything wasn't exactly like "Married with Children" and that we're not all a bunch of morons. . . .

CMW, Sacramento, CA USA 04/12/99

I don't want to apologize for American behavior or ignorance by any means, but I can offer some reasons why I think it is the way it is.

1. We are the richest nation in the world in most regards. Therefore, way too many have a superiority complex.
2. Even though we are a nation of immigrants, we have not needed to learn a foreign language growing up to communicate with people we encounter on a daily basis—English has become the language of business, education, and diplomacy, and too often we expect others to speak it.
3. The rudeness of Americans may be explained by statistics. Perhaps a large percentage of Americans behave well overseas, but there are just so many Americans with the money to travel that we are bound to encounter a large number who behave badly.
4. We grow up in an isolated society. Our neighbors to the north and south seem so far away for most people. For a Frenchman, a German or Italian seems just around the bend. This influences our educational system so that languages, geography, etc., are not emphasized enough. It is amazing how many students can't even tell you where North America is on a map. Size of the country has a real role in this—Russia and China have also

been somewhat culturally isolated during periods in their own histories.

Any other theories on this?

DW, Durham, NC USA 12/03/98

Last December, I returned to the States after having been in charge of a civilian personnel office at a small U.S. Army base in the Netherlands. Almost without exception, the Americans who were stationed there, both military and civilian, were the biggest bunch of ignorant and pigheaded jackasses I had ever seen. For example, I went to a soldier's home (U.S. Army-subsidized in an American mini-ghetto) to buy a table she had advertised for sale. I did not have dollars on me so I offered Dutch guilders instead. But she told me she had NO USE for guilders since she bought everything on base. I was dumbstruck. OK, I thought, you may not have had any choice in being sent to Schinnen (which was in a very pleasant and picturesque part of the Netherlands), but don't you have even the smallest desire to explore your surroundings? Hell, you might learn something. Maybe she was an extreme example, but, in general, I found the Americans to have very little interest in the host country and even less interest in the Dutch people. It was a sobering and saddening experience for me. It is no wonder that we often are perceived as spoiled, bored, superficial and stupid children. Yes, other nationalities can sometimes display these characteristics, but Americans seem to be hard-wired with these negative qualities.

Dave D, Washington, DC USA 04/05/99

My first experience abroad came in 1985 while in the U.S. Marine Corps. I was stationed for seven months in Iwakuni, Japan, and a vast majority of the Marines never left the base or the "100-yard dash" outside the main gate. The worst ugly Americanism I recall was the popular T-shirt with a nuclear mushroom cloud on it with the words, "Made in America, Tested in Japan."

I did everything I could to get as far away from the base as possible, and enjoyed myself and learned more than I thought I would.

Mike S, Everett, WA USA 05/11/99

I was a Navy Lieutenant on active duty in the Mediterranean. I gave a lot of liberty briefings during that time. . . . Prior to any port visit, sailors are educated about the port and usually given a stern warning about getting involved in any trouble. One thing to keep in mind is that these kids off Navy ships aren't taking the summer off to bounce lazily around Europe. They are a long way from home, often for the first time, and when they go ashore they usually just have several hours before they have to go back aboard the ship. They are aware that they represent their country while overseas, and they realize that they are following in a long tradition of U.S. presence in Europe. And they know it is their responsibility to make sure that Navy ships continue to be welcomed.

I would urge any American who is overseas, and spots some sailors or Marines, to go up to them and say hello. The service member might have been gone from the U.S. for several months and would certainly welcome talking to a fellow (civilian) American. And I'm sure most would welcome any advice about what to see or do.

Ed B, Boston, MA USA 12/28/98

My worst (best?) Ug-Am story involved an overweight woman complaining to the staff at the Anne Frank House in Amsterdam that the stairs were too steep and that they should provide an elevator in the house so that elderly and physically challenged people could enjoy the house as well!

Dave E, Morrisville, NC USA 01/07/99

To Dave E: Why are people "ugly Americans" for suggesting that tourist sites be made elderly/disabled accessible? There are people of all nationalities who are not so fortunate as to be able to enjoy many incredible sites around the world, simply because they are unable to ascend a steep flight of stairs.

Shanya D, Boston, MA USA 01/15/99

In reply to Shanya D: We travelling Americans in search of history have much to be thankful for. The European governments have seen fit to preserve the authenticity of historic sites. Why should these sites be "altered" to accommodate overweight (handicapped?) people? If Shanya herself has ever been to the Anne Frank House, she should realize that to alter those narrow steps to the secret apartment would surely destroy the authenticity! I myself, being overweight and out of shape, would never expect that Europeans alter their tourist areas to accommodate me! There are limitations on all of us, whether it is financial, physical or emotional. We have to live with those limits and not foist our disabilities on the rest of the world!

Patsy K USA 03/11/99

Please, folks, no social agendas. Get out there and travel! If we met each other on the streets, we'd probably all be friends. . . . Be good to each other!

Rick USA 04/25/99

I had been traveling for a while and had become disdainful of all other Americans, ignoring them for other nationalities. Boarding my plane to come home, I overheard an older American couple talking with a deep Southern accent. I automatically assumed that they were the typical tourists, minus the huge tour bus encasing them. I didn't say anything or act on this; I'm not a jerk. We got on the plane, and they ended up sitting next to me. I silently sighed. It turned out that they had been living in Holland for thirteen years on a ministry. We talked the entire flight, and they offered me a place to stay if I ever went to Delft. It was one of the nicest flights I have had in ages, and I regretted my UA attitude. I will be better about it from now on.

Jennifer K USA 04/29/99

Jennifer, I usually have the same reaction when I see some American with a Midwestern or Northern accent sitting next to me. ☺

Orange (#1 baby) Sun USA 04/29/99

My first trip to Europe was in 1976. I was delighted to be there; I was impressed by everything I saw. I marveled at how neat and tidy it was. As my husband and I journeyed across southern Germany, suddenly we came across piles of litter and debris. I was shocked. Where was the German orderliness and cleanliness? I was confused and then mortified to learn we had just passed an American military base!

This incident taught me a never-to-be-forgotten lesson. The first bad thing I saw in Europe was American-made. I became determined that no one could ever point at me as an example of the Ugly American.

Diann, TX USA 05/11/99

Okay, equal time for other ugly nationality stories. I lived in England for five years and traveled extensively on the continent. I learned the phrase "You'd think they won the bloody war" in every language when referring to Germans, who, while on holiday, seem to become extremely aggressive and loud. In London, where everyone lines up for their bus, you could count on Germans pushing to the head of the line.

Next, the Brits. As much as I love them, many of them, once they leave the island, seemed to need to get as drunk as possible as quickly as possible . . . . Although loving to holiday in Spain especially, they would . . . have to have their fry-ups and chicken and chips, ignoring local food. So it's not just us ugly Americans, which should be reassuring to some.

Carolyn S, Albuquerque, NM USA 01/03/99

I know there are individual examples of enlightenment among our people and that there are numerous examples of undesirable behavior committed by the English, Japanese or whoever. But the bottom line is this: American society is so different from, say, Dutch or French, that it is not surprising that we come off, typically, as awkward, child-like neurotics who, clad in the ubiquitous rubber clodhoppers and baseball caps that have become our uniforms, roam the world being alternatively shocked and bored. We display the most frightful ignorance of anything beyond our borders. It hurts me to say all this because I am American myself, but have had, by the grace of God, the opportunity to live overseas for about ten years of my life. Please tell me: why are we so awful?

Dave D, Washington, DC USA 12/02/98

The Ugly (whatever) phenomenon is practiced by any culture that feels superior to the other. The Americans do it in Europe, the Europeans do it in Africa and Asia, the Saudi Arabs do it in India. I am an Indian and I see far too many ugly Saudi Arabs in India. Other nationalities are far more guilty of this ugly behavior than Americans. Let's put it all in perspective before we speak.

Manoj D Hong Kong 04/20/99

There's a corollary to all this: The "Ugly Anti-Ugly American." You meet a few Americans in Europe who have turned their contempt for their fellow Americans into a lifestyle. Even if they do condescend to speak to you, they can scarcely conceal their contempt. Anybody else have such experiences?

Many of the people writing these UA comments say they try very hard to pretend they're not Americans (carefully choosing their wardrobe, wearing Canadian flags, etc.) Why? If you're a "Beautiful American," let the world know it! If the only Americans who identify themselves as Americans are the UAs, the rest of the world will think we're all that way.

Jim C, Boulder, CO USA 04/10/99

I couldn't agree more . . . about Americans who bogusly wear Canadian flags. I traveled a lot through Europe and Asia during the late 60s and early 70s, at the height of the Vietnam War, when Americans were sometimes *personae non gratae* because of our government's behavior all over the world. Hiding behind a Canadian flag seemed to me to be cowardly as well as dishonest—and how would people overseas ever learn about what "real" Americans were like if none of the good folks were willing to represent the other sides of our country? I've seen atrocious behavior by Americans, who can be noisy and disruptive but at the same time free-spirited and generous—and although there are times when I've cringed at faux pas, I believe that's simply part of our heritage—we can grate on people, but usually our hearts are in the right place.

Nancy M, San Francisco, CA USA 11/09/99

I am so sick of the "Ugly American" issue! I travel extensively in Europe as a photographer and I can guarantee you that if one hears "excuse me," "sorry," or "please" ANYWHERE it is from an American. NO one is more pushy, rude, and crass as tourists than the Japanese and Germans as a whole. It's not out of any personal prejudice that I write this, it's from experience and polling locals (especially in the service/tourist industry) about whom they would rather have in their country. I am proud to be an American traveling and have been welcomed as such everywhere I've traveled. Even when Americans do make mistakes, they are the ones most apt to make up for it and learn from them. I've been told Americans are the friendliest, smile, tip and treat people better, and are most willing to "get into" the culture of places and talk to the people more than any other nationality. So, there! Be proud of being an American.

Susan S, San Diego, CA USA 08/02/99

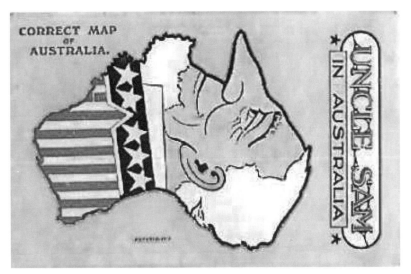

Uncle Sam in Australia, postcard, ca. 1909

Troops fighting the British in the War of 1812 were the first to receive rations in containers bearing a "U.S." label. The letters indicated a federal tax status for shipping, but longshoremen and soldiers apparently joked that these were the initials of the New Yorker who packed them, "Uncle Sam" Wilson. Eventually, Uncle Sam became a national icon. He maintained Wilson's gender, complexion, and beanpole frame, but other traces of his origin were forgotten. As an embodiment of the republic, he grew taller and gained more angular features, stars and stripes, a white beard, and a top hat. Stateside, he was generally portrayed as a kindly father figure, cheerful, patient, and loving but firm in defense of his family. Outside the United States, he was more often portrayed as a bully. This postcard seems to foreclose neither sort of interpretation. It was printed at a time when Australia and New Zealand were gaining autonomy from Britain and when the United States was increasing its presence among navies of the Pacific.

Uncle Sam Welcomes Mexico, commemorative postcard, 1915

The San Diego exposition was part of a U.S. celebration of the completion of the Panama Canal. It was sponsored by the city of San Diego, the first Pacific port in the United States north of the canal. The photo was snapped as a band played in front of the Home Economy Building on the Plaza de Panama.

Chinese Pose as Auto Tourists near San Francisco, postcard, 1910

This pictorial fantasy became the face of a greeting card posted to a San Francisco resident just before New Year's Day, 1911. Thanks to a studio backdrop, Woo Dum and his friends assumed the unlikely pose of sporty tourists. At the time, Chinese in San Francisco were essentially barred from public life outside of Chinatown. In 1910, also, they established the T'ung Meng Hui (Together Sworn Society), one of several stateside organizations that were the main source of funds for the Chinese Nationalist Party. The following fall, San Francisco's Chinese Nationalists celebrated victory when the party defeated the Manchu government and installed a China-born, U.S.-educated leader, Sun Yat-sen, as the republic's first president.

U.S. Tourist Poses by a Bar in Havana, Constantino
Arias, 1948

The photographs by Constantino Arias provide a biting vision of everyday life in
Cuba under dictator Fulgencio Batista, when the nation was also a popular destination for U.S. tourists. Among the positions that Arias held at the time was as a
house photographer for the Hotel Nacional.

E. P. THOMPSON

44 Letter to Americans (1986)

During the 1960s and 1970s social studies in Western universities turned sharply to the left. Broadening 1930s-style socialism and purging Stalinist sympathies, a "New Left" helped make Marxism more attractive to culturally oriented critics in the arts, humanities, and social sciences. In the United States, the University of Wisconsin was a center of innovation (for example, historians such as Frederick Jackson Turner's student Merle Curti, Harvey Goldberg, Fred Harvey Harrington, Gabriel Kolko, George Mosse, George Rawick, and William Appleman Williams). But the movement also included East Coast intellectuals such as C. L. R. James and Eugene Genovese. Key European contributions crossed the Atlantic through the French *annalistes* (sociologists and historians led by Lucien Febvre and Marc Bloch via the *Annales d'histoire économique et sociale*) and critics such as Antonio Gramsci, Eric Hobsbawm, and E. P. Thompson.

Long before the "counter-culture" became fashionable, Thompson was an influential British Communist and labor educator. His 1963 book, *The Making of the English Working Class*, inspired generations of scholars in and around American Studies. In *Annales* tune, it demonstrated an imaginative, less narrowly materialist way to comprehend relations of dominance and oppression. He helped forge links between ideology and economy, academic criticism and political activism, industrial and postindustrial experience, and local and global perspectives. The next generation of radical scholars (such as Mari Jo Buhle, Nancy Shcrom Dye, Ann D. Gordon, Linda Gordon, Herbert Gutman, Vincent Harding, and Manning Marable) readily acknowledged their debt to his work.

In the following essay, Thompson addresses a sequence of violent international events. As usual, as he explains, determining "who started it" requires dating the "start," usually to one side's advantage. In the squabble that inevitably ensues, responsibility for stopping it is apt to be shirked. Nevertheless, no one could doubt the gravity of the events to which Thompson refers.

On April 14, 1986, about one hundred U.S. aircraft from the Sixth Fleet of the Navy and the 48th Tactical Fighter Wing of the Air Force attacked Libya. In justification, representatives of the U.S. government cited a long list of Libyan provocations, chiefly acts of international terrorism. The list, for which they held Col. Muammar al-Qaddafi particularly accountable, began with the same allegations that prompted the United States to close its consulate and then to boycott Libyan oil, beginning in 1981–1982. Recent incidents included airport explosions in Rome and Vienna (December 1985), threats to nearby U.S. forces (March 1986, when the military was testing Qaddafi's "Line of Death" along the northern edge of the Gulf of Sidra), the downing of TWA Flight 840 over Greece (April), and then the bombing of a well-known retreat for U.S. servicemen stationed in Berlin, Germany. The attack on the La Belle Discothèque killed a Turkish woman and two American troops and injured 230 others.

Nine days later, President Reagan ordered retaliation. The National Security Council approved air strikes on Tripoli and Benghazi targets. Although in populous cities, damage was supposed to be limited to command and control centers for terrorism and nearby air defenses such as the Benina airfield. Dubbed "El Dorado Canyon," the operation was complex and bloated, not least because NATO allies France, Germany, Italy, and Spain refused to help. U.S. planes would leave from England, radically increasing the length of flights (for F-111s, up from an average of two hours per sortie to thirteen) and requiring roundtrip support so immense (eight to twelve in-flight refuelings per aircraft) that all chance of surprise attack would be lost.

Although the U.S. air armada hovered near targets for about an hour, the engagement was brief. In just twelve minutes, beginning at 2:00 A.M. Tripoli time, planes dropped sixty tons of munitions.

Representatives of the United States announced that the operation was a success. Although the "efficiency" was low (only four of eighteen F-111s actually dropped their payload), all targets were hit, and all but one of the planes returned safely. "Karma 52" and its crew were apparently shot down. Capt. Paul F. Lorence's remains were lost; Capt. Fernando L. Ribas-Dominicci's were returned to the United States three years later.

Representatives of Libya protested consequences on the ground. Destruction included serious (albeit "collateral") damage to the French embassy and neighboring residences, more than 200 casualties (mostly civilians), and 37 deaths, including Qaddafi's fifteen-month-old adopted daughter.

Worcester, England
22 April 1986

Dear Americans,

I will explain to you why I am, just now, what you call "anti-American."

I have difficulty in being this, since I am, in ethnic origin, half American myself. When I say this, my American friends think I am making some sort of joke. It is supposed that all nations are "ethnic" except Americans, who are in some way post-ethnic. Yet if ethnicity comprises historical and cultural traditions, Americans (of whatever color) are as ethnic as anyone, and are also becoming more nationalistic with each year.

On my mother's side, I can trace American ancestry, along five or six lines, for over 300 years. I have spent pleasant days, reversing the usual genealogical pilgrimage, hunting out simple burial stones of ancestors in Rhode Island field plots.

I'm afraid that most of this ancestry was WASP. My great-great-grandfather, Judge William Jessup, nominated Lincoln at the Chicago Republican Convention and chaired the committee which drew up his campaign platform.

His son, Henry Jessup, was one of the founders of the American Mission in the Lebanon, where my mother was born and grew up. If you read his *Fifty-Three Years in Syria* you will find that there were Americans in those days who did not regard the Islamic world as being made up of "wogs," "gooks," or targets for bombardment. (In 1984 the *New Jersey* lobbed half-ton shells onto the hills around Zahle where my mother spent her childhood.)

You will also find out that the troubles of the Middle East did not start yesterday. They were there before the state of Israel. In that tormented human macédoine (the Lebanon), Druse and Maronites, Moslem and Christian sects, warred with each other 150 years ago.

The British and the French in those days sought to reform the manners of the people by indiscriminate acts of retaliation. The British, in 1841, had the brilliant idea of bombarding Beirut. All this did was to prepare for the ferocious retribution which the Druse visited upon Christian villages in the massacres of 1860.

Since the British gave this example of "diplomacy," I suppose that my British half should congratulate you on following our example. It is the American half of me which rises up in outrage.

What has come over you? What has caused this strange national self-exaltation, this isolationism of the heart, these intrusions upon others' territories and cultures, these Rambo reflexes?

How can a nation which preens itself on its sensitivity to racism in its domestic arrangements behave with brutal racist indifference towards Libyans?

Terrorism is a word for things so terrible that it dulls the brain like alcohol. For the death of one American serviceman in West Berlin—there was also another death, but since it was a Turk and a woman it is rarely mentioned—63 Libyan lives are exacted. Perhaps there was Libyan involvement in the Berlin disco terror, but no one has yet put that to any jury.

An eye for an eye is questionable morality. But by your moral arithmetic, one American pair of eyes equals the eyes of 63 Libyans. Human blood is precious, but my American ancestry did not teach me that American blood is ten times more valuable than European and one hundred times more valuable than Libyan or Nicaraguan, "wog" or "commie" or "gook" blood.

The harboring of terrorists is certainly a foul offence. Each year huge sums are collected in the USA to buy arms for the Provisional IRA. At the St. Patrick's Day parades in New York City, graced by mayors and political dignitaries, the collectors are out, and no doubt my liberal friends have contributed, with no notion of the anguish which this brings to sectarian-tormented Northern Ireland. It is said that American money may have been used to buy Libyan arms, used for IRA terrorism in Ireland or England. It is being asked very widely in Britain today whether this now entitles us to get out our aging Vulcan bombers and bomb New York.

Terrorism is infinitely recessive, like Chinese boxes. Where do we start? With the British bombarding Beirut? With the Druse massacres of Christians? With Mr. Begin's Stern Gang blowing up the St. David Hotel full of Brits? With Israeli bombing strikes on the Lebanon? With CIA-backed adventures, first to install that good anti-Communist, Qaddafi, and then to assassinate him when he turned out to be less pliant? With the drowning by American gunfire of Libyan sailors in the Gulf of Sidra? With the Berlin disco? Or with the state terrorism—and assassination attempt—of your F-111s on Tripoli?

What Druse massacre of the future is now being meditated in darkening hearts throughout the Islamic world? Is it true (as we have been told) that not one voice has yet been heard in Congress, explicitly condemning the terror bombing of the sleeping city of Tripoli? Are all the compassionate and internationally minded Americans whom I used to know now dead? And do their descendants not care?

If my American half feels outrage against my motherland, my British (or European) half regards my fatherland with shame. Those F-111s were launched from the English countryside. You have been told that, while other Europeans are wimps, Mrs. Thatcher is a heroine who "walks tall." I can assure you that she is no heroine to her own people. She is seen as the betrayer of our national integrity and our national honor. Our land has been used to harbor your state terrorism, in exactly the same way as the Libyans are accused of harboring Palestinian agents. The feelings of two-thirds of our nation are those of revulsion and shame, not of fear. To be sure, there is a not-unnatural dislike of the immediate consequences. At a time when the Archbishop of Canterbury's representative, Mr. Terry Waite, has been, at risk to his own life, patiently negotiating the release of American hostages in the Lebanon, your actions have caused the murder of British hostages and turmoil at European airports and sensitive points—which are nearer to the Islamic world than your own.

We understand that Americans, having done their worst to screw our world up, will now abstain from taking their holidays in Europe for fear that they might get hurt. But we are slow to learn our right place, and have not yet concurred in your low valuation of European blood.

There are also—if I may impose on your patience a little longer, as you prepare to take holidays in the safety of Russia and China—some small political objections. Many Europeans don't like U.S. policies in Central America, but we watch them with the resignation proper to our station. After all, you've been going on like that for a century or so. And it is "your" backyard.

But the Mediterranean is not even Europe's backyard. It is part of Europe. It is the cradle of European civilization, and even on its southern shore there are ancient half-European cities, a European diaspora.

It is not your sea and we don't know what you are doing there. Do you? What *are* you doing there? Who invited you? By what right do you blunder and bomb and bombard around its shores?

Don't pretend that something called NATO asked you to do this. It did not. It was not consulted. The NATO allies most closely concerned in that sensitive zone—Spain, Italy and Greece—are appalled.

If you decide to fund and arm terrorists in Nicaragua, maybe that's your own affair, the affair of your victims, and of nations in America, South and North. But if you start bombing around the fringes of Europe, without any consultation with your allies, then NATO is nothing but a hole with an American gun pointing through it.

You have turned my fatherland into the Diego Garcia of the North Atlantic, a launching-base for your state terrorism. Most of my own people agree with me. That is a comfort of sorts. But the comfort will be worth little until your bases have been removed.

That is why both halves of me—the American and the British—unite in what you misrecognize as "anti-Americanism." It is because I value American traditions that I am opposed to the public face of the American state, to the cowardly bombast of its reigning politicians, to the evil which its racist aggression is reproducing, and the dangers into which it is leading the whole world. I am not opposed to Americans. I think it is tragic that they have forgotten their traditions and lost their way, through an overdose from their media of ideological alcohol.

People are asking, up and down Europe, whether this or that nation ought now to leave NATO? My own advice leads to a cleaner and simpler solution. Let the European NATO allies, with courtesy and thanks, invite the United States to leave NATO. If she will not leave, then let them expel her. They can then attend to their own security needs in whichever way best suits them, and engage in their own negotiations for disarmament with the Soviet bloc.

We shall certainly feel safer when your F-111s, Poseidons and battle-fleets have gone home. You will probably feel safer also, and suffer from fewer rushes of ideological blood to the head. You might even find it safe to take your holidays in the Mediterranean again. Where all of you, except for President Rambo, will be heartily welcome.

Yours sincerely,
E. P. Thompson

VI | America as a Culture

Some Guiding Questions

Why look for a particular culture in the United States?
    What is at stake?
    For whom?
        For Americans with or without social privilege?
        For people outside the United States?
    What factors might be expected to account for
        the culture's appearance?
How should the distinctiveness and worth of the
    culture be gauged?
    Of what might it consist?
        How important, for example, is a unified
            tradition of artistic expression?
        Of political and economic institutions?
        Of intimate values?
        Of imagined ideals or regularities in the
            realities of daily life?

How should critics judge the culture that they find?
In what ways—in what respects and from whose perspective—should it be judged relatively good or bad?
For example, how broadly should features of American culture be shared?
Which ones?
How well should it reflect the diversity of individuals or the similarities within groups?
How much should it stay the same or change?
What sorts of invention or preservation are best?

45 The American Scholar (1837)

In the early nineteenth century, North America was an infamously dynamic setting of agriculture, commerce, and nature, diverse languages, folkways, faith, and toil. But it was also considered an intellectual backwater. Native and African-American traditions were under heavy assault. Women's work counted in "a separate sphere." Most schools were poor imitations of those in Europe, requiring rote recitations from Greece or Rome and the churches and courts of monarchs. European immigrants and their descendants tended to mix pride and shame in their liberty from "the learned classes" of the Old World. American leaders longed for a worthy substitute.

For most of U.S. history, they found one in "the man of letters." He was an advocate of literacy, well schooled in European, Protestant tradition but eager to stake out native ground and well connected to the publishers and reviewers who could make it his. He could be counted on for evaluation of almost everything. But he emphasized "American" things, books, fashions, and ideas, what they meant, how they mattered. His strong suit was the essay. Rather than speaking *for* a constituency, profession, or institution, he aimed to speak *of* society, art, and nature—about them, to them, with them—in a voice determinedly his own.

He also bespoke his social position, the particular institutions and traditions with which he traded. The first home of the most famous American men of letters was New England, and their exemplar was Ralph Waldo Emerson. His Brahmin credentials were impeccable. The following address, delivered in Cambridge, Massachusetts, in 1837, was sponsored by the elite brothers of Phi Beta Kappa (short for *Philosophia biou kybernetes*—"Philosophy is the guide of life"). Formed in 1776, it probably qualifies as the very first "Greek" fraternity or sorority in the Americas. Just six years before Emerson's address, it remained a secret society, and it admitted only men until 1875.

Part of the challenge in reading "The American Scholar," no doubt, is due to the exclusiveness of the occasion. And a prose poem from a prior century can be tough going, especially when bathed in the Transcendentalism for which Emerson is famous. He constantly tacks between the common and the cosmic. But the urge for just such a connection has been a persistent feature of American cultural criticism. Here, Emerson provides both a singular illustration and a prototypical defense of the tradition.

Mr. President and Gentlemen,

I greet you on the re-commencement of our literary year. Our anniversary is one of hope, and, perhaps, not enough of labor. We do not meet for games of strength or skill, for the recitation of histories, tragedies, and odes, like the ancient Greeks; for parliaments of love and poesy, like the Troubadours; nor for the advancement of science, like our contemporaries in the British and European capitals. Thus far, our holiday has been simply a friendly sign of the survival of the love of letters amongst a people too busy to give to letters any more. As such, it is precious as the sign of an indestructible instinct. Perhaps the time is already come, when it ought to be, and will be, something else; when the sluggard intellect of this continent will look from under its iron lids, and fill the postponed expectation of the world with something better than the exertions of mechanical skill. Our day of dependence, our long apprenticeship to the learning of other lands, draws to a close. The millions, that around us are rushing into life, cannot always be fed on the sere remains of foreign harvests. Events, actions arise, that must be sung, that will sing themselves. Who can doubt, that poetry will revive and lead in a new age, as the star in the constellation Harp, which now flames in our zenith, astronomers announce, shall one day be the pole star for a thousand years?

In this hope, I accept the topic which not only usage, but the nature of our association, seem to prescribe to this day—the AMERICAN SCHOLAR. Year by year, we come up hither to read one more chapter of his biography. Let us inquire what light new days and events have thrown on his character, and his hopes.

It is one of those fables, which, out of an unknown antiquity, convey an unlooked-for wisdom, that the gods, in the beginning, divided Man into men, that he might be more helpful to himself; just as the hand was divided into fingers, the better to answer its end.

The old fable covers a doctrine ever new and sublime: that there is One Man—present to all particular men only partially, or through one faculty; and that you must take the whole society to find the whole man. Man is not a farmer, or a professor, or an engineer, but he is all. Man is priest, and scholar, and statesman, and producer, and soldier. In the divided or social state, these functions are parceled out to individuals, each of whom aims to do his stint of the joint work, whilst each other performs his. The fable implies that the individual, to possess himself, must sometimes return from his own labor to embrace all the other laborers. But unfortunately, this original unit, this fountain of power, has been so distributed to multitudes, has been so minutely subdivided and peddled out, that it is spilled into drops, and cannot be gathered. The state of society is one in which the members have suffered amputation from the trunk, and strut about, so many walking monsters—a good finger, a neck, a stomach, an elbow, but never a man.

Man is thus metamorphosed into a thing, into many things. The planter, who is Man sent out into the field to gather food, is seldom cheered by any idea of the true dignity of his ministry. He sees his bushel and his cart, and nothing beyond, and sinks into the farmer, instead of Man on the farm. The tradesman scarcely ever gives an ideal worth to his work, but is ridden by the routine of his craft, and the soul is subject to dollars. The priest becomes a form; the attorney, a statute book; the mechanic, a machine; the sailor, a rope of a ship.

In this distribution of functions, the scholar is the delegated intellect. In the right state, he is Man Thinking. In the degenerate state, when the victim of society, he tends to become a mere thinker, or, still worse, the parrot of other men's thinking.

In this view of him, as Man Thinking, the theory of his office is contained. Him nature solicits with all her placid, all her monitory pictures; him the past instructs; him the future invites. Is not, indeed, every man a student, and do not all things exist for the student's behoof? And, finally, is not the true scholar the only true master? But the old oracle said, "All things have two handles: beware of the wrong one." In life, too often, the scholar errs with mankind and forfeits his privilege. Let us see him in his school, and consider him in reference to the main influences he receives.

I. The first in time and the first in importance of the influences upon the mind is that of nature. Everyday, the sun; and, after sunset, night and her stars. Ever the winds blow; ever the grass grows. Every day, men and women, conversing, beholding and beholden. The scholar is he of all men whom this spectacle most engages. He must settle its value in his mind. What is nature to him? There is never a beginning, there is never an end, to the inexplicable continuity of this web of God, but always circular power returning into itself. Therein it resembles his own spirit, whose beginning, whose ending, he never can find—so entire, so boundless. Far, too, as her splendors shine, system on system shooting like rays, upward, downward, without center, without circumference—in the mass and in the particle, nature hastens to render account of herself to the mind. Classification begins. To the young mind, every thing is individual, stands by itself. By and by, it finds how to join two things, and see in them one nature; then three, then three thousand; and so, tyrannized over by its own unifying instinct, it goes on tying things together, diminishing anomalies, discovering roots running under ground, whereby contrary and remote things cohere, and flower out from one stem. It presently learns that, since the dawn of history, there has been a constant accumulation and classifying of facts. But what is classification but the perceiving that these objects are not chaotic and are not foreign, but have a law which is also a law of the human mind? The astronomer discovers that geometry, a pure abstraction of the human mind, is the measure of planetary motion. The chemist finds proportions and intelligible method throughout matter; and science is nothing but the finding of analogy, identity, in the most remote parts. The ambitious soul sits down before each refractory fact; one after another, reduces all strange constitutions, all new powers, to their class and their law, and goes on for ever to animate the last fiber of organization, the outskirts of nature, by insight.

Thus to him, to this schoolboy under the bending dome of day, is suggested, that he and it proceed from one root; one is leaf and one is flower; relation, sympathy, stirring in every vein. And what is that Root? Is not that the soul of his soul?—A thought too bold; a dream too wild. Yet when this spiritual light shall have revealed the law of more earthly natures—when he has learned to worship the soul, and to see that the natural philosophy that now is, is only the first gropings of its gigantic hand, he shall look forward to an ever expanding knowledge as to a becoming creator. He shall see, that nature is the opposite of the soul, answering to it part for part. One is seal, and one is print. Its beauty is the beauty of his own mind. Its laws are the laws of his own mind. Nature then becomes to him the measure of his attainments. So much of nature as he is ignorant of, so much of his own mind does he not yet possess. And, in fine, the ancient precept, "Know thyself," and the modern precept, "Study nature," become at last one maxim.

II. The next great influence into the spirit of the scholar, is the mind of the Past—in whatever form, whether of literature, of art, of institutions, that mind is inscribed. Books are the best type of the influence of the past, and perhaps we shall get at the truth—learn the amount of this influence more conveniently—by considering their value alone.

The theory of books is noble. The scholar of the first age received into him the world around; brooded thereon; gave it the new arrangement of his own mind, and uttered it again. It came into him, life; it went out from him, truth. It came to him, short-lived actions; it went out from him, immortal thoughts. It came to him, business; it went out from him, poetry. It was dead fact; now, it is quick thought. It can stand, and it can go. It now endures, it now flies, it now inspires. Precisely in proportion to the depth of mind from which it issued, so high does it soar, so long does it sing.

Or, I might say, it depends on how far the process had gone, of transmuting life into truth. In proportion to the completeness of the distillation, so will the purity and imperishableness of the product be. But none is quite perfect. As no air-pump can by any means make a perfect vacuum, so neither can any artist entirely exclude the conventional, the local, the perishable from his book, or write a book of pure thought, that shall be as efficient, in all respects, to a remote posterity, as to contemporaries, or rather to the second age. Each age, it is found, must write its own books; or rather, each generation for the next succeeding. The books of an older period will not fit this.

Yet hence arises a grave mischief. The sacredness which attaches to the act of creation—the act of thought—is transferred to the record. The poet chanting, was felt to be a divine man: henceforth the chant is divine also. The writer was a just and wise spirit: henceforward it is settled, the book is perfect; as love of the hero corrupts into worship of his statue. Instantly, the book becomes noxious: the guide is a tyrant. The sluggish and perverted mind of the multitude, slow to open to the incursions of Reason, having once so opened, having once received this book, stands upon it, and makes an outcry, if it is disparaged. Colleges are built on it. Books are written on it by thinkers, not by Man Thinking; by men of talent, that is, who start wrong, who set out from accepted dogmas, not from their own sight of principles. Meek young men grow up in libraries, believing it their duty to accept the views, which Cicero, which Locke, which Bacon, have given, forgetful that Cicero, Locke, and Bacon were only young men in libraries, when they wrote these books.

Hence, instead of Man Thinking, we have the bookworm. Hence, the book-learned class, who value books, as such; not as related to nature and the human constitution, but as making a sort of Third Estate with the world and the soul. Hence, the restorers of readings, the emendators, the bibliomaniacs of all degrees.

Books are the best of things, well used; abused, among the worst. What is the right use? What is the one end, which all means go to effect? They are for nothing but to inspire. I had better never see a book, than to be warped by its attraction clean out of my own orbit, and made a satellite instead of a system. The one thing in the world, of value, is the active soul. This every man is entitled to; this every man contains within him, although, in almost all men, obstructed, and as yet unborn. The soul active sees absolute truth; and utters truth, or creates. In this action, it is genius; not the privilege of here and there a favorite, but the sound estate of every man. In its essence, it is progressive. The book, the college, the school of art, the institution of any kind, stop with some past utterance of genius. This is good, say they—let us hold by this. They pin me down. They look backward and not forward. But genius looks forward: the eyes of man are set in his forehead, not in his hindhead: man hopes; genius creates. Whatever talents may be, if the man create not, the pure efflux of the Deity is not his—cinders and smoke there may be, but not yet flame. There are creative manners, there are creative actions, and creative words; manners, actions, words, that is, indicative of no custom or authority, but springing spontaneous from the mind's own sense of good and fair.

On the other part, instead of being its own seer, let it receive from another mind its truth, though it were in torrents of light, without periods of solitude, inquest, and self-recovery, and a fatal disservice is done. Genius is always sufficiently the enemy of genius by over influence. The literature of every nation bear me witness. The English dramatic poets have Shakespearized now for two hundred years.

Undoubtedly there is a right way of reading, so it be sternly subordinated. Man Thinking must not be subdued by his instruments. Books are for the scholar's idle times. When he can read God directly, the hour is too precious to be wasted in other men's transcripts of their readings. But when the intervals of darkness come, as come they must—when the sun is hid, and the stars withdraw their shining—we repair to the lamps which were kindled by their ray, to guide our steps to the East again, where the dawn is. We hear, that we may speak. The Arabian proverb says, "A fig tree, looking on a fig tree, becometh fruitful."

It is remarkable, the character of the pleasure we derive from the best books. They impress us with the conviction, that one nature wrote and the same reads. We read the verses of one of the great English poets, of Chaucer, of Marvell, of Dryden, with the most modern joy— with a pleasure, I mean, which is in great part caused by the abstraction of all time from their verses. There is some awe mixed with the joy of our surprise, when this poet, who lived in some past world, two or three hundred years ago, says that which lies close to my own soul, that which I also had well-nigh thought and said. But for the evidence thence afforded to the philosophical doctrine of the identity of all minds, we should suppose some pre-established harmony, some foresight of souls that were to be, and some preparation of stores for their future wants, like the fact observed in insects, who lay up food before death for the young grub they shall never see.

I would not be hurried by any love of system, by any exaggeration of instincts, to underrate the Book. We all know, that, as the human body can be nourished on any food, though it were boiled grass and the broth of shoes, so the human mind can be fed by any knowledge. And great and heroic men have existed, who had almost no other information than by the printed page. I only would say, that it needs a strong head to bear that diet. One must be an inventor to read well. As the proverb says, "He that would bring home the wealth of the Indies, must carry out the wealth of the Indies." There is then creative reading as well as creative writing. When the mind is braced by labor and invention, the page of whatever book we read becomes luminous with manifold allusion. Every sentence is doubly significant, and the sense of our author is as broad as the world. We then see, what is always true, that, as the seer's hour of vision is short and rare among heavy days and months, so is its record, perchance, the least part of his volume. The discerning will read, in his Plato or Shakespeare, only that least part—only the authentic utterances of the oracle; all the rest he rejects, were it never so many times Plato's and Shakespeare's.

Of course, there is a portion of reading quite indispensable to a wise man. History and exact science he must learn by laborious reading. Colleges, in like manner, have their indispensable office—to teach elements. But they can only highly serve us, when they aim not to drill, but to create; when they gather from far every ray of various genius to their hospitable halls, and, by the concentrated fires, set the hearts of their youth on flame. Thought and knowledge are natures in which apparatus and pretension avail nothing. Gowns, and pecuniary foundations, though of towns of gold, can never countervail the least sentence or syllable of wit. Forget this, and our American colleges will recede in their public importance, whilst they grow richer every year.

III. There goes in the world a notion, that the scholar should be a recluse, a valetudinarian—as unfit for any handiwork or public labor, as a penknife for an axe. The so-called "practical men" sneer at speculative men, as if, because they speculate or see, they could do nothing. I have heard it said that the clergy—who are always, more universally than any other class, the scholars of their day—are addressed as women; that the rough, spontaneous conversation of men they do not hear, but only a mincing and diluted speech. They are often virtually disfranchised; and, indeed, there are advocates for their celibacy. As far as this is true of the studious classes, it is not just and wise. Action is with the scholar subordinate, but it is essential. Without it, he is not yet man. Without it, thought can never ripen into truth. Whilst the world hangs before the eye as a cloud of beauty, we cannot even see its beauty. Inaction is cowardice, but there can be no scholar without the heroic mind. The preamble of thought, the transition through which it passes from the unconscious to the conscious, is action. Only so much do I know, as I have lived. Instantly we know whose words are loaded with life, and whose not.

The world—this shadow of the soul, or other me, lies wide around. Its attractions are the keys which unlock my thoughts and make me acquainted with myself. I run eagerly into this resounding tumult. I grasp the hands of those next me, and take my place in the ring to suffer and to work, taught by an instinct, that so shall the dumb abyss be vocal with speech. I pierce its order; I dissipate its fear; I dispose of it within the circuit of my expanding life. So much only of life as I know by experience, so much of the wilderness have I vanquished and planted, or so far have I extended my being, my dominion. I do not see how any man can afford, for the sake of his nerves and his nap, to spare any action in which he can partake. It is pearls and rubies to his discourse. Drudgery, calamity, exasperation, want, are instructors in eloquence and wisdom. The true scholar grudges every opportunity of action past by, as a loss of power.

It is the raw material out of which the intellect moulds her splendid products. A strange process too, this, by which experience is converted into thought, as a mulberry leaf is converted into satin. The manufacture goes forward at all hours.

The actions and events of our childhood and youth, are now matters of calmest observation. They lie like fair pictures in the air. Not so with our recent actions—with the business which we now have in hand. On this we are quite unable to speculate. Our affections as yet circulate through it. We no more feel or know it, than we feel the feet, or the hand, or the brain of our body. The new deed is yet a part of life—remains for a time immersed in our unconscious life. In some contemplative hour, it detaches itself from the life like a ripe fruit, to become a thought of the mind. Instantly, it is raised, transfigured; the corruptible has put on incorruption. Henceforth it is an object of beauty, however base its origin and neighborhood. Observe, too, the impossibility of antedating this act. In its grub state, it cannot fly, it cannot shine, it is a dull grub. But suddenly, without observation, the self-same thing unfurls beautiful wings, and is an angel of wisdom. So is there no fact, no event, in our private history, which shall not, sooner or later, lose its adhesive, inert form, and astonish us by soaring from our body into the empyrean? Cradle and infancy, school and play-ground, the fear of boys, and dogs, and ferules, the love of little maids and berries, and many another fact that once filled the whole sky, are gone already; friend and relative, profession and party, town and country, nation and world, must also soar and sing.

Of course, he who has put forth his total strength in fit actions, has the richest return of wisdom. I will not shut myself out of this globe of action, and transplant an oak into a flower-pot, there to hunger and pine; nor trust the revenue of some single faculty, and exhaust one vein of thought, much like those Savoyards, who, getting their livelihood by carving shepherds, shepherdesses, and smoking Dutchmen, for all Europe, went out one day to the mountain to find stock, and discovered that they had whittled up the last of their pine trees. Authors we have, in numbers, who have written out their vein, and who, moved by a commendable prudence, sail for Greece or Palestine, follow the trapper into the prairie, or ramble round Algiers, to replenish their merchantable stock.

If it were only for a vocabulary, the scholar would be covetous of action. Life is our dictionary. Years are well spent in country labors; in town—in the insight into trades and manufactures; in frank intercourse with many men and women; in science; in art; to the one end of mastering in all their facts a language by which to illustrate and embody our perceptions. I learn immediately from any speaker how much he has already lived, through the poverty or the splendor of his speech. Life lies behind us as the quarry from whence we get tiles and capstones for the masonry of to-day. This is the way to learn grammar. Colleges and books only copy the language which the field and the work-yard made.

But the final value of action, like that of books, and better than books, is, that it is a resource. That great principle of Undulation in nature, that shows itself in the inspiring and expiring of the breath; in desire and satiety; in the ebb and flow of the sea; in day and night; in heat and cold; and as yet more deeply ingrained in every atom and every fluid, is known to us under the name of Polarity—these "fits of easy transmission and reflection," as Newton called them, are the law of nature because they are the law of spirit.

The mind now thinks; now acts; and each fit reproduces the other. When the artist has exhausted his materials, when the fancy no longer paints, when thoughts are no longer apprehended, and books are a weariness—he has always the resource to live. Character is higher than intellect. Thinking is the function. Living is the functionary. The stream retreats to its source. A great soul will be strong to live, as well as strong to think. Does he lack organ or medium to impart his truths? He can still fall back on this elemental force of living them. This is a total act. Thinking is a partial act. Let the grandeur of justice shine in his affairs. Let the beauty of affection cheer his lowly roof. Those "far from fame," who dwell and act with him, will feel the force of his constitution in the doings and passages of the day better than it can be measured by any public and designed display. Time shall teach him, that the scholar loses no hour which the man lives. Herein he unfolds the sacred germ of his instinct, screened from influence. What is lost in seemliness is gained in strength. Not out of those, on whom systems of education have exhausted their culture, comes the helpful giant to destroy the old or to build the new, but out of unhandselled savage nature, out of terrible Druids and Berserkers, come at last Alfred and Shakespeare.

I hear therefore with joy whatever is beginning to be said of the dignity and necessity of labor to every citizen. There is virtue yet in the hoe and the spade, for learned as well as for unlearned hands. And labor is everywhere welcome; always we are invited to work; only be this limitation observed, that a man shall not for the sake of wider activity sacrifice any opinion to the popular judgments and modes of action.

I have now spoken of the education of the scholar by nature, by books, and by action. It remains to say somewhat of his duties.

They are such as become Man Thinking. They may all be comprised in self-trust. The office of the scholar is to cheer, to raise, and to guide men by showing them facts amidst appearances. He plies the slow, unhonored, and unpaid task of observation. Flamsteed and Herschel, in their glazed observatories, may catalogue the stars with the praise of all men, and, the results being splendid and useful, honor is sure. But he, in his private observatory, cataloguing obscure and nebulous stars of the human mind, which as yet no man has thought of as such—watching days and months, sometimes, for a few facts; correcting still his old records—must relinquish display and immediate fame. In the long period of his preparation, he must betray often an ignorance and shiftlessness in popular arts, incurring the disdain of the able who shoulder him aside. Long he must stammer in his speech; often forego the living for the dead. Worse yet, he must accept—how often!—poverty and solitude. For the ease and pleasure of treading the old road, accepting the fashions, the education, the religion of society, he takes the cross of making his own, and, of course, the self-accusation, the faint heart, the frequent uncertainty and loss of time, which are the nettles and tangling vines in the way of the self-relying and self-directed; and the state of virtual hostility in which he seems to stand to society, and especially to educated society. For all this loss and scorn, what offset? He is to find consolation in exercising the highest functions of human nature. He is one, who raises himself from private considerations, and breathes and lives on public and illustrious thoughts. He is the world's eye. He is the world's heart. He is to resist the vulgar prosperity that retrogrades ever to barbarism, by preserving and communicating heroic sentiments, noble biographies, melodious verse, and the conclusions of history. Whatsoever oracles the human heart, in all emergencies, in all solemn hours, has uttered as its commentary on the world of actions—these he shall receive and impart. And whatsoever new verdict Reason from her inviolable seat pronounces on the passing men and events of today—this he shall hear and promulgate.

These being his functions, it becomes him to feel all confidence in himself, and to defer never to the popular cry. He and he only knows the world. The world of any moment is the merest appearance. Some great decorum, some fetish of a government, some ephemeral trade, or war, or man, is cried up by half mankind and cried down by the other half, as if all depended on this particular up or down. The odds are that the whole question is not worth the poorest thought which the scholar has lost in listening to the controversy. Let him not quit his belief that a popgun is a popgun, though the ancient and honorable of the earth affirm it to be the crack of doom. In silence, in steadiness, in severe abstraction, let him hold by himself; add observation to observation, patient of neglect, patient of reproach; and bide his own time— happy enough, if he can satisfy himself alone, that this day he has seen something truly. Success treads on every right step. For the instinct is sure, that prompts him to tell his brother what he thinks. He then learns, that in going down into the secrets of his own mind, he has descended into the secrets of all minds. He learns that he who has mastered any law in his private thoughts, is master to that extent of all men whose language he speaks, and of all into whose language his own can be translated. The poet, in utter solitude remembering his spontaneous thoughts and recording them, is found to have recorded that, which men in crowded cities find true for them also. The orator distrusts at first the fitness of his frank confessions—his want of knowledge of the persons he addresses—until he finds that he is the complement of his hearers—that they drink his words because he fulfills for them their own nature; the deeper he dives into his privatest, secretest presentiment, to his wonder he finds, this is the most acceptable, most public, and universally true. The people delight in it; the better part of every man feels. This is my music; this is myself.

In self-trust, all the virtues are comprehended. Free should the scholar be—free and brave. Free even to the definition of freedom, "without any hindrance that does not arise out of his own constitution." Brave; for fear is a thing, which a scholar by his very function puts behind him. Fear always springs from ignorance. It is a shame to him if his tranquillity, amid dangerous times, arise from the presumption, that, like children and women, his is a protected class; or if he seek a temporary peace by the diversion of his thoughts from politics or vexed questions, hiding his head like an ostrich in the flowering bushes, peeping into microscopes, and turning rhymes, as a boy whistles to keep his courage up. So is the danger a danger still; so is the fear worse. Manlike let him turn and face it. Let him look into its eye and search its nature, inspect its origin—see the whelping of this lion—which lies no great way back; he will then find in himself a perfect comprehension of its nature and extent; he will have made his hands meet on the other side, and can henceforth defy it, and pass on superior. The world is his, who can see through its pretension. What deafness, what stone-blind custom, what overgrown error you behold, is there only by sufferance—by your sufferance. See it to be a lie, and you have already dealt it its mortal blow.

Yes, we are the cowed—we the trustless. It is a mischievous notion that we are come late into nature; that the world was finished a long time ago. As the world was plastic and fluid in the hands of God, so it is ever to so much of his attributes as we bring to it. To ignorance and sin, it is flint. They adapt themselves to it as they may; but in proportion as a man has any thing in him divine, the firmament flows before him and takes his signet and form. Not he is great who can alter matter, but he who can alter my state of mind. They are the kings of the world who give the color of their present thought to all nature and all art, and persuade men by the cheerful serenity of their carrying the matter, that this thing which they do, is the apple which the ages have desired to pluck, now at last ripe, and inviting nations to the harvest. The great man makes the great thing. Wherever Macdonald sits, there is the head of the table. Linnaeus makes botany the most alluring of studies, and wins it from the farmer and the herb-woman; Davy, chemistry; and Cuvier, fossils. The day is always his, who works in it with serenity and great aims. The unstable estimates of men crowd to him whose mind is filled with a truth, as the heaped waves of the Atlantic follow the moon.

For this self-trust, the reason is deeper than can be fathomed—darker than can be enlightened. I might not carry with me the feeling of my audience in stating my own belief. But I have already shown the ground of my hope, in adverting to the doctrine that man is one. I believe man has been wronged; he has wronged himself. He has almost lost the light, that can lead him back to his prerogatives. Men are become of no account. Men in history, men in the world of today are bugs, are spawn, and are called "the mass" and "the herd." In a century, in a millennium, one or two men; that is to say—one or two approximations to the right state of every man. All the rest behold in the hero or the poet their own green and crude being—ripened; yes, and are content to be less, so that may attain to its full stature. What a testimony—full of grandeur, full of pity, is borne to the demands of his own nature, by the poor clansman, the poor partisan, who rejoices in the glory of his chief. The poor and the low find some amends to their immense moral capacity, for their acquiescence in a political and social inferiority. They are content to be brushed like flies from the path of a great person, so that justice shall be done by him to that common nature which it is the dearest desire of all to see enlarged and glorified. They sun themselves in the great man's light, and feel it to be their own element. They cast the dignity of man from their downtrod selves upon the shoulders of a hero, and will perish to add one drop of blood to make that great heart beat, those giant sinews combat and conquer. He lives for us, and we live in him.

Men such as they are, very naturally seek money or power; and power because it is as good as money—the "spoils," so called, "of office." And why not?—for they aspire to the highest, and this, in their sleep-walking, they dream is highest. Wake them, and they shall quit the false good, and leap to the true, and leave governments to clerks and desks. This revolution is to be wrought by the gradual domestication of the idea of Culture. The main enterprise of the world for splendor, for extent, is the upbuilding of a man. Here are the materials strown along the ground. The private life of one man shall be a more illustrious monarchy—more formidable to its enemy, more sweet and serene in its influence to its friend, than any kingdom in history. For a man, rightly viewed, comprehendeth the particular natures of all men. Each philosopher, each bard, each actor, has only done for me, as by a delegate, what one day I can do for myself. The books which once we valued more than the apple of the eye, we have quite exhausted. What is that but saying, that we have come up with the point of view which the universal mind took through the eyes of one scribe; we have been that man, and have passed on. First, one; then, another; we drain all cisterns, and, waxing greater by all these supplies, we crave a better and more abundant food. The man has never lived that can feed us ever. The human mind cannot be enshrined in a person, who shall set a barrier on any one side to this unbounded, unboundable empire. It is one central fire, which, flaming now out of the lips of Etna, lightens the capes of Sicily; and, now out of the throat of Vesuvius, illuminates the towers and vineyards of Naples. It is one light which beams out of a thousand stars. It is one soul which animates all men.

But I have dwelt perhaps tediously upon this abstraction of the Scholar. I ought not to delay longer to add what I have to say, of nearer reference to the time and to this country.

Historically, there is thought to be a difference in the ideas which predominate over successive epochs, and there are data for marking the genius of the Classic, of the Romantic, and now of the Reflective or Philosophical age. With the views I have intimated of the oneness or the identity of the mind through all individuals, I do not much dwell on these differences. In fact, I believe each individual passes through all three. The boy is a Greek; the youth, romantic; the adult, reflective. I deny not, however, that a revolution in the leading idea may be distinctly enough traced.

Our age is bewailed as the age of Introversion. Must that needs be evil? We, it seems, are critical; we are embarrassed with second thoughts; we cannot enjoy any thing for hankering to know whereof the pleasure consists; we are lined with eyes; we see with our feet; the time is infected with Hamlet's unhappiness—"Sicklied o'er with the pale cast of thought."

Is it so bad then? Sight is the last thing to be pitied. Would we be blind? Do we fear lest we should outsee nature and God, and drink truth dry? I look upon the discontent of the literary class, as a mere announcement of the fact, that they find themselves not in the state of mind of their fathers, and regret the coming state as untried; as a boy dreads the water before he has learned that he can swim. If there is any period one would desire to be born in—is it not the age of Revolution; when the old and the new stand side by side, and admit of being compared; when the energies of all men are searched by fear and by hope; when the historic glories of the old, can be compensated by the rich possibilities of the new era? This time, like all times, is a very good one, if we but know what to do with it.

I read with joy some of the auspicious signs of the coming days, as they glimmer already through poetry and art, through philosophy and science, through church and state.

One of these signs is the fact, that the same movement which effected the elevation of what was called the lowest class in the state, assumed in literature a very marked and as benign an aspect. Instead of the sublime and beautiful; the near, the low, the common, was explored and poetized. That, which had been negligently trodden under foot by those who were harnessing and provisioning themselves for long journeys into far countries, is suddenly found to be richer than all foreign parts. The literature of the poor, the feelings of the child, the philosophy of the street, the meaning of household life, are the topics of the time. It is a great stride. It is a sign—is it not?—of new vigor, when the extremities are made active, when currents of warm life run into the hands and the feet. I ask not for the great, the remote, the romantic; what is doing in Italy or Arabia; what is Greek art, or Provençal minstrelsy; I embrace the common, I explore and sit at the feet of the familiar, the low. Give me insight into today, and you may have the antique and future worlds. What would we really know the meaning of? The meal in the firkin; the milk in the pan; the ballad in the street; the news of the boat; the glance of the eye; the form and the gait of the body—show me the ultimate reason of these matters; show me the sublime presence of the highest spiritual cause lurking, as always it does lurk, in these suburbs and extremities of nature; let me see every trifle bristling with the polarity that ranges it instantly on an eternal law; and the shop, the plough, and the ledger, referred to the like cause by which light undulates and poets sing—and the world lies no longer a dull miscellany and lumber-room, but has form and order; there is no trifle; there is no puzzle; but one design unites and animates the farthest pinnacle and the lowest trench.

This idea has inspired the genius of Goldsmith, Burns, Cowper, and, in a newer time, of Goethe, Wordsworth, and Carlyle. This idea they have differently followed and with various success. In contrast with their writing, the style of Pope, of Johnson, of Gibbon, looks cold and pedantic. This writing is blood-warm. Man is surprised to find that things near are not less beautiful and wondrous than things remote. The near explains the far. The drop is a small ocean. A man is related to all nature. This perception of the worth of the vulgar is fruitful in discoveries. Goethe, in this very thing the most modern of the moderns, has shown us, as none ever did, the genius of the ancients.

There is one man of genius, who has done much for this philosophy of life, whose literary value has never yet been rightly estimated—I mean Emanuel Swedenborg. The most imaginative of men, yet writing with the precision of a mathematician, he endeavored to engraft a purely philosophical Ethics on the popular Christianity of his time. Such an attempt, of course, must have difficulty, which no genius could surmount. But he saw and showed the connection between nature and the affections of the soul. He pierced the emblematic or spiritual character of the visible, audible, tangible world. Especially did his shade-loving muse hover over and interpret the lower parts of nature; he showed the mysterious bond that allies moral evil to the foul material forms, and has given in epical parables a theory of insanity, of beasts, of unclean and fearful things.

Another sign of our times, also marked by an analogous political movement, is, the new importance given to the single person. Every thing that tends to insulate the individual—to surround him with barriers of natural respect, so that each man shall feel the world is his, and man shall treat with man as a sovereign state with a sovereign state—tends to true union as well as greatness. "I learned," said the melancholy Pestalozzi, "that no man in God's wide earth is either willing or able to help any other man." Help must come from the bosom alone. The scholar is that man who must take up into himself all the ability of the time, all the contributions of the past, all the hopes of the future. He must be an university of knowledges. If there be one lesson more than another, which should pierce his ear, it is, The world is nothing, the man is all; in yourself is the law of all nature, and you know not yet how a globule of sap ascends; in yourself slumbers the whole of Reason; it is for you to know all, it is for you to dare all.

Mr. President and Gentlemen, this confidence in the unsearched might of man belongs, by all motives, by all prophecy, by all preparation, to the American Scholar. We have listened too long to the courtly muses of Europe. The spirit of the American freeman is already suspected to be timid, imitative, tame. Public and private avarice make the air we breathe thick and fat. The scholar is decent, indolent, complaisant. See already the tragic consequence. The mind of this country, taught to aim at low objects, eats upon itself. There is no work for any but the decorous and the complaisant. Young men of the fairest promise, who begin life upon our shores, inflated by the mountain winds, shined upon by all the stars of God, find the earth below not in unison with these—but are hindered from action by the disgust which the principles on which business is managed inspire, and turn drudges, or die of disgust—some of them suicides. What is the remedy? They did not yet see, and thousands of young men as hopeful now crowding to the barriers for the career, do not yet see, that, if the single man plant himself indomitably on his instincts, and there abide, the huge world will come round to him. Patience—patience—with the shades of all the good and great for company; and for solace, the perspective of your own infinite life; and for work, the study and the communication of principles, the making those instincts prevalent, the conversion of the world. Is it not the chief disgrace in the world, not to be an unit—not to be reckoned one character—not to yield that peculiar fruit which each man was created to bear, but to be reckoned in the gross, in the hundred, or the thousand, of the party, the section, to which we belong; and our opinion predicted geographically, as the north, or the south? Not so, brothers and friends—please God, ours shall not be so. We will walk on our own feet; we will work with our own hands; we will speak our own minds. The study of letters shall be no longer a name for pity, for doubt, and for sensual indulgence. The dread of man and the love of man shall be a wall of defense and a wreath of joy around all. A nation of men will for the first time exist, because each believes himself inspired by the Divine Soul which also inspires all men.

VERNON L. PARRINGTON

46 Ralph Waldo Emerson
Transcendental Critic (1927)

In the 1970s, Gene Wise published essays that remain among the most trusted accounts of the history of American Studies in the United States. He identified Ralph Waldo Emerson as the field's premier prophet and Vernon Louis Parrington as its first apostle. Prior to the field's institutionalization as "myth and symbol" (ca. 1950–1965), Parrington's *Main Currents in American Thought: An Interpretation of American Literature from the Beginnings to 1920* (3 volumes, 1927–1930) was, in Wise's estimation, "the most comprehensive expression" of what America is like and how it should be studied: "More than any other Americanist, Parrington gave life to Emerson's vision of 'The American Scholar,' a passionate mind encountering a dynamic world, sans the mediating forms of convention."

Among the ways that the work was unconventional was in its focus on American thought in the first place. Turn-of-the-century universities generally addressed *thought* as a means rather than an object of apprehension and *American* thought as dumb or derivative. Literature was rarely a subject at all. "English" referred to a British language, best acquired through recitation regimens and researched through philology. Interpretation and criticism were the province of non-academic periodicals. Scholars spent their time authenticating manuscripts, meticulously tracking and compiling shifts in vocabulary, syntax, and other linguistic resources. In fact, soon after *Main Currents* won a Pulitzer Prize (1928), literary scholars returned to tracking minutiae under the more empirical, disciplined, and conservative reign of "The New Criticism."

However, Parrington showed just how synthetic and daring a culture critic might be. Admittedly, neither his selection of sources nor his analysis of any one of them was remarkably original or incisive. His approach—charting national progress via a parade of authors—was modeled on Hippolyte Taine's *History of English Literature* (1864). His understanding of the substance of U.S. history never veered far from the then canonical renderings of Carl Becker and Charles Beard, who favorably reviewed his work. His infatuation with some writers and neglect of others (nearly all women and people of color) were scandalous, even by 1920s standards.

His strength, rather, was the clarity and scope of his mode of interpretation. It was great enough to sustain consideration well beyond the particular pages and personalities that he favored. His interest in literature and history was tailored to suit a civic vision.

Unlike his mentors (for example, Barrett Wendell), Parrington was less interested in appreciating individual texts than in drawing contrasts and generalizations from many of them. Writings were prized, not for some "intrinsic" aesthetic worth, but for the views they might afford of myriad other things that, he assumed, moved with the broad, turbulent tide of American culture. In plotting these "main currents," texts were his buoys. One passage might help a reader navigate a novel; another, the life of its author or its social context and implications.

He integrated these readings through a political sensibility that was and remains conventionally unconventional in U.S. academia, ranging from vaguely adversarial or liberal to stridently Marxist. In 1917, for example, he wrote: "Literature is the fair flower of culture, but underneath culture are the deeper strata of philosophy, theology, law, statecraft—of ideology and institutionalism—resting finally on the subsoil of economics." Like the Progressive historians of his day, he tended to see society swinging on a gate. With the passage of each period of time, U.S. thinkers shift from inviting to resisting the advance of social justice. Since these movements seem ever to vary on a small number of themes (for example, democracy versus tyranny, artist versus citizen, wilderness versus city, farm versus factory), their interaction in one period could well provide lessons for another.

In this way, Parrington was unashamedly presentist. Like most of his descendants in American Studies in the United States, he pursued a "usable past" and wore his bias on his sleeve. Of course, the substance of the bias was in some ways distinctly his own. His sense of "manhood" was groomed amid Victorian and Populist influences on the Midwestern Plains where he came of age. He made no secret, for example, of his distaste for Harvard University, which he called "a liability . . . to the cause of democracy" and "the apologist and advocate of capitalistic exploitation." But Parrington's critical standards also seem attuned to common contemporary tastes: his reformist politics, his masculine sense of morality and "reality," his passion for democracy and public affairs, his suspicion of prestige or sentiment and sympathy for revolution. He tended to flatter or dismiss American thinkers in direct proportion to the way that they addressed these variants of U.S. ideals.

Subsequent Americanists have advocated different ideals and considered different texts, but their ethos can still be traced through Parrington back to Emerson and the early republic as well as forward to modern American Studies.

At the age of thirty-six the man who was to become the most searching critic of contemporary America expressed his conception of his mission in the following passage:

What shall be the substance of my shrift? Adam in the garden, I am to new-name all the beasts of the field and all the gods in the sky. I am to invite men drenched in Time to recover themselves and come out of time, and taste their native immortal air. I am to fire with what skill I can the artillery of sympathy and emotion. I am to indicate constantly, though all unworthy, the Ideal and Holy Life, the life within life, the Forgotten Good, the Unknown Cause in which we sprawl and sin. I am to try the magic of sincerity, that luxury permitted only to kings and poets. I am to celebrate the spiritual powers in their infinite contrast to the mechanical powers and the mechanical philosophy of this time. I am to console the brave sufferers under evils whose end they cannot see, by appeals to the great optimism, self-affirmed in all bosoms. (*Journals*, Vol. V, p. 288.)

Seven days before Emerson set down this transcendental pronouncement, he had written in his Journal a different comment:

A question which well deserves examination now is the Dangers of Commerce. This invasion of Nature by Trade with its Money, its Credit, its Steam, its Railroad, threatens to upset the balance of man, and establish a new, universal Monarchy more tyrannical than Babylon or Rome. Very faint and few are the poets or men of God. Those who remain are so antagonistic to this tyranny that they appear mad or morbid, and are treated as such. Sensible of this extreme unfitness they suspect themselves. And all of us apologize when we ought not, and congratulate ourselves when we ought not. (Ibid., Vol. V, pp. 285–86.)

In such comments and others scattered plentifully through his journals, Emerson essayed to make clear to himself the function of transcendental criticism as he felt himself called to practice it. It was to be no trivial or easy duty. In the midst of a boastful materialism, shot through with cant and hypocrisy and every insincerity, fat and slothful in all higher things, the critic proposed to try the magic of sincerity, to apply the test of spiritual values to the material forces and mechanical philosophies of the times. His very life must embody criticism; his every act and word must pronounce judgment on the barren and flatulent gods served by his countrymen. He must be a thinker and as such he must summon to the bar of a nobler philosophy the current standards of value and conduct. Men of the greatest reputation must not be spared; he must "issue a *quo warranto* and revoke the characters of fame," overruling the verdict of newspaper editors and the acclaim of the electorate. Here was a revolutionary business indeed, that the critic was proposing to himself; and the calm serenity with which he set about it was disconcerting. A thinker loose in the America of Daniel Webster, a thinker who proposed to test men and measures by the magic of sincerity, was likely to prove an unpleasantly disturbant factor in a world of pretense. Measured by such standards, the current philosophies must bate and dwindle, and the common ideals shrink to the mean and paltry. The life of an honest thinker laid on the America of 1840 would reveal how far short it came from the stature of intellectual manhood.

Emerson the critic has been too much obscured to common view by Emerson the brilliant dispenser of transcendental aphorisms. The oracular *Essays* with their confident wisdom—the sententious expression of the middle period of a life that came to late maturity—interpose themselves between the young priest whose intellectual interests quietly detached themselves from Unitarian orthodoxy, and the mature critic whose loyalties quietly detached themselves from the gods of his generation. The very brilliancy of the *Essays* conceals the laborious processes by which their abundant wisdom was distilled. One must go to the *Journals* for that—to those intimate records that reveal how patiently he sought for truth and how honestly he followed it. Wisdom did not come to him of its own accord; it was painfully groped for. As an introspective Puritan youth he began early to keep a diary of his intellectual life, gathering into successive journals the savings from his discursive readings. For years as a quiet student he lived in a world of moral aphorisms, a cold, thin atmosphere where gnomic phrases bloomed and ancient oracles uttered judgment. This was the seedtime of his mind. He was making acquaintance with the noble dead, gathering their utterances to make for himself a new testament. . . rich with the thought he has crammed into them.

The cheerful serenity that never deserted him was a triumph of will over circumstance. It was a singularly cheerless world that bred him. . .—the lean aftermath of two centuries of asceticism. The business of plain living and high thinking was a joyless manner of life, and the young Emerson got little pleasure from it. . . . It was a world stricken with tuberculosis. Of the five brothers one was mentally defective, another burnt up his vitality and went to the West Indies to die, a third of brilliant powers succumbed to consumption. His first wife died of the same scourge; his second wife and Emerson himself were long affected with incipient tuberculosis. To ease such anxious lives there was need of a great solace, and that solace was sought in religion. The ascetic youth ran as naturally to religious meditation as a normal child to play. . . . The earlier jottings in the journals, before philosophy came to soften the inherited asceticism, and a transcendental revulsion from the common pessimism had turned him into a serene optimist, often are as bleak and austerely introspective as those morbid human documents that fill the old libraries of Puritanism. Such meditations are thin gruel for the nourishment of a vigorous life, and Emerson must have suffered from innutrition if he had not come upon more substantial food.

Fortunately the old Puritan anchors were already dragging, and Emerson was pretty well adrift when the romantic surge caught him and sent him far along new courses. The Puritan moralizer became the transcendental seeker; the curious-minded loiterer in the gates of the temple, who had studied the moral winds by watching the tiny straws of circumstance—erecting unconsidered trifles into ethical signposts—calmly quitted the church and set forth on his intellectual quest. The ties had long been loosening, but it was his year abroad where he discovered ways of thinking unknown to Concord and Boston, that effectively liberalized his mind and released him from the narrow Yankee provincialisms. On that momentous trip Goethe, Landor, Coleridge, Wordsworth, Carlyle, set him speculating on new themes, stimulating afresh the love of Plato, in whom he had long found inspiration. Continental idealism with its transcendental metaphysics refashioned Emerson and put him upon his life-work. . . .

He had looked within himself and discovered the divinity of the individual soul; but he had not probed the non-self, the great encompassing universe of matter by which the individual is circumscribed and of which he is a part. To discover there the diffused presence of God, to feel his kinship with man, to understand that the soul is a microcosm, were necessary preliminaries to the unfolding of his transcendental philosophy, and he went about the work with painstaking thoroughness. From this creative contact with nature emerged the Emerson we know, radiant with idealism, glad of life; and this radiant gladness he put into his maiden essay, *Nature*.

This was in 1836 when Emerson was thirty-three years of age. In the next two years he published *The American Scholar*, quintessence of transcendental individualism, and the *Divinity School Address*, the bible of transcendental religion. With the appearance of the second series of *Essays*, six years later, the major ideas of his philosophy were fully elaborated. Stripped of its idealistic phraseology, of its beauty and fervor, the master idea of the Emersonian philosophy is the divine sufficiency of the individual. In accepting himself he accepted his fellows, and he accepted God. The universe he conceived of as a divine whole, whereof each man is his own center from whom flows the life that has flowed in upon him, perennially fresh, perennially a new creation. The law for things is not the law for mind; man is unkinged in acknowledging any lesser sovereignty than the sovereignty of self. Statutes, constitutions, governments, schools, churches, banks, trade—the coercing sum of institutions and customs—these things do not signify; they are only idols with clay feet that blind men worship. The true divinity dwells elsewhere, in the soul of man; and that divinity must rule the world and not be ruled by it. The apotheosis of individualism—such in briefest terms was the gospel of Emerson; new only in its radiant dress and idealistic sanctions, the final transcendental form of a doctrine spread widely by the French romantic school. It was the same revolutionary conception that Channing had come upon, that Jefferson had come upon, that Rousseau had come upon—the idea which in the guise of political romanticism had disintegrated the *ancien régime*, and in the form of philosophical romanticism had disintegrated eighteenth-century rationalism—the idea that was providing Utopian dreams for an ebullient democratic faith.

Thus equipped with a philosophy, Emerson was prepared to begin his work as a critic. The ideal he had drunk of was a perennial condemnation of the material. The mean and ignoble ends pursued by a mean and ignoble society were a challenge to the serenity of his faith, and he must set himself to analyze the causes of the low estate to which the potential sons of God had fallen. Lesser revolutions in thought were implicit in this greater one, revolutions which Emerson was bound to go through with. Despite the jaunty optimism of which he was often accused, his eyes were never blind to reality; to see, and measure, and judge, was to become his life business. He did not shrink from the ugliest fact, and the unhappy condition he discovered men to be in would have discouraged a less robust faith. . . .

In seeking an explanation of the tragic gap between the real and the ideal, he came to attribute a large measure of the cause, like the eighteenth-century romantics, to pernicious social institutions which stifle the nobler impulses and encourage the baser; and he became convinced likewise that the work to which the critic was called was the work of liberation, setting the mind free from false and ignoble loyalties that it might serve the true. He prepared therefore to lay his transcendental yardstick on the little world of Yankee reality and judge how far short it came of its potential divinity. New England had never been scrutinized so searchingly, measured so justly. Serene, imperturbable, he set the ideal in one pan of the scales, and all the New England realities in the other, and bade his neighbors see how the balance tipped. For a generation he was the conscience of America, a pricker of inflated balloons, a gauger of the national brag and cant and humbug. With keen insight he put his finger on the mean and selfish and the great and generous. He surveyed his world with the detachment of posterity and anticipated the slower judgment of time. . . .

So shrewd a critic must concern himself greatly with the Jacksonian revolution that was hurrying America towards the acceptance of political equalitarianism. By every compulsion of his transcendental philosophy Emerson was driven to accept the abstract principle of democracy. He understood well what hopes for human betterment were awakened by the principle of majority rule, and as he followed the noise and tumult of the political campaigns he was driven to definition. . . . His deepening concern over the state of politics in America— the property-mindedness of the Whigs and the mob-mindedness of the Democrats—drew him into an analysis of political parties and the nature of the political state. . . .

In his speculations on the nature and functions of the ideal republic—a theme that was much in his mind—he elaborated what we may call the transcendental theory of politics, a theory closely akin to philosophical anarchism. All the elaborate machinery devised by political thinkers like Montesquieu and John Adams, with their schemes of checks and balances to preserve the *status quo*, he calmly throws overboard; constitutions he is not interested in, nor the complicated props of coercive sovereignty. The single, vital, principle on which the true republic must found itself, he insists, is the principle of goodwill. . . .

The doctrine of an ethical sovereignty, he asserts,

> . . . promises a recognition of higher rights than those of personal freedom, or the security of property. A man has a right to be employed, to be trusted, to be loved, to be revered. The power of love, as the basis of a State, has never been tried. . . . There will always be a government of force where men are selfish; and when they are pure

enough to abjure the code of force they will be wise enough to see how these public ends of the post-office, of the highway, of commerce and the exchange of property, of museums and libraries, of institutions of art and science can be answered.

Every man's nature is a sufficient advertisement to him of the character of his fellows. My right and my wrong is their right and their wrong. Whilst I do what is fit for men, and abstain from what is unfit, my neighbor and I shall often agree in our means, and work together for a time to one end. But whenever I find my dominion over myself not sufficient for me, and undertake the direction of him also, I overstep the truth, and come into false relations to him. I may have so much more skill or strength than he that he cannot express adequately his sense of wrong, but it is a lie, and hurts like a lie both him and me. Love and nature cannot maintain the assumption; it must be executed by a practical lie, namely by force. This undertaking for another is the blunder which stands in colossal ugliness in the governments of the world. . . . For any laws but those which men make for themselves are laughable. . . . This is the history of government—one man does something which is to bind another. . . . Hence the less government we have the better—the fewer laws, and the less confided power. The antidote to this abuse of formal government is the influence of private character, the growth of the individual. . . . To educate the wise man the State exists, and with the appearance of the wise man the State expires. The appearance of character makes the State unnecessary. The wise man is the State. *(Essay on Politics.)*

Thus in transcendental fashion does Emerson range himself on the side of Jefferson, in opposition to a coercive sovereignty. A strong and energetic government he feared as an efficient instrument of tyranny; and of the several contrivancies by which it enforced its will, he considered the police power the stupidest. As a sensible man he bore with the state; he would pay his taxes; he would not strain at gnats. But as a free man he would not suffer the state to coerce him; he would destroy it first. . . .

With equal emphasis he rejected the economic interpretation of politics. As a child of the romantic revolution he understood quite clearly how the waves of humanitarian aspiration broke on the reefs of property rights, how economic forces were in league against the ideal republic. There could be no true democracy till this matter of economics was put in subordination to higher values. Both the political parties, the respectable Whigs and the voluble Democrats, he was convinced, were debauched by it; the one served property openly, the other secretly. "From neither party, when in power, has the world any benefit to expect in science, art, or humanity, at all commensurate with the resources of the nation." Emerson did not deny the fact of the universal appeal of economics. He could not, of course, accept the theory of economic determinism; but he was convinced that the whole matter must be probed deeply. . . .

He did not, he said, "look with sour aspect at the industrious manufacturing village, or mart of commerce"; but he would not glorify the machine, nor reduce man to a factory hand. He questioned the sufficiency or finality of the division of labor. . . . The industrial revolution with its factory system must be judged in the light of its effect upon the workingman. . . . The suggestion that "a man should have a farm or mechanical craft for his culture," was an implicit denial of industrialism in the days of its first triumphs. . . .

> We must have a basis for our higher accomplishments, our delicate entertainments of poetry and philosophy, in the work of our hands. . . . Manual labor is the study of the external world. The advantages of riches remains with him who produces them, not with the heir.
>
> I should not be pained at a change which threatened a loss of some of the luxuries or conveniences of society, if it proceeded from a preference of the agricultural life out of the belief, that our primary duties as men could be better discharged in that calling. . . . The doctrine of the Farm is merely this: that every man ought to stand in primary relations with the work of the world, ought to do it himself, and not to suffer the accident of his having a purse in his pocket, or his having been bred to some dishonorable and injurious craft, to sever him from those duties; and for this reason, that labor is God's education; that he only is a sincere learner, he only can become a master, who learns the secret of labor, and who by real cunning extorts from nature its sceptre. (Man the Reformer.)

In all this—in the doctrine of the minimized state, of the sacred rights of the individual, of the wholesomeness of an agricultural life; in his concern for social justice and his tenderness for the poor and exploited among men—Emerson proved himself a child of the romantic eighteenth century, who by his own transcendental path had come upon the Utopia that an earlier generation had dreamed of, and which he sketched in the lovely poem prefacing the *Essay on Politics*. Much of Emerson is compressed in these lines:

> Fear, Craft, Avarice,
> Cannot rear a State.
> Out of dust to build
> What is more than dust. . . .
> When the Muses nine
> With the Virtues meet,
> Find to their design
> An Atlantic seat,
> By green orchard boughs
> Fended from the heat,
> Where the statesman ploughs
> Furrow for the wheat;
> When the Church is social worth,
> When the statehouse is the hearth,
> Then the perfect State is come,
> The republican at home.

The contrast between such Utopian conceptions and the realities of America in the [18]40s was calculated to edge the critical judgment with a certain asperity. The older agrarian simplicity of New England was being submerged by the industrial revolution, and in the midst of the change Emerson quietly pronounced judgment upon the new idols of his generation, upon State Street and Beacon Street, upon Webster and Clay and Douglas, upon Everett and Choate, upon black slavery and white, upon the Mexican War and the Fugitive Slave Bill, upon the stolid poor and the callous rich. His judgment was severe but it was never unjust. . . . It was the crass materialism of America—of the Democrats equally with the Whigs, of the northern capitalists equally with the southern planters—that drove him to exasperation, and tempered his optimism. . . .

To be a critic rather than a fighter, and a critic because he was a poet and philosopher—this was the duty laid upon Emerson; and yet he was sorely troubled when men from the skirmish line of social conflict reported to him the need of leaders. Why should he be privileged to remain in his study when slaves were abducted on the streets of Boston and John Brown was fighting at Harper's Ferry? With the extremest reluctance he was drawn into the struggle—it was not his fight.

> I waked at night [he recorded in his journal] and bemoaned myself, because I had not thrown myself into this deplorable question of Slavery, which seems to want nothing so much as a few assured voices. But then, in hours of sanity, I recover myself, and say, "God must govern his own world, and knows his own way out of this pit, without my desertion of my post, which has none to guard it but me. I have quite other slaves to free than those negroes, to wit, imprisoned spirits, imprisoned thoughts, far back in the brain of man,—far retired in the heaven of invention, and which, important to the republic of Man, have no other watchman, or lover, or defender, but I." (*Journals*, Vol. VIII, p. 316.)

But always in the end he was drawn in, and none spoke wiser or braver words to a careless generation. He never faltered, never compromised; the prophet of the ideal faced the real and told the truth about it, serenely and with clear insight. His heroes were not the heroes of State Street; Horace Greeley, Theodore Parker, Horace Mann, Henry Ward Beecher, he accounted the great Americans of his day, and not Everett and Webster and Clay and Calhoun. A friend of civilization, he was partisan only to the ideal; to justice, truth, righteousness. A Yankee of the Yankees, a Puritan of the Puritans, he had emancipated himself from all that was mean and ungenerous in the one and harsh and illiberal in the other. A free soul, he was the flowering of two centuries of spiritual aspiration—Roger Williams and Jonathan Edwards come to more perfect fruition.

NORMAN FOERSTER

47 Factors in American Literary History (1925)

Scholars now recall the early 1900s as a period when critics of U.S. literature and culture formed two opposing camps: New Humanists versus Literary Radicals. In the pages of popular periodicals and in lecture halls, they argued about the goals and methods of American cultural criticism: Should they be drawn from a European heritage or culled from New World experience? In either case, they could agree, Americans needed more vital ideals. Curiously—since most of them were university educated and affiliated, and since American culture was at that point barely discussed in classrooms—they could also agree that academia was a key source of confusion. Their faith in nationality and their hostility toward intellectuals (at least *other* ones) could be demagogic.

In a famous manifesto for Literary Radicals published in *The Dial* in 1918, Van Wyck Brooks explains:

Our professors continue to pour out a stream of historical works repeating the same points of view to such an astonishing degree that they have placed a sort of Talmudic seal upon the American Tradition . . . put a gloss upon it which renders it sterile for the living mind. . . . The professor. . . comes to fulfill himself in the vicarious world of the dead and returns to the actual world of struggling and mis-educated mortals in the majestic raiment of borrowed immortalities. And he pours out upon that world his own contempt for the starveling poet in himself.

At some times (particularly for Literary Radicals) the villains are stodgy, nostalgic idealists; at other times (particularly for New Humanists) they are stooges of contemporary, commercialized reality. In either case a new generation of critics should fill the void. They should, as Brooks put it, "create a usable past":

The spiritual past has no objective reality; it yields only what we are able to look for in it. . . . From this point of view our contemporary literature could hardly be in a graver state. We want bold ideas, and we have nuances. We want courage, and we have universal fear. We want individuality, and we have idiosyncrasy. We want vitality, and we have intellectualism. . . . But these conditions result largely, I think, from another condition that is, in part at least, remediable. The present is a void, and the American writer floats in that void because the past that survives in the common mind of the present is a past without living value. But is this the only possible past? If we need another past so badly, is it inconceivable that we might discover one, that we might even invent one?

Discover, invent a usable past we certainly can, and that is what a vital criticism always does. . . . Every people selects from the experience of every other people whatever contributes most vitally to its own development. . . . There are just as many histories of America as there are nations to possess them. . . . This, I say, is a commonplace to anyone whose mind has wandered even the shortest way from home, and to travel in one's imagination from country to country, from decade to decade, is to have this experience indefinitely multiplied. . . . By which I do not mean at all that we ought to cut our cloth to fit other people. I mean simply that we have every precedent for cutting it to fit ourselves. . . .

What is important for us? What, out of all the multifarious achievements and impulses and desires of the American literary mind, ought we to elect to remember? The more personally we answer this question, it seems to me, the more likely we are to get a vital order out of the anarchy of the present.

Although usually considered part of the opposing New Humanist camp, Norman Foerster here provides one of the first, most succinct, and comprehensive responses, in effect, to Brooks's call. Originally drafted for the 1925 meeting in Chicago of the new American Literature Group of the Modern Language Association (MLA), the paper helped establish an agenda for American Studies in the rest of the twentieth century.

The conventional mold in which our books and our college courses on American literature are cast indicates that we are not using intelligently the accelerated interest in our literature. We are still thinking in terms of a conception attained about a quarter of a century ago, despite the fact that it was superficial and premature. It is time for us to abandon the paradox involved in our theory that American literature is only a branch of English literature while in practice we treat it as a thing apart. It is time for us to abandon the political and geographic terminology in which we have enshrouded our confusion. The Colonial Period, The Revolutionary Period, The Early National and Later National Periods (or First National, Second National, etc., as if our subject were banks), The East, The West, The South, The New England Group, Knickerbocker Group,

Later New York Group, etc., etc.—these facile terms totally fail to make plain the organic relation of American and European literature, or even that the subject we are dealing with is literature. In a few quarters there has been, since the war, an enthusiastic waving of the flag "Americanism"; but obviously those who rally round this stirring symbol have commonly but the faintest idea of what it symbolizes. It is time for us to seek, in all simplicity and honesty, a more nearly adequate conception of American literature than has yet existed. Throwing our nineteenth century into clearer perspective, the Great War removed from large numbers of Americans the sectional spectacles that had distorted their vision. We are now ready for free and fresh thought, for scientific thought, for the undisturbed use of observation, reason, and imagination.

We have a very special opportunity, moreover, owing to the work of recent American historians. Although literary history is, of course, only a department of general history, we have egregiously failed to keep pace with the historians. Their modification or rejection of old points of view and introduction of new ones started more than thirty years ago, synchronously with the revolt in life and literature that began in the 1890s and is still in full career. Men like Turner, Andrews, Osgood, Adams, and Beard have given us a new vision of the forces dominant in our past. By 1922 it was possible for Professor Schlesinger to publish a book entitled *New Viewpoints in American History*, bringing together some of the results of this re-interpretation. It is time for our literary historians at least to look forward to a book of *New Viewpoints in American Literary History*.

We should also derive stimulation—perhaps some light—from the critics of American culture, or rather the critics who have been deploring the absence of "Civilization in the United States." Although we have long had such critics (including Emerson, Whitman, and other 100 percent Americans), we have never before, I imagine, had so many of them, or so many who were noisy, or so many shades of opinion, or so many readers who applauded or reviled. While our creative energy has expressed itself in Spoon Rivers and Main Streets, our critical energy has naturally expressed itself in Prejudices, Definitions, Americans, Roving Critics, Letters and Leadership, Histories of Literary Radicals. Divine or not, ours is a discontent more insistent and comprehensive than any we have hitherto experienced in this country. The open or experimental mind—even perhaps the empty mind—has never been so widely popular "in the best circles." We are questioning everything, including things that are unquestionable. It is time for us to question our inherited conception of American literature, which is certainly not unquestionable.

I have indicated what seems to me the cardinal symptom of our disordered interpretation of American literature, namely, our tendency to think in terms of political and geographic divisions. I propose to offer a different conception, not with a view to settling offhand so large a problem, but merely to render the problem itself clearer and to suggest the spirit in which it should be approached.

All the factors may be comprised under two heads: European culture and the American environment. American history, including literary history, is to be viewed as the interplay of these two tremendous factors, neither of which has been studied profoundly by our literary scholars. Because they are tremendous, however, they must be divided into a serviceable number of lesser factors, and from such a list (which I must leave hypothetical) I will select the four that seem to me most important. They are (1) the Puritan tradition, (2) the frontier spirit, (3) romanticism, and (4) realism. I can merely sketch their significance.

First, *the Puritan tradition*. This is, of course, only part of a larger factor, viz., the European tradition as it appeared before our Revolution. For we must reckon not only with the Puritan but also with the so-called "Cavalier" tradition, indeed the whole Anglo-Saxon tradition—its habit of mind in matters social, legal, political, economic, esthetic, religious. We must reckon with the rationalism and sentimentalism of the eighteenth century. I have selected the Puritan tradition as probably the outstanding factor in the first century and as a shaping force in the entire development of American civilization down to the present day. No doubt the Quakers, as Dr. Canby has recently asserted (*Saturday Review*, January 2, 1926), "have been neglected as a shaping force"; yet I think we are essentially right in our belief that the Protestant stamp on American life was primarily Puritan. The great problem is, rather, in just what ways Puritanism affected American life, and for the solution we must look mainly to the historians, who have not yet dealt adequately with our religious history.

Secondly, *the frontier spirit*, or (to name this factor in its broadest significance) nature, physical America. While the influence of Puritanism has been amply conceded (though never really demonstrated) by our students of literature, the influence of the frontier has been strangely neglected. Professor Turner's paper on "The Significance of the Frontier in American History" presented in 1893, as Jay B. Hubbell has observed, "has well-nigh revolutionized the study of American history. . . . Yet the literary history of the frontier is still to be written." Whoever writes it will have occasion to follow the steps of Buckle, Shaler, Turner, and Paxson. Since Turner it has been clear that "the most American thing in all America" is the frontier. From Europe we derived Puritanism and, later, romanticism and realism; but the frontier is American—is the key to the definition of "Americanism." In race and tradition we are fundamentally European; but our geography is our own, and the consequences of our geography can scarcely be exaggerated. More truly than Shakespeare's England did America find herself set apart:

> This other Eden, demi-paradise,
> This fortress built by Nature for herself
> Against infection and the hand of war,
> This happy breed of men . . .

The first momentous result of this splendid isolation was political independence, which provided us henceforth with an ever-stimulating sense of an heroic past and a large if not wholly manifest destiny. Isolation led to the Monroe Doctrine, which extended the boundaries of the Garden of Eden to Patagonia. As generation followed generation, the frontier in North America shifted westward, ever renewing itself and ever sending back to the East currents of thought and feeling and power that in large measure determined the development of American democracy. It transformed the European type into such men as Jefferson, Jackson, Lincoln, Roosevelt, or, among the writers, Emerson, Whitman, Mark Twain. It was Emerson who said that "Europe stretches to the Alleghenies; America lies beyond," and it was he who spoke for the frontier, as well as for romanticism, in his address on the American Scholar and his essay on Self-Reliance. The pioneer spirit is as vital in him as are his Puritan background and his kinship with Wordsworth, Coleridge, and Carlyle. In Whitman, the frontier background of Emerson's idealism becomes foreground. "Here is action untied from strings, magnificently moving in masses"; and he sought to create an equivalent poetry. Nothing of Europe here—effete feudal Europe—but instead the primal virtue of the unexhausted West. The imagination of Whitman dwelt with rapture on this other Eden, this truly New World in which a happy breed of men might make a new start:

Have the elder races halted?
Do they droop and end their lesson,
wearied over there beyond the seas?
We take up the task eternal,
and the burden and the lesson,
Pioneers! O pioneers!

Whitman's 1819–1892 cover the flowering and fading of the pioneer spirit; the year of his death coincides almost exactly with the passing of the physical frontier. Both Emerson and Whitman had witnessed, with mingled feelings, the materialistic splendor that followed the frontier. America, as Emerson viewed it, was another name for Opportunity, and opportunity, to most Americans from the Puritan days onward, had meant above all economic opportunity. The conquest of nature by man was succeeded by the conquest of man by nature. More and more, Things were in the saddle, as Emerson saw. "The largeness of the nation," said Whitman even before the great era of industrial expansion, "were monstrous without a corresponding largeness and generosity of the spirit of the citizen." But instead of seeking such a growth of the spirit (for which both Emerson and Whitman steadfastly offered light and leading), America gave herself up, with slight compunction, to materialism—materialism colored with a conventional religiosity, which effected the ascendancy of middle-class philistinism. The chosen race became the children of darkness. The currents of thought and feeling and power that the frontier minority had sent back to the East steadily dwindled, and instead of working out a new national culture under the inspiration of the pioneer spirit, all America lapsed into the comfortable prosperity and philistine tyranny of Main Street.

From the early days, the absence of a national culture had been a problem and a challenge. Political and economic independence could not wholly stifle higher cravings. Necessarily, a frontier people found themselves provincial, and their provincialism took two opposite forms. On the one hand was provincial dependence, a reliance upon the cultural mother across the seas; on the other, provincial self-assertion, a narrow Americanism that extolled itself and deprecated the foreign. And the two forms could coexist in the same person. It would be interesting to discuss the diverse ways in which this problem has been envisaged by recent critics like Van Wyck Brooks, Randolph Bourne, H. L. Mencken, Stuart Sherman, and Henry Canby. I can only remark here, however, that these critics are dealing with a problem that had its origin on the frontier, that they belong in a long succession of critics and creative writers who have been concerned with it, and that they must pass on to future generations of critics and creative writers a problem that, among all the great nations, confronts America alone, because America alone is a frontier nation.

I come now to the third factor, European *romanticism*, which, like the frontier, has been strangely neglected. Despite casual glances at English romanticists, our literary historians have obscured the fact that the literature of the United States from the birth of the nation to the twentieth century is part of the Romantic Movement. We too had our precursors in the eighteenth century, of whom Freneau is the most distinguished; we had our sentimental preparation, our *Werther* fever, our Gothic enthusiasms, our fresh interest in nature, and we had a democratic Revolution before the French. We had our first generation of moderate romantics, writers like Bryant, Irving, and Cooper. At the height of our romantic movement, say between 1830 and the Civil War, we had the group of writers—Emerson, Hawthorne, Thoreau, Longfellow, Lowell, Whittier, Poe, Whitman, etc.—who virtually created American literature. We had in the *Blütezeit* of New England a larger and more compact "school" than the Lakists or Cockneys in England, comparable, rather with the *romantische Schule* in Germany. For inspiration we looked to England and the Continent, as England had looked to Germany, and Germany to France (or Rousseau). We had our lovers of beauty; we were fascinated by the Middle Ages; we wrote ballads; we had disciples of nature; we turned to the national Past, to the Indians, the Puritans, and the Revolution; we cultivated the sense of wonder, the supernatural, the grotesque, the ego, the genius; we were ardent in social reform, and carried out pantisocratic notions at Brook Farm and Fruitlands; we worked out new theories of poetry and art in revolt against pseudo-classicism; we were reverently appreciative of Shakespeare, traveled much in the realms of Elizabethan gold, discovered or rediscovered Homer, Plato, Dante, Calderon, Rousseau, Goethe, Kant, and the *Germans* generally. And at length we had our decadence in Bayard Taylor, Stoddard, Stedman, Aldrich, Lanier, etc.

As in every country that experienced the romantic impulse, the movement was modified by national conditions. When Cabot said that Transcendentalism was "romanticism on Puritan soil," he might have extended his definition by saying that American literature in the nineteenth century was romanticism "on Puritan and pioneer soil." For temporal background, our romanticism has not only the Revolutionary idealism but also the Puritan idealism, an indefeasible possession: for spatial background, our romanticism looks beyond the Alleghenies to the free West. Furthermore, national conditions of more than one kind caused the romantic wave to attain its height nearly a half century later than in England and Germany. When Wordsworth, after living on into an alien age, died in 1850, our Cooper still had one year to live, Irving nine years, and Bryant twenty-eight; and these are our earliest important writers. Again, within the years 1803–19, the English writers who were born include such names as Tennyson, Browning, Thackeray, Dickens, and George Eliot, whom we are accustomed to term Victorians; but the American writers born within the same years are Emerson, Hawthorne, Longfellow, Whittier, Poe, Thoreau, Lowell, and Whitman, our outstanding romantics. And again, the Victorians died, on the average, before the American romantics, three of whom survived into the 1890s. It follows that what we lacked in this country was not, certainly, a Romantic Movement, but a Victorian era at all comparable with England's. Our Victorianism was both brief and undistinguished.

And now the fourth and last main factor, *realism*—the application of the scientific spirit to art—reliance upon the senses and common sense, whether in their naïve working or in that organized working which Huxley describes. Although the scientific spirit gained a secure hold in the century of Benjamin Franklin, it did not really flourish in our literature till after the romantic dispensation. Realism, indeed, had been implicit in romanticism itself: keenness of sense perception, awareness of the complexities of the inner life, exploration of "the near, the low, the common," concern with "the poor, the feelings of the child, the philosophy of the street, the meaning of household life," in a word, "insight into today" as opposed to "the remote, the romantic"—these "auspicious signs of the coming days" which Emerson discerned in 1837, in the full flush of romanticism, only needed emphasis in order to render possible the new literature that came to be known as realistic. To give this emphasis was, historically considered, the prime achievement of Walt Whitman. While he belonged to the romantics by virtue of his splendid personality, his doctrine of individualism and humanitarianism, and his religion of nature and the soul, he unmistakably points forward at the same time to the sophisticated realism of our time, by virtue of his sharp sense perception, his unflinching attitude toward facts of life shunned by what Edward Carpenter termed the "impure hush" of the Victorian era, his revolt from the modes of versification of the past and his experiment with the form now known as free verse. He anticipated our literature, also, in his attitude toward science, despite the mysticism that ever crowned his acceptance of science. Poetry is the child of science, "exuding the greatness of the father." From science he derives authority for his treatment of sex: "The innocence and nakedness are resumed—they are neither modest nor immodest." From science he derives the idea of "vital laws" higher than those of the theology that came out of the Orient: "The whole theory of the supernatural, and all that was twined with it or educed out of it, departs as in a dream." It is everywhere obvious that in science, whose standards underlie all modern realism, Whitman found, or believed that he found, ample support for those aspects of his work which repelled his contemporaries and which attract many readers in our day of science in life and realism in the arts.

I can only touch upon the subsequent development of realism, the result partly of spontaneous reaction against decadent romanticism, and partly of fresh European influence. Between 1870 and 1890, while such men as Burroughs, Muir, and Fiske were demonstrating the claims of science, and while the poets remained predominantly romantic, the cause of realism in literature was advanced by such prose writers as Mark Twain, Howells, James, Eggleston, Miss Murfree, Miss Jewett, and Miss Wilkins (are these our "eminent Victorians"?). In the revolt of the 1890s—in men like Garland, Markham, and Crane—realism attained a bitterness that contrasts with the optimism of Whitman. In Mr. Robinson and Mrs. Wharton it became more rational and satirical and ironic; and at length came the "New Poetry," a poetry not without romantic elements, but distinguished in the main by its subtle sense observation, its rational and satiric outlook on life, and its eager experiment to find instruments of expression in keeping with the new vision. After 1916, when this poetry had reached its highest point, the realistic impulse centered in prose, in the short story, the novel, and the drama, giving special heed to the scientific contribution known as the "new psychology."

Such in brief is my own reading of the factors dominant in the evolution of American literature. Perhaps I have chosen them wrongly; that is not the question. The question is, whether we do not need, for our future historical studies and our criticism, a fresh interpretation of the forces that have directed our literature.

I need not detail our other needs, which are many. Our scholarship will attend, with exemplary patience, to the uncovering of new materials and facts. Professor Pollard, in his recent *Factors in American History*, confesses that he is not tempted "to add to the mass of excellent research which now pours out in such a volume from American historians that one wonders that even the United States can contain it all." Is it not true that American *literary* historians are already threatening to expand our knowledge beyond the power of controlling that knowledge? The danger that confronts the higher study of American literature is an aimless accumulation of small facts. Additions to the sum of knowledge are rarely of value unless they are related with an important end in view. No doubt we could go on forever building mountains of fact to the wonderment of Europeans like Professor Pollard; but our proper task is really to use the materials already at hand, and to seek new materials intelligently.

This cannot be done, I fear, on the basis of our antiquated interpretation of American literature. In order to work intelligently, we need a fresh interpretation, or a number of fresh interpretations—the systematic exploitation of promising points of view. Each possible main factor should be extensively applied to see how much it really explains. Different groups of students could work on different lines: some, for example, on the moral and religious background; some on the Revolutionary tradition; some on the manifold effects of the pioneer spirit; some on the Romantic Movement in America; and some on the realistic and scientific movement since Whitman. Each of these themes merits an extensive and thorough book; and until the books have been made possible by cooperative effort, I do not see how the state of American literary history can be measurably improved.

48 Middletown Faces Both Ways (1937)

The French philosopher Auguste Comte was among the first to argue that systematic social science—what he in 1838 dubbed *sociologie*—could serve civil ends. Once divines lost control of the state, Comte reasoned, policy ought to be guided by methods that were more exacting (*positive*) than theology, closer to physics than metaphysics. As he predicted, positivist, numbers-crunching demographers and criminologists soon proved useful to republican governments in Europe. But around 1900, when the social sciences moved to the academy (led by Emile Durkheim in France and Max Weber in Germany) and established headquarters in the United States, attention returned to more abstract, synthetic concerns. Social scientists aimed not only to analyze particular problems, populations, and institutions but also to understand how society worked as a whole.

For some citizens, of course, society never "works" very well. Their painful experience suggests the limits of the whole and thereby the need for safety nets. So, early twentieth-century sociologists (especially the so-called Chicago School, in league with progressive reformers) tended to focus on ethnic enclaves or deviants—"nuts and sluts"—who were amenable to precise, policy-oriented research. Some also aimed to study the totality of society holistically and head-on, say, in the manner that contemporary anthropologists were studying non-Western "primitives." These discipline-blending scholars looked at Americans with similar, albeit simulated, detachment.

Over the next half-century they identified a set of "norms" (typical ways of acting) or "values" (preferences, conceptions of the important or desirable) that seemed distinctly American. Most of their lists (for example, by Ethel Albert, Cora DuBois, Alfred Kroeber, Clyde Kluckhohn, Florence Kluckhohn, Milton Rokeach, Fred Strodbeck, Robin Williams) included:

- Individualism—a singular, private self as the ultimate locus of responsibility and choice, best free of social control
- Progress—change as, more likely than not, for the better
- Practicality—efficiency, compromise, action, work, improvisation
- The present and the future—time as a perishable commodity to be spent or invested wisely
- Justice—equality of opportunity, peace, discomfort with all-too-common bigotry and snobbery
- Competition—open, merit-based rivalry among "naturally" unequal individuals, groups, ideas, and institutions, especially in the economy
- Friendliness—informality, play, fun, generosity
- Honesty—candor, transparent rules of work and play
- Success—increasing status and wealth, at least up to a "middle-class" ideal
- Faith—worship, charitable community, church

They also began investigating ways that such values interact and change in actual communities. Their most famous and frequently restudied site has been Muncie, Indiana, the city that Robert and Helen Merrell Lynd called "Middletown." The Lynds' sources were multimedia—polls, censuses, documentary and oral histories, journalism, fiction, and fieldwork. On the advice of anthropologist Clark Wissler they sorted observations into six realms: vocation, home, education, leisure, community service, and religion. The Lynds' two books—*Middletown: A Study in Contemporary American Culture* (1929) and *Middletown in Transition* (1937)—were immediately, immensely popular.

The authors were well known both as social scientists and as activists. For more than thirty years they were key on-campus allies of labor and civil rights reformers. As a devout Protestant (with a divinity degree from Union Seminary), Robert Lynd shared with earlier progressives a concern that industrialization, urbanization, immigration, and consumerism threatened the Social Gospel. He aimed to show that modern cities could, in fact, resist the worst temptations of modernity.

Since Muncie (population 37,000) was a midsize slice of middle America but unusually homogeneous (its rapid growth coming as local farmers took factory jobs in town), the Lynds hoped to find there a preserve of "traditional" virtues, a place that was not so much typically as *proto*typically American. In 1930, 88 percent of the city's households were native-born and white, a higher percentage than all but two of the hundreds of U.S. cities equal in size or larger at the time. (The other one of the two was New Albany, Indiana, where Robert Lynd grew up.) If pre-industrial, Christian values could survive anywhere; and if detachment was to be the pose, Muncie would be the place. The Institute for Social and Religious Research (a philanthropy associated with the Interchurch World Movement and the Presbyterian Board of Home Missions) was their patron.

What the Lynds found, however, was that even under such promising circumstances, civic virtues were all but dead. *Middletown* confirmed the dark predictions of Karl Marx and Thorsten Veblen. Like Sinclair Lewis's Babbitt and H. L. Mencken's "booboisie," citizens struggled only to advance material, individual, or class interests; soul and community be damned. The faith or philanthropy of leading industrialists (Muncie's "X family," the Balls) was far less important than their ruthless domination of local affairs. The Lynds' sponsor (which got much of its money from New York's X family, the Rockefellers) found this message so disturbing that they dissociated themselves from the project.

With the onset of the Great Depression (1929–1939), the Lynds' leftist leanings turned yet more strident. In their restudy, *Middletown in Transition*, Muncie fared even worse. Rather than changing with mounting challenges, lame values seem only more entrenched.

Subsequent studies identify several problems in the Lynds' approach. It is certainly hard now to credit their detachment. When faced with Middletown and modernity, they obviously had an axe to grind. Nearly all of their disappointments require a presumption that there once were truly good old days of pre-industrial, native-born, Protestant hegemony. Unlike more cutting-edge colleagues in sociology, they also seemed to count only two social classes: the haves and the have-nots. Hence, the opportunities for advancement that drew so many farm kids to Muncie counted for little in the Lynds' estimation. If they had used finer categories and studied a more typical industrial city (where immigrants supported even greater upward mobility among native-born workers), the Lynds' image of rigid social hierarchy would be impossible to sustain. Even when their perspective was less prejudiced, Muncie proved an unfortunate choice. With the help of home economist Faith Williams, for example, they were sensitive to women's opportunities at home and on the job, but at the time Muncie had a smaller proportion of wage-earning women than 90 percent of the cities in the United States.

In such ways, the Lynds' bias shows. They certainly underestimated the vigor of American workers and women in general. But restudies have also confirmed that the values they found in Muncie were prevalent nationally and that they remain remarkably so even today. Here they assess the continuity of culture from the 1920s to the 1930s.

The preceding chapters have sought to make explicit the elements of permanence and of change in Middletown as the city has met with four types of experience peculiarly conducive to cultural change: sudden and great strain on its institutions, widespread dislocation of individual habits, pressure for change from the larger culture surrounding it, and at some points the actual implementing from without of a changed line of action. These ten years of boom and depression might be expected to leave permanent marks on the culture. . . .

The prosperity of the fat years, while sharpening the disappointments of the depression, also remains today in Middletown in the form of enhanced personal goals and glimpsed new psychological standards of living for many of its citizens. The fact that Middletown does not regard the depression as in any sense "its own fault," or even the fault of the economy by which it lives, makes it easy for the city to think of the confusion following 1929 as "just a bad bump in the road," one of those inevitable occurrences that spoil things temporarily but do not last. The gold-rush scramble back to confidence which the research staff witnessed in 1935 was the inevitable result of such a rationale of the depression. Middletown was in effect saying, albeit soberly and decidedly anxiously: "It's all over, thank God! And now we'll get after all those things we were planning for ourselves in 1928–29!" In a culture built on money, the experience of better homes, better cars, winter vacations in Florida, and better educated children dies hard; and while some people's hopes, especially among the working class, have been mashed out permanently by the depression, the influential business group who determine the wave length of Middletown's articulate hopes are today busily broadcasting the good news that everything is all right again.

The depression experiences contained more outright novelty than did the years 1925–1929:

- A city exultantly preoccupied with the question, "How fast can we make even more money?" was startled by being forced to shift its central concern for a period of years to the stark question, "Can we manage to keep alive?"
- A city living excitedly *at* a future which all signs promised would be golden lived for a while *in* the present with its exigent demands.
- A city living by the faith that everyone can and should support himself lived through a period of years in which it had to confess that at least temporarily a quarter of its population could not get work.
- A city intensely opposed to society's caring for able-bodied people has taxed itself to support for an indefinitely long period one in every four of its families.
- A city that has chronically done without many manifestly needed civic improvements, on the philosophy that it does no good to hunt up and plan desirable things to do because there isn't any money to pay for them, has lived for a time in a world in which not money but ability to plan and carry out progress was the limiting factor.

- A city built around the theory of local autonomy has lived in a world experiencing rapid centralization of administrative authority and marked innovations in the interference by these centralized agencies in local affairs.
- A city that lives by the thought that it is one big cooperating family has had the experience of a wholesale effort by its working class to organize against its business class under sponsorship from Washington.
- A city committed to faith in education as the key to its children's future has had to see many of its college-trained sons and daughters idle, and to face the question as to what education is really "worth."
- A city devoted to the doctrine that "Work comes first," to an extent that has made many of its citizens scarcely able to play, has faced the presence of enforced leisure and heard people talk of "the new leisure." Civicly, the community has begun to state positively the problem of the leisure of the mass of its people and to make wider provision for popular leisure pursuits.
- A city still accustomed to having its young assume largely the values of their parents has had to listen to an increasing number of its young speak of the world of their parents as a botched mess.
- A city in which the "future" has always been painted in terms of its hopes has been forced to add to its pigments the somber of its fears.

Experiences such as these partake in their cumulative effect of the crisis quality of a serious illness, when life's customary busy immediacies drop away and one lies helplessly confronting oneself, reviewing the past and asking abrupt questions of the future. What has Middletown learned from its crisis and partial convalescence?

Chapter I stated some of the larger questions of this sort which the research staff took to Middletown in June, 1935. The broad answer to these questions is that basically the texture of Middletown's culture has not changed. Those members of the research staff who had expected to find sharp differences in group alignments within the city, in ways of thinking, or feeling, or carrying on the multifarious daily necessities of life, found little to support their hypotheses. Middletown is overwhelmingly living by the values by which it lived in 1925; and the chief additions are defensive, negative elaborations of already existing values such as, among the business class, intense suspicion of centralizing tendencies in government, of the interference of social legislation with business, of labor troubles, and of radicalism. Among the working class, tenuous and confused new positive values are apparent in such a thing as the aroused conception of the possible role of government in bolstering the exposed position of labor by social legislation, including direct relief for the unemployed. But, aside from these, no major new symbols or ideologies of a positive sort have developed as conspicuous rallying points. Leadership in the community has not shifted in kind, but has become more concentrated in the group observed in 1925. . . .

Even the fault lines which appear today and show signs of developing into major fissures within the community were faintly visible in 1925. In the main, a Rip Van Winkle, fallen asleep in 1925 while addressing Rotary or the Central Labor Union, could have awakened in 1935 and gone right on with his interrupted address to the same people with much the same ideas.

Such changes as are going forward in Middletown are disguised by the thick blubber of custom that envelops the city's life. The city is uneasily conscious of many twinges down under the surface, but it resembles the person who insists on denying and disregarding unpleasant physical symptoms on the theory that everything *must* be all right, and that if anything really is wrong it may cure itself without leading to a major operation. The conflicts under the surface in Middletown are not so much new as more insistent, more difficult to avoid, harder to smooth over. Many of these latent conflicts, aggravated by the depression and now working themselves toward the surface of the city's life, have been pointed out in the preceding pages: conflicts among values hitherto held as compatible; conflicts among institutions—economic and political, economic and educational and religious, economic and familial; conflicts among groups in the community breaking through the symbols of the unified city; conflicts between deep-rooted ideas of individual and collective responsibility; conflicts, above all, between symbols and present reality.

The physical and personal continuities of life are relatively great in the small community, and the average dweller in such a community probably has a sense of "belonging" that is qualitatively somewhat different from that of the big-city dweller. The institutions in the small city tend to be familiar and, with the help of many assumptions of long standing as to how they are linked together and operate, a quality of simplicity is imparted to them in the minds of local people. By assuming continuities and similarities, this simplicity is interpreted outward to include "American life" and "American institutions."

One of the major elements of conflict imparted by the depression to Middletown has been the injection of a new sense of the inescapable complexity of this assumedly simple world. As indicated earlier, the more alert Middletown people met the depression with an earnest desire to "understand" it—only to be thrown back later, in many instances, with a sense that it was "too big" for them and that all they could do was to try to stick to their jobs and save their own skins. One suspects that for the first time in their lives many Middletown people have awakened, in the depression, from a sense of being at home in a familiar world to the shock of living as an atom in a universe dangerously too big and blindly out of hand. With the falling away of literal belief in the teachings of religion in recent decades, many Middletown folk have met a similar shock, as the simpler universe of fifty years ago has broken up into a vastly complicated physical order; but, there, they have been able to retain the shadowy sense of their universe's being in beneficent control by the common expedient of believing themselves to live in a world of unresolved duality, in which one goes about one's daily affairs without thought of religion but relies vaguely on the ultimates in life being somehow divinely "in hand." In the economic order, however, it is harder for Middletown to brush aside the shock by living thus on two largely unconnected levels, for the economic out-of-handness is too urgently threatening to daily living.

So Middletown tries to forget and to disregard the growing disparities in the midst of which it lives. Its adult population has, through its socially gay youth and busy adult life, resisted the patient scrutiny of problems and the teasing out of their less obvious antecedents and implications. As a local man remarked in 1924 in commenting on the pressure of modern living, "We've lost the ability to ponder over life. We're too busy." And, if in the boom days Middletown was "too busy" to ponder, it was too worried to do so in the depression. It is quite characteristic, for instance, that, as one woman remarked in 1935, "We never get down to talking about things like the coming of fascism. The only time we ever talk about any of those things is when we comment on a radio program." Rather than ponder such things, Middletown prefers either to sloganize or to personalize its problems. And the more the disparities have forced themselves to attention, the more things have seemed "too big" and "out of hand," the more Middletown has inclined to heed the wisdom of sticking to one's private business and letting the uncomfortable "big problems" alone, save for a few encompassing familiar slogans. Where Middletown cannot avoid these big problems and must on occasion present at least the semblance of a balance in this system of non-balancing intellectual bookkeeping, it is resorting increasingly to the suppression of detailed entries and to the presentation of only the alleged totals.

One frequently gets a sense of people's being afraid to let their opinions become sharp. They believe in "peace, but —." They believe in "fairness to labor, but —." In "freedom of speech, but —." In "democracy, but —." In "freedom of the press, but —." This is in part related to the increased apprehensiveness that one feels everywhere in Middletown: fear on the part of teachers, of the D.A.R., and of the Chamber of Commerce; fear by businessmen of high taxes and public ownership of utilities and of the Roosevelt administration; fear by laborers of joining unions lest they lose their jobs; fear by office-holders wanting honest government and of being framed by the politicians; fear by everyone to show one's hand, or to speak out.

But this process of avoiding issues goes on less and less fluently. With a widening gap between symbol and practice in the most immediate concerns of living, there are more forced choices as to where one's emphasis is to be placed. Middletown wants to be adventurous and to embrace new ideas and practices, but it also desperately needs security, and in this conflict both businessmen and workingmen appear to be clinging largely to tried sources of security rather than venturing out into the untried. Middletown people want to be kind, friendly, expansive, loyal to each other, to make real the idea of a friendly city working together for common ends; but, in a business world where one is struggling for self-preservation, or for power and prestige as a supposed means to self-preservation, warm personal relations, like the more fastidious sorts of integrity, may tend to become a luxury and be crowded to the wall. If necessary, one dispenses with affection. People want to continue to live hopefully and adventurously into the future, but if the future becomes too hazardous they look steadily toward the known past.

On the surface, then, Middletown is meeting such present issues and present situations it cannot escape by attempting to revert to the old formulas: we must always believe that things are good and that they will be better, and we must stress their hopeful rather than their pessimistic aspects. This leads to the stating of such social problems that may arise defensively and negatively—rather than to engaging in a positive program for social analysis and reconstruction. It is still true in 1936 that, to Middletown, such things as poverty or a depression are simply exceptions to a normally good state of affairs; and anything wrong is the fault of some individuals (or, collectively, of "human nature") rather than anything amiss with the organization and functioning of the culture. The system is fundamentally right and only persons wrong; the cures must be changes in personal attitude, not in the institutions themselves. Among these personal cures for its social woes are the following six basic qualities needed for a better world outlined in a local address: "faith, service, cooperation, the Golden Rule, optimism, and character." "The typical citizen," says an editorial approvingly, "discounts the benefits of the political and economic New Deal and says that common sense is the answer to the depression. . . . He thinks hard work is the depression cure." Or again, "If profits are low, it is still possible to get a good deal of enjoyment by doing the best possible under adverse circumstances and by taking pride in our work."

This marked tendency in Middletown's thought and feeling to see the place where remedial change is needed in individual people and not in its institutions helps to ease its tension over local political corruption and other shortcomings in the midst of which it lives. Its faith in the ultimate quality and final perfection of its institutions is thus left intact, and its Christian emphasis upon the need to spur on weak and faltering human nature to that perfecting of itself "which all history proves to be slowly taking place" makes the individual shoulder the whole burden of blame. Over and over again one sees Middletown following this line of reasoning. Thus, for instance, the reason Middletown's business class is unable to see any sense in such a concept as "class differences" is that it recognizes no relevant basis for "classes" in the institutional system. And it does not recognize them because, according to its way of viewing things, "getting ahead" is a personal matter. The institutions are there, fixed and final in their major aspects, and the individual must struggle to make them work and to be more worthy of them. Once one gets this point of view, Middletown's rationale of "the rich" as "social benefactors" and of "the iniquity of the New Deal" becomes apparent. One can see why Middletown feels the rightness of recent editorials in its press such as the following:

LET'S GIVE THE RICH A REST

It is popular just now to assail the wealthy, and unpopular to defend them, and yet most of the economic progress that America has made would have been impossible had this not always been a land of opportunity for those who wish to make money without undue restrictions upon their gains. . . . Thousands of boys reared in poverty have become millionaires through their own ability, through their unbridled ambitions, and in becoming so have supplied occupations and the comforts of life to many times the number of thousands who have acquired the millions.

Instead of laying all our troubles upon those who have had the talent and the brains to become wealthy, why not each of us assume our share of responsibility for the economic situation of the nation?

MONEY-MAKING THE BIG INCENTIVE

The way to make both the poor man and the rich man poorer is to tax wealth so greatly that it loses its incentive to produce. . . .

ON THE "SOCKING" OF THE RICH

Who remembers when the American boy was taught he had as good an opportunity to become wealthy as the town's richest man had at the same age? And when the rich, while perhaps they were envied by others, were thought worthy of emulation? When riches were not considered a disgrace but an honor and millions would have died rather than accept charity?

Now the demagogues, the social outcasts, the unsuccessful, the lazy, the ambitionless, the ignorant all join in a swelling chorus in denunciation of those who by their work and ability have acquired more of the world's goods than others have been able to obtain, making no distinction between the wealth that has come by reason of intelligence, hard work, and thrift and that which has been obtained through trickery and fraud. . . . So we preach the doctrine of "socking" the rich, because the majority of us are not rich and are not likely ever to be rich, since the majority have not the ability, even given the opportunity, to acquire great wealth.

But without great accumulations of centralized capital, America today would be almost wholly a nation of farmers, instead of being divided between agriculture and industry. Except for centralized capital, how could great factories be constructed, great buildings be erected, hospitals built and maintained, vast charities be supported, scientific investigations be made, and the results of such investigations given free to the world?

To men holding the philosophy these editorials reveal, efforts in Washington or elsewhere to make changes in *institutions* by which men live constitute a misguided assault on the one source of strength and progress within a nation, namely, the personal drive within the individual to accumulate wealth and to "better himself." "Progress," according to this philosophy, is a by-product of the pursuit of wealth.

The essentially instrumental character of Middletown's living noted earlier—namely, its emphasis upon the "future," "saving," "trying to get somewhere in life," and so on, as against the present quality of living—tends to augment its tension over emerging conflicts. This sort of instrumental living puts a heavy premium upon assumed simplicity and reliability in the underlying institutional system. One can hardly live confidently *at* the future unless one assumes a guaranteed highway; if one assumes the broad, sure highway, one need not concern oneself too much over dusty inadequacies in the present, because the road mounts surely just around the next bend; but if one questions the very existence of a sure highway "as some radicals and long-haired thinkers do," then what is to become of all the virtues of fortitude and hard work? A culture thus committed to instrumental living tends, because emotionally it so badly needs to do so, to do with its present difficulties along the road precisely what Middletown has tended to do with the depression, that is, to regard it as just an unduly stiff bit in the road. And only with great difficulty or as a result of prolonged discouragement will it do what a minority of Middletown's working class are beginning to do—ask whether the road is really leading anywhere, whether after all it is the best possible road, or even whether the present isn't a good time and place to recognize one's difficulties and to begin to face them. . . .

The people learn, unlearn, learn,
a builder, a wrecker, a builder again, . . .
"Precisely who and what is the people?"
Hope is a tattered flag and a dream out of time.

. . . .

Hope is an echo, hope ties itself yonder, yonder.
In the darkness with a great bundle of grief
    the people march.
In the night, and overhead a shovel of stars for
    keeps, the people march:
        "Where to? what next?"

—Carl Sandburg, *The People, Yes*

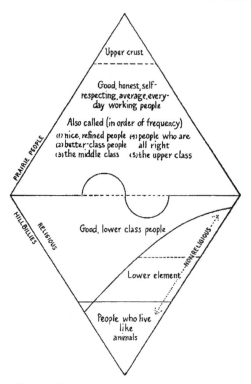

Plainville Social Class, James West (Carl A. Withers), 1945

In 1939 and 1940, Columbia University student Carl Withers conducted field re-search in a Midwestern farm town (population 275). Out of respect for confidants, in print he used only fake names for them, their hamlet, and himself. While col-leagues in anthropology and folklore studied far-off "primitives" or nearby urban-ites, Withers pursued isolated representatives of what he assumed to be America's small-town, self-sufficient past. He explains, "I sought a community with the few-est possible economic and social factors which might complicate the problem un-der scrutiny," namely, the response of "Plainville, U.S.A." to modernization. "I hoped to find a community where people were all living as nearly as possible on the same social and financial plane"—all English-speaking Protestants, no Negroes or foreigners, no resorts or industry, as far as possible from a highway. Plainvillers endorsed his supposition that they were all just ordinary, independent folks. He soon discovered, though, that they depended on a powerful structure of social classes with complex relations to distant institutions of commerce and government. Like many of his peers, Withers often made this point through irony, juxtaposing every-day speech and academic analysis. His diagram here forces words from one into a form of the other, together exposing a myth in Plainville's plainness.

ALICE KESSLER-HARRIS

49 Cultural Locations

Positioning American Studies in the Great Debate (1992)

It is tempting to end this volume with a line of argument—say, with Lionel Trilling's criticism of Parrington's criticism of Emerson's criticism of prevailing views of America. But what ties this work to subsequent American Studies is as much a style as a subject of curiosity and dispute. It is simultaneously past- and present-minded, ethically charged, and self-reflexive. Critics glimpse America as if through a looking glass that the whole world ought to see. At each moment the vision of each observer remains distinct, but nearly all seem to peer anxiously in the same direction—the United States—and to recognize familiar profiles in motion, overlaid with their own reflections.

However, the substance of their impressions—say, of the meaning of "America," how it was allegedly shaped, or the methods and merits of looking—have varied greatly. Particularly since the mid-1950s, when the field became a professional academic affair, disputes have grown ever more intricate and intense. The roots of new and old disagreements burst through American soil.

Parrington's *Main Currents in American Thought* can be considered especially fertile in that respect. It has provided a wealth of sites for grafting and pruning. For example, although very well received at the time of its publication (1927–1930), just ten years later it was widely scorned. Professors of literature, history, and social science found his methods sloppy and his taste—his sampling strategy or aesthetic—incoherent. Leftists found his politics lamely accommodative while conservatives considered him subversive. Subsequent interpretations of American culture have kept Parrington's legacy alive and, I think it is fair to say, vice versa.

Probably the single most scathing and suggestive response was published by Lionel Trilling, first in a 1940 review and then as the opening chapter of his immensely popular book, *The Liberal Imagination* (1950).

Trilling's own career was even more volatile than Parrington's. From the 1930s through the mid-1970s he was a critic whom people loved or loved to hate. He was both an early champion of Marxist criticism (particularly the Trotskyite version that first reigned in *Partisan Review*) and among the first of the "New York intellectuals" to repudiate Stalinism as well as fascism and then liberalism. He was both profoundly suspicious of the academy and a tireless self-promoter. He was the son of immigrants and the first Jew ever to gain a tenure-track job in the English Department of Columbia University, but he was also quick to dismiss Judaism as a significant feature of his own or anyone else's autobiography. Although he had next to nothing good to say about "the New Critics," he shared their affection for irony and close reading and provided much of the sense of cultural crisis to which they coyly appealed. Albeit via the royal "we," he styled himself as the heroic survivor ("the opposing self") in the center of artistic, social, and spiritual conflicts that he took to be fundamental and universal.

In building such a precious place for himself, Trilling and many of his contemporaries slowly began to seem more bourgeois and conservative than they ever styled themselves. That reputation was confirmed in the 1960s when, to his horror, Trilling faced Columbia students who considered "opposition" a bodily and social as well as writerly responsibility. As Nina Baym observed in 1981, the Jezebels with whom Trilling's generation jousted—the unwashed or effete, the New Critics or Romantics, idealists or nihilists, et al.—seem to be projections of misogynist sentiment. Critics conjured such sirens as foils in "melodramas of beset manhood." In the journal of the U.S. American Studies Association, *American Quarterly*, a half-dozen years later, Houston Baker added:

> The questions Trilling finds—correctly or incorrectly—intimately relevant to his life are descriptive only of a bourgeois, characteristically twentieth-century, white Western mentality. . . . In "diasporic," "developing," "Third World," "emerging" . . . territories there is no need to pose, in ironical Audenesque ways, questions such as: Are we happy? Are we content? Are we free? Such questions presuppose, at least, an adequate level of sustenance and a faith in human behavioral alternatives sufficient to enable a self-directed questioning. In other words, without food for thought, all modernist bets are off.

As with Emerson and Parrington, these observations, too, would attract yet more pruning and grafting in the field that became American Studies. Here, Columbia University's Professor Alice Kessler-Harris explains how the field has fared. The occasion is her presidential address to the 1992 meeting of the American Studies Association.

Since we last met, the world has seen momentous changes. . . . Apartheid in South Africa is in the process of crumbling. . . . Communism is shattered. . . . The cold war is no longer. At this speaking, Arabs are sitting down with Israelis. . . . Unemployment insurance, sexual harassment, national health care, abortion rights, family leave, civil rights, and a newly virulent conservatism are all burning issues of the moment. None of them has occupied our daily thoughts more than the issues of multiculturalism.

Now I confess to more than a bit of puzzlement over all this. . . . American free enterprise is a clear victor in the struggle for what we once called the minds and hearts of the people. Yet somehow we have become enmeshed in a battle over the idea of America. What is at stake in this battle? How are we, as students of American Studies, to think about it?

The absence of a common enemy, you might say, makes room for internal dissent. So it seems no more than reasonable that the same year that witnessed the demise of what appeared to be a major threat to the United States should witness the escalation of a fiery internal controversy that has left none of us untouched. Who has not participated in debates over revising the curriculum to meet the changing needs of students with new demographic profiles? Who has not written and read reviews of the several books that indict campuses as hotbeds of political correctness? . . . Let us look a little more closely at the debate and then see if we can't forge an American Studies position.

In its simplest form, multiculturalism acknowledges and attempts to incorporate into the curriculum and campus environment "the wide range of cultures that cohabit the U.S." It represents, as even its detractors acknowledge, "the discovery on the part of minority groups that they can play a part in molding the larger culture even as they are molded by it." The trouble, according to its critics, is that multiculturalism is rarely benign. Rather, critics fear that multicultural courses will displace traditional subjects, depriving students of what they call the heritage of Western culture.

For the purposes of this argument, I want to separate that central issue from arguments about political correctness. Opponents of multiculturalism often argue that codes of conduct and attempts at curricular reform designed to promote tolerance, in practice, inhibit our capacity to speak our minds. They accuse advocates of diversity of imposing particular standards of behavior. But what is often called political correctness detracts from the issues surrounding multiculturalism. Lest we substitute one myth for another, we can and should decry excesses perpetrated in the name of that endeavor. We only need recall some of our earlier experiences as Marxists, feminists, and activists in the 1960s to remember how important it was to be allowed to speak our piece and to despair when we hear reports that, in the name of multiculturalism, students . . . resort to intimidating criticism.

Still, most efforts to achieve a multiculturalism curriculum can hardly be defined as excessive behavior. Though no one would deny the existence of occasional harassment or alarming insinuations, the degree to which intimidation and coercion of the kind that can be defined as politically correct behavior actually exists on American campuses remains an open question. The American Council on Education, the American Civil Liberties Union, and the Carnegie Foundation for the Advancement of Teaching all agree that the problem of coercion from the politically correct is far less prevalent than the rising numbers of incidents of racial intolerance, homophobia, and sexism. So we puzzle about how the issue of multiculturalism got turned into "Left-wing McCarthyism" or "Fascism of the Left."

But the issue of political correctness may be something of a red herring. At the heart of the attack on multiculturalism lies a concern not for rights but for community. To its opponents the idea of what constitutes America seems to be at stake: the meaning conjured up when we think of our nation as threatened. That meaning is intimately tied to ideas about the nature of Western civilization and the particular humanistic values it is said to represent. Those values are constructed in opposition to a feared and unnamed enemy. Thus, what is at stake has two levels: one, a set of Western ideas on which the concept of America as it is defined in these United States is said to rest; and the other, the material set of relations that we see around us and that is in danger of disintegration. They emerge clearly in the language in which the discussion is formulated.

In the spring of 1991, Lee M. Bass gave 20 million dollars to Yale to fund a course of study in Western civilization. The *New York Times* article that announced the gift commented that this was "a field that for more than a decade has been under attack while many colleges and universities increased their emphasis on the study of people and cultures outside the Western tradition." A month later, George Will used the pages of *Newsweek* to rise in defense of Western civilization. The curriculum wars, he declared, were "related battles in a single war, a war of aggression against the Western political tradition and the ideas that animate it.". . . .

Conceiving of the battle of ideas as neither more nor less than a war, those who protest multiculturalism construct powerful enemies against whom they urge resistance. A. M. Rosenthal, in an essay revealingly titled "Suicide on the Fourth," conflated Communists and

Fascists with America's racial bigots and "their emotional cousins" who were members of the Left . . . "new segregationists" . . . .

The war is defensive. It aims to prevent fragmentation and disintegration of something variously called identity or common cultural ground or cultural unity. As Rosenthal put it, the question is "whether this country is to be etched indelibly in the minds of young Americans simply as a strange collection of races and ethnic groups without real identity or purpose in common, or as a great creative action of nationhood in which the building of one became the purpose of many." And in the words of George Will, the forces of multiculturalism "are fighting against the conservation of the common culture that is the nation's social cement."

At the core of protest, then, is the central importance of cultural unity. When a specially appointed committee of New York State educators recommended a dramatic revision of the social studies curriculum in the state's schools last year, the ensuing disagreements echoed arguments all over the nation. The committee . . . concluded "that the teaching of social studies as a single officially sanctioned story was inaccurate as to the facts of conflict in American history, and further that it was limiting for white students and students of color alike." This led critics to suggest that "the old orthodoxies glorifying developments like the Pilgrims' journey to Plymouth Rock or the westward migration might be replaced by a new orthodoxy that would be critical of them." A dissenting committee member commented . . . "The people of the United States will recognize, . . . even if this committee does not, that every viable nation has to have a common culture to survive in peace." Under these circumstances, it was hardly hyperbole for the *Times* to note that "the battle over the New York State social studies curriculum is fundamentally a battle over the idea of America."

A battle over the idea of America? Yes, and one in which the issue is what constitutes "America" and in which fears of fragmentation and loss of identity have replaced the fears of secret enemies conjured up by the old FBI. Those who attack what they call a politically correct stance seem to be supporting the idea of America as something fixed and given, deriving from Western civilization, while those who resist attach themselves to an idea of America that is more fluid and susceptible to change. One side constructs democratic culture as a tradition to be defended, a flag to be protected; the other, as an ongoing process whose meanings are diffuse and changing. One side fears fragmentation of cultural unity; the other derides unity as a myth and protests loss of identity. The issue is joined: how do we preserve cultural unity and still do justice to the multiplicity of American cultures? To accomplish this, we must redefine what we mean by identity.

These are not new issues for American Studies, but their entry into so broad a public sphere pushes us, as scholars (once again) into a posture of self-examination. The political debate calls on myths about a past that we in the field of American Studies have helped to create and interpret, and then popularize among an unsuspecting public. The political battle that rages around us is partly of our making. We, as historians, as cultural critics, as intellectuals who shape image and self-image, have (if you will forgive the metaphor) built the bombs being used in a battle we now seek to avoid.

And so, perhaps reluctantly, we must take on the task of asking how we construct ourselves as a nation. In the past . . . we have . . . desperately wanted to see unity. Our great heroes have been scholars such as David Riesman, David Potter, Frederick Jackson Turner, and Henry Nash Smith who have chosen to present images of a shared and stable identity. Our eagerness to see through their eyes has shaped not only our field, but also the conception of America now in dispute.

In the late 1940s and 1950s, Lionel Trilling noted, "even the most disaffected intellectual must respond to the growing isolation of his country amid the hostility which is directed against it." The desire for unity inhibited public critique of institutions that accepted the tempting funds offered by foundations like Carnegie and Rockefeller to develop American Studies programs with the explicit aim of shoring up national identity in the face of a perceived totalitarian threat. Institutions like Yale, Barnard, Brown, and the University of Wyoming benefited from grants—grants that only became controversial in the 1960s and after. Then, the impact of funding sources on the shape of intellectual life generated a controversy that brought to consciousness an ongoing debate about the relationship between culture and politics. That debate is perhaps responsible for the relatively hospitable response of the American Studies Association to demands for political voice from those seeking cultural representation in that period.

For American Studies has another tradition that parallels the search for unity. In a much-discussed presentation at the 1990 meeting of the association, Leo Marx argued that American Studies had a long heritage of efforts to deal with the complexity of cultural differences—a heritage that extended back to the 1920s when distinguished scholars such as F. O. Mathiessen challenged then-accepted universalisms. Past presidents Allen Davis and Linda Kerber, among others, have pointed to the recent efforts of the discipline of American Studies to pay attention to calls of opening doors of intellectual inquiry. In her 1988 presidential address, Kerber traced the efforts of the American Studies Association to integrate diversity into its organizational structure and scholarly enterprise. I came into the association on the wings of that change. Just out of graduate school, I was invited to give a paper at the Washington convention in 1971. It took only a day to realize that my connections in the association would be with the radical caucus—the group actively seeking to reconcile the style, form, and content of American Studies with new understandings of the world around them. With the women's movement in full throttle, I joined the efforts of women for greater representation on the council. Arguably the search for diversity has constituted the creative dynamic of American Studies for many years.

But in recent years efforts to look at the lives of people of color, of members of various ethnic groups, and of women have lost some of their legitimacy—some of the impetus they provided for a continuing dialogue over the meaning of culture. The difficulties are rooted in the efforts of scholars to reconcile our rich new knowledge about previously neglected groups with the challenges they offer to cherished notions (myths, if you will) about the American past. In an earlier moment, we simply insisted on the importance of certain myths and defended them as legitimate efforts to construct a persuasive narrative around which to develop an estimable national identity. . . . Our predecessors could and did succeed in defining what they called the American Character. They constructed images of national identity with such concepts as individualism, pragmatism, ambition, idealism, and progress and attributed them variously to the influence of the frontier, affluence, and a classless and nonhierarchical society. The effort to put these together into a manageable whole resulted by the early twentieth century in a celebration of liberalism as the apotheosis of the democratic ideal. As Americans, we celebrated an aggressive individualism, nurtured by political democracy and producing economic prosperity as its much-desired offspring.

But this interpretation of our past was built on silences—silences that were rudely shattered when in the 1960s the search for identity exacerbated differences among us and destroyed our faith in the union of individualism and democracy. The events of that decade (the civil rights movement, feminism, Vietnam, the search for authenticity, and the cry for participatory democracy) called the parameters of cultural homogeneity into question, pushing many American Studies practitioners into a critical stance and encouraging the development of new social and cultural theory that relied heavily on revisionist history, women's studies, and a new consciousness of racial and ethnic divisions. By themselves, these concerns might have been temporary phenomena—we had, after all, absorbed immigrant groups for many years. But the shift to a new pluralism was accompanied by a simultaneous disavowal of notions of common identity, a fragmentation of any unified meaning to the word "American." The result was a search for the sources of individual and group identity in the lives of ethnics, blacks, women, and poor and working-class people, as well as of elite businessmen and socially prominent reformers. The 1970s and 1980s witnessed the simultaneous discovery of the nonpowerful and a refusal among many historians to fit the newly discovered into old myths about the past. The new narrative, they insisted, could not simply suggest that those who were different were "other." It had to incorporate some understanding of . . . how differences among individuals and groups moved the historical process forward.

The twin rebellion against conceptions of common identity and the new pluralism proved to be crucial in the development of a relational stance. Black history, for example, which had not proved especially troublesome when it evoked the moral possibilities of Frederick Douglass, Harriet Tubman, or Martin Luther King, became contentious when historians started to ask how it had shaped the white mind and the dominant economy. In that guise, it raised questions not only about a common vision, but about the role of domination in constructing economic and political democracy as well. It also called into question the plausibility of the liberal idea of inevitable progress. The study of women, hardly a threat when it spoke to the accomplishments of great women like Jane Addams, Eleanor Roosevelt, or even Elizabeth Cady Stanton, created a backlash when it asked about how a gender system sustained racial and class divisions. From that standpoint, the study of women constituted an attack on the very definition of "American," identifying as masculine (rather than universal) metaphors derived from such stalwarts as Whitman and Melville, and raising questions about the gendered content of individualism, self-reliance, pragmatism, and optimism. . . . Writing women and people of color into our understandings of culture required redefining "American" to incorporate multiple definitions of identity. . . . Members of the American Studies community now see efforts at social generalization as merely a thin camouflage of power relations.

The result, by the 1980s, was methodological ferment. . . . Criticism of what later became known as multiculturalism had already begun, and calls for "synthesis" could be heard everywhere. Even social critics longed for the old history—a clear narrative line with a little literature or anthropology thrown in to help define culture. Alas, an easy synthesis was no longer possible. The search for the particular that had underlined and identified a fully pluralist America had repudiated old certainties of consensus, centrality, and truth without creating anything to replace them.

If some of us in American Studies have incorporated the disturbing results of this new knowledge, we have not yet conveyed it to the world. Somehow we need to argue that to construct a new identity does not mean to abandon the concept of American identity. Rather, it should spur us to think about democratic culture as a continuing and unending process. The easiest way to illustrate this is with a personal example.

If you ask me where I come from, I'll tell you I was born in England during World War II of refugee parents who were Hungarian-speaking Czech citizens. We (my brothers and I) grew up speaking first Hungarian, then German—the language of the refugee community. Finally, we were sent to school to learn English—an event that happened shortly before we all moved to Wales, where I lived until we emigrated to the United States. By then I was a teenager. How do I construct myself? It depends on the circumstance. Neither Hungarian nor Czech, neither English nor Welsh, I claim identities as my sense of otherness requires. I suppose that makes me a certain kind of American. For I fully understand the advantages of my other persona—after all, the transformation from an immigrant outsider in Britain to a British émigré in America brought with it instant privilege and insider status that transcended and covered up other disadvantages.

That story is filled with silences. Listen to how loudly they scream a contradictory tale that undermines the urbane and cosmopolitan image I want to construct for you. My father, whom I like to imagine was no ordinary worker, nevertheless worked with his hands all his life. My mother, who died when she was barely forty, left three children to be defended from the good intentions of the British state authorities. Imagine now the refugee father with his tattered English trying to hang on to what was left of his family. I reconstruct myself as orphan child, desperately shamed by a parental heritage from which I could not wait to distance myself; I am revealed as a grammar school product who bore the weight of many exceptionalisms in a country unified by a language and culture I thought I would never fully possess. The saga of emigration becomes an escape that parallels those of my immigrant forebears. It is the transformation from undifferentiated alien to ethnic identity, from state protection to visible poverty, ultimately from unwanted outsider to the constructed self you see before you.

Like the process of construction on a personal level, creating a national image requires us to make conscious and unconscious decisions about what to include and exclude. It asks of us a negotiation between our efforts to retain the particular sense of self that links us to a special tradition and the efforts of such cultural forces as schools and the mass media to impose a sense of commonality that threatens to reduce each of us to what we share. . . .

When we construct ourselves, we do so out of a sense of what makes us distinctive. Those of us who are immigrants, African American, Latin, gay or lesbian, or any combination of these and a dozen other identities have no difficulty seeing in ourselves the otherness out of which we construct the persona that faces the world and limits or expands our vision. As powerful as these perspectives are in shaping a sense of well-being or grievance, they provide us with only partial visions—visions that each of us daily reconciles with the larger culture.

Our insistence on a multicultural curriculum, on a multicultural view of American experience, grows out of the clarity with which we see the pitfalls of adopting an image of anything as complex as America as a unified enterprise. "Who cuts the border?" asks Hortense Spillers in the introduction to a new collection of essays. "Who has the right to claim America?" she asks angrily. America has been constructed out of

> a dizzying concoction of writing and reportage, lying and "signifying," jokes, "tall tales," and transgenerational nightmare, all conflated under the banner of Our Lord . . . [It exemplifies] for all intents and purposes the oldest game of trompe l'oeil, the perhaps-mistaken glance-of-the-eye, that certain European "powers" carried out regarding indigenous Americans.

America, she suggests, was "made up" in the gaze of Europe . . . as much a "discovery" on the retinal surface as it was in the appropriation of land and historical subjects.

Nearly thirty years ago, John Kouwenhoven asked us to think about how common our common culture was, as he put it, to "determine the limits of our community of experienced particulars." When we have heeded this warning, we have been able . . . to see the differences between essentially political patterns within which we reside and daily experiences that we continually create. The result is less fragmentation than it is a richer view of culture as the double effect of the given and self-generated. The perspective draws on the deeply rooted ambiguity that has allowed American Studies practitioners to see the relational ways in which a culture operates—to observe the frictions and tensions that serve both to name particular experiences and to trace the products of social consensus . . . .

The questioning of universalism has led to an exciting search for a common vocabulary. It encourages us to enter into a conversation about whether there is still a "we" at the heart of American culture and to wonder how "we" is constituted. It requires us to reconstruct the disembodied voice—sometimes known as "the American people"—. . . in a way that will simultaneously provide a more inclusive framework and take a standpoint that distinguishes our perspective from that of an earlier and narrower notion of the American persona. It creates the possibility that "we" can unify around the search for a democratic culture, instead of finding ourselves incorporated into a set of tropes such as individualism and equality from which many feel excluded. Tom Bender illustrated how that had been done by Lionel Trilling, who moved from a radical "we" to one that represented an intellectual middle class and in the process extended the reach of his audience by thousands of people. Though Trilling remained caught in a narrow world of narrow definitions, the process enables us to see how he reconstructed himself.

But if the old universalisms have gone, can we find a "we" that experiences culture in shared ways, that encompasses some sense of common identity? Surely that is our task. We can be helped to it by drawing some lessons from postmodernism and particularly from feminist theory. . . . Asking whose claim to knowledge we are validating reminds us of what we lose when we are exclusive—reminds us that the answer depends on a fuller vision that incorporates all of our lives, and urges us to operate from an intellectual position that takes such a stand.

Speaking of the uses of theory for black feminist academics, Patricia Hill Collins has noted that, while black women possess a unique standpoint that produces "certain commonalities of perception," individual differences result in diverse experiences of common themes. The outsider/within status produces a creative tension that enables women of color to see the limits of the insider's knowledge and to attempt to redefine it. Barbara Johnson warns us of the fragility of such identities: the insider, she suggests, becomes an outsider the minute she steps out of the inside. To some extent, every student of American Studies participates in the profoundly political process of determining a stance from which to see. Collins's advice is not dissimilar from that of John Fairbank, who, in his presidential address to the American Historical Association, asked historians to look at America from the outside. . . . "What image have we of our self-image?" Fairbank asked. "What do we think we are doing in the world?"

If the fight for multiculturalism is a request for inclusion, if the heart of American Studies is the pursuit of what constitutes democratic culture, then we need to see the struggle over multiculturalism as a tug of war over who gets to create the public culture. For too long that culture has been the province of a narrow sector of society—its universals shaped our sense of the world, turning each of us into a problematic other. But the effort to alter a static and unitary notion of America has persisted for too long to be denied. Just as I construct myself in relation to my audience, just as American Studies constructs itself in relation to the politics of time and place, so America will reconstruct itself both in response to our multiple identities and in response to our efforts as scholars to describe it.

In that sense, we are all "other." The particular standpoints from which we operate may be differently revealing, but they all participate in the construction of the self (collective and individual) that will become the "other" of the next generation. Our project can be neither a false universalism, nor the reification of pieces of the culture at the expense of the whole. Rather, we need to explore how people become part of, not separate from, the unified whole called America. As students and scholars of American Studies, we are called on to engage in, to facilitate, the conversation that occurs in the public marketplace by ensuring the perpetuation of a processual notion of America.

Far from undermining the search for unity, identity, and purpose, the multicultural enterprise has the potential to strengthen it. It provides a way of seeing relationally that is consistent with the early founders of American Studies as well as with its more recent protagonists. If it redefines identity from a fixed category to a search for a democratic culture, if it refuses to acknowledge a stable meaning or precise unchanging definition of America, multiculturalism nevertheless opens the possibility of conceiving democratic culture as a process in whose transformation we are all invited to participate.

SUGGESTIONS FOR
FURTHER READING
ON THE ROOTS OF
AMERICAN STUDIES

"American Studies: A Critical Retrospective," special issue of *American Studies* 40:2 (Summer 1999).

Bellah, Robert, et al. *Habits of the Heart: Individualism and Commitment in American Life*. Rev. Ed. Berkeley: University of California Press, 1996.

Bender, Thomas. *Intellect and Public Life: Essays on the Social History of Academic Intellectuals in the United States*. Baltimore, MD: Johns Hopkins University Press, 1992.

Bender, Thomas, and Carl E. Schorske, eds. *American Academic Culture in Transformation: Fifty Years, Four Disciplines*. Princeton, NJ: Princeton University Press, 1998.

Bercovitch, Sacvan. *The Rites of Assent: Transformations in the Symbolic Construction of America*. New York: Routledge, 1993.

Bodnar, John, ed. *Bonds of Affection: Americans Define Their Patriotism*. Princeton, NJ: Princeton University Press, 1996.

Ceaser, James W. *Reconstructing America: The Symbol of America in Modern Thought*. New Haven, CT: Yale University Press, 1997.

Dickstein, Morris. *Double Agent: The Critic and Society*. New York: Oxford University Press, 1992.

Fishwick, Marshall W., ed. *American Studies in Transition*. Philadelphia: University of Pennsylvania Press, 1964

FitzGerald, Frances. *America Revised: History Schoolbooks in the Twentieth Century*. New York: Vintage Books, 1979.

Fox, Richard Wightman, and James T. Kloppenberg, eds. *A Companion to American Thought*. Cambridge, MA: Blackwell, 1995.

Georgi-Findlay, Brigitte, and Heinz Ickstadt, eds. *America Seen from the Outside—Topics, Models and Achievements in the Federal Republic of Germany*. Berlin: The Free University, 1990.

Gilroy, Paul. *The Black Atlantic: Double Consciousness and Modernity.* Cambridge, MA: Harvard University Press, 1993.

Graff, Gerald. *Professing Literature: An Institutional History.* Chicago: University of Chicago Press, 1987.

Greene, Jack P. *The Intellectual Construction of America: Exceptionalism and Identity from 1492 to 1800.* Chapel Hill: University of North Carolina Press, 1993.

Gunn, Giles. *Thinking Across the American Grain: Ideology, Intellectuals, and the New Pragmatism.* Chicago: University of Chicago Press, 1992.

Gutman, Huck. *As Others Read Us: International Perspectives on American Literature.* Amherst: University of Massachusetts Press, 1991.

Hartshorne, Thomas L. *The Distorted Image: Changing Conceptions of the American Character Since Turner.* Cleveland, OH: Press of Case Western Reserve University, 1968.

Horwitz, Richard P., ed. *Exporting America: Essays on American Studies Abroad.* New York: Garland Publishing, 1993.

Kammen, Michael. *In the Past Lane: Historical Perspectives on American Culture.* New York: Oxford University Press, 1997.

_____. *Mystic Chords of Memory: The Transformation of Tradition in American Culture.* New York: Random House, 1991.

Kockemans, Joseph J., ed. *Interdisciplinarity and Higher Education.* University Park: Pennsylvania State University Press, 1979.

Kuper, Adam. *Culture: The Anthropologists' Account.* Cambridge, MA: Harvard University Press, 1999.

Levine, Lawrence W. *Highbrow/Lowbrow: The Emergence of Cultural Hierarchy in America.* Cambridge, MA: Harvard University Press, 1988.

Lipset, Seymour. *American Exceptionalism.* New York: W. W. Norton, 1996.

Lipsitz, George. *Time Passages: Collective Memory and American Popular Culture.* Minneapolis: University of Minnesota Press, 1990.

Lubiano, Wahneema, ed. *The House That Race Built: Black Americans, U.S. Terrain.* New York: Pantheon, 1997.

Maddox, Lucy, ed. *Locating American Studies: The Evolution of a Discipline.* Baltimore, MD: Johns Hopkins University Press, 1998.

Madsen, Deborah L. *American Exceptionalism.* Edinburgh: Edinburgh University Press; Jackson: University Press of Mississippi, 1998.

McGiffert, Michael, ed. *The Character of Americans: A Book of Readings.* Rev. Ed. Homewood, IL: Dorsey Press, 1970.

Merideth, Robert, comp. *American Studies: Essays on Theory and Method.* Columbus, OH: C. E. Merrill, 1968.

Pachter, Marc, and Frances Wein, eds. *Abroad in America: Visitors to the New Nation, 1776–1914.* Reading, MA: Addison-Wesley for the National Portrait Gallery, Smithsonian Institution, 1976.

Parrington, Vernon L. *Main Currents in American Thought: An Interpretation of American Literature from the Beginnings to 1920.* New York: Harcourt, 1927–1930.

Pells, Richard. *Not Like Us: How Europeans Have Loved, Hated, and Transformed American Culture Since World War II.* New York: Basic Books, 1997.

Rosenzweig, Roy, and David Thelen. *The Presence of the Past: Popular Uses of History in American Life.* New York: Columbia University Press, 1998.

Ross, Andrew. *No Respect: Intellectuals and Popular Culture.* New York: Routledge, 1989.

Rothenbert, Paula S., ed. *Race, Class, and Gender in the United States: An Integrated Study*. 4th Ed. New York: St. Martin's Press, 1997.

Salzman, Jack, ed. *American Studies: An Annotated Bibliography of American Civilization of the United States*. New York: Cambridge University Press, 1990.

Shumway, David R. *Creating American Civilization: A Genealogy of American Literature as an Academic Discipline*. Minneapolis: University of Minnesota Press, 1994.

Skard, Sigmund. *American Studies in Europe: Their History and Present Organization*. Philadelphia: University of Pennsylvania Press, 1958.

Smith, Henry Nash. *Virgin Land: The American West as Symbol and Myth*. Cambridge, MA: Harvard University Press, 1950.

Tate, Cecil F. *The Search for a Method in American Studies*. Minneapolis: University of Minnesota Press, 1973.

Turpie, Mary, and Joseph Kwiat, eds. *Studies in American Culture: Dominant Ideas and Images*. Minneapolis: University of Minnesota Press, 1960.

Walker, Robert H., ed. *American Studies Abroad: Contributions in American Studies*. Westport, CT: Greenwood Press, 1975.

Wilkinson, Rupert. *American Social Character: Modern Interpretations from the '40s to the Present*. New York: Icon Editions, 1992.

_____. *The Pursuit of American Character*. New York: Harper and Row, 1988.

Williams, Raymond. *Keywords: A Vocabulary of Culture and Society*. Rev. Ed. New York: Oxford University Press, 1983.

Wise, Gene. *American Historical Explanations: A Strategy for Grounded Inquiry*. 2nd Ed. Minneapolis: University of Minnesota Press, 1980.

Yetman, Norman, ed. "American Studies: From Culture Concept to Cultural Studies?" special issue of *American Studies* 38:2 (Summer 1997).

CREDITS FOR SELEC-
TIONS, CITATIONS,
AND VISUALS

American Legion. *Constitution of the American Legion*, adopted in Saint Louis, Missouri (1919).

Arias, Constantino. "U.S. Tourist Poses by a Bar in Havana" (1948). Reprinted at the opening of George Black, *The Good Neighbor: How the United States Wrote the History of Central America and the Caribbean* (New York: Pantheon Books, 1988). The original is in the collection of the Center for Cuban Studies in New York City.

Blackwell, Alice Stone. *Objections Answered* (New York: National American Woman Suffrage Association, 1913). Reprinted in *Woman Suffrage: History, Arguments, And Results: A Collection Of Six Popular Booklets Covering Practically the Entire Field Of Suffrage Claims And Evidence, Designed Especially For The Convenience Of Suffrage Speakers and Writers and For the Use of Debaters and Libraries*, rev. ed., ed. Frances M. Björkman and Annie G. Porritt (New York: National Woman Suffrage Publishing, 1916), 161–202.

Blashfield, Edwin Howland. "The Spirit of the West," mural in the Governor's Reception Room, State Capitol, Pierre, South Dakota (1910). Photograph courtesy of Mary Anne Beecher.

Bourne, Randolph. "Trans-National America," *Atlantic Monthly* 118 (July 1916): 86–97.

Brooks, Van Wyck. "On Creating a Usable Past," *Dial* 64 (April 11, 1918): 337–41.

Ceaser, James W. *Reconstructing America: The Symbol of America in Modern Thought* (New Haven, CT: Yale University Press, 1997), 241.

"Chinese Pose as Auto Tourists," postcard from Woo Dum and friends to Mary Edwards in San Francisco (December 31, 1910). From the collections of the California Historical Society, reprinted in Laverne Mau Dicker, *The Chinese in San Francisco* (New York: Dover Publications, 1979), 92.

Christy, Howard Chandler. "Americans All!" (1919), poster for the Bureau of the Public Debt, War and Conflict No. 526, Control Number NWDNS-53-WP-4C, in the Still Picture Branch, National Archives, College Park, Maryland.

Clifford, James. *Routes: Travel and Translation in the Late Twentieth Century* (Cambridge, MA: Harvard University Press, 1997), 302.

Continental Congress. *The Declaration of Independence of the Thirteen Colonies*, adopted in Philadelphia, Pennsylvania (July 4, 1776).

Crèvecoeur, J. Hector St. John de. *Letters from an American Farmer; Describing Certain Provincial Situations, Manners, and Customs, Not Generally Known; And Conveying Some Idea of the Late and Present Interior Circumstances of the British Colonies in North America, Written for the Information of a Friend in England by J. Hector St. John de Crèvecoeur* (Dublin: John Exshaw, 1782). Reprinted in *Letters from an American Farmer* (New York: Fox, Duffield and Co., 1904), 48–91.

DeMent, Iris. "Wasteland of the Free," from *The Way I Should* (Warner Bros., 1996). Copyright © 1996 by Songs of Iris. Used by permission. All rights reserved.

Douglass, Frederick. "What to the Slave Is the Fourth of July?" delivered in Rochester, New York (July 4, 1852). Published as a pamphlet (July 1852) and reprinted in *Frederick Douglass, the Orator*, ed. James M. Gregory (Springfield, MA: Willey, 1893), 103–6.

DuBois, W. E. B. (William Edward Burghardt). "Of Our Spiritual Strivings," *The Souls of Black Folk; Essays and Sketches* (Chicago: A. C. McClurg, 1903), 1–12.

Dylan, Bob. "Ballad of a Thin Man," *Highway 61 Revisited* (Sony/Columbia Records, 1965).

Emerson, Ralph Waldo. "The American Scholar," delivered in Cambridge, Massachusetts (August 31, 1837), published as *The American Scholar; An Address, Delivered by Ralph Waldo Emerson Before the P B K Society, at Cambridge, August, 1837* (New York: The Laurentian Press, 1901). Reprinted in *Nature, Addresses and Lectures* (Boston: J. Munroe, 1849; Boston: Houghton, Mifflin and Company, 1903; and New York: AMS Press, 1968), 79–115.

European Back Door Travelers. "Ugly American Sightings," Internet bulletin board (http://www.ricksteves.com/graffiti/graffiti78.html, 2001). Reprinted with permission of the moderator, Rick Steves. Rick Steves is the author of *Europe through the Back Door* (Avalon Travel Publishing).

Foerster, Norman. "Factors in American Literary History," adapted from a paper delivered before the American Literature Group of the Modern Language Association, Chicago, Illinois (December 27, 1925), in *The Reinterpretation of American Literature: Some Contributions Toward the Understanding of Its Historical Development*, ed. Norman Foerster for the America Literature Group of the Modern Language Association (New York: Harcourt, Brace and Company, 1928), 23–38.

Gast, John. "American Progress," original oil on canvas, widely reproduced in lithograph, Gene Autry Museum of Western Heritage, Los Angeles.

Gobineau, Joseph-Arthur, comte de. "Les Colonisations Européennes en Amérique," in *Essai sur l'inégalité des races humaines* [Essay on the Inequality of Races] (Paris: Pierre Belfond, 1853, 1855), Book VI, Chapter 8, translated for this volume by Mary Roberts and Richard Horwitz (2001) from the French reprint, ed. Jean Gaulmier with Jean Boissel (Editions Gallimard, 1983), 1130–42. Abridged English translations of *Essai* include *The Moral and Intellectual Diversity of Races, With Particular Reference To Their Respective Influence In the Civil and Political History of Mankind, From the French of Count A. De Gobineau* (Philadelphia: J. B. Lippincott, 1856), reprinted as Joseph-Arthur de Gobineau, *The Moral and Intellectual Diversity of Races* (New York: Garland, 1984).

Goethe, Johann Wolfgang von. "Den Vereinigten Staaten" ["To the United States"] (1827), translated for this volume by Astrid Schnitzer and Richard Horwitz (2000) from the German collection, *Johann Wolfgang Goethet Edicthe 1800–1832* (Frankfurt am Main: Deutscher Klasssiker Verlag, 1988), 739.

Guthrie, Woody. "This Land Is Your Land" (February 23, 1940) in *Woody Guthrie Songs*, ed. Judy Bell and Nora Guthrie (New York: Ludlow Music, 1992), 5. *This Land Is Your Land*, words and music by Woody Guthrie. © Copyright 1956 by TRO (Renewed), 1958 (Renewed), 1970 (Renewed) by Ludlow Music, Inc., New York, New York. Used by permission.

Haggard, Merle, and Roy Burris. "Okie from Muskogee." Copyright © 1969 by Sony/ATV Songs LLC. All rights administered by Sony/ATV Music Publishing, 8 Music Square West, Nashville, TN 37203. All rights reserved. Used by permission. The context surrounding this composition is purely conjecture.

Handsome Lake. "How America Was Discovered," as told to Arthur C. Parker by Chief Cornplanter, in *Seneca Myths and Folktales*, ed. Arthur Caswell Parker (Buffalo, NY: Buffalo Historical Society, 1923), 383–85. Reprinted by permission of the Buffalo and Erie County Historical Society.

Ho Chi Minh. *Declaration of Independence of the Democratic Republic* [now The Socialist Republic] *of Vietnam*, presented in Hanoi (September 2, 1945), reprinted in *Selected Works* (Hanoi: Foreign Languages Publishing House, 1961), 3:17–21; and in *Ho Chi Minh, Selected Writings* (1920–1969), 53–56. Reprinted by permission of Xunhasaba, Vietnam National Corporation for the Export and Import of Books, Periodicals and Other Cultural Commodities.

Hoover, Herbert. "The American System," delivered in New York, New York (October 22, 1928). From Public Statements, Box 91, Herbert Hoover Library, West Branch, Iowa. Reprinted by permission of the Herbert Hoover Library.

Hughes, Langston. "Puerto Ricans," from *The Best of Simple* (New York: Hill and Wang, 1961), 216–18. Copyright © 1961 by Langston Hughes. Copyright renewed 1989 by George Houston Bass. Reprinted by permission of Hill and Wang, a division of Farrar, Straus and Giroux, LLC.

James, Henry. "Americans Abroad," *The Nation* 27:692 (October 3, 1878): 208.

Kessler-Harris, Alice. "Cultural Locations: Positioning American Studies in the Great Debate," *American Quarterly* 44:3 (September 1992): 299–312. Copyright © 1992 by The American Studies Association. Reprinted by permission of The Johns Hopkins University Press.

Kipling, (Joseph) Rudyard. "The White Man's Burden," *McClure's Magazine* 12:4 (February 1899): 290–91.

Lange, Dorothea. "Dust Storm at this War Relocation Authority center where evacuees of Japanese ancestry are spending the duration," and "Manzanar Relocation Center, Manzanar, California" (July 3, 1942) for the War

Relocation Authority of the Department of the Interior. Control Numbers NWDNS-210-G-10C-839 and NWDNS-210-G-C840 in the Still Picture Branch of the National Archives, College Park, Maryland.

Lehrer, Tom. "National Brotherhood Week," recorded at the hungry i, San Francisco, California (1965) for *That Was The Year That Was* (Warner/Reprise, 1966). Reprinted by permission of the performer.

Lincoln, Abraham. "Gettysburg Address," delivered in Gettysburg, Pennsylvania (November 19, 1863).

Linton, Ralph. "The One Hundred Percent American," *The American Mercury* 40:160 (April 1937): 427–29.

Lynd, Robert S., and Helen Merrell Lynd. *Middletown in Transition: A Study in Cultural Conflicts* (New York: Harcourt, Brace, and Co., 1937), Chapter 13, 487–96, 511. Copyright © 1937 by Harcourt, Inc., 1965 by Robert S. Lynd and Helen M. Lynd. Reprinted by permission of the publisher.

Mao Tse-tung. "Cast Away Illusions, Prepare for Struggle" (August 14, 1949), reprinted in *Selected Works of Mao Tse-tung*, 5 vols. (Beijing: Foreign Languages Press, 1961), 4:425–31. Reprinted by permission of China Books and Periodicals, Inc.

McKay, Claude. "America," in *Selected Poems of Claude McKay With a Biographical Note By Max Eastman* (New York: Harcourt, Brace and World, 1953), 59.

"The Melting Pot," postcard from Wethersfield, Connecticut (July 4, 1913). Courtesy of Wethersfield Historical Society.

Mencken, Henry Louis. "On Being an American," in *Prejudices: Third Series* (New York: Alfred A. Knopf, 1922), 9–64. From H. L. Mencken, *Prejudices: Third Series*. Copyright © 1922 by Alfred A. Knopf Inc. and renewed 1950 by H. L. Mencken. Reprinted by permission of Alfred A. Knopf, a Division of Random House, Inc.

"Mexican Embassy Heard, Believes That Baseball Could Further International Ideals," *New York Times* (April 7, 1946), Section 5, p. 3. Reprinted by permission of The Associated Press.

Monroe, James. "The Monroe Doctrine," State of the Union Address, Washington, DC (December 2, 1823).

Montaigne, Michel de. "Of Cannibals," trans. John Florio (1603). Reprinted in *The Essays of Montaigne, Done Into English by John Florio, Anno 1615, With an Introduction by George Saintsbury* (London: D. Nutt, 1892–93).

O'Sullivan, John L. "Annexation," *United States Magazine and Democratic Review* 17 (July 1845): 5–10.

Paddy's Lament. Traditional folksong performed in the Atlantic world since ca. 1865.

Parrington, Vernon Louis. *Main Currents in American Thought: An Interpretation of American Literature from the Beginning to 1920, Volume II, 1800–1860* (New York: Harcourt, Brace and Company, 1927–1930), 2:386–99. Copyright © 1927 by Harcourt, Inc., and renewed 1954 by Vernon L. Parrington, Jr., Louise P. Tucker, and Elizabeth P. Thomas. Reprinted by permission of Harcourt Inc.

Pattee, Fred Lewis. "Introductory Note," *Century Readings for a Course in American Literature* (New York: The Century Company, 1919), v.

Peters, Gretchen. "Independence Day" (1992), recorded by Martina McBride on a single RCA Records release (1993). Copyright © 1992 by Sony/ATV Tunes LLC and Purple Crown Music. All rights administered by Sony/ATV Music Publishing, 8 Music Square West, Nashville, TN 37203. All rights reserved. Used by permission. The context surrounding this composition is purely conjecture.

Publius (Alexander Hamilton). "The Utility of the Union in Respect to Commercial Relations and a Navy," *New York Independent Journal* (Saturday, November 24, 1787). Reprinted in *The Federalist Papers*, Number 11.

Quinney, John Wannuaucon. "Independence Day Speech" in Reidsville, New York (July 4, 1854), reprinted in *The American Indian* (January 1928) and in *Great Documents in American Indian History*, ed. Wayne Moquin and Charles Van Doren (New York: Praeger Publishers, 1973), 166–70.

Rockwell, Norman. *Freedom from Want* (1943). Posters featuring this image were commissioned by the Office of Government Reports, Division of Public Inquiry, Bureau of Special Services, Office of War Information. Control Numbers NWDNS-44-PA-78 and NWDNS-44-PA-261 in the Still Picture Branch of the National Archives, College Park, Maryland. Copyright © 1943 by the Norman Rockwell Family Trust. Reprinted by permission of the Norman Rockwell Family Trust.

Roosevelt, Franklin Delano. "The Four Freedoms," State of the Union Address, Washington, DC (January 6, 1941).

Rosenthal, Joe. "Flag Raising on Iwo Jima" (February 23, 1945) for the Naval Photographic Center of the Department of the Navy. Reprinted by permission of AP/Wide World Photos.

Sandburg, Carl. Excerpt from Carl Sandburg, *The People, Yes* (New York: Harcourt, Brace, 1936), 223, 30, 29, 286. Copyright © 1936 by Harcourt, Inc. and renewed 1964 by Carl Sandburg. Reprinted by permission of the publisher.

Shakespeare, William. *The Tempest* (1611; first published in London, 1623), Act 5, Scene 1, Lines 182–185, and Act 1, Scene 2, Lines 319–374.

Sondheim, Stephen, and Leonard Bernstein. "America," from *West Side Story* (United Artists, 1961). Copyright © 1956, 1957, 1959 by Amberson Holdings LLC and Stephen Sondheim. Copyright renewed. Leonard Bernstein Music Publishing Company LLC, Publisher, Boosey & Hawkes, Inc., Sole Agent. Reprinted by permission.

Sundblom, Haddon. " 'Give and Take,' Say I" (1937) and "Cheers" (1944) for The Coca-Cola Company. "Coca-Cola" is a registered trademark of The Coca-Cola Company.

Supreme Court of the United States. *Bowers v. Hardwick*, 478 U.S. 186 (June 30, 1986).

Supreme Court of the United States. *Engel v. Vitale*, 370 U.S. 421, 82 S. Ct. 1261 (June 25,1962).

Supreme Court of the United States. *Loving v. Virginia*, 388 U.S. 1 (June 12, 1967).

Thompson, E. P. (Edward Palmer). "Letter to Americans" (April 22, 1986), in *Mad Dogs: The U.S. Raids on Libya*, ed. Mary Kaldor and Paul Anderson (London: Pluto Press in association with European Nuclear Disarmament, 1986), 11–15. Reprinted by permission of Pluto Press.

Truth, Sojourner. *"Ain't I a Woman?"* delivered in Akron, Ohio (May 1851). Reprinted as "Reminiscences by Frances D. Gage of Sojourner Truth," in *History of Woman Suffrage*, 6 vols., ed. Elizabeth Cady Stanton, Susan B. Anthony, and Matilda Joslyn Gage (New York: Fowler and Wells, 1881), 1:115–17.

Turner, Frederick Jackson. "The Significance of the Frontier in American History," delivered before the American Historical Association in Chicago

(July 12, 1893), published in the *Proceedings of the State Historical Society of Wisconsin* (December 14, 1893): 199–227.

"Uncle Sam in Australia," postcard (ca. 1909).

"Uncle Sam Welcomes Mexico," commemorative postcard, San Diego Exposition, Balboa Park, Plaza de Panama (1915). San Diego Historical Society Photograph Collection, Number PC4-399.

Vega, Ana Lydia. "Wrestling with the Hard One." Copyright © 1994 by Ana Lydia Vega. English translation of "Pulseando con el difícil," originally written in Spanish and included in the author's essay collection, *Esperando a Loló y otro delirios generacionales* (Río Piedras: Editorial de la Universidad de Puerto Rico, 1994), 11–19.

Wang Guangyi. "Great Castigation Series: Coca-Cola," Beijing, People's Republic of China (1993). The original (oil on canvas, 79 inches square) is in the artist's collection and reprinted with his permission.

Wang, Peter. Publicity poster for *A Great Wall: An American Comedy Made in China*, produced by Shirley Sun for Orion (1986).

Warhol, Andy. Excerpt from *The Philosophy of Andy Warhol (From A to B and Back Again)* (New York: Harcourt Brace Jovanovich, 1975), 100–101. Copyright © 1975 by Andy Warhol, reprinted by permission of Harcourt, Inc.

Warhol, Andy. *Five Coke Bottles* (1962). Copyright © 2001 by the Andy Warhol Foundation for the Visual Arts/ARS, New York.

Warhol, Andy, and Pat Hackett. *POPism: The Warhol '60s* (New York: Harcourt Brace Jovanovich, 1980), 39.

Weber, Max. *The Protestant Ethic and the Spirit of Capitalism*, trans. Talcott Parsons (New York: Scribner's Press, 1958, © 1930), 47–48. *Protestant Ethic and the Spirit of Capitalism* by Weber, © 1980. Reprinted by permission of Prentice-Hall, Inc., Upper Saddle River, New Jersey.

West, James (Carl A. Withers). "Plainville Social Class." Reprinted from James West, *Plainville, U.S.A.* (New York: Columbia University Press, 1945), 129. Copyright © 1945 by Columbia University Press. Reprinted by permission of the publisher.

Wilson, Woodrow. "Americanism and the Foreign-Born," delivered in Philadelphia, Pennsylvania (May 10, 1915). Reprinted in *American Ideals*, ed. Norman Foerster and William W. Pierson, Jr. (Boston: Houghton Mifflin Company, 1917), 178–82.

Winthrop, John. "Modell of Christian Charity" (1630). Reprinted in *Collections of the Massachusetts Historical Society* (Boston, 1838), 3rd series, 7:31–48.

Woman's Rights Convention. *Declaration of Sentiments and Resolutions*, adopted in Seneca Falls, New York (July 19, 1848). Reprinted in *History of Woman Suffrage*, ed. Elizabeth Cady Stanton, Susan B. Anthony, and Matilda Joslyn Gage (New York: Fowler and Wells, 1889), 1:70.

Zhou Yan. "Goddess of Democracy under Construction" (1989). Photograph courtesy of Zhou Yan.